Sociology and Social Research

. . . Research . . .

AN INTERNATIONAL JOURNAL

American Culture Themes 3
WILLIAM TORRENCE AND PAUL MEADOWS

Labor Under Review: 1957 8
MELVIN J. VINCENT

Concerning Marriage and Family Life . . 16
V. A. CHRISTOPHERSON AND J. WALTERS

Social Class in Philadelphia Methodism . . 23
FREDERICK A. SHIPPEY

Art and Communication 28
BRUCE A. WATSON

Anomie and Religious Orthodoxy 34
T. C. KEEDY, JR.

Direction of Sociological Research 38
EMORY S. BOGARDUS

News Notes 42

Peoples and Culture . . . 44
Social Problems and Welfare 51
Social Theory and Research 61
Other Publications Received 76

VOL. 43 SEPTEMBER-OCTOBER 1958 No. 1
YEARLY SUBSCRIPTION, $3.50 SINGLE COPIES, 70 CENTS

Sociology and Social Research

AN INTERNATIONAL JOURNAL

PUBLISHED BIMONTHLY AT THE UNIVERSITY OF SOUTHERN CALIFORNIA
UNIVERSITY PARK, LOS ANGELES 7, CALIFORNIA

YEARLY SUBSCRIPTION, $3.50 SINGLE COPIES, 70¢

Entered as second-class matter March 31, 1936, at the post office at Los Angeles, California, under the act of March 3, 1879.

PUBLISHED BY

UNIVERSITY OF SOUTHERN CALIFORNIA PRESS

UNIVERSITY PARK LOS ANGELES 7, CALIFORNIA

SOCIOLOGY AND SOCIAL RESEARCH

September-October 1958

AMERICAN CULTURES THEMES: AN ANALYSIS OF FOREIGN OBSERVER LITERATURE

WILLIAM TORRENCE
AND
PAUL MEADOWS
University of Nebraska

The general purpose of this paper is to present a thematic analysis of the observations of American culture by certain foreign observers. Specifically, this study identifies, by means of a given definition, prevailing culture themes of American society selected from the works of these foreign observers.

It is, of course, a commonplace that the task of culture analysis becomes more complicated when one turns to the more industrialized, heterogeneous national societies.[1] A suggestion to meet this problem has been advanced by Opler. He asserts:

> In every culture are found a limited number of dynamic affirmations, called themes, which control behavior or stimulate activity. The activities, prohibition of activities, or references which result from the acceptance of a theme are its expressions. Such expressions may be formalized or unformalized. Limiting factors, often the existence of other opposed or circumscribing themes and their extensions, control the number, force, and variety of a theme's expressions. The interplay of theme and counter-theme is the key to the equilibrium achieved in a culture, and structure in culture is essentially their interrelation and balance.[2]

It is proposed here to examine a sample of foreign traveler literature in terms of the preceding suggestion of culture themes. Such an investigation represents, it must be pointed out, a type of culture analysis.[3]

[1] Concerning problems and methods of national culture analysis generally, cf. Margaret Mead, "National Character," A. L. Kroeber, editor, *Anthropology Today: An Encyclopedic Inventory* (Chicago: University of Chicago Press, 1953), pp. 642-67.

[2] Morris E. Opler, "Themes as Dynamic Forces in Culture," *American Journal of Sociology*, 51: 198.

[3] Bernard Berelson, *Content Analysis in Communication Research* (Glencoe, Illinois: The Free Press, 1952).

Two very general approaches are available for use in the content analysis of any given media. These are the a priori and the a posteriori departures. According to McGranahan, the a priori approach is one "which sets up logical categories (of culture characterizations) in advance." The a posteriori approach is one "which derives categories from the specific material examined."[4] The latter method has been chosen for this study. The frame of reference used in establishing the a posteriori categories has been suggested by Opler's definition of culture themes as previously noted. The specific categories of analysis were obtained by induction from the culture theme assertions of these foreign observers. These culture theme assertions constitute the collected data of this study.

Eleven foreign traveler reports were consulted.[5] Initially, in the case of each book every statement considered to be within the scope of culture themes as defined above was abstracted from the text. For example, from Andre Siegfried's *America Comes of Age* there are these assertions:

> Organization appeals to the American, for he loves teamwork and cooperation with machinery. He is perfectly at home wherever it is possible to use machinery, and if he is aware that his excessive division of labor limits his personal interest in the final achievement, he does not seem to regret it.[6]

The themes were then examined in order to determine the presence of similarities; these made possible a tentative list of classes of themes. At this point the "sort" was examined for overlapping, ambiguities, and misfits. The final classification thus derived and elaborated and offered below is not regarded as definitive but only as tenable because empirical; it is an inductive, derivationally a posteriori classification.

The class (a) is given first in the summary that follows and is italicized; after the class statement the codal summary (b) appears.

I. (a) *Americans love practicality.* (b) Theory is discounted by Americans; intellectual activities seem inconsequential; only self-expression in tangible ways is acceptable.

---

[4] Donald V. McGranahan, "Content Analysis of the Mass Media of Communication," in M. Jahoda, M. Deutsch, and S. Cook, editors, *Research Methods in Social Relations: with Especial Reference to Prejudice,* Part Two: *Selected Techniques* (New York: The Dryden Press, 1952), p. 554.

[5] The eleven reports were: Hilaire Belloc, *The Contrast* (1924); Paul de Constant, *America and Her Problems* (1915); Walter L. George, *Hail, Columbia* (1921); Geoffrey Gorer, *The American People* (1948); Hermann Keyserling, *America Set Free* (1929); Wyndham Lewis, *America and the Cosmic Man* (1949); Hugo Munsterberg, *The Americans* (1904); Lucien Romier, *Who Will Be Master, Europe or America?* (1928); Andre Siegfried, *America Comes of Age* (1927); Peter Vay De Vaya, *The Inner Life of the United States* (1908); Tingfang Wu, *America, Through the Spectacles of an Oriental Diplomat* (1914). A survey was made of reviews written by American authors about these books. Of 88 critiques, approximately three fourths were favorable toward them.

[6] *Op. cit.*, p. 152.

II. (a) *Mechanization, organization, and efficiency appeal to Americans.* (b) Cooperative or organized effort is a good thing per se; the mechanical is prized; the machine is the embodiment of impersonal control.

III. (a) *Americans insist on standardization.* (b) If it can't be mass produced, it loses its appeal; unity and uniformity are equated; conformity is prized above creativity.

IV. (a) *Americans prefer individualism and freedom from authority.* (b) It is displayed in the repugnance felt toward authority, which is regarded as per se bad, in the fear or contempt for holders of authority.

V. (a) *Americans are fond of bigness and quantity.* (b) Americans love excess, power, superlatives, size, headlines; quantity is a measure of achievement; monopoly is admired though resented.

VI. (a) *Americans demand competitive effort.* (b) America is the land of new chances; American qualities are products of competition, status should be competitively earned, unearned status is scorned.

VII. (a) *Some superior-inferior relationships are acceptable.* (b) Isolationism reflects disdain for the rest of the world; customers are properly objects of deception; Americans accept or assume the authority of American civilization.

VIII. (a) *Americans admire productivity.* (b) Trade and industry are admired because they are productive; production sets a premium on all things; (production) takes priority over all things.

IX. (a) *Americans prize creature comforts.* (b) Americanism is equated with goods; tangible gain is a supreme goal; acquiring goods leads to no further drives, no other motivations are really necessary.

X. (a) *Americans love to moralize their economic interests.* (b) Moral values are abstract terms, attached freely and dogmatically to concrete realities; the business frame of reference is the social frame of reference; exploitation of resources is legitimized into terms of civic value.

XI. (a) *Work is regarded as of moral value.* (b) Worklessness is embarrassing and immoral; work is a value in itself; unworked-for status is despised.

XII. (a) *The achievement of wealth is held to be a test of worth.* (b) Wealth is a path to distinction; wealth is equated with superiority; the greater the wealth, the greater the achievement.

The reader will have noted that each of the major classes of culture themes covers, within each class, a range of theme statements. It was thought that a subgrouping of theme statements within each class would prove to be a useful method of further summarizing the observations of these foreign observers. In other words, it was hypothesized that modalities could be established within each class, just as modalities, in the form of major classes, had been established for the entire collection of culture themes. This, as a phase of the study, was done.[7]

Next, the rank-order distribution of the theme classes and the original numbering of the theme classes (in Roman numerals and in parentheses), followed by the frequency of each class, appear below:

1. Americans prefer individualism and freedom from authority (IV), 76.
2. Some superior-inferior relationships are acceptable (VII), 39.
3. Americans love to moralize their economic interests (X), 32.
4. The achievement of wealth is held to be a test of worth (XII), 26.
5. Americans demand competitive effort (VI), 25.
6. Americans insist on standardization (III), 23.
7. Work is regarded as of moral value (XI), 18.
8. Mechanization, organization, and efficiency appeal to Americans (II), 17.
9. Americans love practicality (I), 17.
10. Americans are fond of bigness and quantity (V), 13.
11. Americans prize creature comforts (IX), 12.
12. Americans admire productivity (VIII), 9.

It would be too much to expect of any report of a modern culture that it be free from contradictions and conflicts in the material reported. Even a casual examination of the culture themes which our foreign observers have noted will locate major disagreements among the themes of American culture. Because of these disagreements, the authors have sought to present some of the more obvious contradictions as follows:[8] (1) conformity versus autonomy, (2) egalitarianism versus inegalitarianism, (3) antiracism versus racism, (4) American superiority versus American protectionism, (5) materialism versus antimaterialism, (6) isolationism versus intervention.

---

[7] Because of space limitations the 36 subcategories are not presented here. Interested readers can secure copies by writing to the authors. It should be understood, however, that this identification of intraclass modalities does not involve the assumption of a continuum of culture theme statements within each class; instead, the identification involves only clusters based upon obvious similarities.

[8] Again due to space limitations, the theme and countertheme presentation is reported on the basis of main headings. However, the specific content is available to interested readers by writing the authors.

On the basis of the study, it appears that culture themes may, by using the definition advanced by Opler and certain of the methodological tools used in content analysis, be identified in a sample of foreign observer literature. There were 307 culture theme assertions identified in the works of the eleven foreign observers selected for this study. It was possible to sort this group of culture theme statements into 12 general classes. Each general class was conceptualized in terms of similarities of statement. Finally, it proved to be possible at this point to determine subcategories of culture themes within each general class. This subcategorization developed 36 distinct subclasses. It seems, therefore, that the general methodology of content analysis, with the refinements posed in this study, can be used as a method of identifying culture themes in literature dealing with American or other culture phenomena.

Some definite future research projects appear feasible on the basis of the present study. Thus, content analysis, using the theme as the dimensional unit, can be applied to the material of native American writers in order to determine the extent of agreement or disagreement with the theme assertions found in this study. In addition, a desirable investigation involves the construction of a precoded or uncoded questionnaire or interview schedule followed by a fielding of such an instrument in order to determine, among a representative sample of Americans, the extent of their acceptance or rejection of the theme assertions found in this study. Such a fielded instrument would, without question, disclose many other culture themes held by Americans but not apparent to foreign observers, however well trained and observant they might be. That such data would be enormously useful to institutional leaders as well as culture theorists goes without saying.

LABOR UNDER REVIEW: 1957

MELVIN J. VINCENT
University of Southern California

The year with the economic dip at its end: 1957. Despite the glowing promises made at the beginning, it did not take too long to reveal some weak spots in the United States economy. The Eisenhower Administration made publicity efforts to scare away any reports of a recession in the making: "leveling off of the greatest boom the country ever enjoyed," "ironing out soft spots for the steady onward growth," "the nation can never again get into economic trouble and the new forthcoming balance will bring greater prosperity." These were phrases designed to comfort the urbanites, the "exurbanites," and the farmers. In February the worst jolt came to all this publicity when the Secretary of the Treasury reported that "unless we mend our ways we will see a depression that will curl your hair," thereby embarrassing the Administration. Demands for recantation filled the air. Mending what ways? Creeping steadily upward were prices, and union rumblings for increased wages were heard, business costs were advancing, government spending went on apace, and the stock market met all these with a cruel downward trend. As if more were needed, the United States Department of Commerce announced early in February the biggest seasonal decline in employment since 1949, reporting an employment drop of 1,700,000.

Along with the economic and political dip, organized labor also took a nice dip and a precipitous one at that. March had no sooner appeared than the public became aware that Senator John L. McClellan had been elected as chairman of the new bipartisan Senate Select Committee on Improper Activities in the Labor and Management Field, a committee which was to be occupied for over 100 days listening to nearly 500 witnesses relate how terrorism had entered into certain areas of union-management relationships. The revelations were markedly shocking even to AFL-CIO President George Meany, who lost no time in inaugurating plans to clean the stables of corrupt unionism. The publicized accounts of the misuse of union funds by the President of the Teamsters' Union, Dave Beck, led to the further examination of some other union funds, mishandled by union officers.

Coupled with this was the sad reflection that during the last few years organized labor had not been doing too well at the hands of the

Eisenhower-appointed members of the National Labor Relations Board. In 1950, 4,223 representative elections were won by the unions (73%), while in 1957 only 2,988 were won (61%). The employees represented in 1950 numbered 759,038, but in 1957 were down to 269,050, a sharp decline in labor victories. Labor claims this has been due to an "anti-labor climate" caused by steady pressures of managerial forces following up their Taft-Hartley victory in 1947, the new "free speech" powers given to employers by the NLRB, and some adverse NLRB decisions of recent vintage. Whatever the causes, organized labor has lost ground during the last few years. Not all of this can be blamed upon the Republican-dominated NLRB, since some of it must be showered upon those misleaders of unions who have so harmed the cause that at any moment a new crop of right-to-work laws may bloom and bear fruit.

The following selected record of labor events has been compiled from press dispatches, newsweeklies, labor newspapers, labor pamphlets, and the Department of Labor's *Monthly Labor Review.*

January

Year begins with apparent prosperity holding over from 1956. Employment set at 64.6 million, average pay $2.05 an hour. Prices begin to move upward. Major stock issues take a tumble, reason given as pessimistic outlook caused by huge inventories and slow auto sales.

International Union of Electrical Workers' President James Carey adopts an ethical practices code and calls on all unions to recognize right of Congress to investigate labor racketeering and corruption. Declares that any of his officers pleading the Fifth Amendment would be placed on trial by union.

U.S. Supreme Court unanimously holds that unions can strike to back up demands made under reopener clauses in long-term contracts, even though the contract has not expired, if the sixty-day notice under Taft-Hartley provision has been given.

February

AFL-CIO executive council goes against James Beck and his Teamster's Union for its defiance of the Senate Committee investigating union corruption and for its upholding of labor officials pleading Fifth Amendment. Beck goes to Europe while the Senate Committee pries into suspected manipulation of welfare funds by union officials.

Eisenhower disturbed over growing signs of inflation due to higher wage demands, price advances, and increased business costs. Secretary of Treasury Humphrey threatens a depression unless all this is curbed.

Department of Labor and Department of Commerce report rise in unemployment of nearly half million during January.

David J. McDonald re-elected President of U.S. Steelworkers. First time a running president had been opposed in the union's twenty-year existence, Philip Murray having been its president until he became head of the CIO.

Congressional Joint Economic Committee criticizes the Eisenhower admonition to labor and industry to limit price and wage boosts, and calls for a reduction in the budget.

March

Indiana passed a Right-to-Work Act, called by unions Right-to-Wreck act. Indiana became the eighteenth state to have such a statute; two other states having once passed such legislation withdrew the acts. Indiana Governer allowed the act to become law without his signature.

Secretary of Labor Mitchell wants extension of minimum wage to cover 2½ million more workers.

Senator John L. McClellan elected chairman of new bipartisan Senate Select Committee on Improper Activities in the Labor and Management Field. FBI arrests James Hoffa, ninth president of Teamsters' Union for attempted bribery in order to get information from Senate Investigating Committee by planting a spy in the Committee. Dave Beck accused of using union funds for his own personal investments. Walter Reuther of AFL-CIO shocked at revelations. Robert F. Kennedy, brother of Senator John Kennedy, appointed as chief counsel of the Investigating Committee.

April

AFL-CIO executive council orders Beck to appear before it on May 20. Union leaders definitely worried over exposures. Dave Beck appears before the Senate Committee and pleads both the Fourth and Fifth Amendments. His Teamsters' executive board meets at Galveston and declares that no notice will be taken of the AFL-CIO Ethical Practices Committee attempt to suspend Beck.

Unions reported to be treasury-rich to the extent of over a billion dollars; union welfare and pension funds placed at about 25 billion. No Federal regulation of these funds obtains, although AFL-CIO is said to favor Federal legislation proposed by Senator Paul Douglas' Senate investigating subcommittee to impose such regulation.

United Auto Workers' Convention is held in Atlantic City and goes on record for shorter work week and same pay. If automation is going to displace human labor, two things must happen—shorter work week and maintenance of purchasing power.

First-quarter profits promising despite lessening of steel production and some layoffs in railroading. Consumer price index reaches an all-time high with living costs up 3.7 per cent in year. Means one-to-three-cent an hour raise for 1,400,000 workers tied to escalator clauses. Labor blames management and vice versa.

Secretary of Labor Mitchell confers with Eisenhower over the growing demand to curb power of union leaders. "A gangster economy" may be in store for the country unless union racketeering is stopped, avers Senator McClellan. American Lithographers Association at a New York meeting tells how one of its locals has paid $8,700 in support of a two-day clinic to show how labor-savings techniques can help speed up production.

May

Senator Joseph McCarthy, who once charged that there were fifty-seven Communist members in the U.S. Department of State, dies.

Federal Grand Jury in Tacoma, Washington, indicts Dave Beck for dodging more than $50,000 on his 1950 income tax and for preparing a false tax return for his Teamsters' Building Association. Teamsters' executive council declares Beck must go; he is also scheduled to appear before the AFL-CIO Ethical Practices Committee and the Senate Investigating Committee. Later, the AFL-CIO expels Beck as a vice-president and elects as his successor John F. English, treasurer of the Teamsters' and an anti-Beck man.

General Motors claims that spring car sales are not up to expectations; TV sales way below.

June

Senate Investigating Committee turns its attention to James Cross, President of International Bakery and Confectionery Workers, for dipping into the union's funds.

Reuther sends his UAW officials a note stating that any of them using the Fifth Amendment will be automatically suspect.

Supreme Court holds that Dupont Company's ownership of 23 per cent of General Motors' stock constitutes an illegal monopoly, decision being based upon the 1914 Clayton Act. Also reverses contempt-of-Congress conviction of labor organizer John Watkins for refusing to answer before House Un-American Activities Committee in 1954. Supreme Court now noted for its broadening of civil liberties in U.S.

Orders acquittal of five of the fourteen California communists and orders new trials for nine.

Industrial production falls in May for third straight month—may be an omen pointing to a recession.

July

Steelman Ernest F. Weir dies. His National Steel Company is one of the last with a company union.

James Hoffa being tried on charges of bribery in a Federal Court in Washington, but found not guilty.

Reconstruction Finance Corporation, set up by Hoover, goes out of existence. Made $640 million on 130,000 loans.

U.S. Steel executives decide to raise price of steel $6 a ton to offset a 6 per cent rise in wages. Eisenhower asks both labor and management to temper demands on account of inflationary tendencies. Huge first half-year profits for oil and steel, but slumps in paper, airlines, and housing industries.

"Moonlighting"—holding two jobs at one time—rises from 1,800,000 to 3,700,000 in last six years. Problem to be faced—do workers who engage in it want shorter hours after all?

Dr. Edwin C. Nourse claims that both "administered prices" and "administered wages" cause inflation. First exists when a company is big enough or dominant enough to maintain prices even in face of slackened demand.

August.

Gallup Poll finds that 61 per cent of the Americans polled rejected the four-day week.

Lack of buoyancy noticed in many businesses. Tighter money in sight with discount rate raised from 3 to 3½ per cent by Federal Reserve Board.

Reuther proposes to halt wage-price boosting by cutting prices of 1958 cars by $100. Industry shocked by proposal and asks Reuther to extend his present contract two years beyond May 29, 1958.

AFL-CIO's professional organizers, numbering 225, petition NLRB to certify their organization as an official bargaining agent. Makes a union within a union in reality.

Economic boom in its last-rose-of-summer stage. Stock prices tumble as living costs hit a new high with a decline of 20.8 per cent in spending power of dollar since 1939.

September

Major fringe benefits for industry will top $12 billion for 1957, or 6 per cent of total wages, according to U.S. Department of Commerce.

AFL-CIO Ethical Practices Committee tells Teamsters' to get rid of both Beck and Hoffa or have union expelled. Gallup Poll shows public regard for labor unions has slipped from 76 per cent in February to 64 per cent in September.

U.S. Department of Agriculture claims American farmer richest in world, since his land values have jumped to a huge $109.5 billion.

John L. Lewis announces his UMW's union with its employer-financed Welfare and Retirement fund took in $157 million for year ending June 30, 1957. Has paid out $138 million in $100-a-month pensions to widows. Reserve fund set at $145 million and its beneficiaries number 215,702.

Democrat Edward W. Proxmire sworn in as U.S. Senator from Wisconsin to succeed the late Joseph McCarthy.

Railroads in a sharp slump with profits declining $61 million from 1956 during first six months of 1957.

October

Sputnik of USSR orbits and sends gloom over the United States, signaling the beginning of a satellite race.

Secretary of Defense Charles Wilson resigns; Attorney General Herbert Brownell leaves the Cabinet and is replaced by William Pierce Rogers, who at 44 becomes the youngest Cabinet member.

Senator Knowland of California wants to restrict irresponsible and corrupt labor union practices by legislation.

NLRB examiner charges Kohler Company (longest strike in U.S. history—since April 1954) with unfair labor practices. Company will appeal his decision to the full Board.

Hoffa wins the presidency of the Teamsters' Union. By court order he is refused the presidency for the time being.

Teamsters' suspended by Executive Council of AFL-CIO.

November

President Meany of AFL-CIO orders United Textile Workers to get rid of its secretary-treasurer, who the McClellan Committee revealed had used union funds. Both the president and the secretary-treasurer resigned. AFL-CIO suspends Bakery and Confectionery Workers for like reasons.

Unemployment set at 2½ million, with pessimism about the business future beginning to grow. Downturn causes Federal Reserve Board to lower discount rate. Steel production down from 100 per cent capacity to 81 per cent.

Democrats win several gubernatorial elections and cause Republican gloom. Secretary of Labor states that profits are being squeezed and that collective bargaining in 1958 will be tougher.

Dave Beck, Jr., found guilty in a Seattle court for collecting on sale of two Cadillacs owned by Teamsters' Union.

December

AFL-CIO Convention in Atlantic City dismisses Teamsters' Union. Secretary Mitchell tells it about a labor legislation program: (1) lay down rules for democratic procedures and conduct of unions; (2) require periodic reports of finances. Administration will not recommend a right-to-work law nor ask for application of antitrust legislation to unions. President Gray of Building and Construction Trades makes a plea for a one-year voluntary wage freeze to keep prices stable, and Meany accuses him of adopting the big-business idea that wage boosts cause inflation.

Steel production now down to 67 per cent of capacity. The downturn in business now labeled plainly as recession but a "gold-plated" one. Unemployment set at 3,188,000, highest since 1949. Reuther's platform: higher wages, increased leisure, bigger health and welfare benefits as cure for recession.

Dave Beck found guilty of larceny in Seattle.

Supreme Court refused to reconsider its denial of a review of a Court of Appeals decision upholding an NLRB finding that the discharge of supervisors unlawfully interfered with rank-and-file workers' rights. Also rules that a state court has no authority over a suit for reinstatement and wages brought by former employees of an interstate commerce employer.

For unionism in general, 1957 has not been a propitious year. The revelations of the McMillan Senate Labor-Management Investigating Committee have placed organized labor on the defensive. President George Meany has left no doubt in the minds of those loyal to labor that under his direction the AFL-CIO will clean its own house even at the cost of losing over a million dues-paying members as noted in the expulsion of several large unions. The formation of Ethical Practices Committees by the AFL-CIO and several of its member unions would seem to be a step in the right direction for union preservation. Labor may be thankful for the "liberal" members of the United States Supreme Court, which in March ruled that a state court does not have jurisdiction over organized picketing and that it does not have power to enjoin Taft-Hartley violators, and in May, reversed the Supreme Court of Tennessee, which had held that the right-to-work law in that state permitted the state to prevent picketing an employer in interstate commerce who refused to employ union labor. So far as strikes were concerned, they totaled about 16 million man-days, or less than one half of those in 1956. Collective bargaining may be "tough" in 1958, according to Secretary of Labor Mitchell, because of the mounting unemployment which began to manifest itself through the latter half of 1957. Organized labor may be said to be at the crossroads, many things depending upon the length of the downswing in production and what Congress may do in the way of labor legislation in 1958.

RESPONSES OF PROTESTANTS, CATHOLICS, AND JEWS CONCERNING MARRIAGE AND FAMILY LIFE

VICTOR A. CHRISTOPHERSON
University of Connecticut

JAMES WALTERS
Florida State University

It is commonly believed that socialization in a particular religious group significantly influences the expectations, values, and behavior of the members of the group, although it is recognized that personal experiences profoundly modify and, in many instances, reverse the expected influence of a particular religion. It has long been known that the several religions differ in terms of the degree to which their official views toward various aspects of marriage and family life are institutionalized. For example, the official Catholic view on some of the methods widely used to prevent conception is known to be in rather sharp contrast with the attitudes of most Protestants and Jews. Moreover, it is generally conceded that Jews and Catholics are more opposed to interfaith marriage than are Protestants.

The present study was undertaken upon the assumption that the viewpoints expressed by the members of each of the three religious groups utilized would reflect more unanimity and similarity within the groups than between them.[1] It was the purpose of the study to examine the responses of each group in order to extend existing insights into the behavior and into the "unofficial" perceptions and attitudes of the members of the three religious groups in the areas of religion, parental and in-law relationships, marriage expectations, and children.

A total of 222 women participated in the study: 80 Protestants, 75 Catholics, and 67 Jews. The criteria for the selection of the subjects were as follows: (1) white, (2) single, (3) female, (4) undergraduate student beyond the freshman year, (5) 18-23 years of age. Freshmen were excluded from the study in order that the subjects would have had

---

[1] It was assumed that this would hold sufficiently true, even though no attempt was made to control such obviously important variables as degree of ardency on the part of the respondents, or particular religious subgroups among the Protestants and Jews.

some opportunity to become oriented to the college culture. Eighty-four per cent of the Jews, 80 per cent of the Protestants, and 80 per cent of the Catholics came from an urban background. As a group, the subjects were predominantly middle-class.

The items included in the instrument developed for this exploratory study were framed from questions from students enrolled in the senior author's classes over a period of several years. The items were phrased in a similar form, e.g., "Subject would postpone marriage if it were necessary to live with either set of parents," "Subject feels that the family finances should be controlled by the husband," "Subject would consider marriage in spite of objections from one or both sets of parents," "Subject would consider it right for parents to continue financing her education after she was married."

To these questions the subject responded as follows: (1) statement describes me very accurately, (2) statement is quite descriptive of me, (3) statement is both true and untrue of me, (4) statement is generally not true, (5) statement is decidedly false.

In the present analysis of the data, however, categories 1 and 2 were combined and considered to reflect a positive response to a given item, and categories 4 and 5 were combined and considered to reflect a negative response.

Originally, 25 questions in each of four subscales were included. Those questions most frequently asked were used in the final revision of the instrument to reduce the number of questions to 10 in each subscale.

The expressions used frequently by the students in their questions were purposely left intact in the development of the items. It was believed that by including the expressions characteristic of the group for which the instrument was intended, interest would be stimulated and truthful responses elicited.

In the development of the instrument, 15 subjects participated in pretest trials. After responding to the questionnaire, the 15 subjects were interviewed to obtain information concerning the ambiguity of the items and to note the extent to which the verbal replies agreed with the written responses of the subjects. Although the interview has been used as a criterion for rating the validity of the questionnaire,[2] several in-

[2] See Lois Ackerley, "The Information and Attitudes Regarding Child Development Possessed by Parents of Elementary School Children," in G. Stoddard, editor, *University of Iowa Studies in Child Welfare* (Iowa City: University of Iowa, 1935), pp. 115-67; James Walters and Ralph H. Ojemann, "A Study of the Components of Adolescent Attitudes Concerning the Role of Women," *Journal of Social Psychology*, 25:101-10.

vestigators have indicated the limitations of utilizing this criterion in obtaining indices of validity. Kelly and Fiske,[3] for example, present impressive evidence which indicates the fallibility of the human observer in an interview setting. Metzner and Mann, and Kahn,[4] on the other hand, noted satisfactory similarity between responses obtained by questionnaire and by interview. However, when Kahn compared differences between replies in an interview and responses on questionnaires, he found the responses on the questionnaires were more highly predictive of an outside criterion of productivity than were the responses obtained in the interview.

Although many investigators believe that the advantages inherent in the interview—the alleviation of misconceptions in meaning, the opportunity for supplementing questions, investigating generalities and obscure points or evasions, the opportunity for more detailed responses, and the opportunity for spontaneous answers—make it a more valuable research technique than paper-and-pencil questionnaires, it was believed that the validity of the data to be obtained in the present study would be supported by insuring anonymity to the subjects. In any event, the agreement between responses obtained in the interview setting and on the questionnaires was sufficiently high to suggest that the use of the questionnaires in the collection of the data was warranted. That the rationale for such a procedure has limitations is apparent: the authors were able to discover little evidence supporting the claim that anonymity is important to the validity of responses to items such as those included in this study.[5] Also, the benefits derived from using students' expressions rather than presenting them in more "polished" form are based upon a priori judgment as was the assignment of items to specific subscales.

Within the four areas studied—Religion, Parental and In-Law Relationships, General Marriage Expectations, and Children—there

---

[3] E. Lowell Kelly and Donald W. Fiske, "The Prediction of Success in the VA Training Program in Clinical Psychology," *The American Psychologist,* 5:395-406.

[4] Helen Metzner and Floyd Mann, "A Limited Comparison of Two Methods of Data Collection: The Fixed Alternative Questionnaire and the Open-ended Interview," *American Sociological Review,* 17:486-91; Robert L. Kahn, "A Comparison of Two Methods of Collecting Data for Social Research: The Fixed-alternative Questionnaire and the Open-ended Interview," *Dissertation Abstracts,* 12:382.

[5] However, Ellis noted a greater likelihood for "damaging admissions" in a questionnaire than in an interview. Albert Ellis, "Questionnaire *versus* Interview Methods in the Study of Human Love Relationships," *American Sociological Review,* 12: 541-53; Albert Ellis, "Questionnaire *versus* Interview Methods in the Study of Human Love Relationships. II. Uncategorized Responses," *American Sociological Review,* 13: 61-65.

were important omissions. Inclusion of an item in the questionnaire was based solely upon the frequency with which questions had been asked. Thus, the present study fails to present evidence on many significant questions in each of the areas investigated because of the criterion used in the selection of the items.

The questionnaires were administered in two ways. The questionnaires were administered to approximately half of the subjects by student assistants, who delivered the questionnaires to the residents in several women's dormitories who met the criteria for selection outlined above. Each subject was supplied with a blank envelope along with the questionnaire, and she was instructed to seal the completed form. The envelopes were placed in an unattended cardboard box with a slit in the top. Each subject was asked to complete the form when she was alone to insure anonymity.

The remaining subjects were given the questionnaires by the senior author to complete during regular sociology, child development, and English class sessions. Following the procedure described above, the subjects sealed the completed questionnaires in envelopes and deposited them in a cardboard box.

RESULTS

Religion. Although only 10 per cent of the Catholics indicated that they would marry a person of a different faith, 64 per cent reported that they frequently date men of other faiths. In contrast, 15 per cent of the Protestants said they would marry a person of another faith, while 52 per cent stated they frequently dated men of other faiths. Reflecting a more conservative viewpoint, 4 per cent of the Jewish women evidenced a willingness to consider marrying men of other faiths. However, 14 per cent of them admitted having dates with men of other faiths.

More Catholics and Protestants attended church than indicated on explicit acceptances of their religious doctrines, i.e., were in agreement with the official doctrines of their respective churches. The opposite was true of the Jews. Ninety-two per cent of the Catholics attended church, while 59 per cent accepted their religious doctrines explicitly. Comparable percentages for the Protestant subjects were 62 per cent and 33 per cent. Only 13 per cent of the Jewish subjects reported that they attended synagogue, while 26 per cent of them accepted their religious doctrines explicitly.

That the Protestant group seemed most flexible with regard to converting to the spouse's religion is seen by the rather large percentage differences. Seventeen per cent of the Protestants indicated that they would be willing to change, while only 3 per cent of the Jews and 1 per cent of the Catholics so indicated.

A larger percentage from each religious group indicated that they would marry a person of "no religious faith" than of a different faith. Forty-five per cent of the Protestants so indicated, 26 per cent of the Jews, and 22 per cent of the Catholics.

Twenty-three per cent of the Protestants indicated that they would allow their children to be brought up in a different faith, while 14 per cent of the Catholics and 9 per cent of the Jews would agree.

Parental and In-Law Relationships. The Protestants were the least inclined to live with their future parents-in-law; the Jews were the most favorably disposed. Fifty-one per cent of the Protestants indicated that they would postpone marriage if it was necessary to live with their in-laws. Forty-four per cent of the Catholics responded in a like fashion, as did 26 per cent of the Jews.

With regard to receiving financial aid from either set of parents after marriage if it was offered, 18 per cent of the Jewish subjects indicated they would, while 14 per cent of the Protestants and of the Catholics responded affirmatively. When the financial aid was specifically earmarked for a college education after marriage, the percentage of affirmative responses increased slightly: Jews, 28 per cent; Protestants, 17 per cent; Catholics, 15 per cent.

Forty-three per cent of the Catholics indicated they would confide in their mothers-in-law concerning marital problems, while 40 per cent of the Jews and 31 per cent of the Protestants indicated they would do so. On the other hand, 76 per cent of the Protestants would be willing to accept advice from their mothers-in-law, while 62 per cent of the Catholics and 56 per cent of the Jews indicated they would do so. Eighty per cent of the Jews would consider calling their in-laws "Dad and Mom" as would 79 per cent of the Catholics and 78 per cent of the Protestants.

Marriage Expectations. With regard to a question concerning whether the husband should help with household chores including child care, 62 per cent of the Catholics responded affirmatively as compared with 46 per cent of the Jews and 42 per cent of the Protestants. The Jewish subjects reflected a slightly stronger leaning toward a patriarchal pattern when the matter of who should control the family purse strings was considered. Thirty-five per cent of the Jews thought the husband should exercise this control, while 21 per cent of the Catholics and 20 per cent of the Protestants so indicated.

Thirty-four per cent of the Protestants felt that quarreling was a good way to relieve feelings in marriage as did 26 per cent of the Catholics and 19 per cent of the Jews. Indicating their understanding of the importance of solving problems before marriage, only 7 per cent of the Jews, 3 per cent of the Protestants, and 2 per cent of the Catholics thought that problems having to do with birth control, finance, and in-laws could be settled as well after as before marriage. However, 19 per cent of the Protestants, 16 per cent of the Jews, and 2 per cent of the Catholics considered divorce a suitable way out of marriage if things did not go well.

When asked whether the subject would consider working after having a baby, 24 per cent of the Jews and 11 per cent of both other groups indicated that they would.

Children. Ten per cent of the Catholics indicated they desired a "large family," while only 5 per cent of the Protestants and 1 per cent of the Jewish subjects indicated a similar desire. One of the largest differences reflected had to do with the use of contraceptives to control the birth of children: 85 per cent of the Jews, 58 per cent of the Protestants, and 18 per cent of the Catholics responded that they would consider the use of contraceptives. In response to a question asking whether the subject would marry someone who does not desire children, 38 per cent of the Protestants, 7 per cent of the Jews, and 2 per cent of the Catholics reported that they would. However, 89 per cent of the Catholics, 84 per cent of the Protestants, and 81 per cent of the Jews thought children were essential in order to have a happy marriage.

Twelve per cent of the Catholics, 9 per cent of the Protestants, and 2 per cent of the Jews indicated that they would consider having a child in order to stabilize a "rocky" marriage. In response to a question concerning whether children should be allowed to express their opinions concerning family problems, 85 per cent of the Protestants, 76 per cent of the Catholics, and 72 per cent of the Jews responded affirmatively.

SUMMARY

1. Even though the percentage of Catholic women who dated outside their religion was slightly greater than that of the Protestants, the Protestants indicated that they were most inclined to marry across religious lines and the Jews, least inclined. All three religious groups indicated a greater disposition to marry spouses of "no religious faith" than to marry across religious lines. The Protestants evidenced the least resistance of the three groups to the idea of having their children brought up in a different faith.

2. The Jewish subjects were more willing than the other two groups to receive financial aid from parents after marriage, they were more prone to confide in their in-laws concerning marital problems, and they evidenced greater willingness to live with their in-laws rather than postpone marriage. Less than half of the subjects in each of the three groups evidenced a willingness to confide in their mothers-in-law concerning marital problems; however, the Protestant women evidenced the least resistance to accepting advice from their mothers-in-law.

3. Less than half of the Protestants and Jews felt that the husband should help with household chores. The Catholics, on the other hand, evidenced a greater acceptance of husbands assuming responsibility for household chores. Over a third of the Jewish students thought the husband should control the family money, while approximately a fifth of the Catholics and Protestants expressed this point of view. The majority of the students reported they felt that quarreling was not a good way to relieve feelings in marriage; and, for the vast majority of the members of each of the three religious groups, divorce was an unsuitable solution for an unhappy marriage. The percentage of Jewish subjects who indicated a disposition to be gainfully employed after having a baby was more than twice as great as either the Protestants or Catholics.

4. Very few of the subjects reported a desire for a "large family"; however, twice as many Catholics desired a "large family" as Protestants. The Catholics were, as might be expected, more opposed to the use of contraceptives than either the Protestants or the Jews. Although few of the students reported that they would have a child in order to stabilize a "rocky" marriage, over four fifths of the subjects in each of the groups thought children were essential for a happy marriage.

SOCIAL CLASS IN PHILADELPHIA METHODISM

FREDERICK A. SHIPPEY
Drew Theological Seminary

An important datum respecting a religious movement, particularly a denomination, is its occupational composition. Because social stratification has come to be closely identified with vocation, occupation is considered to be one of the reliable indices of class affiliation.[1] Thus a study of the functional role of church members in society, according to gainful employment, can yield significant findings for the sociology of religion.

The present empirical investigation is a pilot study projected to discover, if possible, how a major denomination functioning in a large metropolitan area is embedded in the class structure of the community. To accomplish this exploration, materials were procured from 201 local Methodist congregations covering 32,689 gainfully employed church members who reside in greater Philadelphia. Field materials were gathered in the conventional categories utilized by the U.S. Bureau of Census.

I

The Philadelphia materials which are the basis for the present pilot study were assembled, the customary scientific precautions in field methodology and in laboratory procedure being utilized. Data respecting the occupational composition of the general population were procured from the 1950 U.S. Bureau of Census publications. The scope of the survey is found in three geographical elements: the city of Philadelphia, plus three counties (Bucks, Delaware, and Montgomery) in Pennsylvania and two counties (Camden and Gloucester) in southern New Jersey. Taken together, they comprise a territory regarded by definition here as greater Philadelphia.

Information on the occupational composition of a major denomination (Methodism) was not as readily available. Indeed, such data do not exist in any written records. Under the circumstances, it was necessary to set up a survey procedure by which the desired information could be

[1] Liston Pope, "Religion and the Class Structure," in Bendix and Lipset, *Class, Status and Power* (Glencoe, Illinois: The Free Press, 1953); A. B. Hollingshead, *Elmtown's Youth* (New York: John Wiley & Sons, 1949); Wheeler, *Social Stratification in a Plains Community;* Malcolm McAfee, *Social Class and Social Control in the Protestant Church* (unpublished Ph.D. thesis, Yale).

gathered reliably. First, the local church was designated as a dependable means of access to the information sought. Next, local committees were formed in each of the 201 Methodist churches. (Data are lacking from the remaining 12 churches in the territory.) Then these groups were provided uniform tabulation sheets and instructed in a pretested methodological procedure. The over-all laborious task was carried to completion in 1952, placing at last in the surveyor's hands virtually complete information on employed members of Methodist churches in greater Philadelphia. The 201 local congregations reported gainful employment (in the 1950 U.S. Census categories) for 32,689 affiliated persons. This means that 34.9 per cent of the denomination's members (93,590) were gainfully employed.

To achieve the limited objectives of this pilot study, it was necessary to locate a monograph which would afford the possibility of a conversion of occupational materials into a class system. Eventually the choice fell upon *Elmtown's Youth* by August B. Hollingshead (New York: Wiley & Sons, 1949). This work became the basis for the development of a sixteen-cell percentage distribution table which correlates social classes with standard occupational categories. The Hollingshead system is structured into five classes[2] which can be described briefly as follows: Class I, persons born to wealth and high lineage; Class II, persons of exceptionally high income and dignified occupation; Class III, industrious persons engaged as foremen, independent professionals, and owners of small businesses; Class IV, the "poor but honest" wage-working common people; and Class V, the poorly paid and erratically employed persons. Type of gainful employment ranks high generally in this arrangement. Classes I and II are elided in the present analysis. However, the remaining three strata appear as Hollingshead has them everywhere in *Elmtown's Youth.*

II

The results can be scrutinized in at least two ways: first, a local comparison can be drawn between the denomination and the general population in greater Philadelphia. Second, an interproject comparison can be made among various monographs which report a class distribution for Methodism. Space limitations force these comments into a very short Procrustean bed.

---

[2] The pattern compares favorably with the Warner scheme based upon the latter's Index of Evaluated Participation (Hollingshead, *Elmtown's Youth, op. cit.*). Also it bears a strong resemblance to the strata reported recently in Denmark. See Svalastoga, Hogh, Pedersen, and Schild, "Differential Class Behavior in Denmark," *American Sociological Review*, 21: 435-39.

The local comparison can be noted from an inspection of the following four statistical distributions.

In Philadelphia the percentage of persons in Classes I and II was 9.1 for Methodists and 6.3 for the population; in Class III, 39.3 for Methodists and 32.1 for the population; in Class IV, 35.5 for Methodists and 40.4 for the population; and in Class V, 16.1 for Methodists and 21.2 for the population.

In Pennsylvania suburbs the percentage of persons in Classes I and II was 10.0 for Methodists and 8.1 for the population; in Class III, 39.6 for Methodists and 34.5 for the population; in Class IV, 34.8 for Methodists and 38.2 for the population; and in Class V, 15.6 for Methodists and 19.2 for the population.

In New Jersey suburbs the percentage of persons in Classes I and II was 10.1 for Methodists and 6.7 for the population; in Class III, 41.0 for Methodists and 33.0 for the population; in Class IV, 33.9 for Methodists and 40.0 for the population; and in Class V, 15.0 for Methodists and 20.3 for the population.

In the grand totals for all three areas, the percentage of persons in Classes I and II was 9.7 for Methodists and 6.8 for the population; in Class III, 39.7 for Methodists and 32.8 for the population; in Class IV, 34.9 for Methodists and 39.8 for the population; and in Class V, 15.7 for Methodists and 20.6 for the population.

It is evident that Methodism is prominently embedded in Classes I, II, and III in greater Philadelphia, even exceeding the general population by approximately 10 per cent (9.8%). This finding is borne out as one observes the location of the churches, the level of lay leadership, and the financial capacity of the congregations. Among subdivisions of the survey territory, the percentage range of overembeddedness runs from 7.0 to 11.4. However, Methodist entries for Classes IV and V reveal the opposite effect. Methodism is underembedded in these classes. While one half of the denomination's persons are found in the two lowest classes, more than 60 per cent of the population is in those categories. The progressive withdrawal of congregations from areas of blight and transition during the past fifty years may be reflected in these findings. The least advantaged population groups find Methodist churches few and far between. A dearth of the denomination's buildings is found in the inner city.

Turning now to an interproject comparison of the denomination's class orientation, we encounter great difficulty in finding comparable data. Many monographs have been written in which no serious attempt has been made to relate class findings to other literature in the field. Therefore rough approximation will have to suffice until adequate refinements become available. Here then is presented the proportion of Methodists assigned to various classes in Elmtown, Jonesville, and Philadelphia. Contrasts are clearly evident. The percentages of Methodists assigned to classes in Elmtown were 5.4 to Classes I and II, 33.3 to Class III, 48.4 to Class IV, and 12.9 to Class V. In Jonesville the percentages were 22.4 to Classes I and II, 39.8 to Class III, 31.7 to Class IV, and 5.9 to Class V. In Philadephia the percentages were 9.7 to Classes I and II, 39.7 to Class III, 34.9 to Class IV, and 15.7 to Class V. Generally speaking, the Philadelphia statistics fall between Elmtown and Jonesville.

Further, the findings of Havighurst and Morgan in Social History of a War Boom Community (New York: Longmans, Green & Co., 1951), a four-class system in Seneca, Illinois, point definitely to the dominant penetration of Methodism in middle and upper classes. Among the least advantaged groups even under "boom" conditions, the denomination was relatively unsuccessful in reaching the lowest classes. Liston Pope and other scholars emphasize the middle-class orientation of Methodism. But no study known to the writer reverses the findings disclosed in the present conversion of Methodist materials on greater Philadelphia. The results of the present study appear to be in the same direction, although much more precision is desirable in determining the configuration of Methodism in the class structure of society. Many additional research explorations may be required to solve the technical problems which now stand in the way of precision.

III

In summary one may cite at least four implications for further study.

1. The use of the Hollingshead monograph raises at least two important questions which merit further investigation: (a) Is the Elmtown class system applicable to a large metropolitan area? If not, then what other system is more relevant? (b) Is the sixteen-cell percentage table adequate to convert data from occupational classifications into a class system? What bias is introduced by a pattern developed strictly from the occupations of the fathers of high school students? Does this pattern really approximate occupational composition of an entire community?

2. What constellation of psychological, sociological, economic, and religious traits belongs to each stratum in a social class system? Some intimation of the manifold intertwining of aspects of life in an advantaged suburb may be noted from the five-year study of *Crestwood*

Heights by Seeley, Sim, and Loosley (New York: Basic Books, 1956). Must the inference be drawn that no single factor index approach, not even occupation, can be utilized in studying the class system at the community level?

3. In utilizing a single factor index, in the study of religion and social stratification, is occupation of sufficient importance to justify additional research projects of this type? If it is not, then what characteristic is more important? To what extent does the choice depend upon investigative interest in personal or institutional religious phenomena?

4. What effects does occupational mobility have upon social class? To what extent is a single denomination or sect involved in such changes? How is this complicated by religion's own propensity to gravitate toward class levels of highest prestige? Perhaps the complicated dynamic character of both society and religion deserves more research attention.

ART AND COMMUNICATION

BRUCE A. WATSON
East Contra Costa Junior College

One of the necessary characteristics of social interaction is communication, the transference of meanings and feeling-states from one person or group to another.[1] When, for one reason or another, the clarity or continuity of communication is blocked, the patterns of interaction become confused and disorganized and role impairment may result. This paper is a study of art—painting and sculpture—as a means of communication between the modern artist and the viewer and the results of this means of communication to the social roles of them both.

In studying painting and sculpture as means of communication three assumptions were made: first, the period of modern art from the beginning of the Romantic movement to the present has been characterized by far-reaching experimentation with materials and subject matter; second, such experimentation has been possible only because of the breakdown in the traditional means of art patronage, such as church, guild, and ruler; third, the consequence of experimentation and freedom from authority has been the shift from representational or exoteric art to increasingly abstract or esoteric art.[2]

I

The problem of communication between the artist and the viewer is a perplexing one, for never has so much art reached so many people in such great variety. Museums and community art shows have enjoyed capacity crowds.[3] Inexpensive reproductions and books on art fill the stores. Television has brought the art critic into the home. And amateur painters dot the landscape in profusion. Yet the reactions of the public[4] to the symbols of modern art do not seem to indicate that the mere

---

[1] Arnold Rose, *Sociology* (New York: Alfred Knopf, 1956), p. 559.

[2] A great amount of material has been gathered by art historians to account for and to describe this change. Some sociologists also have been interested in this area of research. See Radhakamal Mukerjee, *The Social Functions of Art* (Bombay: Hind Kitabs, 1948); Pitirim Sorokin, *Fluctuations in Art Forms,* Vol. I of *Social and Cultural Dynamics*, 4 vols. (New York: American Book Company, 1937-41); D. W. Gotshalk, *Art and the Social Order* (Chicago: University of Chicago Press, 1947).

[3] "Picnic Time," *Time*, LXI: 72, June 15, 1953.

[4] Excluding the so-called critical elite. Cf. H. A. Bloch, "Toward the Development of a Sociology of Literary and Art Forms," *American Sociological Review*, VIII: 313-20.

viewing or acquisition of a work of art leads necessarily to an understanding of that work.[5]

It would seem that the more esoteric the work of art, the less likely would communication take place. In order that the symbols in a work of art communicate, there must be an awareness of the symbols in the work and their significance in relation to previous learning on the part of the person making the symbols and the person responding to them. Unless such previous awareness of the particular symbols and their meaning is evidenced, there can be no foundation for a response, and neither communication nor understanding will take place.[6]

This lack of communication because of the inability, or unwillingness,[7] of the artist to communicate often has resulted in quite militant misunderstandings. The art critic F. W. Ruckstull was very sure that modern art was responsible for increases in immorality and crime[8] and that it was the creation of egomaniacs and sadists.[9] The now famous Armory Show, which introduced modern art to America, was the subject of a vice inquiry when it was shown in Chicago.[10] This does not mean that the artist has been free from misunderstanding on his own part. Often not realizing why the public has reacted to his work in confusion and, as did Ruckstull, in fear and disgust, the artist has reacted, in turn, by dehumanizing his work still further.[11]

The above discussion does not mean to imply that the immediate receptivity of the viewing public is necessary to ultimate communication and understanding. Instead, there appears to be something of a lag in

---

[5] Random comments which the writer has gathered from gallery-goers fall into the following categories: bewilderment ("What is it?"); rationalization ("My two-year-old boy can do that well."); humor ("It looks like something I'd hang on my shower door."); chagrin ("How could anyone paint something like that?").

[6] See George Mead's discussion of significant symbols in *Mind, Self and Society*, edited by Charles Morris (Chicago: University of Chicago Press, 1934), pp. 46 and 71 ff. See also Ernst Cassirer, *An Essay on Man* (New Haven: Yale University Press, 1944), Chap. II, *et passim*. There would seem to be, moreover, two dimensions to the symbolism in a work of art: first is the internal symbolism, such as a lamb or fish in a religious work, which aids in conveying the story; second, the external or *gestalt* symbolism composed of the total effect of the work upon the viewer.

[7] Balcomb Greene, "The Artist's Reluctance to Communicate," *Art News*, 55, January 1957, p. 44.

[8] *Great Works of Art and What Makes Them Great* (New York: Garden City Publishing Company, 1925), p. 22.

[9] *Ibid.*, p. 21.

[10] Russell Lynes, *The Tastemakers* (New York: Harper & Brothers, 1955), pp. 198-210.

[11] Mukerjee, *op. cit.*, p. 276.

modern art between the development of new techniques and understanding by the public. Certainly this has been true with reference to the Impressionists of the 1880's, who were despised in their own day and who are quite revered today.

II

The lack of communication between the artist and the viewer and the consequent problems which emerge from it have had profound effect upon the social role of the modern artist.

The artist as a kind of occupational subculture, characterized by a common core of values, sentiments, and beliefs,[12] has largely broken down. Once the life of the artist was inextricably bound to the life of the community in which he lived. The artists of the late Middle Ages, as Joseph van der Elst has noted,[13] were strictly regulated by the guilds, which not only set standards of quality and price but demanded, as well, from prospective apprentices certificates of legitimate birth and recommendations attesting to their honesty. Nor was there any distinction apparently made between the useful and the fine arts. Melchior Broederlam, for example, court painter to the first Duke of Burgundy, decorated the duke's fleet, repaired some apparatus at the castle at Hesdin used for wetting guests with water, and designed a carriage for the duchess.[14] The artist, as a consequence of the broad view taken of his talents, had a sense of community. That sense of community has disappeared during the last century under the impact of experimentation, the breakdown of traditional patterns of authority, and the distinction apparently being made today between the useful and the fine arts.[15]

Because of the loss of a sense of community, the modern artist—as artist—finds himself between two philosophically antagonistic worlds, those of freedom and of authority, and not really at home in either one. It is in this sense that the artist is a type of marginal man,[16] for the capacity to identify with a meaningful occupational and social role has disappeared.

---

[12] Richard La Piere, *A Theory of Social Control* (New York: McGraw-Hill Book Company, 1954), p. 39.

[13] *The Last Flowering of the Middle Ages* (Garden City, New York: Doubleday, Doran and Company, 1944), p. 35-37.

[14] Johan Huizinga, *The Waning of the Middle Ages*, trans. F. Hopman (London: E. Arnold, 1924), p. 226.

[15] See the discussion of art for art's sake in the *Encyclopedia of the Arts*, edited by D. D. Runes and H. G. Schrickel (New York: Philosophical Library, 1946), p. 69.

[16] See Robert Park's definition of marginality in E. V. Stonequist, *The Marginal Man* (New York: Charles Scribner's Sons, 1937), p. xv. It may be noted that interest in the estrangement of intellectuals in general has been exhibited in modern social thought since Saint-Simon.

True, many modern artists have sought a sense of community for their talents. In the 1930's many of them joined various associations, such as the American Artist's Union, the United American Artists, and the American Artist's Congress.[17] Through these organizations they hoped to find a means of solving their common problems and gaining commissions; however, like so many depression era organizations, their influence diminished with the approach of World War II. Other attempts to find a sense of community have been made through what Russell Lynes terms "corporate taste,"[18] i.e., the patronage of art by business and industry, and through the patronage of government.[19] These have been little more than fair weather friendships, however, lasting only as long as they have had utility to both parties. Moreover, such alliances could mean a return to the regulation of creative activity from which the artist so long struggled to free himself.

But the world of freedom also has its tyrannies. As Dostoevski somewhere said, "Nothing is more seductive for man than his freedom of conscience. But nothing is a greater cause of suffering." For the freedom of the modern artist to create as he pleases, without the restrictions imposed by ruler, guild, or patron, has not been necessarily an advantage. Not always has it been a self-made choice or what David Riesman and his associates recently referred to as "autonomy."[20] Such an artist as Michelangelo, living out his old age in a one-room garret, may have been autonomous, and so might have been Rembrandt. Yet, although these two artists stood apart from the mainstream of community life, they could still know the purpose, the end for which they created. Not so the modern artist. While the quest for freedom began with the Romantics as an individually motivated, self-conscious drive for freedom, it soon became inseparably bound to those other social changes—particularly urbanism and industrialization—which bloomed with the beginning of the nineteenth century and which created the division of labor and the atmosphere of anonymity now so characteristic of Western civilization. No longer does the artist know specifically for whom or

---

[17] Horace Kallen, *Art and Freedom* (New York: Duell, Sloane, and Pearce, 1942), II: 895.

[18] *Op. cit.*, Part III.

[19] George Biddle, "An Art Renascence Under Federal Patronage," *Scribner's Magazine*, XCV: 429-30; Jacques Villon, "The Painter in Modern Society," *7 Arts*, No. 2, edited by Fernando Puma (New York: Permabooks, 1954), pp. 20-32.

[20] David Riesman, Nathan Glazer, and Reuel Denny, *The Lonely Crowd* (New York: Doubleday Anchor Books, 1956), pp. 276 and 286 f.

for what he creates. Where once he sold a specific service, he now sells a commodity. Where once a particular patron purchased the service, an anonymous public now buys the commodity.

Tied to the vagaries of price and public taste, divorced from the ends of the creative process, the self-conception of the artist has been that of isolation and uselessness.[21] The result often has been the attempt to become still further estranged from the community by seeking refuge and in-group recognition in the artists' quarters of San Francisco, New York, London, or Paris.[22] Under such conditions even the most esoteric innovations of the artist have been rationalized into a system or school of art and militantly defended against the reactions of the public.[23]

As a consequence, there has developed something of a cycle between the artist and the viewing public: the experimentation of the modern artist has led to esoteric symbolism; that, in turn, has led to blocked communication, misunderstanding by both the artist and the viewer, and feelings of mutual rejection—all resulting in a greater loss of community by the artist, resulting in still further experimentation.

III

As this study of the communication between the role of the modern artist and that of the viewer through the media of painting and sculpture was necessarily heuristic in its conception, a number of avenues of research may be suggested:

1. Whether or not the problem of communication described in this study also characterizes other artists such as writers, musicians, composers, and dancers presents an interesting area of research. If parallels can be made, then do degrees of marginality exist within these art forms? Is there a difference between the painter of the so-called fine arts and the commercial artist? What differences, if any, exist between the composer of esoteric scores for string quartets and a composer of popular tunes?

2. It would seem necessary also to discover the extent to which this analysis is a valid description of all modern artists. Unfortunately for the purposes of this study, art history and criticism have been mostly con-

---

21 Cf. Gian-Carlo Menotti, "A Plea for the Creative Artist," *7 Arts*, edited by Fernando Puma (New York: Permabooks, 1953), p. 39. See also the allegory of the dwarfs Hercules and Filomena in Aldous Huxley, *Crome Yellow* (New York: Bantam Books, 1955), Chap. XIII.

22 For a discussion of so-called bohemianism, see Caroline F. Ware, *Greenwich Village* (New York: Houghton Mifflin Company, 1935), Chap. VIII.

23 Cf. Horace Kallen, "Modernism," *Encyclopaedia of the Social Sciences*, X: 567; also Riesman, Glazer, and Denny, *op. cit.*, pp. 295-96.

cerned with artists of high caliber—a definite numerical minority. In consequence, the attitudes and feelings of many, indeed most, modern artists seldom find their way into the pages of history. On the other hand, tremendous possibilities exist to fill the void through research among the many artists who are to be found working today.

3. Do the apparent consequences of these problems of communication differ from one nation to another? Are there problems of communication between the artist and the viewer in England or in France? If not, is the character of the viewing public different in these nations? If so, are the marginality and anomie of the artist greater in these countries than in the United States?

4. Another area of research suggests itself in determining the extent to which the social role of the artist is dependent upon the means of communication, upon other factors of social conditioning,[24] upon the stereotyped conception of the role of the artist, or upon some combination of these factors. Case studies of individual artists might afford an excellent starting point.

5. Further insight into the process of communication through the media of painting and sculpture could be gained by determining the extent to which changes in artistic technique and subject matter are social in origin,[25] are determined by the psychological predisposition of the artist, or are a product of the blending of the two. Only shrewd speculations exist so far to bring any light on this problem. Valuable as these speculations are in formulating hypotheses, only sound research can develop them into a comprehensive and objective system of data.

---

[24] An interesting study of the recruitment of music composers may be found in Dennison J. Nash, "The Socialization of an Artist: The American Composer," *Social Forces*, 35: 307-13.

[25] For a survey of theories of the social determination of art, see Paul and Mary Meadows, "The Social Determination of Art," *Sociology and Social Research*, 35: 310-13.

ANOMIE AND RELIGIOUS ORTHODOXY

T. C. KEEDY, JR.
University of Maryland

This study was undertaken to test the relation of anomie, as measured by the Srole scale, to religious orthodoxy. Modern religion has been considered as a factor in social and personal disorganization as well as in ethnocentrism.[1] And ethnocentrism, in turn, has been found correlated with anomie.[2] Logically, it follows that anomie and religious adherence are correlates; however, a recent study has not supported this. Bell[3] found no differences in anomie between frequent and infrequent church attenders, at regular religious services, when neighborhood economic status was held constant. Bell's criteria of church attendance rates is, however, a partial indicator of adherence to religion.[4] In the present investigation an aim was to measure religious adherence by means of a scale which would give attention to overt behavior such as church service attendance as well as to covert behavior such as acceptance of and conformity to church doctrines.

RESEARCH DESIGN

A pretested questionnaire was administered to 138 middle-class Protestant undergraduates of a small liberal arts, denominational college in the "Bible Belt" area of the South. Of these 138, 36 were female and 102 were male. The average age of the subjects of this study was 19.8 years. The questionnaire consisted of 5 anomie items,[5] 5 authoritarianism items,[6] 10 ethnocentrism items,[7] and a 10-item religious

[1] T. W. Adorno *et al.*, *The Authoritarian Personality* (New York: Harper & Brothers, 1950), Chaps. VI and XVIII; B. Bettelheim and M. Janowitz, *Dynamics of Prejudice* (New York: Harper & Brothers, 1950), pp. 50-52, 155-56, *passim.*; R. K. Merton, *Social Theory and Social Structure* (Glencoe, Illinois: The Free Press, 1957), pp. 28-30; R. L. Roy, *Apostles of Discord* (Boston: Beacon Press, 1953); J. M. Yinger, *Religion in the Struggle for Power* (Durham: Duke University Press, 1946).

[2] A. H. Roberts and M. Rokeach, "Anomie, Authoritarianism, and Prejudice: A Replication," *American Journal of Sociology*, 61: 355-58; L. Srole, "Social Integration and Certain Corollaries: An Exploratory Study," *American Sociological Review*, 21: 709-16.

[3] Wendell Bell, "Anomie, Social Isolation, and Class Structure," *Sociometry*, 20: 113.

[4] G. M. Vernon, "An Inquiry into the Scalability of Church Orthodoxy," *Sociology and Social Research*, 39: 324.

[5] L. Srole, *op. cit.*, pp. 712-13.

[6] *Ibid.*, p. 713.

[7] T. W. Adorno *et al.*, *op. cit.*, p. 128.

orthodoxy scale which was developed for the purpose of this investigation. For the anomie, authoritarian, and ethnocentrism scales, each item was scored 3 if the respondent agreed, 2 if he was undecided, and 1 if the subject indicated disagreement. The range of scores possible for the anomie and authoritarianism items was from 5 to 15, and for the ethnocentrism scale the range possible was from 10 to 30.

The orthodoxy items each had a 5-choice pattern of agreement and disagreement. Each item was scored 4 if the subject strongly agreed, 3 for indicating agreement, 2 for indicating being undecided, 1 if he disagreed, and 0 if the respondent strongly disagreed. Therefore, the possible range of scores for the religious orthodoxy scale was from 0 to 40.

The items contained in this scale were: (1) God assists your denomination in its mission upon earth. (2) God assists some or all ministers in their representation of God to man and man to God. (3) The Bible was written with God's assistance. (4) Your denomination's interpretation of the Bible is right. (5) I attend church on Sundays if it is possible. (6) I regularly say grace before meals. (7) I abstain, because of church teaching, from the consumption of alcoholic beverages. (8) I tithe to the church or give as much as I can. (9) I regularly participate in family worship or regularly worship with friends other than at church services. (10) I regularly participate in church activities other than attendance at church services.

The orthodoxy scale, upon pretesting, did not fully meet the 90 per cent level of reproducibility. The difference between the means of low - and high - scoring respondents was significant beyond the 1 per cent level of confidence for each item, and the split-half reliability, corrected for double length, was .83. No systematic error patterns were displayed. This scale, while not strictly unidimensional, does have a consistent focus.

FINDINGS

The expectation that anomie and religious orthodoxy are correlates is supported. A correlation of .25, which is significant beyond the 5 per cent level of confidence, was found between the two variables. However, this relationship was statistically significant only when the variates of ethnocentrism and authoritarianism were held constant by the method of partial correlation. This finding raises questions as to interrelations among the variables of anomie, religious orthodoxy, authoritarianism, and ethnocentrism.

Religious orthodoxy and ethnocentrism correlated .35, and with anomie partialed out the correlation remained significant at .33. A statistically significant correlation of .38 was found between religious orthodoxy and ethnocentrism when the operation of authoritarianism was held constant.

Authoritarianism and ethnocentrism were found to correlate at .60. When the variable of anomie was held constant, the correlation became .59. Authoritarianism and ethnocentrism, with the effects of orthodoxy partialed out, correlated at .62.

A correlation of .23 was found between anomie and ethnocentrism. This became statistically insignificant when either religious orthodoxy or authoritarianism was held constant by the method of partial correlation.

Anomie and authoritarianism correlated at .20. When either ethnocentrism or orthodoxy was held constant, this correlation became statistically insignificant. With the variable of ethnocentrism not held constant, but with religious orthodoxy partialed out, the correlation between anomie and authoritarianism was .19, which is just short of statistical significance.

Religious orthodoxy and authoritarianism were not found to be significantly correlated. This lack of relationship remained when anomie and ethnocentrism were partialed out.

DISCUSSION

These data indicate that religious orthodoxy is a correlate of anomie. This offers support to the contention that modern religion is not entirely supportive or integrative in its social functions. Ethnocentrism was found to be related to religious orthodoxy. This finding is in agreement with researches into the area of the authoritarian personality in which it was shown that those who adhered to an organized religion were more ethnocentric than those who rejected it.[8]

Although religious orthodoxy was found to be a correlate of anomie and of ethnocentrism, yet anomie was not found to be independently correlated with ethnocentrism. The correlation between anomie and ethnocentrism was accounted for by the operation of religious orthodoxy and authoritarianism which are correlates of ethnocentrism independently of each other. These findings disagree with Srole's contention that

---

[8] Adorno, *op. cit.*, Chaps. VI and XVIII.

anomie is a determinant of ethnocentrism.[9] The results of this study further disagree with Srole's findings[10] in that the relationship between anomie and authoritarianism was spurious and was accounted for by the operation of ethnocentrism which was, in turn, independently and highly correlated with authoritarianism.

It is concluded (1) that Srole's variable of anomie is a correlate of religious orthodoxy, (2) that anomie is not an independent correlate of ethnocentrism or of authoritarianism, and (3) that religious orthodoxy and authoritarianism are both important and independent correlates of ethnocentrism.

---

[9] Srole, "Social Integration and Certain Corollaries: An Exploratory Study," *op. cit.*, p. 715.

[10] Srole, "Social Dysfunction, Personality, and Social Distance Attitudes," *op. cit.*, p. 7.

THE DIRECTION OF SOCIOLOGICAL RESEARCH

EMORY S. BOGARDUS
University of Southern California

An examination of the fifteen papers published in the preceding July-August issue, 1958, of *Sociology and Social Research*[1] on areas for research by sociologists gives some indications regarding the direction in which sociology is tending at the present time. While that group of papers does not cover all the fields of sociological research, it discloses important trends.

The areas for research that were reviewed were social stratification, sociology of art, the family, deviant behavior, social disorganization, racial relations, small groups, population, medical sociology, international sociology, rural sociology, collective behavior, and sociology of religion.

Cutting across these fields to a greater or less extent, certain emphases, or directions, may be noted. These are (1) roles, (2) social and group structure, (3) social stratification, (4) deviant behavior, (5) social tensions, and (6) social change. These directions will be considered in order.

1. *Roles.* The study of personality roles in group life is at a peak in sociological research today. Research is called for concerning types of roles, nature of roles, role expectations, roles reacting to roles, function of roles—in all aspects of human relations and institutions. More studies are called for concerning role playing and role taking in every expression of everyday life of every person. Social life appears to be made up of roles and role playing and role taking. There is a call to examine life in social groups in terms of how a person plays different roles in different situations, of how and why different persons play the same roles, of how roles are played according to the role playing and role taking of other persons. Investigation is called for regarding the "why" as well as the "how" of role playing. To understand the meaning of social and group life, sociologists are trying to find out the "why" and the "how" of each person's repertoire of roles.

2. *Social and Group Structure.* In one way or another the various papers on research indicate that, since persons play and take roles within social and group structures, one needs to study further the nature of

[1] Volume 42, No. 6.

these structures. Further research is needed of social structure where it is closely constructed, as in the case of dyads, triads, and other small groups, or as found in each of the established social institutions. It is also needed in the study of loosely constructed social groupings, for example, the crowd and the public. More understanding is required concerning the ways by which social structure affects role playing. The "whys" in this field are in special need of research.

However, there seems to be a minimum of research attention being given to study of the procedures and processes by which persons influence or make over social structure. The role of leader in influencing the behavior of others, as well as being influenced by his social and group life, is another field for more research. The role of anyone making over social structure invites research. Data are needed in answering the question, Why do capitalist and communist structures defy the best efforts of statesmen and politicians in breaking the deathlike grip in which these social structures are seemingly locked today?

3. *Social Stratification.* Since social stratification is an important aspect of social structure, one way to study structure is to begin with social stratification. Recent research has thrown this field wide open to further investigation. Since structure may be likened to a kind of layer cake, several problems may be posed for research: What are the human values in stratification? How far do strata hinder upward mobility in a democracy? How can strata be modified? In what ways are they socially delimiting? Are they intrinsically democratic?

The activities of the "power elite," that is, of those persons who exercise control over the elected representatives of the people, provide many hypotheses for research. A better understanding is needed of how the power elite acquire power in the first place. What is the source of their authority to usurp power? In what different ways are they adept in exercising social power? Are they essential in a democratic society? What may take their place?

4. *Deviant Behavior.* As an area for research, deviant behavior has many aspects. Is deviant behavior increasing faster than the population? When is behavior deviant? Is there more deviant behavior in some areas of life than in others? If some social institutions experience more deviant behavior than others, why? Why is deviant behavior sometimes destructive and sometimes constructive with reference to group values? How can a group control its members so as to stimulate constructive deviant behavior? So as to keep destructive behavior at a minimum? Is destructive deviant behavior sometimes of social value?

What is the relation of deviant to standard behavior? How can studies of standard behavior throw light on deviant behavior? By what methods can deviant behavior best be studied?

Closely related is the area for research connecting deviant behavior and social disorganization. When does social organization produce deviant behavior? When does deviant behavior lead to social disorganization? And vice versa? Is there an interplay between deviant behavior and social disorganization? Can changes be made in social structure so as to reduce both deviant behavior and social disorganization?

5. *Social Tensions.* Accompanying deviant behavior and changes in social structure are social tensions, which create social problems and which suggest many research topics in all fields of social life. For example, what brings about tensions in family and marriage relations, and how may they be reduced or anticipated? In racial relations? In industrial relations? In religious relations? and so on. Are there common characteristics of tensions? Of their origins? Of their reduction? What is the relation of tensions in any social institution and the personality problems of the members? What are the connections between tensions and the structure of a given social institution? When are tensions indicative of need for social change?

6. *Social Change.* Social change involves problems for research, such as changes in social structure and social organization, changes in function of groups, changes in tensions in any group relationship, changes in social values. Perhaps the last-mentioned field of social change is the most difficult to investigate because of its subjective nature. If values, as Karl Mannheim points out, are not abstract entities and not "intrinsic qualities of an object," but exist as an "expression of the valuating person or group" for which they are valid,[2] they may not be too difficult to be reached by sociological methods of research.

Related research themes are: What is the connection between social values and individual values and role playing and role taking? Which comes first, change in social values or change in personal values, or do changes in a given social field occur in terms of their interaction? What are the origins of the social values of any social group or institution? What is the nature of the social valuation process in any social situation where tensions and conflicts are active? Perhaps here is one of the aspects of behavioral science where sociologists and psychologists need most to join their research forces.

---

[2] *Systematic Sociology* (New York: Philosophical Library, 1958), pp. 131 ff.

It is to be noted that the current direction of sociological research also calls (1) for an examination of the methods of interviewing with a view to making them more objective and of the uses of statistical techniques in studying interpersonal relations, (2) for further investigation of the meanings of interpersonal relations, (3) for examination of the ways in which the results of research are affecting the development of sociological concepts, and (4) for more multivariable studies and more multicultural studies. The findings in the various areas of research now being conducted by sociologists point in the general direction of a reliable and adequate system of sociological thought.

NEWS NOTES

University of Washington. The 53rd annual meeting of the American Sociological Society was held at the University, August 27, 28, 29, with Professor Robin M. Williams of Cornell University giving the Presidential Address on the subject "Continuity and Change in Sociological Study." One of the special events of this meeting was a program "honoring the Centenary Year of Emile Durkheim and George Simmel," a French and a German contributor, respectively, to the founding of sociology. The University was host at the same time, also, to the Rural Sociological Society and the Society for the Study of Social Problems.

Whittier College. Dr. Charles J. Browning of Pasadena College has joined the sociology faculty of Whittier College.

Los Angeles State College. Professor Joseph B. Ford has received a Fulbright appointment to teach and do research in Austria; he is teaching at the University of Vienna.

University of Arizona. Dr. I. Roger Yoshino of the State College of Washington has accepted a position in sociology at the University of Arizona. Professor R. R. Ireland is the head of the Department.

Los Angeles City College. Professor Robert C. Williamson has received a Smith-Mundt assignment for the year to the University of San Salvador where he will do research in the School of Economics and teach in the School of Humanities (in the Spanish language).

El Camino College. Dr. Dempster Dirks made a study tour this past summer in Japan, the Philippines, and India.

Arizona State College. Henry L. Manheim who recently completed a "small groups" study for the Ph.D. degree at the University of Southern California has been appointed to the sociology staff of Arizona State College.

The University of Southern California. Edward C. McDonagh assumed the chairmanship of the Department of Sociology, effective September 1, 1958. Robin M. Williams, President of the American

Sociological Society, served as visiting professor during the Summer Session. Dennis McElrath (Ph.D., Yale University) joined the department as a visiting assistant professor and will specialize in medical sociology. Georges Sabagh is on leave-of-absence to administer a study of selected ecological factors associated with mental deficiency at Pacific Colony Center. Three graduate students successfully passed the Final Oral Examination for the Ph.D. degree in sociology: Attilio Parisi, Nathan Hurvitz, and Henry Manheim. Harvey J. Locke headed several sections on family behavior at the national meetings held at Seattle.

The University has received a grant of $700,000 from the Ford Foundation to organize a Youth Studies Center in a community to be selected in the Los Angeles area. Donald Van Arsdol will be released from some of his teaching load to gather basic ecological data concerning the community selected. A number of departments in the behavioral sciences will be actively involved in the Ford project over the next five years, principally public administration, sociology, and psychology. Edward C. McDonagh represents the department of sociology on the interdiscipline university committee administering the grant.

Martin and Esther Neumeyer published the third edition of their *Leisure and Recreation* (Ronald Press). Melvin J. Vincent's *Industrial Sociology* is in press (Van Nostrand). James Peterson's (with E. Metheny) *The Trouble with Women* was published during the spring (Vantage Press). John E. Nordskog's *Social Change* is being prepared for publication (McGraw-Hill Book Company). E. S. Bogardus' *Principles of Cooperation* (second edition) was published in the summer. Edward C. McDonagh (with Sven Wermlund of Gothenburg University, Sweden, and Jack Crowther of Compton College, California) completed the analysis of data on the differential statuses of selected professions as perceived by Swedish and American university students.

San Jose State College. Qualified students are being admitted this year for the master's degree in sociology.

State College of Washington. Professor John B. Edlefson has returned from a three year assignment to Pakistan where he had the responsibility of establishing sociology as a teaching and research subject at the University of Panjab in Lehore.

PEOPLES AND CULTURE

THE INSTITUTIONS OF ADVANCED SOCIETIES. Edited by Arnold M. Rose. Minneapolis: University of Minnesota Press, 1958, pp. ix+691.

Professor Arnold M. Rose has directed the assemblage of ten analytic discussions of the institutions of "advanced" societies by leading behavioral scientists representing several parts of the world. There has been a lack of material available to the behavioral scientist concerning the comparativeness of various modern societies and their cultures. Rose is correct in observing that most of our knowledge on the cross cultures has dealt with primitive or preliterate peoples and almost none with contemporary societies. Perhaps it should be added that the editor is one of the few behavioral scientists competent by training and experience to undertake the direction of this important task.

The introductory chapter by the editor points up the weaknesses in the "functionalist analogy" when applied to selected aspects of modern society. Rose insists upon a causal relationship between variables and finds fault with some of the tightrope walking of some of the functionalists. The first chapter becomes a setting for an analysis of the institutions and ways of life of the United Kingdom (Anthony H. Richmond), Australia (Ronald Taft), Finland (Heikki Waris), Poland (Jan Szczepanski), Yugoslavia (Oleg Mandich), Greece (John Koty), Israel (S. N. Eisenstadt), France (François Bourricaud), Brazil (Emilio Willems), and the United States (Jessie Bernard). Most of the collaborators have had the advantage of living in the United States for a period of time and are thus able to relate their observations to our own country in a number of particulars. There is an attempt in each chapter to follow a frame of reference with special attention to population trends, ethnic and regional subcultures, social class and status mobility, economic organization, social control, politics, religion, public opinion, family, education, national character, and the community.

Readers of this work will be surprised to see the two descriptions of societies dominated by communist ideology (Yugoslavia and Poland). There seems to be emerging a conflict between nationalism and communist ideology of the Soviet brand. It is much too early to be certain, but it appears that nationalism is a greater force of unity than either political ideology or religious conviction. There thus seems to be some evidence that the Poles and the Yugoslavs want their own brand of nationalistic communism, and the unsuccessful uprising of the Hungarian people nearly two years ago may give further substance to this point of view.

This work by a number of behavioral scientists attests to the importance of integrating effort to produce a document of enormous reference value to the academic and lay public. Anyone contemplating travel to the countries and societies analyzed in this book would do well to inspect this work. E.C.M.

INDIA'S CHANGING VILLAGES. Human Factors in Community Development. By S. C. Dube. Ithaca: Cornell University Press, 1958, pp. x+230.

This book describes and analyzes some of the problems involved in a Community Development Project conducted in a "block of 153 villages" in recent years in India. The villages ranged in population from about 200 to over 5,000. They were relatively advanced "agriculturally and economically." "Kinship, caste, and territorial affinities are the major determinants that shape their structure and organization." The "development program" included irrigation, distribution of improved seed, sale of improved implements, distribution of fertilizer, animal husbandry, improved health and sanitation conditions, social education, youth welfare, cooperatives, improved roads. The achievements were extensive and many, but not all will be lasting. This survey deals with eighteen months of activity which covers only the first half of the Project. The results are appraised in terms of two villages, one being large and the other small.

Several problems were encountered. The people accepted some aspects of the Project more readily than they did other activities. Motivations for acceptance included (1) economic advantage, (2) prestige of the individual, family, caste, village, (3) novelty, and (4) compliance with wishes of official leaders. The obstacles to acceptance were (1) apathy, (2) suspicion, (3) inadequate communication with villagers, and (4) tradition and culture.

Three methods of communication were used: (1) contact, (2) demonstration, and (3) people's participation. Three kinds of leaders were utilized: (1) representatives of the government, (2) local elite, and (3) "model farmers," who are "obscure and apolitical" but whom the people are most likely to follow. The last named appear to be more influential than the "power elite." This study has far-reaching implications for anyone who is interested in offering aid to the people of underdeveloped countries. E.S.B.

MAN IN THE PRIMITIVE WORLD. By E. Adamson Hoebel. New York: McGraw-Hill Book Co., 1958, pp. xvi+678.

This is an enlarged (543 to 678 pages) second edition of a general text in anthropology. The first version, which appeared in 1949, has long since proved its usefulness in introductory courses. There are four major sections. Part One briefly reviews the scope and aims of anthropology; Part Two outlines present knowledge concerning ancient man and prehistoric cultures; Part Three describes the races of mankind and examines possible relationships between race and cultural capacity. In the remaining portion of the book is found most of the traditional material of cultural anthropology, with 21 chapters devoted to discussions of various aspects of primitive life such as food getting, housing, handicrafts, social and political control, religion, and magic. This section also includes an analysis of the nature of culture and chapters covering the relationship between language and culture, the influence of culture upon personality formation, and cultural growth and evolution. A useful adjunct is a 20-page glossary.

An evaluation of this book might be made by answering the question, How does it differ from the previous edition? Anyone familiar with the earlier version will readily recognize that this book has entailed a great deal of rewriting as well as enlarging and is far superior to the first effort. The section on ancient man has been considerably expanded (from 58 to 94 pages) and incorporates important new data and ideas. The treatment of race uses the recently developed genetic approach to classification, which may or may not be an improvement. Chapters dealing with primitive life have been only moderately revised. The chapter on language and culture is new as is the one on culture and personality. Brief summaries and short lists of readings have been added at the end of each chapter. The latter includes easily obtainable sources and will prove valuable to the rare beginning student who is interested in going deeper into particular topics. Illustrations have been doubled and some striking full-page photographs are reproduced.

As with any text, some reservations can be expressed. Although the book is well written, the author sometimes becomes wordy or even a little pedantic. Occasionally he overgeneralizes. The glossary is cluttered with terms of restricted usage and with others for which there are more familiar synonyms. There are several ways in which the volume might have been improved. Distribution maps of primitive economics and languages, for example, would be helpful. These are minor faults, however. The book as a whole is well conceived and written with competence. It covers the fields of anthropology adequately with some attention to theoretical as well as factual data. As a text it is not too difficult reading and will serve to acquaint the beginning student with the science of man and his works.

WILLIAM J. WALLACE
University of Southern California

MODERN RUSSIA. By John Long. New York: Philosophical Library, 1958, pp. 180.

The author ties up the present with the past and proceeds to discuss the physical setting of Russia, the peoples of the U.S.S.R., the one-party system, the planned economy, and Soviet Russia in the world today. He writes a brief factual commentary on post-Stalinist Russia. While objecting "to many aspects of the Soviet experiment," he admits that he has "an admiration for certain extraordinary qualities which the Russian people display." He concludes that the peoples of Russia are numerous and determined, possessing "great physical stamina, courageous in adversity and strong in a sense of their destiny." There is a great danger "of Western miscalculation" regarding Russian potential. While the Soviet leaders believe in capitalism's downfall because, for example, of its "increasing need of artificial stimulants," they would have few advantages from going to war, especially since by their propaganda procedures they are able to win nation after nation. The chapter on the peoples of Russia shows their great diversification and also a number of social levels in Soviet society. The book is clearly written. A.R.R.

POPULATION IN ITS HUMAN ASPECTS. By Harold A. Phelps and David Henderson. New York: Appleton-Century-Crofts, Inc., 1958, pp. xvi+512.

"Get wisdom but also try to get understanding." This Bible quotation is the theme of the book. Professors Phelps and Henderson have developed a human approach for their study of population. A series of well-supported trends are given which are not likely to be voided by temporary variations in census counts or new vocabulary. Their study of population from the insights of many disciplines has the purpose of "combining an understanding of measurements and other numerical contributions with an interpretation of people and societies in their demographic relationships."

The text is divided into six sections with a brief, meaningful introduction to each section which prepares the reader for the discussions that follow and points to possible future trends and studies. The sections are Growth, Distribution, Composition, Balance, Quality, and Perspectives. Each group of chapters is complete but organized to introduce the section that follows. The authors open with a discussion of "World Prospects," which is the usual concluding topic of most books on population. This introduction develops the reader's interest in the facts, theories, and discussions of the different population groups and the questions of birth, death, marriage, and population quality. The last section, "Perspectives," relates national and world population trends, the ideas of early demographers, and closes with present and possible future population planning and policies of a national and world nature. The charts, graphs, and quotations make the presentation meaningful and thought provoking. The authors have developed a fresh approach which may be examined by all individuals interested in social studies.

WOODROW W. SCOTT
George Pepperdine College

WITH ALL DELIBERATE SPEED. Segregation-Desegregation in Southern Schools. Edited by Don Shoemaker. New York: Harper & Brothers, 1957, pp. 239.

The series of papers in this treatise on racial problems constitute "a journalistic summation of three turbulent years since the U.S. Supreme Court decision against segregation in the public schools." A large part of the materials have been drawn from the *Southern School News*, which is published each month under the direction of the Southern Education Reporting Service (established in 1954 by six southern newspaper editors and six southern educators). The materials aim to be "neither pro-segregation nor anti-segregation." They seek to report the facts as they are found, "state by state." A brief biographical sketch is given in the book of the eleven contributors.

In the "editor's afterword" interesting data are given: for example, of 9,015 school districts in the 17 southern states, only 3,008 had children of both races in 1956, that is, only 38 per cent. In three years, 1954-57, 685 districts, or 18 per cent of those having children of both races, "had begun or accomplished the desegregation process." Eight states have no integration below the college level and five "at no level whatever." Since the 1954 Decision, 138 legislative measures have been adopted "designed to slow down or arrest any movement toward segregation." School officials have "tended to look upon the problem as local

—with perhaps an assist from the state capitol." There has been a pitting of white people against white to an extent, a deterioration of racial relations between whites and Negroes in industrial and urban areas, a rise of hostility between North and South, a confinement of conflict to nonbloodshed activities, and a growing restlessness and even agony within the churches over the problem. Moreover, the southern states involved are undergoing an industrial revolution, and the editor declines to answer the question: What comes next? The book is valuable as a source book in the study of racial conflict and change. E.S.B.

OTHER MEN'S SKIES. By Robert Bunker. Bloomington: Indiana University Press, 1956, pp. 256.

This book discusses the United States policy in dealing with the American Indian since the early 1930's. Robert Bunker served with the United Pueblo Agency at Albuquerque, New Mexico. This agency administers the eighteen Pueblo tribes of New Mexico, the Zuni, the Ramah Navajos, and the Navajos to the east and southeast edge of the Navajo country. As a result of this experience, Mr. Bunker gained an insight into the problems facing the American Indian, and consequently recognized the necessity of developing a philosophy and a program of helping the Indian to help himself.

Other Men's Skies reads like a novel. Yet it is very informative in presenting the relation of the American Indian to the Federal Government, and in portraying the culture and the various aspects of Indian life in the Southwest. From the very beginning of the book as the reader follows the experiences and thinking of the author, he becomes acquainted with the Indian's way of life, he learns to appreciate the Indian's pride and dignity, he sees how his psychology differs from white man's psychology, he becomes aware of the potency of Indian traditions, and he senses the depth of Indian philosophy.

Mr. Bunker seems to have a rare understanding of and a keen insight into the needs of the Indian. He ably presents the necessity of the goal of self-government, and he cheerfully and optimistically reshapes old ways and traditions into a new way of life for the American Indian. The author's sensitive awareness and his understanding of the special problems of the Pueblos make his book a unique contribution, which will appeal especially to those interested in the welfare of America's minority peoples.

FLOYD A. POLLOCK
Stephen F. Austin State College

THE NEW JAPAN. Edited by Elizabeth and Victor A. Velen. New York: The H. W. Wilson Company, 1958, pp. 203.

This book contains important selections from a variety of sources dealing with social change in "new Japan," characterized by the contests of conflicting social forces for power. With the defeat of Japan in 1945, a social vacuum was created—the regime of imperialist forces was overthrown and new social developments had not come into power. Under the "occupation" forces, a new democratic government was organized, ownership of land was widely distributed, women were released from traditional bondage to men, and so on. Now, ten years later, a political recession is becoming established due to several facts: (1) the new democratic order was not chosen by the people but "imposed," (2) economic pressures and need for "world markets have increased," (3) communists have made much of economic maladjustments. A great deal is at stake, for Japan's influence among large Asian peoples will increase. An observation is made that Japan's success with the democratic pattern of life might well prove the most important psychological factor "in the spread of democracy in Asia." Hence, it is important that the United States offer a great deal of help in building democracy among the Japanese.

E.S.B.

SOCIAL PROBLEMS AND WELFARE

REHABILITATION: A Community Challenge. By W. Scott Allan. New York: John Wiley & Sons, Inc., 1958, pp. xvi+247.

The concept of rehabilitation as developed in this book is inclusive in definition. "It refers to a combination of disciplines, techniques, and specialized facilities which are intended to provide physical restoration, psychological adjustment, personal and vocational counseling, job training and placement." According to the National Council on Rehabilitation, it involves "the restoration of the handicapped to the fullest physical, mental, social, vocational and economic usefulness of which they are capable."

The author discusses the size of the problem and the tools utilized in rehabilitation such as programs, services, personnel, facilities, equipment, coordination and integration of services on a community-wide basis with local responsibility accepted. Essential to success is teamwork of the various specialists, such as physician, nurse, therapist, counselor, social worker, psychologist, and vocational adviser. Also necessary in this cooperative endeavor are the lay volunteers, the fund raisers, along with representatives of labor and management and of civic, service, fraternal, charitable, and religious groups.

Principles include the consideration of the whole person, not splitting his needs into categories, not seeing the person as merely a medical, a social, a psychological, or a vocational problem. Like other people, the handicapped have multiple needs, not a single need. There should be concern for the patient at the onset of his disability, not only when it has resulted in severe limitations. Special attention is given to "services for the home-bound," one of the greatest and most overlooked needs of those disabled by disease or injury. Preparation of the family as well as of the patient for return from a hospital is a definite factor in rehabilitation. Another principle is that actual employment of a handicapped worker should be based upon its productivity for both employer and employee.

The facilities of hospitals and rehabilitation institutions are discussed and differentiated, and a number of floor plans are pictured. Attention is given to social laws and rehabilitation, to health insurance and medical care plans. Programs of public assistance, social security, workmen's compensation, and veterans' services are reviewed and related to the promotion of rehabilitation by helping to remove handicaps rather than to its retardation by rewarding the continuance of the disabilities.

The author points up the need for recognizing the value of inter-agency activity among the many groups which are interested in special problems, such as chronic illness or some one physical or mental disability. Besides, "crippling disease and injury respect no international boundary" and "rehabilitation" has world-wide significance.

The author lists twelve challenges for the future as requiring consideration and comments that the convictions of human worth and of value of human welfare and social responsibility are linked "to the insistence that disability should not mean inability, that misfortune should not remove opportunity." The book is a thorough and scholarly review of the entire process of rehabilitation. It is well organized and well documented and contains an excellent bibliography. B.A.MCC.

CRIMINOLOGY AND CRIME PREVENTION. **By Lois Lundell Higgins and Edward A. Fitzpatrick. Milwaukee: The Bruce Publishing Company, pp. xxvi+471.**

Crime prevention is the major aim of the authors in producing this book. With this in mind, the material is selected and analyzed to provide the reader with factual data that may be useful for this purpose. After discussing briefly the nature, extent, and costs of crime, and the legal aspects, the various explanations and causal factors are analyzed. Special chapters are devoted to the biological and psychological factors, what the environment may contribute, and the relative influences of the individual and environmental causes of delinquency and crime.

The major portion of the book is devoted to such aspects of criminology as organized crime, racketeering, white-collar crime, drug addiction, alcoholism, and the treatment and preventive agencies. Police services, criminal courts, correctional institutions and the new penology, probation and parole, pardoning power, juvenile delinquency, society's reaction to delinquency, women and crime, the military and criminology, and the prevention of crime constitute the concluding chapters.

A great deal of material is packed into the book, with numerous headings and subheadings. Each chapter has a summary put in the form of "main propositions," which is followed by questions and problems and a special bibliography. The opinions of the authors are frequently expressed, but numerous studies are cited to support their main contentions.

However, in many instances only one paragraph is devoted to an important phase of the subject. Fewer subheadings and more concrete data would have been desirable. But the authors never lose sight of their main objective, namely, crime prevention, which is conceived of as a science with the dual purpose of deterring crime and prohibiting the formation of the criminal personality. M.H.N.

WITH THIS RING. Louis H. Burke. New York: McGraw-Hill Book Company, Inc., 1958, pp. xxiii+280.

Here is a unique book on marital difficulties. It is based upon the actual procedures and practices of cases referred to the Conciliation Court, a department of the Superior Court of Los Angeles County, which deals with marital problems. Mildred and Gordon Gordon worked closely with Judge Burke in the writing of the book; Dr. Everett L. Shostrom, a clinical psychologist, acted as a consultant. Each chapter describes a type of marital or family problem, including one or more cases, with a description of the main conditions and problems involved in each case and the steps taken in dealing with the case. Many problems were new and needed new solutions, but others were old and familiar types. The cases fall into two main categories: (1) the problems within the family, such as immaturity, sexual incompatibility, jealousy, children, stepchildren, gambling, and alcohol; (2) problems which grow out of conditions that are chiefly or partly without the family, including interference from in-laws and house guests, finances, the working wife, and religion. Some of the problems are vague, such as simply "falling out of love," while others are specific.

One of the unique features of the procedures of the Court of Conciliation is the "Reconciliation Agreement," which is prepared for each case and signed by both husband and wife. This agreement was often arrived at after a period of investigation and counseling, and a hearing in the court itself. The judge himself interviews both husband and wife, individually and together, and others who are directly involved in the case.

It is one of the most enlightening and unique accounts of cases of family difficulties. Many of the couples had already filed for divorce or were in the process of separation or obtaining a divorce. It is the kind of treatment of cases of marital difficulties that should help couples facing similar problems. M.H.N.

AMERICA'S CHILDREN. By Eleanor H. Bernert. New York: John Wiley & Sons, 1958, pp. xiii+185.

This study was carried out under the sponsorship of several agencies, the purpose being to simplify the data recorded by the United States Census and to make them available to the people.

The significant facts are analyzed under captions dealing with the number of children, living arrangements, school enrollment, educational attainment, retardation, and employment. The figures show that where the proportion of minor children is greatest, the median family income is low. Here also school facilities are inadequate and the rate of retardation is high. Living arrangements reveal considerable alteration in recent years. In 1950 more than 2.5 million children lived in families broken by widowhood or divorce and 1.5 million in other broken homes. A large number lived in institutions or foster homes. These maladjustments and departures from normal home life are increasing.

School enrollment has enjoyed a phenomenal increase in fifty years, and now nearly all children aged seven to thirteen attend school. A general striving for a high school education is also clearly apparent. Variation in the advance of children through the grades confronts the educator as a serious problem. Both the schools and the community are affected. In 1950 more than 4,000,000 children were reported to be retarded in grade, some of them by two or more years. Nevertheless, emphasis is being placed on more hours of schooling and an adapted curriculum content. The poor performance of so many children raises some important questions: Are standards too high? Is the age-grade standard fallacious in principle? Are the schools overcrowded? Other factors also affect the progress of the children, among them being broken homes, economic pressures, illness, change of residence, and disinterest in education.

Work after school hours was carried on by one eighth of high school students in 1950. Many were enrolled in school and also engaged in part-time work. Agriculture provides the largest field of employment for the male "teen-ager." Females serve as household workers and salesgirls. Among the nonwhites the high rates of participation in the labor force are coordinated with low educational attainment in the case of boys. For girls the reverse seems to be the case. G.B.M.

INDUSTRIAL SOCIETY AND SOCIAL WELFARE. By Harold L. Wilensky and Charles N. Lebeaux. New York: Russell Sage Foundation, 1958, pp. 384.

The development of voluntary and public social services in this country has been inextricably a part of the industrial development of the United States. Those who believe that the practice of social work is deeply enriched by knowledge of the social, economic, and cultural context within which social welfare services exist and by which they are influenced will welcome this volume.

The authors—Harold Wilensky, associate professor of sociology at the University of Michigan, and Charles N. Lebeaux, associate professor of social work at Wayne University—have presented their material in three parts. The first deals with the development of urban-industrial society and the emergence of social problems. It moves from the traditional praise and criticism of the industrial revolution, through a consideration of capitalism and the American culture, to an appraisal of industrialism and modern urbanization. The second part is concerned with social problems and the supply of welfare services in the United States. Here are traced some of the links between changes in technology and the social problems these create. They concentrate upon the universal effects of advanced industrialism—a large mobile labor supply, complex specialization, stratification, large-scale organization, and the concentration of people in metropolitan centers. These massive changes in American society are pointed to as the major determinants of the social problems which create the demand for social welfare services. In this regard are discussed family breakdown and deviant behavior, particularly juvenile delinquency.

Part three considers the organization of welfare services as these have resulted from changes in the social order. It considers, too, the emergence of the social work profession, with some of its strivings and obstacles. A particularly valuable contribution of this book is the extensive bibliography, even though, regrettably, there is no grouping by subject or otherwise. This volume draws heavily, and with pertinence, upon the social sciences.

FRANCES LOMAS FELDMAN
School of Social Work
University of Southern California

FREE TIME: Challenge to Later Maturity. Edited by Wilma Donahue, Woodrow W. Hunter, Dorothy H. Coons, and Helen K. Maurice. Ann Arbor, Michigan: The University of Michigan Press, 1958, pp. 172.

The University of Michigan Tenth Anniversary Conference on the Aging, held June 24 to 26, 1957, was devoted to the problem of leisure as a major challenge of the later years of life. The book contains ten of the papers presented at the conference, with a Foreword by Wilma Donahue and a Preface by Clark Tibbitts, the initiator of the Michigan Conferences on Aging. The papers deal with a variety of aspects of the problem, presented by representatives from the fields of anthropology, sociology, mental health, psychology, economics, education, religion, and related areas of study. As might be expected, the papers are unequal in value and objectivity. They contain many generalizations, some of which are not based on objective studies but were drawn from observations and general knowledge of the subject. However, the concrete data presented give certain aspects of the problem and indicate the broad outline of the necessary preparation for the leisure of later maturity. "Putting the free time to work could well make the later years one of life's most rewarding periods." M.H.N.

COMMUNITY IN DISASTER. By W. H. Form and S. Nosow, with G. P. Stone and C. M. Westie. New York: Harper & Brothers, 1958, pp. xiv+273.

In a sense, this book is a study in community organization when the routine type of community organization is disrupted. It is a study of the victims of a community disaster, such as destruction of life and property by a tornado. It is a study of how the survivors of a community disaster go about rescue and rehabilitation work. It is a study of how the staff of a disaster relief organization perform after disaster has hit a community. It is a study of relief organizational performance. It is a study of the interaction of various community agencies and subagencies in a disaster situation.

Among the findings are these: (1) the crisis behavior of individuals "may be predicted from a knowledge of the roles that individuals play in everyday life," and (2) the crisis behavior of community organizations depends on the degree to which the community and organizations have converged and the degree to which organizational structures were "integrated into the broader community." This study needs to be supplemented for comparative purposes by similar inquiries into other disaster situations. E.S.B.

POPULATION: AN INTERNATIONAL DILEMMA. A Summary of the Proceedings of the Conference Committee on Population Problems, 1956-1957. By Frederick Osborn. New York: The Population Council, 1958, pp. ix+97.

After discussing population growth throughout the world during recent decades, this book takes up briefly the problems related to overpopulation in various countries. To get the underdeveloped but overpopulated countries to tackle the overpopulation problem is difficult. It is still considered in many countries that size of population is an index of national strength, and hence it is not popular in these countries for their governments to put measures into effect that will reduce fertility; in fact, "no government has yet dared a comprehensive policy that is openly, enthusiastically, and fully implemented." However, even in China the communist leadership has been converted "to the necessity of limiting family size," widely publicized 'as a health and welfare measure." It also appears that family limitation in any country will not come about "because of pressures from the outside." The change must come from internal education.

The United States is viewed "as a backward country with respect to population policy." It is claimed that American political leaders are either "unaware of the problems or are afraid to face them." The increasing populations of the United States and Russia are a source of some anxiety to the rest of the world, partly because of the increasing demands on the world's food. The book makes its main thesis plain, although not all of the ramifications are fully explored. E.S.B.

GRUNDLAGEN DER REHABILITATION IN DER BUNDESREPUBLIK DEUTSCHLAND. By Kurt-Alphons Jochheim. Stuttgart, Germany: Georg Thieme Verlag, 1958, pp. viii+203.

Medical problems are discussed here in their interrelationship with social and economic situations, as they form the basis (*Grundlage*) for the rehabilitation of the physically and mentally disabled. The author, in his first chapter, presents a general survey of the development and execution of rehabilitative programs in such countries as the United States, England, France, Sweden, Holland, Austria, and Switzerland. Several chapters are devoted to social legislation. There are chapters on employment counseling and placement and Germany's inaugurative efforts of *Arbeitstherapeutischer Einrichtungen fuer die Gutachtertaetigkeit* (foundation of work-therapy in order to establish or make possible social and work diagnosis). A final and important chapter deals with the sponsors of the rehabilitative programs. HANS A. ILLING

BUILDING YOUR MARRIAGE. Revised Edition. By Rex A. Skidmore and Anthon S. Cannon. New York: Harper & Brothers, 1958, pp. xxiv +700.

This textbook has a practical emphasis, designed particularly to help students in preparing for marriage. The first fourteen chapters are devoted exclusively to this subject, including discussions of why one should prepare for marriage, the maturation of personality, love, dating, courtship, mate selection, religion in marriage, biological and medical factors, legal aspects, parents and relatives as resources, when to marry, engagement, and morality in relation to marriage. The second part deals with the achievement of happiness in marriage, including the wedding and honeymoon, blending romantic and conjugal love, the use of money, solving conflicts, and avoiding divorce. The final section is devoted to the enrichment of family life, especially through the coming of children, being successful parents, and growing old gracefully. Much of the material is organized around the basic questions asked by more than 8,000 students since 1939. The tables and other statistical data are up to date, including 1957 statistics. Two new chapters are devoted to family life today and the relation of personality factors to mate selection. Case summaries, reports of original research, and cartoons, charts, and drawings add to the interest in and the understanding of the problems discussed.

The authors are interested in the solution of marital problems and present valuable suggestions. The maturing of personality and the ways in which such maturity may be achieved are stressed throughout the book. Matured personalities constitute the main factor in marital success.

M.H.N.

COOPERATION AMONG COOPERATIVES. Chicago: The Cooperative League of the USA, 1958, pp. 22.

Outstanding among the characteristics of the present time are "automation, merger, integration, concentration of economic bargaining power"; the key to economic independence for small-scale producers, small businesses, and consumers is "the cooperative form of economic organization." But what are the cooperatives going to do about this threatened loss of free enterprise? This attractively planned and illustrated document suggests "cooperation among cooperatives." Moreover, it specifically proposes (1) joint ownership of facilities, (2) encouraging patronage of other types of cooperatives by members, (3) development of integrated services, (4) joint campaigns to promote all local co-op services, and (5) consumer co-ops promoting marketing co-ops' products and services.

A surprisingly succinct and clear-cut description is given of cooperative business in the United States and of "their present and potential mutually helpful relationships." The exhibit includes farm supply and rural consumer cooperatives, farm marketing cooperatives, the cooperative farm credit system, rural electric cooperatives, town and city consumer cooperatives, credit unions, cooperative mutual insurance, cooperative health plans and cooperative home ownership. A constructive picture is the result, and the need for cooperatives to work together is made clear and urgent. E.S.B.

CASE HISTORIES IN COMMUNITY ORGANIZATION. By Murray G. Ross. New York: Harper & Brothers, 1958, pp. 259.

The paucity of available case recordings illustrating the community organization method has caused a serious limitation in teaching this subject. Dr. Ross has done an excellent and timely job in compiling this book of such records. It should find a wide use as a companion volume to his *Community Organization: Theory and Principles,* published by Harper & Brothers, in 1955.

This second book is introduced by a first chapter, entitled "Conceptions of Community Organization." This makes more explicit and carries further the philosophy that the author professed in his first book and serves to give the reader a frame of reference for evaluating the case material that follows. The material has been classified according to the separate nature of the work done with individuals, with groups, and with intergroups.

The case records are well selected, carefully edited to remove extraneous writing, and limited in scope to what might be considered episodic presentations rather than complete histories. They represent the practice in both American and Canadian communities. They have been chosen to provoke thought about theory as it relates to this practice. This thought is guided by questions in point, following each chapter. The author makes no evaluation of the work they represent, leaving it to his readers to understand and judge the material. He does ask that it be done according to the conceptions presented in the first chapter.

Whenever Dr. Ross writes about community organization, he is thoughtfully writing about people—those who do it, those involved in it, and those who are served by it. Because he has this human approach, he brings this special field to life, giving a dynamic quality to the same kind of material that has so often been presented in a sterile way. This particular book should do much to enhance the teaching of community organization as a process.

JOHN G. MILNER
School of Social Work
University of Southern California

SOCIAL THEORY AND RESEARCH

IN SEARCH OF MAN. By Andre Missenard. Translated from the French by Lawrence G. Blockman. New York: Hawthorn Books, Inc., 1957, pp. 348.

This book is a report on the results of the studies by Dr. Alexis Carrell and the author while they were collaborating at the French Foundation for the Study of Human Problems. The author presents the fundamental hypothesis that man is the resultant of joint action of "all environment" upon hereditary patrimony. Environment is defined as the physical (climate and geographic), chemical (nutrition and respiration), and psychic (educational and social). Conscience, transcendental interference, and spiritual influences are also included as aspects of the environment. The book is divided into four parts. The first concerns genetics and heredity; the second, nutrition; the third, the physical milieu; and the fourth, the social milieu, particularly education. Reports on research in genetics, nutrition, intelligence, character building, education, and other areas are given.

Missenard says the present dilemma in the world is the result of man's having lost track of the fact that "the highest purpose of any civilization is man himself, and that whether a civilization is good or bad depends upon whether it makes man better or worse." He states man is becoming worse for two reasons. First, "moral values have come to be more and more disdained. . ." Man today is so intelligent that he will not submit to any laws save those of his own pleasure. Second, humans are keeping the weak and defective alive to reproduce while the intellectual and ruling classes are less fertile. The solution to this situation according to Professor Missenard is for "the scholars of the world to set aside 'materialistic works' and elaborate a program of research for the intrinsic improvement of mankind." Students of social relations will find this report on the thinking of two Frenchmen interesting and thought provoking.

WOODROW W. SCOTT
George Pepperdine College

MILLWAYS OF KENT. By John Kenneth Morland. Chapel Hill, North Carolina: The University of North Carolina Press, 1958, pp. xxiii+291.

Millways of Kent is another in the growing series of studies of American "communities." As these studies become more numerous, sociologists and anthropologists view critically the progress toward a number of goals, but toward two in particular. One of these goals is the emergence of a definitive concept of "community," accompanied, of course, by a clarification or at least standardization of contingent concepts. The other major goal is to understand the processes of social organization at the "grass roots" level. Morland, working under the guiding genius of John P. Gillin, raises some points for serious consideration with regard to the first goal, but it is with regard to the second that he makes a greater contribution.

Kent is the same southeastern town whose Negro community was described by Hylan Lewis in *Blackways of Kent,* and which, we are told, will be further described in *The Townways of Kent,* a forthcoming book by Ralph Patrick, Jr. *Millways* is focused on the community—or communities—of workers in the cotton mills of Kent, their life ways, their values, their ideologies. The Negroes and the other townspeople receive occasional mention, but only as a part of the general background. The emphasis on social cleavages is dramatized by the appearance of these works as a trilogy rather than as a single volume. There is no confusion between the other residents of Kent and the mill "class." In fact, the cleavage is so apparent that the use of the term *mill class* by the author would seem to be more misleading and less appropriate than *mill enclave.* Not only is the present meaning of the word *class* subject to dispute but also the whole perspective of the book emphasizes the insulation of the mill village society from the other enclaves in Kent.

This book has many superior features. Morland makes a greater effort to relate his findings to existing theory than seems to be the habit of many other social anthropologists. The population used is sufficiently small and homogeneous that it is clear that groups, rather than categories, are being studied. Instead of attempting to stratify the mill enclave by gradients of income, education, occupation, etc., applied externally, the stratification pattern is deduced by the author from the ways in which people actually behave—a perspective which seems both justifiable and realistic. Generally, Morland's style is first rate; much of it even bears reading aloud. All in all, it is an excellent book.

THOMAS ELY LASSWELL
Grinnell College

THE CRIMINAL AREA. A Study in Social Ecology. By Terence Morris. London: Routledge & Kegan Paul, Ltd.; and New York: Humanities Press, 1958, pp. xi+235.

This is a concise summary of the theory and methods of social ecology, especially as they have been utilized in criminological research. The author likewise presents a background of criminological theory. Possibly the most important contribution of this treatise is the examination and critical evaluation of the ecological studies of crime and delinquency over the last 150 years. These are related, in particular, to the theory of urbanism. Besides the detailed and critical account of the so-called "Chicago School" of ecological research in criminology, a description of the British studies is presented. Much of this material is normally inaccessible except to readers of the British Museum. Against this documented background, the author presents the results of his own study of delinquency in the County Borough of Croydon.

Croydon is a large British town with special suburban as well as urban characteristics. Information on 997 offenders was assembled and the delinquency rates of the different areas of the city were tabulated. Croydon has not developed radially as so many American cities appear to have done and there are no well-defined zones to which variations in rates can be meaningfully related, but the three highest ward rates occur in those areas which make up and immediately surround the central business district. These areas are spatially separated from the central district and are highly varied in their ecological characteristics. The evidences seem to suggest that the physical characteristics of a delinquency area are of little relevance except that they indirectly condition the social status of the area.

Considerable space is devoted to an analysis of case materials, including some case histories. The case studies amplify the ecological analysis of certain measurable social indices in that they make it possible to examine the processes whereby individuals interact with others in a common environment. Twenty-three factors were used in analyzing the cases. These variables have been extensively stressed in the literature dealing with the social, psychological, and biological factors commonly associated with delinquency. Since no control group was used for comparative purposes, it is difficult to appraise the significance of the different variables as possible causal factors. However, the case studies reveal certain more or less common features. The delinquent is not always maladjusted. His family seems more often to be one characterized by low aspirations and to be resident in an area where similar types of families are found. Family disorganization and other forms of family problems are fairly prevalent. The companions in delinquency are almost invariably members of a local street group or children who attend the same school. Many of the delinquents and their families are in the lower socioeconomic classes which are composed chiefly of unskilled and semiskilled workers.

In the concluding chapters the author points out that delinquency is not only a function of social class, which confirms the basic hypothesis of Albert K. Cohen (*Delinquent Boys: The Culture of the Gang,* 1956), but that it is importantly related to conditions of housing and to social policy. On the whole, this book gives one of the best reviews of the literature on the social ecology of delinquency and crime; and some new material is added, which is based chiefly on the study of Croydon.

M.H.N.

THE PSYCHOLOGY OF RELIGION. By Walter Houston Clark. New York: The Macmillan Company, 1958, pp. xii+485.

Dean Clark of the Hartford School of Religious Education offers through this book an excellent and comprehensive psychological view of religious experience and behavior. Defining religion as "the inner experience of the individual when he senses a Beyond, especially as evidenced by the effect of this experience on his behavior when he actively attempts to harmonize his life with the Beyond," the author proceeds with what might be called a most valuable organization for the development of the text and for his theoretical considerations about the psychology of religion. He reviews well those writers who have attempted to lay foundations for the study. To the final chapter dealing with his conclusions, there is about the whole a fine sense of logical development. For those who need to be informed of the practicality of subjecting the scientific method to the study, there is included a chapter on methods of study, offering some of the more important approaches in methodology that seemingly are utilitarian.

The book is divided into three parts, namely, the approach to the subject, religious growth, and aspects of the religious life. Dean Clark presents ten stimulating questions for appraising mature religion. These center around its primary derivatives, the sense of compelling need, freshness, self-criticism, freedom from magic, meaningful dynamic, integrating social effectiveness, demonstration of humility, constant growth, and creativeness. The most pervading reason for the eternal appeal of religion is that religion, more than any other human function, satisfies the need for meaning in life, declares the author. M.J.V.

HUMAN RELATIONS AND POWER. Socio-political Analysis and Synthesis. By Albert Mueller-Deham. New York: Philosophical Library, 1957, pp. xxi+410.

The author contends that social relations and processes contain all social attitudes and activities. Therefore, the reader is supplied with a thorough theoretical analysis of social relations. Those relations are classified as (1) unition, i.e., we-group, (2) relations based upon reciprocity and conformity, (3) work-association, (4) relations of selfishness, (5) exclusion of the out-group, and (6) relations of divergence. The concept of power plays an important role as a basic analytical tool in the investigation of such sociological formulations as those of "group" and of "institution." Mueller-Deham defines power in its widest sense as ". . .a directed influence or its possibility and potentiality."

This book is composed of four parts. Part I attempts to supply a basis for general sociology through arranging doctrines of social relations, structures, and social processes in a new framework. Part II is devoted to a definition, classification, and analysis of power in the social realm. Part III deals with political theory. Considered are political institutions and forms and types of governmental structures. Part IV treats of ethical problems. In this section Mueller-Deham develops the principle of ethical balance. "It is based on the analysis of every ethical conflict on discernment of the preferential ethical claim in an actual situation. It simply means the putting of primary things first. In scientific research truth is paramount, be the cost what it may; in community relations solidarity is the great fundamental; in business we have honesty; while justice rules the courts."

The book possesses an admirable unity and is written in a highly readable style.

THOMAS C. KEEDY, JR.
University of Maryland

AN INTRODUCTION TO THE STUDY OF SOCIETY. By Blaine E. Mercer with Robert K. Merton as general editor. New York: Harcourt Brace & Company, 1958, pp. xvi+640.

The Study of Society familiarizes the reader with the basic sociological data, the methods by which they were obtained, and how these concepts apply to today's American society. The principal focus is upon the analysis and understanding of social institutions, social processes, and social organization. Each chapter, besides presenting the main ideas, concepts, and problems appropriate to its subject, offers many case studies and examples of research which help to anchor these topics in the students' minds. Outstanding among these are "Jackie Robinson and the Brooklyn Dodgers: Racial Conflict in the Sports World," and the examples of the solidary family, the family in conflict, the public, and the mob.

As an introductory text, it necessarily covers a great deal of territory not too deeply; however, the presentation is such that the student is able to understand the meaning and application of the concepts as well as the strengths and weaknesses of sociology. This reviewer fully agrees with Robert K. Merton, who states, "There is no good reason why a textbook should be tedious. There is wisdom in the adage that interest can be sustained without the sacrifice of serious content." *The Study of Society* is such a book. Another merit is the outstanding use of illustrations to further solidify the meanings of the concepts of sociology as they apply in "real life."

STUART A. BRODY

CONCEPTS AND METHODS OF SOCIAL WORK. Edited by Walter A. Friedlander. New Jersey: Prentice-Hall, Inc., 1958, pp. ix+308.

This book consists of an introduction to the values, goals, and principles of social work followed by descriptions, documented with case illustrations, of social casework, social group work, and social community organization work.

In his presentation of social casework, Henry S. Maas defines the concepts of social role, adaptation to stress, and ego and analyzes their use in the study, diagnostic, and treatment processes. He also relates them to the goals and to the basic and differential principles of casework. Gisela Konopka describes social group work, giving less detailed attention to a larger number of concepts about human behavior and principles of practice as applied to fact finding, diagnosis, and treatment. She thinks that the formulation of combined knowledge about individuals and groups and its translation into principles of action is group work's specific contribution. Genevieve W. Carter's analysis of community organization indicates that social work method is only one means of solving community health and welfare problems. In addition to concepts and principles of social work, such facilitating processes as promotion, research, consultation, public relations, and social action are used by the social worker in carrying out the reconnaissance, diagnostic, planning, and implementation phases of the method.

It was disappointing that the contributors did not use a more uniform approach and terminology so that readers might more easily compare the generic and specific elements of the primary social work methods. The concluding chapter by Friedlander only partially succeeds in synthesizing the content. This book is nevertheless a valuable addition to social work literature, and sociologists will be particularly interested in the use that social workers are making of sociological theory and research findings.

HELEN NORTHEN
School of Social Work
University of Southern California

SOCIAL PSYCHOLOGY. Second Edition. By S. Stanfield Sargent and Robert C. Williamson. New York: The Ronald Press, 1958, pp. x+649.

The first edition of this book by the senior author has been revised, enlarged, improved, and illustrated in this second edition, bearing the subtitle, "An Introduction to the Study of Social Relations." Much of the material of the first edition has been retained as well as the basic plan, but new chapters dealing with group dynamics and ethnic and international relations have been added. The definition of social psychology is still a study "dealing with individual behavior as it affects and is affected by the behavior of others," which definition omits much of the phenomena belonging to collective behavior. The text, however, includes some of the aspects of collective behavior, and satisfies the claim made that it offers an "integrated and practical approach to social psychology," meaning the "bringing together of psychological, sociological, anthropological, and psychiatric techniques and findings," as well as "the application of social psychology to the solution of social problems." The authors have taken advantage of some of the more recent research experiments in the field and presented them appropriately. Some good chapters appear on the subjects of culture, motives, and social roles. Not much space is given to social process or to the various social processes as such. The final chapter reviews the preceding chapters, deals briefly with the present and future of social psychology, and engages in some interesting speculation. The text is lucidly written, although sometimes weighted unevenly as to materials offered.

M.J.V.

THE SOCIAL PSYCHOLOGY OF MUSIC. By Paul R. Farnsworth. New York: The Dryden Press, 1958, pp. xiv+304.

Devoted more to a certain type of psychological study of musical techniques than to the real social-psychological effects of musical compositions as a whole, this attempt to subject music to a kind of scientific inquiry should be nicely rewarding to those interested in the juncture of psychology and music. A recitation of many experiments with such musical effects as tone, melody, and measures of musical tastes and abilities serves to cover the content of several interesting chapters. One, dealing with the language aspects of music, is stimulating in that the old problem of the universality of art is indirectly suggested, and the author reaches the conclusion that the "images music arouses are specific to the experiences of the listener." But so is language itself! Music, he concludes, is not "listening to a language in the fullest sense of the term." This is in accord with the results of many experiments made on listeners who have represented varied cultures.

The final chapter examines the applications that have been made in therapy and industry. Professor Farnsworth avers that while music "can undeniably alter both moods and some basic physiological processes of many persons," the medical value of music remains to be tested in research-oriented hospitals. The book is furnished with what would appear to be a complete guide to the numerous experiments already made. One field of social psychology omitted as such is that of social control through such types of music as "military" or war and religious or spiritual. Most of the experiments reported upon are more of a true psychological nature than strictly social psychological. M.J.V.

HOUSING. A Factual Analysis. By Glen H. Beyer. New York: The Macmillan Company, 1958, pp. xii+355.

The author, who is the director of the Housing Research Center of Cornell University, summarizes a vast amount of concrete data on housing, particularly the housing situation in the United States. He discusses the demand and supply factors in the housing market, the home building industry, home ownership and financing, housing design, neighborhood standards, urban renewal, government's role in housing, rural housing, and housing research. The descriptive material is supplemented by 69 figures and 93 tables, and a series of drawings by Zevi Blum to give a visual picture of the housing situation.

Social scientists are especially interested in the summary of data depicting the economic base of communities, population factors, the growth of cities and metropolitan areas, the social structure of cities, mobility and migration, families and households, family income, standard of living, problems of housing the aged, and regional differences in population and housing. In short, the author tries to show that the "whole basis for our housing is to provide for the shelter requirements of our population." M.H.N.

THE COMMUNITY. An Introduction to a Social System. By Irwin T. Sanders. New York: The Ronald Press Company, 1958, pp. xx+431.

The book, designed primarily as a textbook for undergraduate courses in sociology, is of general value for any person interested in the characteristics of various types of communities, whether large or small, industrial or rural, at home or abroad. The "main stress is upon orientation and the general conceptional framework"; the central theme of the book is that a community is essentially a system of social interaction. After an introductory statement of why communities should be studied and the ways they may be studied, the author describes in detail the social traits of the community, including the community as a place, the people, as a service center, communication network, traditions and values, social layers, types of groups, an arena of interaction, social change, social control, and as a social system. This is followed by a series of chapters on the major systems at work in the community, including local government, the economy, family life, religion and morality, education, health and social welfare, and recreation. The concluding section deals with physical planning and zoning and community development.

The descriptions of the different phases of the community, the definitions of the basic concepts, and the illustrative materials are presented in a simple, understandable, and effective manner. As a general textbook on the community it is one of the best. M.H.N.

THE MAN ON YOUR BACK. By Wyatt Marrs. Norman: University of Oklahoma Press, 1958, pp. 289.

This definitive analysis of the art of living without producing in modern society is certain to attract the attention of all persons seriously concerned with the extent of "freeloaders," spongers, and other human parasites who have arisen within our society. The philosophy of "getting something for nothing" and the development of an attitude that honest work must be left to those persons who have no imagination or creativity seem to be basic assumptions underlying professional parasitism. Marrs views the parasitic as composed mainly of the chronically dependent (the beggar), the predatory (the cunning thief), and the entrenched (who exploit some privileged position).

Special attention is devoted to the institutionalization of social parasitism in contemporary American society. Almost every major institution has developed within it some peculiar form of parasitism; hence, it is not surprising to find institutionalized parasites in the family, church, economic enterprises, and the government. The philosophy of looking toward the government as almost a "white father" who can solve individual problems by handouts has become widely accepted. Marrs levels his heaviest blows at economic and political parasitism. Some very thoughtful implications to our society are raised by the author when he discusses the effects of the "man on your back." Parasitism is a luxury that spoils the giver and the receiver alike. The difficulty of getting rid of known parasites is not easy, inasmuch as there seems to be a type of "contagion" broadcast by their very presence. This excellent book because of its unique and important theme will take its place in a select list of classics about the American scene. It deserves a wide readership to alert the public to the extent and techniques of the parasitic.

E.C.M.

SYSTEMATIC SOCIOLOGY. An Introduction to the Study of Society. By Karl Mannheim. Edited by J. S. Eros and W. A. C. Stewart. New York: Philosophical Library, 1958, pp. 169.

The first three parts of this book deal with man and his psychic equipment, with elementary social processes, and with social integration, respectively. They have been adapted from lectures delivered by Mannheim in 1933-34 in London. Part III, on the different forms of human integration and on the process that leads to integration, is the core of this treatise on systematic sociology. The fourth and concluding part discusses social stability and social change and is based on lectures given during the World War II years.

Established groups—for example, the family—are viewed as being "the integrations of diverse forces and tendencies." The two-person group, the dyad, the couple relationship are considered to be "the most intensive group relationship because the whole personality can enter into it." The discussions of social distance include "fear distance," "power distance," "status distance," and so on; they are all subject to a basic unity in society. Mannheim does not believe that class struggles are inevitable. He considers Marxism as a challenge and gives his reasons. The discussion seems to leave the book uncompleted, for it would appear that a "systematic sociology" needs at least a few well-developed and organized conclusions. E.S.B.

INTERNATIONAL BIBLIOGRAPHY OF SOCIOLOGY. By a Board of Editors from Nine Different Countries. Paris: Unesco, 1958, pp. 272.

Academic and research institutions in many countries have contributed to this bibliography, for example, the institutions of learning in the following centers: Athens, Belgrade, Brussels, Cologne, Jerusalem, Lisbon, Madrid, Mexico City, Oslo, Paris, Perugio, Tokyo, Utrecht, Warsaw, and Washington. A total of 4,240 bibliographic references are given and classified under the following headings: history and organization of social studies, theories and methods of sociology, social structure (the largest section), social control and communication, and social change. A complete subject index and author index are appended to this valuable reference work with its many international as well as national values. E.S.B.

THE SOCIOLOGY OF KNOWLEDGE. An Essay in Aid of a Deeper Understanding of the History of Ideas. By Werner Stark. London: Routledge & Kegan Paul, Ltd., 1958, pp. xi+356.

The author endeavors "to re-think the whole subject of the sociology of knowledge" and "to clarify its issues." In the rethinking process the author reviews a large portion of the literature on the subject, particularly those aspects that have been contributed by Mannheim, the Webers, Pareto, Marx, Nietzsche, and Durkheim. He makes a substantial contribution to the history of the sociology of knowledge.

In discussing the various ways in which there is a "social determination of culture, of thought and feeling, of scholarship and art," the author expresses "due respect for the spontaneity and even the greatness of the individual personality," and does not undertake to argue away "the creativeness of the individual mind." He recognizes, however, that "no one is an island." Within the societary and cultural framework, that is, within social determination, there appears to be a considerable degree of freedom for individual thought and even for creativeness. In this connection an important question is raised: Does the closeness of integration with social reality affect the degree of determination? Another question may be raised: How far can individual freedom affect or make over social determination? Still another is: How far does social determination extend beyond class and party? One more: Is extension of social determination related to intensity of such determination? These and other far-reaching questions are raised but not always answered in this stimulating work. E.S.B.

VEBLENISM: A NEW CRITIQUE. By Lev E. Dobriansky. Washington: Public Affairs Press, 1957, pp. xii+409.

The preface of this new critique of Thorstein Veblen's thought indicates that Professor Dobriansky, taking a cue from a growing revival in the interest of institutional economics, regards this revival as concomitant with Veblenism. Moreover, he holds that "the fundamental and foremost problems of our society" are "social philosophical in nature" and hence undertakes to present the ideas of Veblen as a kind of systematic body of thought. By so doing he attempts to provide an analytic approach with the objective of offering "some contribution to urgent problems bearing upon the integration of the social sciences and the formation of liberal educational curricula designed to conserve the values of Western society and man." Ideas, not vested interests, are "dangerous for good or evil" wrote John Maynard Keynes, and Dobriansky holds that "in a sense these contain within themselves a power of determination."

In the difficult task of exploring systematically the philosophical ideas of Veblen, the author begins with a historical account of the metaphysical roots of Veblenism, widely spread from Descartes to William James. He successfully reveals the views of Veblen on such phenomena as natural rights, class struggle, private property, and machine technology. Interestingly presented, too, are Veblen's views on education.

Veblen does not always fare well in this critique. Often, declares the author, he did not reveal any great profundity of thought and his intellectual orientation was marked by frequent imbalances. His chief strength lay in the attention that he paid "to the proliferous discordant and disturbing factors significant in the modern alteration and redirection of developments and events." Unlike Marx, Veblen recognized the subordination of economic relations to the broader social relations, and many of his predictions have been fulfilled, regardless of his lack of what today would be called a modern social science methodology.

M.J.V.

EXPLORATIONS IN ROLE ANALYSIS: STUDIES OF THE SCHOOL SUPERINTENDENCY ROLE. By Neal Gross, Ward S. Mason, and Alexander W. McEachren. New York: John Wiley & Sons, Inc., 1958, pp. xiv+379.

The analyses of the problems induced by the concept "role" and "role conflict" in these studies are of general significance for social psychology and the behavioral sciences in general. The book comes as a result of some of the findings of the School Executive Studies, a Harvard University research program, the particular area under examination here being the role of "school superintendent in terms of the social structures in which it is involved."

Part One of the report consumes five chapters in exploring the various definitions of the "role" concept as it has been formulated or used by such men as Linton, Parsons, Davis, Newcomb, Sarbin, and others. While similarities appear, there are some differentiations in the usages, including some vagaries. The authors of this volume conclude that for their purpose the definition of role should be restricted to a set of expectations, and hit upon the following: "A role is a set of evaluative standards applied to an incumbent of a particular position," or "a role is a set of expectations." This would seem to be a specific for the ordering of the research design and the accompanying research based upon it. As such, it makes for definiteness. Why so much ado is made about a simple concept by social scientists is difficult to know when role simply refers to the part being played, if one notes that its origin came from the drama. The authors' definition does not separate role expectation then from role, nor do they indicate its relationships to such terms as role behavior, the twofold aspects of role expectation, role playing and role fulfillment.

The research studies of the role of school superintendent have been accomplished with meticulous care, nonetheless, and the research design stands out in excellent relief. At the end, the reader has become aware of the complexities of the role of school superintendent, his strains and tensions both on and off the job, his relationships with community pressures, with teachers and their salary demands, with parents, and even with religious interests involving both the general community and school board members. The studies reveal some major hypotheses concerned with a theory of role conflict resolution and their testing. One such hypothesis: The greater the homogeneity among or between position incumbents, the more consensus they will have on the expectations for their own and others' positions. As a lesson in how to demonstrate and report empirical research, the book serves as an excellent model.

M.J.V.

SOCIOLOGY. Revised Edition. By George A. Lundberg, Clarence C. Schrag, and Otto N. Larsen. New York: Harper & Brothers, 1958, pp. xix+200.

This is the revised edition of a text by exponents of the neopositivist school in contemporary American sociology. This viewpoint emphasizes the basic processes of communication and interaction, and that mathematics, social measuring instruments, operational definitions, a consistent frame of reference, and a logically coherent, empirically verifiable system of concepts are indispensable for the discovery of predictable sociological generalizations and laws. The present text fosters this viewpoint.

New content in the present edition is supplied by three new chapters: "The Process of Social Interaction," "The Nature and Interrelationship of Institutions," and "Sociology and Social Policy." Other new content includes materials on the social basis and functions of communication, the role of communication in socialization and personality development, the social functions and effects of mass communication, the role of religion in the development of human values, group life in urban communities, the origin of research problems and development of hypotheses in sociology, and the field of sociology and its applications.

There are also modifications in the organization of the material, and the presentation has been simplified through explanatory discussions and clarification of basic concepts. Recent research findings and essential statistical data have been incorporated and other factual information has been brought up to date. New illustrative materials such as pictures, graphs, and tables, as well as a glossary of basic terms have been added.

A system of numbered paragraphs and cross references to other pertinent and associated paragraphs throughout the book gives this text special interest.

NATHAN HURVITZ
University of Southern California

MATE-SELECTION. A Study of Complementary Needs. By Robert F. Winch. Boston: Harper & Brothers, 1958, pp. xvii+349.

"*Mate-Selection* is the outcome of a research project in which the author tested the hypothesis that men select wives and women select husbands on the basis of complementariness of emotional needs." The author explores the various studies of love, marriage, and complementary needs, including the studies showing homogamy and some evidence in support of heterogamy. A chapter by Linton C. Freeman shows that mate-selection in non-Western societies may take place without love. The various theories of complementary needs are explored, the general hypothesis of complementary need is stated, and the method of gathering and analyzing data obtained from twenty-five couples is described. Considerable space is devoted to the theoretical formulation as the basis for the analysis of complementariness.

The case studies are classified and analyzed under four main types of complementariness: (1) "Mother-Son," (2) "Ibsenian," (3) "Master-Servant," and (4) "Thurberian." In the first type the wife nurtures her husband in the sense of taking care of him, providing for his wants, and giving him service; and the husband looks to his wife for guidance and direction. "In the Ibsenian marriage there is much the same type of relationship except that the nurturant-dominant parent is the husband and the receptive-submissive one is the wife." In the "Master-Servant" type it is the husband who commands and is the dominant person, the wife serves him and is nurturant; whereas in the "Thurberian" type the reverse conditions and relationships occur. Various complications (levels, ages, and external events) are explored and the implications of the basic hypothesis are pointed out and described.

Considerable attention is given to the general theory of complementariness by the development of a typology of complementary matings and through the use of case materials to illustrate the different kinds of complementariness. One may question the adequacy of the sample, especially with respect to the total number of cases studied and the selection of cases for illustrative purposes. At any rate, the theoretical formulations as well as the case materials provide a basis for further research and exploration.

M.H.N.

OTHER PUBLICATIONS RECEIVED

A STUDY OF HISTORY. By Arnold J. Toynbee. Abridgment of Volumes VII-X, by D. C. Somervell. New York: Oxford University Press, 1957, pp. xiv+414.

The last four volumes of this monumental Study of History have been completed, and, whether or not one reads them in their original form, this abridgment will be found complementary and as invaluable as the abridgment to the first six volumes. The principal subjects developed in the four volumes and the abridgment include Universal States, Heroic Ages, Contacts between Civilizations in Space, Contacts between Civilizations in Time, Law and Freedom in History, and the Prospects of the Western Civilization. The concluding section explains how the *Study* came to be written, and presents an imposing summary of the ten volumes of the original. Toynbee commends Somervell especially for this summary, while at the same time praising his collaborator for both of the abridgments. Toynbee's international pre-eminence as a historian should be sufficient inducement for one to read the complete *Study*, or at least the abridged version. J.E.N.

CURRENT SOCIAL RESEARCH. An Inventory. Compiled by Community Research Associates, New York, 1957, pp. ix+205.

This selected inventory of research and demonstration projects in fields related to the interests of the Federal Department of Health, Education, and Welfare contains reviews of 372 research studies. Each review gives the aim of the research project, the methods of study as far as possible, reference to the findings, and who conducted and who financed the project. About one half of a printed page on the average is given to each review.

The major classifications are (1) behavioral research, (2) socioeconomic research, (3) research on professional education, (4) research on rehabilitation services, (5) research on health services, (6) research on welfare services, (7) program research, and (8) administration research. The first two categories will be of interest to the sociologist. Three indexes are provided: (1) organizations conducting or cooperating in research, arranged by states of the Union, (2) principal researchers (about 350), and (3) subjects. Careful attention has been given to details as well as to the main research emphases in this important reference work. A.R.R.

GEOGRAPHY IN THE 20TH CENTURY. Edited by Graham Taylor. New York: Philosophical Library, 1957, pp. xi+674.

In this study of the growth, fields, techniques, aims, and trends of geography by a total of twenty-two geographers, interesting chapters are included on such subjects as settlement by modern pioneer, racial geography, urban geography, the relations of geography and history, geography and aviation, and the sociological aspects of geography. Especially interesting are the discussions of air photography and the dozen plates illustrating air photography. It is pointed out that the character of a region "depends not on the influence of natural material force in the environment, but on social forces which re-adapt and re-organize the areas and give it a unique character."

THE ART OF OVERSEAMANSHIP. Edited by Harlan Cleveland and Gerard J. Mangone. Syracuse: Syracuse University Press, 1957, pp. 150.

Eleven papers constitute the contents of this report of a conference sponsored by the Maxwell School of Citizenship. It is concluded that the increasing thousands of Americans who work in one capacity or another abroad need the training that is called for in similar occupations at home plus an undesignated factor—perhaps a broader viewpoint of life in all its vital aspects, perhaps "a keen sense of institutional environment," or perhaps helping "to build effective governments as well as healthy and productive peoples."

THE STORY OF HUMAN EMOTIONS. By George M. Lott. From a Teen-Age Viewpoint. New York: Philosophical Library, 1958, pp. 228.

This is a popular presentation by a psychiatrist that is designed to help teen-agers and their parents observe the rules of mental hygiene in the home.

THE MEANING IN YOUR LIFE. By S. Rosenkranz. New York: Philosophical Library, 1958, pp. 146.

Dr. Rosenkranz develops his idea of the role of freedom as giving meaning to life.

THE ANGEL IN THE STONE. By Charles Edwin Butterfield. New York: Comet Press Books, 1957, pp. 171.

A lifetime of advanced thought permeated by imagination has gone into the creation of these sonnets and poems, many of which speak deep human-service messages.

THE JEWISH POPULATION. By Louis Rosenberg. Montreal: Canadian Jewish Congress, Bureau of Social and Economic Research, 1958, pp. 40.

In this statistical summary from 1851 to 1941, with supplementary figures for the period 1951-54, it is concluded that this minority group, "overwhelmingly urban, keenly appreciative of the cultural, economic, and social opportunities, with immigration restricted, with a low rate of intermarriage, and with high tenacity in retaining its religious and cultural identity" has "rapidly adapted itself to the social, educational, and political environment of the country." E.S.B.

HOME CONDITIONS. A Sociomedical Study of 1,066 Hospitalized Patients with Skin and Venereal Diseases. By Esbern Lomholt. Copenhagen: Rosenkilde and Bogger, 1958, pp. 100.

ENROLLMENT STATISTICS, Colleges and Universities, State of Washington, Fall Term, 1957-58. By Calvin F. Schmid. Seattle: Washington State Census Board, 1958, pp. 34.

THE PROMISE OF MODERN LIFE. By D. W. Gotshalk. Yellow Springs: Antioch College, 1958, pp. 116.

The author divides modern time into three periods: (1) one whose outlook emphasized individuality, (2) one in which creativity emerged to accentuate individuality, and (3) the recent period in which interdependence is believed to be in ascendance. We are in need today of developing "the value possibilities of the interrelational principle."

ASIAN WOMEN AND EROS. By Millicent Pomerenke. New York: Vantage Press, 1958, pp. 337.

SOCIAL STATUS AND PUBLIC HEALTH. By Ozzie G. Simmons. New York: Social Science Research Council, 1958, pp. 34.

EFFECTS OF SOCIAL AND CULTURAL SYSTEMS IN REACTIONS TO STRESS. By William Caudill. New York: Social Science Research Council, 1958, pp. 34.

Sociology and Social Research

AN INTERNATIONAL JOURNAL

□

Articles in Forthcoming Issues . . .

November-December and later

Computers and Social Research .... E. F. BORGATTA
Empathy in the Dating Situation .... R. L. STEWART & G. M. VERNON
Social Distance Scales and Stratification .... F. R. WESTIE
Group Processes and Prohibition .... NORMAN JACKSON & M. SHERIF
Self Tattooing Among Delinquents .... JOHN H. BURMA
Occupations of Sociology Majors .... MARGARET L. HELBRICK
Effectiveness in Teaching Sociology by TV .... MARVIN SUSSMAN
Techniques in Teaching Sociology by TV .... R. A. SCHERMERHORN
Changing Attitudes in China .... THEODORE & WEN-HUI CHEN
Lower Levels of Industrial Leadership .... AMITAI ETZIONI
Social Influence on Children .... R. G. HUNT & V. SYNNERDAHL
Job Satisfaction and Leisure .... A. T. W. MATHEWS & B. LABAN
Economic Motivation in Ethnic Relations .... R. R. IRELAND
A Note on British Health Service .... J. B. MONTAGUE, JR.
Measuring Group Opinion .... L. K. NORTHWOOD
Areas for Research in Leisure and Recreation .... M. H. NEUMEYER
Administrative Role in Desegregation .... R. R. DWYER
Social Work and Sociology .... JOSEPH W. EATON
Teaching Sociology by Television .... THOMAS F. HOULT
The Concept of the Group .... MARIE L. BORGATTA

Articles in Preceding Issue . . .

July-August 1958

In Social Stratification .... BERNARD BARBER
In Sociology of Art .... JAMES H. BARNETT
In Sociology of the Family .... JESSIE BERNARD
In Teaching Sociology .... W. BROOKOVER & W. D'ANTONIO
In Deviant Behavior .... MARSHALL B. CLINARD
In Social Disorganization .... ROBERT E. L. FARIS
In Race Relations .... E. FRANKLIN FRAZIER
In Small Groups .... A. PAUL HARE
In Demography .... PHILIP M. HAUSER
In Medical Sociology .... E. GARTLEY JACO
In International Sociology .... ARNOLD M. ROSE
In Industrial Sociology .... EUGENE V. SCHNEIDER
In Rural Sociology .... WALTER M. SLOCUM
In Collective Behavior .... RALPH H. TURNER
In Sociology of Religion .... J. MILTON YINGER

Sociology and Social
. . . Research . . .

AN INTERNATIONAL JOURNAL

The Concept of the Group 83
MARIE L. BORGATTA

Areas for Research in Leisure 90
MARTIN H. NEUMEYER

Teaching Sociology by Radio and Television 97
THOMAS F. HOULT

Teaching Sociology via Television 102
MARVIN B. SUSSMAN

Teaching Sociology by Means of Television 108
R. A. SCHERMERHORN

Measuring Group Opinion 113
L. K. NORTHWOOD

Economic Motivation in Ethnic Relations . 119
RALPH R. IRELAND

Racial Distance Changes in the United States 127
EMORY S. BOGARDUS

Pacific Sociological News 136

Social Problems and Welfare 137
Peoples and Culture . . . 150
Social Theory and Research 156
Social Fiction 166

VOL. 43 NOVEMBER-DECEMBER 1958 No. 2

YEARLY SUBSCRIPTION, $3.50 SINGLE COPIES, 70 CENTS

Sociology and Social Research

AN INTERNATIONAL JOURNAL

PUBLISHED BIMONTHLY AT THE UNIVERSITY OF SOUTHERN CALIFORNIA
UNIVERSITY PARK, LOS ANGELES 7, CALIFORNIA

YEARLY SUBSCRIPTION, $3.50 SINGLE COPIES, 70¢

Entered as second-class matter March 31, 1936, at the post office at Los Angeles, California, under the act of March 3, 1879.

Contributed materials which appear in *Sociology and Social Research* do not necessarily express the opinion or the policy of the editorial staff and publisher.

Articles published in this journal are indexed in *The International Index to Periodicals*, and abstracted in *Sociological Abstracts* and *Psychological Abstracts*.

PUBLISHED BY

UNIVERSITY OF SOUTHERN CALIFORNIA PRESS

UNIVERSITY PARK LOS ANGELES 7, CALIFORNIA

SOCIOLOGY AND SOCIAL RESEARCH

November-December 1958

THE CONCEPT OF THE GROUP
A Brief Consideration

MARIE L. BORGATTA
New York University

The rise of interest in group behavior since World War II suggests the need for consolidation of knowledge. However, any attempt to systematize theory about the group faces a situation which might be paraphrased from Gertrude Stein—A group is a group is a group. The term has been used with many sets of adjectives: open and closed, formal and informal, sentiment-oriented and interest-oriented, voluntary and compulsory, etc. Structure, in a relatively static sense, may be emphasized as the appropriate approach in one analysis while in another the attempt may center around some notion of a dynamic process or functional description.

There seems to be no argument as to whether "the group" exists as long as the term is used in a nongeneric sense. For all practical purposes we have as common knowledge that people have always lived in aggregates of one sort or another and probably will continue to do so. In the past some interest has been displayed in the origins of "the group," and both past and current interest sometimes has centered on the end forms the group may or should take. Discussion of either extreme invariably is metaphysical, and while provocative is also frustrating in its dependence upon speculation with no opportunity to either go back and recapitulate or go forward and see.

There is a rich literature comprising a basic core of descriptive materials on the group and group functioning. Further, implicit in most sociological writing is the assumption that what is being discussed is aggregate human action, first in one complex, then in another, but recognizing the same processes and the same characteristics which reoccur. However, the group as a concept did not become a target for organized study until the advent of sociology as an independent work area. Nevertheless, the Greeks had explicit formulations about society and the division of labor, and certainly throughout recorded history, absence of sociological terminology notwithstanding, there has been recognition that outgroups compete with ingroups for political and military power; that there has been extensive differentiation of group structure in the religious domains; that kinship has ordered and controlled complex relationships among family members and between families; that in the economic sphere activities are both regulated and manipulated; and, more generally, that social life is normative. Until the development of organized sociological thought, however, there has not been the common ground necessary for analysis of qualities of structure and process.

What then is a group, sociologically speaking? Probably a conservative minimum definition is that a group consists of two or more persons in some form of interaction, and recognizable as possessing a unity. More specific definitions might involve considerations of size of the aggregate, intensity of participation, emotional quality of relationships, the kind of structural relationships, the stability of the internal structure, the complexity and interdependence of the members, the purposes served by the aggregate, and the relationship to other aggregates. But what is important to keep in mind is the minimum necessary for a group to exist at all. There cannot be a group without persons and there cannot be a group without interaction.

Some Early Variations of Group Definitions. One of the early characteristics of the discussion about group form was that it was tied in with some other topical consideration, such as social evolution, social control, social conflict, or social ethics. Further, *post hoc* it is obvious that sociologists tended to build comprehensive social theories, emphasizing general philosophical systems, so that teasing out material pertinent to the group concept becomes a task of bringing together odds and ends.

Following the work of Hegel, Comte, and Spencer and identification of the idea of social interaction as the group fabric, group phenomena were no longer commonly accounted for solely by reference to the individual members or solely attributed to the existence of some mystic bond which was imbued with a reality of its own. Since then in Europe the approach has been toward a definitional clarification of the concept of the group, while in recent years in America emphasis has been more on direct observation and empirical research.

Many of the early sociologists emphasized particular assumptions about group phenomena. Gumplowicz, for example, felt that the individual is a group product, and hence the group rather than the individual is the basic unit of society. People bound by similar interests into groups tend to think and act as units, rather than as individuals, in their response to other groups. As an evolutionist he conceived of a selective process in which those groups most suited would survive in society. The realist point of view which Gumplowicz represented was maintained as an important emphasis in the work of a number of others, LeBon and Vierkandt as early examples and McDougall as a later one.

Durkheim also believed in the reality of the group beyond the individual members. He felt that "social facts" were irreducible to individual facts and that the collective beliefs and practices of a group determine the distinguishing behavior of an individual. The group pattern, once established, becomes "real," exercising restraint over the individual by means of a "collective consciousness." According to Durkheim, group structures could be examined on the basis of "mechanistic solidarity" and "organic solidarity." He believed that the relatively undifferentiated type of group (mechanical solidarity) inevitably became more complex through a division of labor and a concomitant differentiation of parts. This latter polar type of group characterized by organic solidarity is based on mutual interdependence through specialization of functions. The collective conscience, being a product reinforced by many similarities, is most pronounced when mechanical solidarity prevails, and repressive law (rather than restitutive law) becomes the legal extension of the collective conscience. Thus, for Durkheim the group possesses a reality of its own which is distinguished from individual expressions and transcends any direct sum of them.

Similarly, Giddings assumes the group as a starting point. Groups may arise unconsciously as a natural product of individual activity which he calls "social composition" (e.g., the family). Contrasted with this are cooperative interest-oriented groups, which he calls "social constitution" (e.g., the state). Within the group, selection factors operate—social values—which affect ultimate survival of the group. "Consciousness of kind" refers to recognition of others as being similar, but the social mind to which he attributed a concrete reality is not given the prominence in his work which, for example, Durkheim gives to collective consciousness.

Thus, while some theorists emphasized the reality of the group, others assumed the reality and concerned themselves more with descriptive distinctions. Toennies, for example, places the emphasis of his analysis on a twofold classification of groups: (a) a group where interrelationship of members is based on sentiment and personal interest is described by the term *Gemeinschaft*; (b) a group based on rational and objective self-interest and the calculated wish to participate as a means to an end is characterized by the term *Gesellschaft.* Toennies used these constructs for descriptive and elaborative purposes in much the same way that Max Weber employed his "ideal type" approach in his comparison of collectivities.

Max Weber, in his intensive use of the "ideal type" construct, focused on logically pure descriptive abstractions. The reality of the group is submerged in his conception, since action exists as the behavior of one or more individuals, and the group is the direct resultant of such action. His emphasis on manifestations of social behavior has caused him to be called "probabilistic" in his approach.

Emphases on Interaction Processes. The analysis of group behavior in terms of forms of interaction gets its firm start with Georg Simmel. Simmel displayed interest in the analysis of many phases of group form, and, while his treatment was not entirely systematic, it was broad in scope even in its briefness. For example, he considered such aspects as the relation of group size to the form of organization and its effect on the individual. He gave detailed attention to the dyad and the triad and their manifestations in society. He also discussed at length the forms of superordination and subordination, providing illustrations exhibiting them in society. In the process of studying secrecy and the secret society, he indicated the part played by knowledge of one another and communication among members and their influence on the forms of interaction. Although primarily interested in form, Simmel nevertheless discussed content and its relation to form. In a modern research sense, Simmel cannot be considered an empiricist; however, many of his theoretical formulations furnish a base for recent small group research.

Von Wiese also has conceptually anticipated many of the modern approaches to group study on an empirical basis. He emphasized attention to form, and used an ideal type approach to categorize (certain) patterns of social interaction within the group. The contributions of von Wiese are frequently considered to overlap those of Simmel.

Cooley may be considered representative of another emphasis framed in interaction theory. In contrast with Simmel and von Wiese, Cooley stresses in his analysis a joint consideration of personality factors and their relationship to the form of the group. His approach, which is commonly associated with the identification of the "primary group" concept, led to the recognition of the importance of the coexistence of informal and formal group structures. The present-day emphasis of small group research on interaction process is most reminiscent of the approach Cooley typifies.

Present-Day Approaches. A reading of current sociological materials pertinent to the group concept is likely to be disappointing to anyone expecting to find radically new contributions to the subject. The present period seems to be characterized by an extensive and intensive attempt to test and develop theory on the basis of empirical observation. This is not different from what Cooley did; it is only "bigger and better." Essentially the difference is that today there are available many tools that make it possible to gather kinds and quantities of data not hitherto within the grasp of the social scientist. Thus, what is new is not theory, but technology. It may be that through technology it will be possible to refine and develop the earlier wisdom into more adequate empirically based theory. On the other hand, the availability of resources does not mitigate the necessity of intelligent and imaginative thought, since machines can't think.

On this score, it is useful to recall Wilson's comment on the present status of the group concept, which ". . . is seen in the more careful definition of terms, the use of controlled observation, the diminution of a tendency toward unfounded generalization, the common realization of a need for systematization, the development of more effective methods and techniques of study, and the conjoining of theory and application.[1]

Thus, we have specialized areas that help to fill in gaps in the general knowledge about the group. For example, the researcher has attempted to get closer to the people he studies. Participant observation techniques became popular largely as a result of volumes like Whyte's *Street Corner Society*. A current example of this approach is *When Prophecy Fails*.[2] The anthropological approaches and the clinical orientation on case material of the therapeutic professions have also influenced this development. In a sense, participant observation is an extension of the careful approach into a culture by the anthropologist who wishes to do effective field work. As an example of the direct cross-fertilization, we may view Strodtbeck's research in the small group area dealing with parallel family situations in several cultures.[3] This indicates the possible range of adaptation of the rigorous sociologist to the broadening of knowledge about the

---

[1] Logan Wilson, "The Sociography of Groups," in G. Gurvitch and W. E. Moore, Eds. (New York: Philosophical Library, 1945), p. 168.

[2] Leon Festinger, Henry W. Riecken, and Stanley Schachter, *When Prophecy Fails* (Minneapolis: University of Minnesota Press, 1956).

[3] Fred L. Strodtbeck, "Husband-Wife Interaction over Revealed Differences," *American Sociological Review*, 16: 468-73.

group through contact with anthropology. Conversely, the influence of sociology is apparent in the primarily anthropological study, *Three Navaho Households: A Comparative Study in Small Group Culture*, that was done by J. M. Roberts.[4]

Another area that has grown in recent years is situational testing. While there have been many forerunners, it was with the publication of the OSS volume, *Assessment of Men*, that interest was stimulated in the observation of actual behavior in test situations, rather than in test scores on paper and pencil questionnaires. An early article by Bronfenbrenner and Newcomb[5] suggested a potential for research which has yet to be realized. Situational observation is broadly related to interests in many other areas, including (1) the group therapy approaches stemming from Roger's nondirective therapy and Moreno's psychodrama; (2) educational approaches, such as Harvard's case study method and the democratic leadership emphasis stemming from Dewey's philosophy and Lewin's experiments in authoritarian and democratic organization; and (3) industrial and military approaches such as Bass's leaderless group discussion.

A great deal of interest in recent years has gone into improving observation techniques. Probably the first to receive wide attention was Chapple's chronograph recording,[6] but by far the most known system of observation at this point is Bales's Interaction Process Analysis. Bales's recording system was not only an explicitly ordered one but was based on a substantial theoretical framework. It also came at a time when other material facilities for the laboratory were readily available, including observation or interview rooms with one-way mirror setups, inexpensive sound recording equipment, etc. Other observation systems that have achieved some prominence in research include those of Benne and Sheats[7] and Carter,[8] but additional systems or modifications will continue to be constructed to meet the needs presented by specific research.

---

[4] J. M. Roberts, *Three Navaho Households: A Comparative Study in Small Group Culture* (Cambridge, Mass.: Peabody Museum of American Archeology and Ethnology, 1951).

[5] Urie Bronfenbrenner and Theodore M. Newcomb, "Improvisations—An Application of Psychodrama in Personality Diagnosis," *Sociatry*, 1: 367-82.

[6] E. D. Chapple, "Measuring Human Relations: An Introduction to the Study of Interaction of Individuals," *Genetic Psychology Monographs*, 22: 2-147.

[7] K. D. Benne and P. Sheats, "Functional Roles of Group Members," *Journal of Social Issues*, 4: (Issue 2) 41-49.

[8] L. F. Carter, "Recording and Evaluating the Performance of Individuals as Members of Small Groups," *Personnel Psychology*, 7: 477-84.

Concomitant with the development of laboratories has been the increase in testing of models and limited range theory. On the one hand, there have been quite systematic approaches to testing theory such as is exemplified by Festinger and his associates.[9] On the other, there has been model construction of the more limited and restricted type as represented by a paper such as Hays and Bush's "A Study of Group Action."[10]

The interest that arose in the sociometric test approaches has led to much serious work. Early in the development of this area, Jennings made an important contribution in her systematic study *Leadership and Isolation*, and since then many other contributions have been published. At this point much of the interest in sociometric research seems to have abated, to be replaced by a more systematic and purposive use of peer and other ratings.

A final area we may mention here is that of social perception or interpersonal perception, largely arising from the work of Cottrell and his students.[11] The literature in this area is growing rapidly, but severe criticisms and limitations exist as challenges to current research.[12]

Topics of interest in small group research continue to be leadership, morale, efficiency, solidarity, sociability, structure, etc. Not all the activity, however, is productive. Some sociologists still feel it is important to justify their assumptions on the basis of philosophical "reasonableness," when the issue may be one which can be resolved by empirical test. For example, the affirmation of a recent author that groups are real may be contrasted with the approach of researchers who have assumed that groups are real and then proceeded to measure consequences that cannot be attributed to the group members as individuals.

In the past, fruitful insights have been gained with limited resources, and it is hoped that increases in empirical knowledge will lead to crystallization of systematic theory. In terms of the definition of the group, the historical perspective seems to point up a simple lesson. Any definition of the group is arbitrary, but the definition in any specific instance must be determined by its usefulness, with full awareness of the limitations involved.

---

[9] L. Festinger, "Theory of Social Comparison Processes," *Human Relations*, 7: 117-40.

[10] David G. Hays and Robert Bush, "A Study of Group Action," *American Sociological Review*, 19: 693-701.

[11] Leonard S. Cottrell, Jr., and Rosalind F. Dymond, "The Empathic Responses: A Neglected Field for Research," *Psychiatry*, 12: 355-59.

[12] Lee J. Cronbach, "Processes Affecting Scores on 'Understanding of Others' and 'Assumed Similarity,'" *Psychological Bulletin*, 52: 177-93.

AREAS FOR RESEARCH IN LEISURE AND RECREATION

MARTIN H. NEUMEYER
University of Southern California

Leisure and recreation are fruitful fields for social research. Sociological studies of these areas of research are not nearly as numerous as research developments in other phases of inquiry.[1] The ramifications of these subjects provide abundant opportunities for every scientific discipline to explore certain phases, including the social aspects with which sociology is primarily concerned.

The literature of leisure and recreation ranges from reports of serious and authoritative studies to publications which may be characterized as "moralistic," designed to bring about specific reforms. The great body of publications is of a more or less practical nature, including administrative types of research undertaken to improve the organization, personnel, facilities, planning, and programs of activities. Publications on sports, games, hobbies, and numerous other forms of leisure pursuits are voluminous.

Various disciplines have participated in both empirical research and in conceptional or theoretical clarification. The specific techniques of research used in a wide variety of studies include the historical, statistical, survey, ecological, case study, interview, questionnaire, participant observational, experimental, comparative, or a combination of these. The three most common methods of research used to study recreation interests, activities, facilities, and resources are (1) the recreation survey, ranging from comprehensive studies to those limited to specific items; (2) the questionnaire, including check lists, the pooling of information or opinions, and the collection of a variety of numerical data; and (3) the recreation interview or case study method.

It is difficult to classify the major areas for research. Denney and Meyersohn,[2] in classifying the literature on leisure, point out that there have been seven major streams of research since 1900: (1) general consumer research; (2) numerous historical studies; (3) a variety of studies stimulated by education, social work, and recreation; (4) the

---

[1] Cf. *Sociology and Social Research*, 42:396-472.

[2] Cf. Reuel Denney and Mary Lea Meyersohn, "A Preliminary Bibliography on Leisure," *The American Journal of Sociology*, 52:602-15. The entire issue is devoted to "The Uses of Leisure."

"Play Movement," studied on its individual rather than its social side; (5) psychological research of leisure and the media of mass communication; (6) studies influenced by sociopolitical theories; and (7) the production and control side of mass media of amusements. They found it convenient to classify the variety of scattered studies under twenty more specialized headings, including a bibliography of bibliographies.

In order to simplify the classification and to abbreviate the descriptions of the areas of research of special interest to sociologists, eight major categories will be used. This list is not complete, for it does not indicate the wide ramifications of the subject, but it points out certain focal points for further investigation.[3]

1. *Leisure and Recreation in a Changing Society.* One cannot understand the significance of the "new leisure" without a consideration of the impact of a changing society. Social changes, historic events, and a new spirit have affected both the quantity and the uses of leisure. Automation is one of the outstanding trends in modern society. Its implications are not as yet fully realized, nor have they been sufficiently explored. The two world wars, the depression of the 1930's, and postwar eras of prosperity produced revolutionary changes. None of these eras of rapid social change have been adequately studied from the point of view of leisure. It is obvious that both the extent of leisure and the recreation trends have been affected by such factors as the geographic setting and the changing physical environment, population growth and mobility, urbanization, science and technology, socioeconomic conditions, political factors, the expansion of education, and the changing community life. Few objective studies of these variables have been made.

2. *Historical Studies.* Studies of the historical developments of recreation have been made for some time. Publications dealing with

[3] For a study of leisure and recreation in their sociological aspects, including suggestions for further study and bibliographies, see Martin H. and Esther S. Neumeyer, *Leisure and Recreation* (New York: The Ronald Press Company, 1958), especially Chap. XV on "Recreation Research." For suggestions for further research on special subjects, consult Harold D. Meyer and Charles K. Brightbill, *Recreation: Text and Readings* (Englewood Cliffs, N.J.: Prentice-Hall, Inc., 1953), pp. 410-27 on "Planning and Research," and *Community Recreation* (Englewood Cliffs, N.J.: Prentice-Hall, Inc., 1956); Florence G. Robbins, *The Sociology of Play, Recreation, and Leisure Time* (Dubuque, Iowa: William C. Brown Company, 1955); Jesse F. Steiner, *Americans at Play* (New York: McGraw-Hill Book Company, Inc., 1933); and George A. Lundberg, Mirra Komarovsky, and Mary Alice McInerny, *Leisure: A Suburban Study* (New York: Columbia University Press, 1934).

popular recreation are listed by Dulles.[4] John Durant and Otto Bettman[5] give a graphic picture of the development of sports in America. Clarence E. Rainwater[6] traces the origin, stages, transitions, and trends of the playground movement in the United States. Others have attempted to bring the data regarding the recreation movement up to date. Few studies have been made of the recreation developments in other lands and of world trends, which are fields of research of major importance.

3. *Recreation Interests, Activities, Habits, and Attitudes.* Numerous studies have been made of recreation preferences and interests, types of leisure activities, and recreation habits and attitudes. What people do during their leisure time represents a dynamic clue to their preferences and wishes, but it is not always possible for them to engage in the best-liked activities. The questionnaire technique is the most common research device used to ascertain the recreation interests and activities of groups of people. Quite often questionnaires include lists of items for checking purposes to discover which activities are most commonly engaged in, those best liked, and the ones that consume the greatest amount of time. When the data are correlated with such variables as age, sex, race, social class, intelligence, education, season of the year, and community conditions, it is possible to get at the dynamic factors that influence what people do during their leisure.[7] Recreation interviews make it possible to obtain similar results, also personal reactions of the interviewees, but the method is more time consuming. Few studies of this type have taken into consideration the multifarious background variables of the groups studied.

4. *Personality and Group Factors.* Sociologists have described personality as the sum and organization of all the traits that make up the person and that condition his role in society. These include the physical, intellectual, emotional, motivational, character, social expressional, and related aspects. It is apparent that what one does during one's free time has a profound effect on personality, and personal traits and conditions

---

[4] Foster R. Dulles, *America Learns to Play: A History of Popular Recreation, 1607-1940* (New York: Appleton-Century-Crofts, Inc., 1940).

[5] *Pictorial History of American Sports: From Colonial Times to the Present* (New York: A. S. Barnes and Company, 1952). Compare Bellamy Partridge and Otto Bettman, *As We Were, 1850-1900* (New York: McGraw-Hill Book Company, Inc., 1946); and Robert W. Henderson, *Early American Sport* (New York: A. S. Barnes and Company, 1953).

[6] *The Play Movement in the United States* (Chicago: The University of Chicago Press, 1922). Compare Charles F. Doell and Gerald B. Fitzgerald, *A Brief History of Parks and Recreation in the United States* (Chicago: Athletic Institute, 1954); and George Hjelte, *The Administration of Public Recreation* (New York: The Macmillan Company, 1940).

[7] One of the early quantitative measurements of the play life of children, using a check list and other items, was made by Harvey C. Lehman and Paul A. Witty, *The Psychology of Play Activities* (New York: A. S. Barnes and Company, 1927).

affect leisure pursuits. The effects and relationships are reciprocal. Few investigators have endeavored to discover the numerous possible relationships between recreation and the total personality.[8] The uses of leisure may either integrate or disintegrate personality, depending upon the kinds of activities engaged in and the responses to them. Conversely, the degree of integration of personality affects the uses of leisure. Standard tests of intelligence, temperament, and the broader personality inventories enable investigators to ascertain some of the possible relations of recreation to personality traits, but these instruments of research have their limitations. They must be accompanied by other types of studies, especially those designed to measure the effects of social relationships.

Group aspects of recreation are of special importance to sociologists. Recreation in the primary or small groups and the larger secondary groups; the impact of the underlying social processes, notably competition; social differentiation and stratification, accommodation and assimilation; suggestion and imitation; the crowd phases, such as amusement fads and the "band wagon" tendency; and the effects of culture: all these afford unique opportunities for social research. Even though the group aspects are usually regarded as the core of sociological research, with few exceptions, these areas for research remain largely unexplored. Their ramifications include nearly all of social life.

5. *Problems of Leisure.* The literature on leisure is replete with discussions of the problems involved, but much of it is of a "reformistic" rather than scientific nature. The broader aspects of social disorganization and social deviation have been explored, but their relationship to leisure is difficult to ascertain. However, certain problems of the uses of leisure have been studied. Gangs and peer groups have been analyzed by Thrasher, Whyte, Hollingshead, Cohen, and others, but there are many unexplored aspects. Differential studies of gang and youth groups in different social strata of society and cultural settings, the conditions and processes of gang formation, and the effects of increased leisure need further consideration. The Chicago study[9] of the relation of recreation to delinquency was comprehensive, but no comparable study has been made of any other community. Alcoholism, drug addiction, vice, and related problems of social deviation have become national concerns. Typological studies of conditioning factors, better research techniques and sampling procedures, and more careful delineation of research projects are needed before extensive progress can be made in the analysis of be-

[8] A notable effort in this direction has been made by S. R. Slavson, *Recreation and the Total Personality* (New York: Association Press, 1946).

[9] Cf. Ethel Shanas and Catherine E. Dunning, *Recreation and Delinquency: A Study of Five Selected Chicago Communities* (Chicago: The University of Chicago Press, 1942).

havior problems, especially from the point of view of leisure.

Considerable progress has been made in the use of recreation therapy for the physically and mentally handicapped. These studies have been made chiefly by those who have had special training in recreation therapy, psychiatry, physical education, and related fields.[10] Scientific studies of the phenomena of old age (gerontology) have advanced considerably; but the leisure aspects, as compared with the problems of income and health, have been neglected until recent years. What forms of vocational, avocational, and related activities are best suited to the aged?

6. *Commercial Aspects.* Commercialization in the field of leisure is phenomenal. Estimates of the total annual expenditures for recreation goods and services range from less than ten to more than twenty billion dollars a year.[11] Why do people go to commercial amusement places? What types of entertainment do they prefer? What are the effects of commercial recreation on individuals and on social groups? These and related questions remain partially unanswered.

7. *Mass Media of Entertainment.* Mass media of entertainment and communication represent perhaps the most significant recent development in recreation, some of which are highly commercialized. Television, radio, printed matter, and motion pictures are among the most popular means of mass entertainment today. They are characteristic aspects of our mass culture.

Except for certain specialized studies,[12] few investigations have dealt

---

[10] Cf. Virginia Mae Axline, *Play Therapy: The Inner Dynamics of Childhood* (Boston: Houghton Mifflin Company, 1947); Valerie V. Hunt, *Recreation and the Handicapped* (Englewood Cliffs, N.J.: Prentice-Hall, Inc., 1955); Clark E. Moustakas, *Children and Play Therapy: A Key to Understanding Normal and Disturbed Emotions* (New York: McGraw-Hill Book Company, Inc., 1953); George T. Stafford, *Sports for the Handicapped* (Englewood Cliffs, N.J.: Prentice-Hall, Inc., 1947); and Fritz Redl and David Wineman, *Children Who Hate* (Glencoe, Ill.: The Free Press, 1951).

[11] Cf. J. Frederic Dewhurst and Associates, *America's Needs and Resources: A New Survey* (New York: Twentieth Century Fund, 1955), XI, "Recreation"; Harold D. Meyer and Charles K. Brightbill, *Community Recreation*, op. cit., 53-66; and *Road Maps of Industry, No. 1080* (New York: The National Industrial Conference Board, Inc., 1956).

[12] The series of studies of motion pictures and children, made during the 1930's under the auspices of The Payne Fund, Inc., were fairly extensive. Radio and television audience measurement concerns are continuously testing the advertising potentials of these media. Examples: C. E. Hooper, Inc., A. C. Nielson Company, American Research Bureau, Pulse, Inc., Trendex, Inc., and Viodex, Inc. Summaries of television audience studies are found in a recent study by Leo Bogart, *The Age of Television: A Study of Viewing Habits and the Impact of Television on American Life* (New York: Frederick Unger Publishing Company, 1956). For a regional study, see Everett C. Parker, David W. Barry, and Dallas W. Smythe, *The Television Radio Audience and Religion* (New York: Harper and Brothers, 1955). For a world-wide survey of mass communication, see *World Communications: Press, Radio, Film, Television* (New York: Department of Mass Communication, UNESCO, 1956).

specifically with the impact of mass communication and recreation. The difficulties in ascertaining the personal and social effects of mass entertainment are obvious, but some progress is being made in certain phases of the subject. The opportunities for research in this field are almost limitless.

8. *Community Recreation.* The community forms of recreation, including both public and semipublic or private agencies, have been studied extensively. Much of this type of research may be broadly defined as administrative research, but various academic disciplines (education, physical education, psychological and social sciences) have found fruitful areas for study.[13] Various studies of public recreation, from local surveys to studies on the state and national levels, have been made; yet basic research programs are still inadequate. Likewise, there are unexplored areas for research in school-centered and church-centered recreation, in youth-serving and group-work agencies, adult leisure activities, especially industrial recreation, and the play life in homes. Few authentic studies of family recreation have been made.

Recreation leadership and personnel qualifications have been a major concern of all types of recreation agencies.[14] The types of leadership, the basic qualifications of each type, the functions and influences, the training program, and the relative responsibilities of leaders in this field provide opportunities for various types of studies.

The importance of fact finding in leisure and recreation can hardly be exaggerated. This is true in other phases of life, but its significance has been emphasized more in some fields than in others. It is difficult to account for the lag in recreation research, except that the public has not fully recognized its importance. Possibly the greatest shortcoming in this field is the lack of basic research. Sociological research is primarily concerned with the social aspects of leisure and recreation, including the historical developments, institutional factors, types of leisure pursuits, social impact of free-time activities, and agencies of social control.

---

[13] See references in footnotes 1, 2, 3, 6, 9, and 11. Compare George D. Butler, *Introduction to Community Recreation* (New York: McGraw-Hill Book Company, Inc., 1949); Howard G. Danford, *Recreation and the Community* (New York: Harper and Brothers, 1953; John H. Jenney, *Introduction to Recreation Education* (Philadelphia: W. B. Saunders Company, 1955); Harold D. Meyer and Charles K. Brightbill, *Recreation Administration: A Guide to Its Practice* (Englewood Cliffs, N.J.: Prentice-Hall, Inc., 1956); and Jackson W. Anderson, *Industrial Recreation: A Guide to Organization and Administration* (New York: McGraw-Hill Book Company, Inc., 1955).

[14] Cf. H. Dan Corbin, *Recreation Leadership* (Englewood Cliffs, N.J.: Prentice-Hall, Inc., 1953); Gerald B. Fitzgerald, *Leadership in Recreation* (New York: The Ronald Press Company, 1951); and M. Vannier, *Methods and Materials of Recreation Leadership* (Philadelphia: W. B. Saunders Company, 1956).

In this brief description of the areas of research germane to the sociology of leisure and recreation, some aspects and details have been omitted or mentioned only in passing. New developments are occurring in every field of endeavor. For instance, the new age of automation affects nearly every phase of recreation and provides opportunities for studies of its various aspects, including the fields of research mentioned in this article.[15] The above sketch is indicative of the main framework of research. Well-executed studies along these lines will contribute enormously to the understanding of the problems of leisure in modern society.

---

[15] Cf. *The Annals of the American Academy of Political and Social Science,* 313 (September 1957). The entire issue, including 28 articles, is devoted to the major aspects of this subject.

TEACHING SOCIOLOGY BY RADIO AND TELEVISION

THOMAS FORD HOULT
Wayne State University

When departments of sociology begin using radio and television courses as an answer to the question of crowded classrooms and the teacher shortage, they must solve completely new problems. Perhaps the experience of the Wayne State University Department of Sociology and Anthropology can give guidance to those departments which have not yet begun using these mass media of communication. Our use of radio and TV began in the spring of 1956 and has continued to date without interruption—but not without controversy.

I

In the fall of 1955 our departmental chairman was asked by the radio department if introductory sociology would make a suitable radio course, and he consulted with me in my role as director of our junior college work. It was my feeling, and he concurred, that since sociology deals largely with abstractions, it is particularly appropriate for radio presentation. But some members of the departmental staff were not enthusiastic. Among the objections mentioned were fears about the exploitation of instructors and potential effects on on-campus enrollment, predictions that radio teaching would be ineffective because good teaching must be a two-way process, and the belief that instructors would inevitably water down their material (which, it was claimed, is inherently controversial) for fear of treading on the toes of important members of the community. Nevertheless, staff approval for a one-semester experiment, with me as the instructor, was obtained when possible ways of meeting the various objections were suggested.

The next question was that of teaching credit for the proposed course. This can be a real source of controversy, particularly where—as at Wayne—radio classes are broadcasts of tape recordings made in a live classroom situation. Some economy-minded administrators might claim that such an arrangement is little if any extra work for the instructor and should therefore involve no additional compensation. To forestall this type of claim, Wayne's faculty radio-TV committee has established the principle that instructors whose classes are taped for later broadcast should receive twice the normal teaching credit as a minimum, with more for radio sections having a large number of registrants. The justification is that radio instructors are under an increased strain while being recorded, and they must make special arrangements to bridge the physical gap between radio students and the classroom.

Another point that should be settled in advance is the disposition of used tapes. Before I agreed to undertake the radio course, I found that I could have the tapes destroyed or erased shortly after broadcast. I did not wish to have them used, without recompense to me, in some subsequent semester. This attitude is approved by our faculty radio-TV committee, which upholds the view that one should have the right to control use of one's lectures much as authors and publishers control copyrighted material.

II

Conducting a class that is being tape-recorded involves only a few minor differences from the ordinary class. Timing—with the Wayne setup—is no problem, since the broadcast time allotted to each credit class is one hour whereas classes run only fifty minutes. Studio personnel use music to fill in any amount of time that is not used by instructors.

Students in the live class must, of course, be oriented to the situation, but it does not take them long to ignore the neck microphone worn by Wayne radio instructors. They do not even seem to mind the fact that their questions and comments must be repeated in essence by the instructor for the benefit of the radio listeners. Some instructors have tried to handle this problem by having floor microphones set up in several places around the classroom, but I did not care for this solution, since it meant that the recording would pick up all the extraneous classroom noises.

One problem that had to be solved was use of the blackboard. Although sociology is largely abstract, occasionally it is handy to write unfamiliar phrases and words on the blackboard or to sketch diagrams. Therefore, I continued this practice even when recording, but while writing or sketching I would describe the process for the radio listeners. I soon found, however, that some things were so complex I was confusing the radio audience. This necessitated careful advance planning that involved going through my lecture notes well in advance and preparing mimeographed reproductions of the more complicated blackboard diagrams I wished to use. These were sent out to members of the radio class, helping me to keep in fairly constant touch with them.

Other contacts helped to lessen the physical isolation of the radio students. For example, soon after registration I obtained a list of the radio registrants (only sixteen the first semester) and sent each a semester plan including test dates, names of the texts, and reading assignments. The assignments were relatively easy to handle, since our department uses a common text and a book of outside readings for all introductory sections. Thus, the radio students did not have to come in to the library for outside work. They *were* required to come to the campus four times for tests on the evenings of the days when no recordings were made because the classroom students were being tested. (Incidentally, radio and classroom students did equally well on the tests.)

In addition to the foregoing types of contact, I urged radio listeners to write or phone me if they had questions or wished to make comments. I answered as many of these as seemed appropriate at the recording session following their receipt. Others I answered with a personal letter or phone call. Many communications were received from noncredit listeners. A few were critical, but most were enthusiastic about the insights gained from the sociological point of view.

Even though tape-recording a class for later broadcast creates the problems mentioned, it has had at least one salutary effect on my own teaching. The thought that some of my colleagues might listen to the broadcasts encouraged me to be particularly careful about the claims I made and the material I introduced. I found that I was no longer tempted to make generalizations for which there is little empirical support but which create student reaction that is ego-satisfying to the instructor. This probably helps to explain the complete absence of pressure from the community to tone down my lectures, even though, with the exception mentioned, I made absolutely no subject-matter changes from the lectures I formerly gave in unrecorded classes. Sex, including some of the more startling details about deviant patterns, religion, business, ethics, and segregation and class stratification in Detroit were all explored. Despite use of such topics, and despite my own permissive attitudes and liberal socioeconomic orientation, no demands were made to take me off the air. This suggests that sociology classes conducted with a reasonable regard for the standards of scientific accuracy can be publicly disseminated because they will create light, not heat, and thus will not arouse partisan emotions unduly.

III

When I reported to our staff on the results and procedures of the first semester's radio class, they agreed to let the experiment continue on a more or less indefinite basis. I therefore gave another radio section during the following semester. Since then we have offered courses in anthropology and criminology, and all of them have been received enthusiastically. Many of us hope to continue the program if funds and university policy permit.

Meanwhile, several of my colleagues and I have begun some television work. In television we find the same problems as in radio, except that the problems and strain are tenfold at least. To compensate, our university radio-TV committee has decided that we should receive three hours teaching credit for every half hour on TV. This is a minimal standard that other schools would do well to emulate.

For my initial television effort, I agreed to moderate a series of noncredit programs on great inventions. I hoped to promote the sociological point of view regarding the part played by the culture base, social change, and the like, in the invention process. I found, however, that even educational television stations are staffed by professionals who, though friendly and interested, are mainly concerned with technical smoothness rather than depth. This explains the details of their suggestions for a television presentation of introductory sociology that is now in the planning stage here. Most of them want it to consist of a lecturer alone. They feel a classroom situation would present technical problems for which there is no good solution. But it seems important to convince them that good education is indeed a two-way process and that the interest and stimulation of a live classroom situation not only would compensate for poor camera angles, but would help prevent an instructor from simply pouring out his own thoughts unchecked by student reaction. It also seems vital that we hold to the idea that members of our department alone, not professional TV producers and directors, are competent to decide what should be presented. The latter, however, will be helpful in solving the problem of visual aids. Even with a subject as abstract as sociology, there appears to be little excuse for using TV if visuals do not play a large part in the presentation. Just how this difficulty can be handled I do not yet know. We may have to evolve a whole new approach that will eventually have a significant impact on regular classroom teaching.

IV

To summarize, then, the use of radio and television for teaching sociology is stimulating, but creates many new problems. Advocates of the new media must convince those who resist change and they must face up to the consequences of the change. Radio and television may, for example, become a real threat to marginal instructors and, in the absence of proper control, they can be used by economy-minded administrators as a technique for exploiting the more capable. To be effective, they must include special measures to overcome the handicap of physical distance between teacher and student, and to remain sociologically meaningful instructors must resist suggestions that they should concentrate on being "smooth" rather than profound. These are knotty problems, but the Wayne experience has shown that, with sufficient effort, they can be solved.

TEACHING SOCIOLOGY VIA TELEVISION: GAINS AND LOSSES

MARVIN B. SUSSMAN
Western Reserve University

Explanatory Note. The authors of the following two papers, Marvin B. Sussman and Richard A. Schermerhorn, on the problems of teaching sociology via television are members of the same department of sociology and have been "TV professors," teaching sociology over station WEWS-CBS in Cleveland, Ohio. Professor Schermerhorn in the spring of 1954 gave Introductory Sociology, while Professor Sussman in the spring of 1957 offered Urban Sociology, both courses being a regular part of Western Reserve University's telecourse program. Since 1951, W.R.U. offers regular University courses on TV for credit.[1] Students who desire credit purchase a Telecourse Guide (abstract of all 45 lectures) prepared by the instructor[2] and any textbooks that may be used and then view lectures, each for a half hour 3 times a week for 15 weeks. During the course, the instructor usually requires extensive written work, and at the completion of the course a final examination is taken by credit students.

Many other persons view the lectures, and by purchasing the Telecourse Guide (sales range from 100 to 900) they can follow the lectures more closely. These individuals would be the equivalent of audit students attending a regular University course. In addition, the course attracts many other viewers, numbered up to 20,000, of which the homemaker predominates.[3] The type of programing at Western Reserve over a commercial station is different from a closed TV circuit in which a TV picture is beamed to a given class or number of classes within a school. At Western Reserve two courses are conducted each semester (a M.W.F. or T.Th.S. sequence), and each course carries three hours of University credit. At present the University, which has pioneered in this field of communication, is in its sixteenth series of college credit courses on TV.

---

[1] For a full report of this program see *Telecourses at Western Reserve University: A Summary Report of the First Three Years, 1951-1954* (Cleveland: Western Reserve University, September 1954) (mimeographed).

[2] While the supply lasts, a copy of the syllabus may be obtained by writing to the authors.

[3] N. G. Halpern, *The Western Reserve University Telecourse Audience* (Cleveland: Western Reserve University, 1953) (duplicated).

Introduction. This paper is concerned with some of the pedagogical and professional problems of teaching sociology on TV. The methods used in obtaining data include (1) being a TV professor in the spring of 1957 and presenting a course called Urban Sociology three times a week, each presentation lasting a half hour, for a 15-week academic year; (2) conducting a series of informal interviews with colleagues who have taught on TV and with administrative personnel; and (3) survey of the literature concerned with various problems of television as a medium for mass education.

Growth of Educational TV. The growth of TV in education, while somewhat slow and spasmodic, has paralleled the general growth of the medium. News stories indicating new ventures in educational TV appear weekly. In the spring of 1958 Ohio State University initiated its first formal course of study for students in mathematics.[4] This is a remedial course required for all those who do not pass the mathematics placement test for entrance to the University. Approximately a thousand students, or 25 per cent of the freshman class, were enrolled.

Learning and the problems of learning via television have attracted the attention of students in psychology and communications.[5] Research reports present contradictory evidence, but generally indicate that learning of subject matter is equally good or often better via TV than in the classroom. These studies are "one shot" researches made at a given point in time and do not treat the intriguing problem of retention of learning. Does TV outdo the traditional instructional course in the retention of learning or vice versa?

Other questions for study concerning the effectiveness of teaching by TV include learning by the casual viewer. What kind of learning takes place when a casual viewer "catches" a few programs of a series in which there has been a continuous build-up of knowledge and concepts which have established the framework for current discussions? What kind of interpretations will a casual viewer make of a lecture on marital relationships in a family course if he did not see or hear the presentations concerned with the institutional setting in which family and marital relationships evolve? In our classrooms we "build up" knowledge, and presentations during the sixth week are based on the work of the previous

---

[4] George E. Condon, "Hint of Future Seen in Ohio State Mathematics Course on TV," *Cleveland Plain Dealer*, March 22, 1958.

[5] For a useful summary of the literature on learning via television up through 1956, see Hideya Kumata, *An Inventory of Instructional Television Research* (Ann Arbor: University of Michigan Press, 1957). Modified from a paper given at the twentieth annual meeting of the Ohio Valley Sociological Society, May 3, 1958, Cincinnati, Ohio.

five. On TV we are expected to teach, not necessarily to entertain, as is the case in a commercial program; so continuity in learning is anticipated from one program to the next. The invidious effect (if any) of casual viewing upon the learning and attitude formation is a fascinating area for future research.

Most television teaching sessions are telescoped into 30-minute periods. We need research as to whether this shortened time period does actually produce equal increments of learning when compared with the 50-minute classroom period and whether it is at all possible to condense into a 30-minute period materials which require 50 minutes to present.

Research in these areas is continuing at an accelerated rate by those who have pioneered in the development of the medium as an instrument for mass education and by others who are concerned about teacher shortages, improvement in teaching techniques, and costs of education.[6]

Pedagogical Gains and Losses. What does TV teaching mean to the professor in terms of preparation, relationships with students, use of materials, and his personal motivations and gratifications?

Teaching on TV requires far more intensive preparation than that required for the lecture hall. Even though most Western Reserve University telecourse professors do not present a Hollywood production, each has reported that extra effort has to go into the planning and presentation of materials.[7] It is not that teaching in the classroom is poorer, but that teaching on TV literally means that the show must go on! The teacher is controlled by time, and, whether he feels like lecturing or not, he has to! Under TV conditions the professor cannot substitute a group discussion or a question period for the required lecture. Each presentation must be carefully prepared and timed. While professors will vary in the amount of time given to preparation (some write out every word and others simply outline their lecture and then speak extemporaneously), the lecture nevertheless has to be organized so as to maximize audience attention. A flip of the dial may tune the listener to a competitor's program of "John's Other Wife's Girl Friend." Even in the classroom, it is only the accomplished student who can learn to sleep with his eyes open. On TV the instructor has to fight to hold the audience by effective use of style, content, and visual aids.

---

[6] Discussion of future research needs are found in H. Kumata, *An Inventory of Instructional Television Research.*

[7] F. G. Macomber and Associates, *Experimental Study in Instruction Procedures: A Progress Report* (Miami, Ohio: Miami University, 1956). Macomber and his associates indicate that TV teaching demands three times as much time and energy of the teacher as that required in a discussion type of class of 30 students (p. 45).

A part of the audience that the professor is now working with is quite different from the one he faces in the classroom. Since the TV educational audiences are not all credit students, more careful attention must be given to the use of sociological terms. There is no way of knowing that "norm" is understood unless time is taken to define and describe it. One serious problem is that the professor does not know whether the students are getting the material; and, because time is limited, the material is likely to be more concentrated and less repetitious than classroom presentations. As a consequence, students may not be able to take notes as rapidly as the material is presented. Delivery is important here. Moreover, the student is in no position to ask the professor to repeat what he said if it is unclear or ambiguous. The professor speaks to the camera. It is his student, and one which does not ask questions. Moreover, the professor does not have the intimate relationship with students that he can develop in the classroom. In the traditional instructional course, students have the opportunity to ask questions and engage in discussions in or after class. No such possibility exists on TV.

TV makes no allowance for the fast or slow learner. The student who catches on quickly may soon become bored with the seeming slowness with which new materials are presented. The slow learner may feel a sense of isolation and even desperation. The professor cannot do much about this, since he is controlled in part by the technical demands of the medium and the need to be consistent in delivery. It has been suggested that it would be helpful if slow learners could tape record each lecture and then replay these broadcasts as needed.[8]

Television is the finest medium for the presentation of pictorial data and for demonstrating experiments, displaying material artifacts, sections of maps, charts, graphs, film clips, and other items. Blackboard work requires precision printing. Objects that are no larger than an inch can be blown up to fill a 24-inch screen. It is in this area that television presentation is most outstanding and far superior to classroom presentation of the same type of materials.

Professors who teach on TV probably do so for a variety of reasons. This is an area which ought to be studied as we move into the sociology of our own profession. Some professors are motivated by the desire to experience teaching on TV, to explore its possibilities, and in this sense

[8] Professor Schermerhorn reports that one of his TV credit students in his Introductory Sociology course did not view a single lecture, since he was working at the time of presentation. His wife viewed and taped the lectures and played them back to him afterwards. He received a grade of C in the course. "But of course," Professor Schermerhorn comments, "there could have been other reasons for that (C) too."

they are innovators and movers in this area of social change. Others are more concerned with appealing to a wide audience and transmitting knowledge of their fields to large groups of people. Probably the television audience of the typical credit course would be the equivalent of a capacity house three times a week in the largest public hall in the city from which the program is emitting. There is some intrinsic gratification from the knowledge that you are talking to such a large audience, particularly when you are doing a good job.

Professional Relationships and Problems. Extra remuneration or time off from regular teaching responsibilities comes to the TV professor. Most universities realize that the professor should receive extra compensation for some of the additional time he spends on preparation and presentation.[9]

A good TV professor can use the medium (as in the past the Ph.D. has been used) as the prehensile tail for climbing the academic ladder. Administrators who are keenly interested in TV programing for educational and for public relations purposes (the latter function is very important, especially from the viewpoint of administration) are very quick to recognize the "star" performer and will make efforts to keep him at the institution with increases in rank and salary. Besides, other institutions may be interested in him, and in one sense he becomes "hot property." In all probability, the professor's success on TV will in the future be considered equally with scholarship, research, community service, and other tangible and intangible factors used in determining academic advancement. Also, it may be possible to become another Frank Baxter (University of Southern California).

TV allows the professor to be his college or university representative to a very large public. In this way he becomes a public relations representative. In Cleveland, Western Reserve University has 244 half-hour periods during a given year before an audience ranging from 15,000 to 30,000. Besides providing an enriching educational experience and continuing education for these viewers, it also is inexpensive publicity for the institution.[10] Professors as part of the institutional complex of academia represent that institution in all their activities. It is difficult

---

9 At Western Reserve University teaching on TV is equivalent to six hours of the regular teaching load. If a professor elects to receive only three hours off his regular teaching responsibilities, he is paid for three hours overload. He also has the option of teaching his normal load and doing the TV course as "extra." For this he receives six hours of overload pay. See the American Council on Education, *Credit Courses by Television: Conference Report* (East Lansing, Michigan, 1955), p. 15, for a discussion of this problem.

10 *Credit Courses by Television*, p. 27. See remarks of Dean Leslie Brown.

to separate the citizen and professional roles. Appearing on television gives the professor an opportunity to serve his institution in another area. The results may be more students, funds for the institution, and community good will.

The TV professor is a pioneer and innovator experimenting with a new medium and in this sense is challenging the traditional methods of teaching. To some of his colleagues he may be viewed as a popularizer who is trying to simplify a difficult subject. Others feel that if he continues his ways in this push-button age, he will soon do away with his own teaching job. It is feared that tapes and filmed lectures will ultimately replace him. Therefore, he is a "professional rate buster," jeopardizing existing standards, and therefore has to be cut down to size. Cogent arguments on the other side maintain that the TV professor ultimately will have more time to meet and work with students and their problems. TV teaching can release the professor from repetitious presentations for important counseling, research, and scholastic activities. In any event, the professor contemplating teaching on TV should weigh its probable effect upon his colleague group.

Teaching on TV requires the coordinated efforts of a team of specialists. In the classroom the professor has complete control over his materials and his captive audience. On TV he has to work with camera men, engineers, producers, and supervisors. What he can or cannot do is determined by the technical limitations of the medium and perception of his team as to what is a good program, their interest and abilities. Thus, best teaching and success on TV is possible only when harmony and cooperation exist among all the specialists.[11] It may be necessary for the professor to utilize some of the findings of small group research in building a harmonious teaching team.

In conclusion, teaching via TV is no fad. It has proved itself and has reached its maturity. In the future it will loom large in the programing of all educational institutions. Sociologists should consider its implications for pedagogy, the problems it creates in professional relationships, and the opportunities it affords for creative teaching and expression.

---

[11] Lawrence E. McKune, "Teachers and Teaching" in a *Report on Educational Television*, prepared by The Subcommittee on Television of the Commission on Research and Service of the North Central Association of Colleges and Secondary Schools, p. 2.

TECHNIQUES AND INSTRUCTION IN TEACHING SOCIOLOGY ON TELEVISION

R. A. SCHERMERHORN
Western Reserve University

If sociology and the allied sciences are to flourish, they can do so only in a favorable climate of opinion, when increasing numbers of citizens feel the need for an accurate, tested body of knowledge on which to base life decisions. The new medium of television makes it possible for the sociologist to reach a greater audience than ever before, to familiarize them with the findings of social science research, to show them the relations between sociological data and their daily living, and finally dispel the mystery, the rumor-mongering, or the adulation that clings to his profession.

On the basis of the author's experience, it appears that the teacher is required to keep his attention constantly focused on three levels of the communication process: (1) capturing and holding interest, (2) television techniques, and (3) instructional adequacy. The rest of this discussion will be devoted to these three areas, based on the inestimable values of hindsight.

To begin with the first item, capturing and holding interest, it may seem axiomatic that the purpose of a course is to instruct rather than to entertain; before the camera, the television lecturer soon learns that this is not an absolute dichotomy. Personally speaking, the writer's own lecture came immediately after a home economics demonstrator, who had been preceded by a session of popular music; it soon became evident, therefore, that it might be more important to *keep* the attention of a mass audience, as well as *get* it. The professor in the classroom has a captive audience; on the air he has not. The televiewer can turn off the instructor at the switch of a knob. *O felix potentia!* Can we hypothesize that this very power may have beneficial consequences for sociology teaching in general?

But abandoning these perhaps unduly hopeful speculations, we may note a few specific measures for attracting and sustaining interest: (1) The use of an opening narrative, aphorism, or allusion to current news events related to the topic of the day. (2) Constant use of pictures, maps, graphs, board outlines and diagrams which help to give vividness and clarity to the presentation. Pictorial statistics are superior to statistical tables. An arresting picture at the outset may establish an interest before words are spoken—the television lecturer soon learns, as the classroom lecturer too often has not, that words may be secondary to a total impression. (3) A continual use of films or film strips. Arnold Green has made a good beginning in this area, but far more needs to be done.[1] (4) Frequent use of guests on the program to give the advantages of expertness and fresh approaches in different aspects of the field. (5) Making use of camera men and technicians in the control room so that they ask questions or comment afterwards, a method by which the lecture will probably succeed in capturing the interest of the wider mass audience.

With regard to the second factor, television technique, the following clues have been found useful: (1) The picture should be kept from becoming static. The author's own experience has been that it is useful to have two desks, one with lectern and one without, and two blackboards. Movement from one desk to the other, and from desk to blackboard to easel where charts and pictures were shown, helps to break up the tendency to remain in a stationary position. (2) An experienced director in the control room can do much to manage frequent shifts of camera, close-ups, and movement of cameras back and forth, giving variety to the picture. At Western Reserve this is done by the University director of drama and television. (3) The blackboard cannot be used in the usual classroom style because close-ups that pick up the writing clearly enough for the viewer cover only half the blackboard. Hence everything must be reduced to half the blackboard size; this requires much condensation of outline or point headings. Diagrams and statistics have to be kept within the same framework. (4) The lecturer cannot allow his eyes to wander away from the camera too long; the director in the control room, if he is worth his salt, will keep urging the speaker to focus on the camera directly most of the time. (5) Change of pace is a necessity to avoid a monotonous presentation: constant variation in speed of articulation, in modulation of the voice, and in emphasis keeps the viewer from surfeit. (6) Time restrictions are more exacting than the ringing of classroom bells; leniency to wander

[1] Note also the *WOI-TV Directory of Non-Royalty Films for Television* obtainable from Richard B. Hull, Director of Radio and Television at Iowa State College. Another source of information valuable for television instruction is the Educational Television Newsletter, published by the Committee on Television of the American Council on Education, 1785 Massachusetts Ave., N.W., Washington 6, D.C. A volume reviewing television education on all levels of instruction is authored by Jennie Waugh Callahan, *Television in School, College and Community* (New York: McGraw-Hill Book Company, 1953).

on for just a few minutes more is no longer a special privilege of the pampered professor. Sanctions are now in other hands and overstepping the bounds of time leaves the teacher talking to thin air—even the studio staff are now moving to the next set. It is therefore imperative to observe the clock at intervals, estimating ahead how much to improvise, how much to delete, when to speed up or to slow down, so that the "wind-up" signal will bring the speaker to a natural conclusion. No matter how carefully time intervals are prepared beforehand, some flexibility is required in the time adjustment for practically every television performance.

Finally, and most important, is instructional adequacy. Let us consider this from the standpoint of *organization* and of *content*. As an organizational device the introductory sociology syllabus (available while they last) has fifty-three pages containing instructions for the course, an introduction by the instructor with study habits, an outline of lectures and assignments with dates, a short abstract of each lecture in paragraph form, some "warm-up" questions for use after assignment reading and before the lecture, a complete description of the six written assignments to be sent in by mail at intervals, a bibliography, and some sample examination questions. Reports by credit students who had taken regular classroom instruction at the University almost uniformly showed that the televiewers put in more hours of actual work to complete their assignments than they had done for classroom courses.

A retrospective glance at the experience of teaching introductory sociology on television leads to the following reflections on content somewhat in the vein of hindsight recommendations. It goes without saying that the content of good teaching in TV lectures should be the same as it is in the classroom. But what are the features of this content which deserve special emphasis in a TV presentation? In the writer's opinion, the presence of a wider audience may justify special attention to the following items.

Some rationale for the use of an adequate technical terminology must be given at the same time so that the lectures do not dissipate into jargon. For example: "If two statuses have conflicting roles, thereby making them incompatible statuses when occupied simultaneously, it is assumed that these statuses would be less frequently occupied simultaneously than would two statuses with roles that do not conflict."[2] This sentence will not only lose the television audience entirely, but will also open the

[2] Author to remain nameless. Quotation from *American Sociological Review.*

floodgates of criticism from our colleagues in the humanities who have had to learn to write felicitously while we have not. The castigations of Stringfellow Barr in *Purely Academic* are surely not without point; his account of sociological jargon in the English classroom is a ghastly example; our British confreres have much to teach us about clarity and straightforwardness of expression in social science. Television presents the sociologist with a first-rate opportunity to make his subject clear and compelling for a lay audience. Is it only gleeful sadism to imagine such an apprenticeship for all sociological writers of books?

Another topic of some concern is the impression left on the neophyte that there is general agreement among sociologists on the major conclusions and generalizations in the field. It is a mistake to give the audience the impression that all is harmonious in sociology. Surely the controversies of science are of absorbing interest, not only to the insider but to the layman. Is it too much to ask that at least a secondary place be found for a discussion of the positivistic as contrasted with the humanistic division within sociology? Or would it be entirely out of place, in the analysis of method which regularly appears, to indicate what has been discovered by the historical and cultural method, the clinical method, or the logic-experimental method? Perhaps this will give the layman a new appreciation of the alternatives in science, a more adequate perspective on the issues in scientific controversy, and certainly a more sophisticated notion of what social science is about—which is likely to mean a more sustained interest in the subject for the future.

Another central aim of the introductory course—and the more widely disseminated this is by television, the more salutary will be its effects—is to heighten the awareness of people regarding the sources of bias in themselves, as observers of the social scene. The effects of group loyalties on ideologies—class, ethnic, or associational—can be pointed up clearly enough in every case so that the relativity of judgment in terms of social position will be thoroughly absorbed by learners as a permanent part of their intellectual legacy. This can also be emphasized as a function of historical trends as the interests of the thirties in social problems and social change are contrasted with the security-mindedness and "adjustment" philosophy of Organization Man in the fifties. As Page has so aptly phrased it, "Students today—though no less than many of their teachers—are interested in organization rather than disorganization, adaptation rather than change, and especially those skills that seem to spell conventional success in work, family and leisure pursuits."[3] By focusing attention on these trends, the introductory course in sociology may at least stimulate the effort at self-correction and make the student aware of certain issues in the sociology of knowledge, even though not labeled as such at this stage.

Finally, a word about method as related to research. Continuous sampling of audience reactions by the techniques of communications research will make it possible to keep a constant check on the results of telecasting, and to judge the effectiveness of the instructor's presentation. As yet this research has been on too small a scale to provide reliable data. The author sampled over 50 per cent of his noncredit students and 80 per cent of his credit students with telephone interviews to obtain some preliminary information and found that over 90 per cent of both groups were married women with the noncredit students older (median 25 years out of school). Noncredit students, who were probably more similar to the mass audience, desired more visual aids, while the credit students as a whole did not. On the other hand, credit students sometimes complained that blackboard shots were too brief for note-taking, while others had no comment. Also the credit students evinced a strong desire to meet with the instructor and other students occasionally throughout the term.[4]

On the basis of this limited experience, it would seem that evaluation a month or two after the telecast program is distinctly a second-best method. A more ideal procedure would be to incorporate research into the structure of the telecourse itself and to sample reactions immediately, before the distorting effects of memory set in. Determination of class and status positions, group membership, etc., of the viewers in the samples would afford a much more precise knowledge of differential effects inherent in certain types of program. And, finally, to insure continuity, the same instructor should teach the course and direct the research for a number of years so that accumulated knowledge could be built up on audience reactions related to absorption of subject matter, attitudinal changes, and how these are connected with the techniques employed on the air.

[3] Charles H. Page, "Sociology as a Teaching Enterprise: Some Problems and Trends," unpublished paper read before the American Sociological Society, Washington, D.C., August 29, 1957.

[4] A typewritten copy of this study can be obtained by request and minor typing costs from the office of Cleveland College of Western Reserve University. The title is "A Sampling of Student Reactions to the Western Reserve University Telecourse in Principles of Sociology—Spring Semester 1954." Note also the Miami University (Ohio) research in effects of closed television teaching, footnote 7, Sussman's paper above.

MEASURING GROUP OPINION BY EXPERT ESTIMATES

L. K. NORTHWOOD
School of Social Work, Columbia University

The orthodox trend in sampling theory, as indicated in principal tests on research methods and in the journals, seems to contain the discussion of sampling within a description of the relative merits of quota sampling vs. probability sampling.

In this paper, sampling is considered as a measurement technique. By sampling is meant a process of selection of cases—not necessarily providing a statistical measure of probable error. In other words, sampling procedure is not absolutely equated with probability sampling.

The purpose of this paper is to try to promote a more flexible view toward sampling procedures in sociological research, especially in relation to estimating group opinion. It will challenge at least one of the basic assumptions of both quota and probability samples.

Each of these modes of sampling strives to achieve a replica of the larger universe being sampled. The glory of the probability samplers, they say, is that they are able to apply statistical tests of reliability because their samples are selected in such a way as to be representative of the population about which generalizations are desired.[1] The quota samplers, unable to provide such a statistical jeweling for their method at the present time, claim that the results obtained by probability samples are not much different from those obtained through quota techniques. They have produced a series of experiments to show this.[2] Moreover, they assert that quota techniques are less costly, less time consuming,

[1] Morris R. Hansen and Philip M. Hauser, "Area Sampling—Some Principles in Sampling Design," *Public Opinion Quarterly*, 9: 183-93. For a discussion of the two sampling methods, see Chap. 7 in Mildred B. Parten, *Surveys, Polls and Samples* (New York: Harper and Brothers, 1950), pp. 219-45; Eleanor E. Maccoby and Robert R. Holt, "How Surveys Are Made," *Journal of Social Issues*, 2: 44-56.

[2] Among the most recent articles are: Joseph R. Hochstim and Dilman M. K. Smith, "Area Sampling or Quota Control—Three Sampling Experiments," *Public Opinion Quarterly*, 12: 73-80; Norman C. Meier and Charles Haner, "Is the Probability (Area) Sampling Method Superior to the Quota Method?" *American Psychologist*, 4: 254; Charles Haner and Norman C. Meier, "The Adaptability of Area Probability Sampling to Public Opinion Measurement," *Public Opinion Quarterly*, 15: 335-52; H. Durant, "Experiences in Random Probability Sampling," *Public Opinion Quarterly*, 15: 765-66.

and for these reasons more frequently used than probability samples. The quota samplers go to much pains to demonstrate that their samples are as representative of the universe as the probability sample.

In this paper is proposed another method of selecting respondents in which it doesn't matter whether the respondents are representative of the universe or not. The proposed method is called the *quota of experts* method of sampling (QE method).

Under the quota of experts method, the respondent is asked *not* to give his own opinion, but an estimate of what he thinks is the group opinion on the issue at hand. Thus, the sample of respondents need not be representative of the population whose attitudes are being measured. It is necessary only that the sample contain a quota of expert judges who are able to make accurate estimates about group opinion.

There is nothing really new about this idea. Experts have been hired to advise administrators for a much longer period than we have had refined sampling techniques. However, since experts are wrong on occasions, the assumption of many is that expert judgments are inferior to the results of polling a well-selected sample. Little research has been expended toward defining areas in which expert judgments may be as good as, or superior to, the findings taken from representative samples. It is only recently that scientists have become interested in the ability of judges to estimate group opinion. To my knowledge, this literature has not been applied in the present context, and that is the function of this paper.[3]

How feasible is the QE method? Is it possible to select expert judges of group opinion? Here is a brief summary of some of the research:

Newcomb demonstrated that "spontaneously chosen leaders will be better judges of the degree to which norms are shared than will most other group members" in a secluded college community of 250.[4] Chowdhry extended this generalization to sociometrically chosen leaders in a series of small homogeneous groups, numbering 30-40 persons each.[5] The

---

[3] Two exceptions which deal with similar areas are: Herbert Stember, "Which Respondents Are Reliable?" *International Journal of Opinion and Attitude Research*, 5: 473-79; Arnold M. Rose, "Communication and Participation in a Small City as Viewed by Its Leaders," *International Journal of Opinion and Attitude Research*, 5: 367-90.

[4] Theodore Newcomb, *Social Psychology* (New York: The Dryden Press, 1950), p. 658. See the same author's *Personality and Social Change* (New York: The Dryden Press, 1943).

[5] Kamla Chowdhry and Theodore Newcomb, "The Relative Abilities of Leaders and Nonleaders to Estimate Opinions," *Journal of Abnormal and Social Psychology*, 47: 51-57. See also K. Chowdhry, "Leaders and Their Ability to Evaluate Group Opinion," Ph.D. dissertation, University of Michigan, 1949.

present author duplicated the findings for top leaders and officeholders in a heterogeneous, highly stratified housing project of 12,000.[6]

In these three studies it should be noted that persons in top leadership positions are superior judges only in estimating well-crystallized group opinions that are relevant, i.e., important and familiar, to the group which they are judging; they are not expert on all kinds of items about the group.

There are contradictory findings as well. Hites and Campbell and others did not note differences between top officeholders and nonleaders as cited above. However, these contradictory conclusions may be resolved by reclassifying the items in terms of their norm productive potential. The author attempted such a reclassification and found that in most cases the contradictions were alleviated. The evidence now available supports the view that top officeholders are superior judges of group relevant norms.

What implications do these findings have for the QE method? They would seem to place at least the following restrictions on the sampling procedure: (1) the quota of experts may be drawn from persons in top officeholding positions and (2) these top officeholders can be expected to give accurate estimates only of crystallized relevant group norms.

A third restriction, pertaining to the nature of the group, is suggested by the contradictory findings. Perhaps there are populations for which the estimates of top officeholders will not excel other judges. Namely, if the sample is a statistical aggregate with little or no group cohesion, consequently no leader offices or crystallized group norms (other than the societal norms), then it would seem that the selection of judges could not be made on the basis detailed above. On the other hand, there may be groups with such a high degree of homogeneity that all judges, regardless of leader status, will be equally expert in judgments about relevant group norms, or as a matter of fact, about any items to do with the group.

In the current research cited above it was noted that not all top officeholders are expert judges of group opinion. Some are very poor judges. On the other hand, some are experts at judging all kinds of group norms and statistical scores about the group—not just relevant group norms. Moreover, some nonleaders were as expert as any leaders in judging all kinds of items. The conclusion is drawn that expertness in assessing group opinion is not necessarily a leadership trait, as has often been suggested.

[6] Lawrence K. Northwood, *Leaders and Nonleaders as Expert Judges of Community Opinions*, Ph.D. dissertation, University of Michigan, 1953.

Rather, expertness is the property of all roles or social categories which have easy access to communications within the group. One category of roles with superior access to communication is the top offices which administer and control social organization, hence the expertness frequently found in persons holding top offices.

The author tested this hypothesis for several social categories known to have superior access to community information in Willow Village. Home-centered wives were more accurate judges of community information than their work-centered husbands, whereas there were no differences between male leaders and female leaders, both having equivalent access to community information. White judges excelled Negro judges, who were socially and physically segregated into one section of the community. Student judges, who were a favored class in the community, encouraged to participate in community affairs, were superior to working class judges, both Negro and white, who were somewhat isolated from community life for a number of reasons, including administration policy.

These findings suggest that a quota of experts might be drawn from any roles with superior access to communications within the group. There are, however, additional reasons that recommend the use of top officeholders: (1) they can be easily identified in the social structure of the group; (2) they are usually influential in the group, thereby furnishing an effective channel for feeding back the findings of the survey.

So far, we have been concerned with designating the classes of judges in a group which have the greatest likelihood of containing large proportions of expert judges. The expert can further be pinpointed by other pertinent research. Hovland and Sherif point out that:[7] "Individuals with strong personal involvement will tend to see issues pretty much in 'all black or white' rather than with fine distinctions, and that statements even mildly critical of their position will be judged to be more hostile to them than by more neutral persons."

This statement was made in reference to judgments on ambiguous items on Thurstone scales. A similar phenomenon was found by the author in the study cited above. Leaders in Willow Village were rated on the extent of their participation in formal organizations and informal cliques, on their attitudes toward participation, and the attitudes of others as to "how actively" the leaders participated in community organization. The most expert judges seemed to be those who had *not* been in

---

[7] Carl Hovland and Muzafer Sherif, "Judgmental Phenomena and Scales of Attitude Measurement: Item Displacement in Thurstone Scales," *Journal of Abnormal and Social Psychology*, 47: 824-25.

their present offices for a great length of time, who were *not* active partisans of inner-clique struggles, who were *not* wrapped up heart and soul in organizational activity. In other words, the most expert judges were not so *intensely* involved in organizations as top officeholders, but more so than nonleaders. They were somewhat removed from policy making, while still being more active, slightly dissatisfied participants than the rank-and-file member of Willow Village organizations.

Similar findings have been pointed to by other authors. For example, Hinckley and Rethlingschafer showed that judgments of the average height of a subject is influenced by the height of the man making the judgment.[8] Others have demonstrated that judgments of group opinions are influenced by the judge's own opinions.[9] However, Hinckley and Rethlingschafer indicate that the egocentric influence is partially controlled by objective facts. In the case of judgments of group opinion, knowledge of group norms and of facts about the group, it is suggested, will lead to more accurate judgments.

The application of these research findings to selecting a quota of experts is this: don't select the quota from among judges who are most deeply involved in the outcome of the issue; they are liable to project their desires into their estimates. This sounds like a principle of law: judges who are prejudiced on an issue should disqualify themselves from sitting in judgment.

In some cases the selection of the quota of experts will be complex. Perhaps this suggests another of the limits of the QE method; it may be adaptable only where the sample is of a known social structure. In regard to this point, it should be noted that both quota and probability samplers are advising extensive presurvey analysis so as to assure the proper proportions of groupings and strata within the sample. Thus all the QE method is doing is to extend this practice.

Furthermore, survey teams have found that an extensive social structural analysis is necessary in order to facilitate the feedback of survey findings to the client. Again, what the QE method is doing is to have this structural analysis largely completed *before* the survey is started, rather than *after* it is completed. The proposals made in this paper may

---

[8] E. D. Hinckley and D. Rethlingschafer, "Value Judgments of Heights of Men by College Students," *Journal of Psychology*, 31: 257-62.

[9] Travers, *ibid.*, pp. 23-28. See also Richard Wallen, "Individual's Estimates of Group Opinion," *Journal of Social Psychology*, 17: 269-74. One of the best discussions of the Oklahoma work in this area is summarized by Muzafer Sherif, "Integrating Field Work and Laboratory," *American Sociological Review,* 19: 759-70.

be considered as consonant with other researchers, suggesting that there is a convergence now taking place in the quota and probability techniques.

To conclude, in the brief time allotted this paper, I urge that alternative modes of sampling to the familiar quota and probability techniques be considered. This challenge has taken the form of suggesting an alternative, the quota of experts technique. The paper has avoided duplicating major criticisms that have been made of the usual techniques elsewhere. It has stressed by example the utilization of current theoretical findings in the field of social psychology in perfecting another mode of sampling.

Two general conclusions from a range of social-psychological experimentation are seen as pertinent to the selection of expert judges: (1) Expertness in judging group opinion largely is a property of those roles with easy access to communications within the organization, especially the roles of top officeholders. This expertness is conditional upon the type of item and the type of group. (2) Most judges slant their group estimates in the direction of their own judgments. However, those judges who lack strong personal involvement in the outcome of the issue, or in organizational commitments, tend to make more accurate estimates. These estimates may be bettered by knowledge of objective facts.

This paper should be interpreted as an attack on the statistical basis of sampling only to the extent that statistical criteria are made the prime determiners of sampling procedures. Space limitations have restricted the presentation of pertinent social-psychological theory in its application to the QE method.

THE ROLE OF ECONOMIC MOTIVATION IN ETHNIC RELATIONS*

RALPH R. IRELAND
University of Arizona

The purpose of this study is to examine French-English social relations in Quebec in order to see how the social and cultural heritage, the status, and the economic role of the French-Canadians have been modified through contact with the dominant English-Canadian culture. The theoretical approach is based upon the conceptual frame of reference set forth by Talcott Parsons in his discussion of "The Motivation of Economic Activities."[1]

The social heritage and structure of any given society determine to a large extent the content of the motivations and the resulting activities of its members. In turn, these are organized into an institutional pattern. Changes in the social structure will produce concomitant changes in individual interests and behavior, though the process may be impeded if the new patterns are incompatible with the old. Other factors besides the objective and the material culture may be involved in social change. However, the emphasis in this paper is on the importance of institutional patterns in the formulation of interests, values, and beliefs rather than to imply that all human behavior is necessarily economically determined. This is particularly apparent when a comparison is made of two contrasting cultures existing side by side, such as is the case with the French and English in Quebec.

---

*Some of this research was undertaken at the University of Toronto, where the author collaborated with Mr. D. McKay and Miss B. Plewman. The late President Charles S. Johnson of Fisk University encouraged and assisted in the presentation of the study, which was originally reported in part at a meeting of the Institute of Race Relations at Fisk University.

[1] Talcott Parsons, *Essays in Sociological Theory, Pure and Applied* (Glencoe, Ill.: The Free Press, 1949), pp. 200-17. Parsons maintains that all human activity, including economic activity, takes place within the institutional framework of society. The societal institutions serve to organize and integrate the subjective aspects of human social action, i.e., the underlying motivational forces. These motivational forces are comprised of disinterested moral sentiments (status, rights, roles) and self-interest. Self-interest expresses itself in economic motivation by a desire for recognition and a desire for self-respect. Insecurity in the economic world may be manifested by such traits as overaggressiveness, acquisitiveness, or an unwillingness to participate in entrepreneurial activities.

SOCIAL AND CULTURAL HERITAGE

Prior to the rapid industrialization of Quebec about half a century ago, the bulk of the people lived on the land under the Seigneurial system, a semifeudal social structure dominated by the Catholic Church. Although this system was formally abolished in 1854, vestiges are still apparent. The self-sufficiency and isolation which had characterized the seigneurie persisted under the Parish system. Many factors combined to maintain the status quo and to hinder agricultural progress. The original shape of the seigneuries and the mode of inheritance resulted in the formation of long, narrow holdings, no longer divisible nor subject to efficient cultivation. Little information on advanced techniques penetrated into the isolated parish from the outside world, nor was it particularly welcome. Traditional methods were thought to be the best.

The average rural French-Canadian family is a closely knit unit which follows a traditional pattern both in the education of the children and in matters of inheritance. This pattern is reinforced by the family's close parochial ties. Although the familial ties are loosened in the industrialized urban areas, the traditional conception of the family still exerts its influence. Most French-Canadians spend their informal social lives within their family circles and cliques. When French-Canadians make non-French contacts or join mixed associations, their activities are usually either formal or superficial.

The dominating influence in the social and cultural life of French Canada has always been the Roman Catholic Church. Historically, the relation between the church and the upper classes in Quebec has been diplomatic. The two groups have developed a division of labor and an integration of leadership rather than a competitive relationship.

In marked contrast to the English-Canadian group with its tradition of separation of church and state and its emphasis on the Protestant Ethic, the influence of the Catholic Church permeates French-Canadian life—in the family, education, social activities, and, to some extent, in government. The clergy and public officials appear together at official functions. The tendency of the French-Canadian to regard Quebec as a "Catholic state" rather than a secular one was symbolized in recent years by placing a crucifix over the Speaker's chair in both Houses of the Quebec legislature.

The majority of the educational institutions in the province are run by the Catholic Church. Until very recently these institutions offered little in the way of technical or commercial training. Traditionally, advanced education has prepared candidates for the priesthood or one of the learned professions. Elementary education has been conducted along lines calculated to instill traditional modes of thought and behavior appropriate to life in a close-knit rural economy. The urbanized or uprooted habitant has not been trained for success in the industrial world.

STATUS OF THE FRENCH-CANADIAN

In French Canada, in the course of three centuries, there has grown up a deep-rooted set of mores regulating the relations of its status groups with each other. Any attack or encroachment upon these mores could be construed by the French as an attack upon their status, upon their social structure. It would, in Parsons' terms, arouse in them "disinterested" feelings of moral indignation, and at the same time might prevent them from achieving satisfaction of their "self-interested" motives in the traditional manner.

French-speaking Canadians are very sensitive about their status. A clear indication of this was brought out by a question on a public opinion poll conducted during World War II which invited the French-Canadians to indicate what they disliked most about English-speaking Canadians. The favorite response was: "Their arrogant, domineering attitude." The English-speaking group, when asked the same question about the French-Canadians, replied: "Their bigotry, prejudice, and provincialism." The French reply betrays a militancy regarding their own status in contrast to the self-assuredness implied in the English response. Parsons explains this by saying that where a conflict of motivation exists, i.e., where a group such as the French-Canadians with its own traditional modes of behavior is expected to act in accordance with an alien and incompatible institutional pattern, its "insecurity" may be manifested in increased aggressiveness.

The concrete expression of these mixed feelings of the French may be interpreted in the light of their heritage. In the past, and to some extent today, the French-Canadian has been subjected to the soil under a feudal system which has been approved by the State and Church alike. The system of land-holding proved to be both a waste of land and human incentive. As the population increased and the family farms could not be further subdivided, emigration to the other provinces, and especially to the United States, provided an outlet for the more enterprising.

Neither his traditional economic system nor his church has prepared the French-Canadian for a prominent role in an industrialized society.

Some observers have stressed the importance of position and status as they affect the French-Canadians in modern industrial towns. The traditional objectives of their culture—small businesses, real estate, and the practice of law or medicine—no longer afford the security or status they gave in a rural society. This has caused the French-Canadian to have his traditional ambitions frustrated in the industrialized communities of his own territory. Only those who feel they have no status to lose dare move out into the secular, industrial, non-French world. In Parsons' terms, the *content* of motives must be in keeping with the social structure if they are to be satisfied. Interpolation of an alien element in the structure will threaten the traditional mode of achieving satisfaction and may even require a change in the direction in which satisfaction is sought.

Frustration in the social, economic, and political spheres seems to play a major role in shaping French-Canadian attitudes. Its power for projection into other spheres, in either a sublimative or compensative form, has been for the most part overlooked. Hughes[2] noted that formerly the professional and merchant classes wielded the greatest influence and had the highest status in a town. Now, the managerial and technical classes possess the power to decide a town's fate. There are few points of actual competition between these classes, represented by the French and English respectively. However, the obviously more advantageous position of the English has made the French all too conscious of the threat to their status in the social structure. Nor is this situation peculiar to the small town, formerly semirural and now highly industrialized. It is evident even in such a metropolis as Montreal.

Today, in the national sphere, many French-Canadians are still convinced that Canada is a dependent nation and subject to the whims of Westminster regardless of the wishes of the people. This point is hotly denied by English-speaking Canadians who assert that Canada is absolutely independent and free to take any course of action it chooses on any matter without having to obtain Britain's sanction. Canada's participation in the last two world wars has obviously not helped the French-speaking population to alter its views. They still believe that Canada would not have become involved in either of these wars had it not been for Britain.

---

[2] E. C. Hughes, *French Canada in Transition* (Chicago: The University of Chicago Press, 1943), pp. 46-83. Hughes suggests that the insecurity of the French-Canadians with respect to their status creates a milieu conducive to listening to attacks on the English and the newly introduced economic system. Thus, an agitator often had no difficulty in persuading his French listeners that they were being *exploited* by an industrial system *imposed* on them by the English.

The French-Canadian's firm belief that Britain ultimately has authority to meddle in Canadian internal and external affairs remains a bone of contention. To the French-Canadian it epitomizes his domination by a victorious race. He feels that he has to play the role of a conquered subject. If this is not true, he argues, then why is it necessary to conscript men except for the defense of Canada? The roots of this problem lie deep in the early history of the country.

In the domestic field also, the French-Canadian feels that he is dominated by his English-speaking compatriots. It is true that he has a proportionate representation in the federal government, but he believes that this representation is more apparent than real. Whenever a motion is introduced by a French-Canadian member of parliament, it can be defeated by the English-speaking majority if it does not meet with their approval. Many French-Canadians feel that their representation in the federal government is ineffective, that, in the final analysis, they have practically nothing to say in controlling or governing the country. That is, French-Canadians believe that the laws they have to obey are enacted without regard for their wishes or interests, as though they were a negligible, instead of the second largest, ethnic group in the population.

THE ECONOMIC ROLE OF THE FRENCH-CANADIAN

The whole structure of the French-Canadian economy in the past has been centered around the home, the farm, and the small business enterprise. Until very recently Quebec escaped most of the direct effects of the Industrial Revolution. What benefits it received came indirectly. However, with the culmination of the Industrial Revolution in the present century in the form of monopolies, interlocking directorates, stupendous profits, etc., even the most isolated regions began to feel its impact. The coming of large industrial firms to Quebec may be considered from many angles. Here were to be found abundant natural resources and a vast reservoir of cheap labor—resources which were readily available and labor that was docile and unsophisticated.

With the advent of the Industrial Revolution in the province, new enterprises were encouraged by both State and Church because of the increase in revenue they would bring and because they would provide an outlet for the overflow of population which the agricultural economy could not absorb. The late development of industry in Quebec favored principally those establishments with relatively large capitalization, and whose well-developed mass-production methods and corporate forms of organization enabled them to compete successfully in the world market. On the whole, it was not a propitious setting for the entrepreneur with a small amount of capital.

It was not until 1901 that the first opposition was raised to the encouragement of "foreign" capital into Quebec. Errol Bouchette urged his people not to neglect industry in their concern for their agricultural and pioneering tradition. However, it was not until the late 1920's that the economic point of view was generally adopted by the elite of French-Canada. This economic development has had profound social consequences. During this period the traditional respect of the habitant for the highly educated and highly placed was gradually supplanted by the class consciousness of the newly urbanized and industrialized masses. This urban proletariat today constitutes more than two thirds of the population of Quebec.

In other ways the social structure of Quebec is feeling the impact of this modern industrial movement. The attraction of the landless sons of farmers to the large towns and cities in search of employment has to some extent weakened the influence of the family unit. The usually static population has become more mobile. The Roman Catholic Church has viewed this situation with increasing concern. So long as the family unit remained static and kept its strong parochial ties, the Church played a prominent role in its life. The urbanized worker often weakened his connections with the Church. He found it possible in this new situation to remain a "good Catholic" without being completely under the thumb of the priest. Statistics show that there has also been a marked decline in the number of children born into the families of nonrural French-Canadian workers. Always in favor of large families and bitterly opposed to birth control, the clergy has communicated its disapproval of this decline in the urban birth rate to the faithful in no uncertain terms.

Another cause for concern on the part of the Church is the influence of trade unionism on the newly urbanized French-speaking workers. The Church is outspoken in its hostility to communism, and it views socialism with much suspicion. The clergy constantly warns the people of the reputed evils inherent in left-wing politics. To counteract this seeming danger, the Church has sponsored such purely Catholic labor organizations as the Syndicates and the Young Catholic Workers. This has caused a certain degree of friction between the Church and the upper-class French-Canadians, who dislike all trade unionism, whether Church-sponsored or not. Nevertheless, the spread of unionism has paralleled the expansion of industry in Quebec. Today, the French-Canadian workers are much less willing to accept lower wages and poorer working conditions than those available to English-Canadians or American workers.

Industry in Quebec increased with technological advancement, especially the development of hydroelectric power; and with this progress skilled technicians and executives were required to operate the concerns. As the French-Canadian educational system had almost completely neglected technological and scientific training, it was necessary to obtain these technicians and executives from the more industrially advanced parts of Canada or from other countries. Generally, such personnel were recruited from the English-speaking group. Today, however, the trend is toward increasing technical education. Engineering courses are well filled at the University of Montreal and L'Ecole Polytechnique. French-Canadians are also to be found in the engineering courses at McGill University. It would thus appear that many of the French group are beginning to seek status through advancement in industry.

A survey of the occupational studies which have been made shows an increasing predominance of English-speaking Canadians as the jobs progress from unskilled labor to top management, the French-Canadians being concentrated at the lower end of the scale. Most of the French who hold high managerial posts are found in the smaller industries. The field of big business is almost entirely dominated by the English.

When considering French-Canadians for positions of foremen and supervisors, the English employers and executives have a real fear that once the French are put into authority they may yield to claims made on them by their families. They claim that every family acts as a lobby for its members. Such a situation is most conducive to feelings of jealousy and discontentment, with the result that these foremen may not be able to maintain discipline and morale. On the other hand, there is ample evidence to show that many French-Canadian businessmen manage to operate successfully despite these alleged familial claims. This may indicate that jealousy appears mainly at the moment of promotion and dies out as soon as the position has been established.

The development of the modern industrial economy, including the American type of urban life and institutions, constitutes a serious threat to the old French semirural economy. Unless this old economy is modernized, it will perish in our present economic structure. This situation is distasteful to most French-speaking Canadians. They realize that most industry is under the control of the English. Seldom do the English work under French authority. Although both French and English are official languages in Canada, the business world conducts its affairs primarily in English. This is a constant irritant to the average French-Canadian, a mark of his minority role. The French-speaking Canadians are now in the process of trying to adjust to these latest and most revolutionary changes introduced in their midst by their English-speaking compatriots.

SUMMARY

The relations between the French-Canadians and English-speaking Canadians frequently take the form of clashes not only on the objective level, that is, between the traditional institutional patterns and an alien and incompatible economic superstructure, but also on the subjective motivational level. The accepted modes of achieving recognition and the symbols of status, or, as Parsons terms them, the specific motives, were formerly widely divergent between the two groups. Today, however, the sustained impact of the modern industrial system is having its effect on the attitudes of the French-Canadian whose life is controlled by it. It is becoming increasingly impossible for him to achieve satisfaction of his "self-interested" motives in the old ways; and, unless he turns his back on the cultural patterns instilled in him in childhood, he finds it difficult to succeed in the new industrial world. Inevitably, in the individual, as in society, there is a conflict of motives between deeply ingrained "disinterested" elements and "self-interest" as defined by economic necessity.

RACIAL DISTANCE CHANGES IN THE UNITED STATES DURING THE PAST THIRTY YEARS

EMORY S. BOGARDUS
University of Southern California

In order to study changes in racial distance reactions a time element is necessary. This factor is represented in this report, which is based on three related pieces of research, the first being made in 1926, the second in 1946, and the third in 1956.

In all three of these studies the same Racial Distance Scale was used.[1] In the 1926 research the reactions of 1,725 persons from 32 different locations in the United States were obtained to a list of 36 different racial groups. While "ethnic groups" would be a more accurate term, since it signifies cultural factors, the respondents for the most part were accustomed to thinking in terms of "races," and hence the latter term was used. The 1,725 respondents were divided almost equally between men and women. Their ages fell between 18 and 35, with a few persons being over 35. Almost one half were enrolled in college courses, while nearly all of the other half were college graduates who were professionally employed but taking one or more postgraduate courses at the time. Approximately one half were enrolled in one or more courses in sociology; and the others, in courses in a wide range of fields. The reactions were obtained from 32 well-distributed areas over the United States, through the aid of faculty members in colleges and universities in these different regions. The respondents from each one of the 32 institutions of higher learning came from many different parts of the United States. Hence the lines of residence of each respondent from his college or university to his home crisscrossed with the lines of residence of respondents from most of the other 31 institutions. Hence there was a rather comprehensive distribution of the 1,725 subjects who participated in this research project. Negroes constituted 10 per cent of the total participants, a percentage similar to the percentage that they constituted of the total population of the United States. In utilizing the data of the

[1] The initial paper by the writer concerning this scale was entitled "Measuring Social Distances" and appeared in the March-April 1925 issue of the *Journal of Applied Sociology*, IX: 299-308. The procedure involved in making the scale was described by the writer in "A Social Distance Scale," *Sociology and Social Research*, XVII: 265-71, January 1933.

1926 study, the writer has drawn upon his report that was published in 1928.[2] This study did not purport in any sense to represent a sampling of the population of the United States, but it was rather a selection of subjects between the ages of 18 and 35 for the most part, representing given educational levels, living in a large number of different areas in this country.

In 1946, twenty years later, the writer made a similar study, obtaining racial distance reactions from 1,950 persons selected in the same way as were the respondents in 1926. These reactions were secured in the same way as in the earlier study. They were obtained from an equal number of men and women, from the same or similar areas in the United States, from persons of the same educational levels and interests, and so on. The respondents belonged to a later generation and were not of course the first group, who had in the meantime grown twenty years older and who would not have been a comparable group in case they could all have been located. The list of "races" had two additions, namely, second generation Mexicans and second generation Japanese. The same Racial Distance Scale was used as in 1926, although in the meantime it had been refined to state the human relationships by which distance reactions were being measured, by socially equidistant intervals as determined by the arithmetic mean of the ratings of 100 judges, and as described in some detail elsewhere by the writer.[3]

In 1956 the writer made a racial reactions study similar to the two preceding ones, specifically for comparative purposes. The same scale was used and the list of "races" included 30 of the 1946 study and 28 of the 1926 project. The respondents belonged to the same educational levels, approximately the same areas of the United States, and were almost equally divided between the sexes. The same method of obtaining the racial reactions was used. This time racial reactions to each of the 30 racial groups were secured from 2,053 respondents, 1,005 of whom were men and 1,048 were women. The comparisons in all cases were made in terms of arithmetic means.[4]

---

[2] *Immigration and Race Attitudes* (Boston: D. C. Heath and Company, 1928).

[3] "A Social Distance Scale," *Sociology and Social Research*, XVII: 265-71.

[4] In making this study the writer is indebted to a large number of persons, especially the following: Alan Bates, Charles Bowerman, Therel Black, Morris Caldwell, Ames Chapman, Frederick Conrad, Joseph Gaiser, Robert Gray, Harry Harmsworth, Harold Hodges, Jr., Thomas Hoult, Harold Jacoby, Donald Kent, Joseph Lagey, Thomas Lasswell, Rose Hum Lee, Samuel Leger, Edward McDonagh, Louise McDonagh, Frances Merrill, Milton Mittelman, Jerome Myers, Philip Nogee, John Owen, Louis Petroff, Floyd Pollock, Eugene Richards, Arnold Rose, Georges Sabagh, James Schellenberg, Hugh Smythe, Woodrow Scott, Vernon Snowbarger, Preston Valien, and I. Roger Yoshino.

Thus, the three studies were conducted in ways designed to be comparative at intervals of ten years (1946-1956), of twenty years (1926-1946), and of thirty years (1926-1956). In presenting comparisons for the years 1926 and 1946, the writer has drawn upon an already published report.[5]

Some of the points at which comparisons of the findings can be made will now be noted. The data on which these observations rest are presented herewith in tabular form.

1. The races in the upper or nearness third of the total group of races toward which reactions are expressed are about the same for the three different dates, 1926, 1946, and 1956. They represent in the main the north European races and those lighter in color.

2. While the distance scores for the races in the nearness third are about the same for the years 1956 and 1946, they are a little higher for the same races in the 1956 study. In order to obtain an explanation of this increase in distance reactions, the interview materials were examined, with the result that at least one point came to the surface, namely, that in recent years the darker colored races seem to be developing an increasing degree of race awareness and are reacting more than earlier against the "superior" attitudes of some of the white races. Further study is needed in order to test this explanation.

3. In comparing the rank order of the 30 racial groups toward whom reactions were expressed by the 2,053 respondents, it may be observed that the Germans went down in rank order (greater distance) in 1946, reflecting, according to interviews, attitudes developed during World War II. The Germans were not accorded any decrease in distance score by 1956, although their rank order was less.

4. The Spanish fell in both the rank order and the distance accorded them in 1946. Interview data suggest that this increase was related to the association, in the minds of some respondents, of Franco with Mussolini and Hitler at that time, as being a dictator.

5. In 1946 the Russians had maintained their rank order and their distance score of 1926, but by 1956 they had fallen decidedly. Interviews pointed definitely to the shift of the Russians from being allies in 1946 and earlier to the leading protagonists in the cold war that developed after 1946, as a major explanatory factor in the marked increase in distance score given them. Some respondents indicated that they would distinguish between Russians as people and Russians as communists, and

---

[5] "Changes in Racial Distances," *International Journal of Opinion Research*, 1:55-62.

that in the first instance they would give them a greater nearness score than they would in the latter case, but that the friendly feeling toward the Russians as people was overcome by the type of government to which they were subject.

6. The Italians fell in rank order and in distance score in 1946. Interviews were uniform in accounting for this increase in distance reactions on the basis of their preceding fascist government under Mussolini. However, the antagonistic feeling reactions did not remain strong, for the 1956 data show that they received a marked decrease in distance and that their rank order was also less.

7. The Czechs had risen in rank order and had been given a decrease in distance score by 1946 (they had fought against the Germans). By 1956 they had fallen in rank order and were given a greater distance score, because of "the communist regime to which they are subject."

8. The Jews received the same rank order and about the same social distance score in 1946 as they did twenty years earlier. However, the interview data showed two different sets of distance reactions by the respondents in 1946. In one type of interview materials deep sympathy was expressed for the Jews because in Europe they had been brutally persecuted by the Nazis. In the other type of reactions, evidences of fear were expressed lest the immigration bars be lowered and Jewish immigrants by the thousands be admitted to the United States. These objectors expressed fear because of what they called the "aggressiveness" of some Jews and of "their tendency to dominate any organization." It appeared that the friendly reactions and the unfriendly ones just about offset each other, for the total distance score toward Jews remained about the same.

In 1956 the Jews received a definitely higher rank order and an increased nearness score. According to the interviews, less marked distinctions between Jews and non-Jews were being drawn in 1956 than earlier, and to some respondents it seemed as though "Jews are undergoing assimilation into American life" and that "they are less conspicuous in actions than they used to be."

9. The Mexicans fell in rank order and received an increased distance score in 1946. By 1956 they slipped down again in rank order, but were given a decreased distance score, which may mean that other racial groups received an even greater decrease in distance. The publicity given in the press in the western part of the United States to the large number of Mexicans who have allowed themselves in recent years to be enticed to

come across the Border illegally to work on farms chiefly, and who had been labeled "wetbacks," aroused adverse reactions. Some respondents think of Mexicans as "peons" and as "unclean laborers."

10. The second generation Mexican, that is, Americans of Mexican parentage received a higher rank order and an improved nearness score in 1956 than they did ten years earlier. The respondents were distinguishing between Mexicans and the second generation Mexican Americans, in favor of the latter.

11. The Japanese fell greatly in rank order and in distance score in 1946 (following the attack on Pearl Harbor and the war). It is noticeable that the reactions toward them changed in the nearness direction after their defeat and their shift toward democracy, as evidenced by their rank order and their distance score in 1956.

12. The second generation Japanese, that is, the Americans of Japanese parentage (Nisei), were for the first time included in the list of groups in the Racial Distance Scale, as was also the case with the second generation Mexican Americans in racial distance experiments in 1934. At that time trial studies showed that they were given practically the same distance score as were the first generation (Issei), despite the fact that they were American citizens by birth whereas their parents could not become citizens. By 1946 the second generation Japanese were given a higher rank order and a greater nearness score, showing that the respondents were distinguishing between the Issei and the Nisei in favor of the latter. This nearness differential was related to the remarkable record for bravery in battle shown by the Nisei soldiers in the American military forces, especially in Italy. By 1956 the Americans of Japanese parentage had been accorded a still better rank order and a lesser distance score.

13. Filipinos moved up in rank order and in nearness score between 1926 and 1946. Their loyalty as a whole to the cause of independence and to the United States during World War II is one explanatory factor, judging by the interviews. In the 1956 study the Filipinos moved up the rank order and received an increase in nearness reactions, which was explained in part at least by some of the respondents as a result of the Filipinos' continued resistance to communism and to the continued friendliness of the Philippines under President Magsaysay for the United States.

14. Between 1926 and 1946 Negroes slid down the rank order and distance score. Some respondents showed resentment toward the increasing militancy of some Negro leaders and toward the latter's insistence on their "rights." This resentment was shown even more by some of the

participants in the 1956 study particularly with reference to the desegregation movement, but this resentment was more than offset by the reactions of many respondents who were slowly becoming adjusted to the idea of at least gradual integration up to a certain point, and hence the total distance score given the Negroes in 1956 was significantly less than in 1946, especially for many parts of the United States outside the South, and for many persons in the 18 to 35 year age group.

15. Sympathetic interest on the part of Americans in the Chinese prior to 1946 in their long defense against Japanese military forces and propaganda would explain in part the upward jump given them in rank order and in nearness reactions in the 1946 study. Their association with the United States in World War II suggests an added explanation. While the rank order and the distance score given them in 1956 show a farness trend, due to the coming of the communist rule over China, yet there is evidence in the interview data that many persons are distinguishing between the Chinese as a people struggling toward democracy and the Chinese communist regime.

16. In looking at the racial group given the greatest distance score in each of the three years, 1926, 1946, and 1956, it will be noted that there is a decline in distance reactions represented by the figures 3.91, 3.61, and 2.83. The aggravations affecting attitudes during World War II would seem to explain why the decline in distance score was limited between 1926 and 1946. It is seen that the large decrease in distance score for 1956 occurs in the reactions toward the eight races given the highest scores. This decrease more than offsets a small increase in distance accorded the races in the nearness third of the total list. The decrease given the darker races is found in interviews to be related to a greatly increased acquaintance with, understanding of, and interest in these racial groups that has developed in the last decade of years on the part of at least a considerable number of the 2,053 respondents in 1956.

17. The arithmetic means of the reactions toward all the racial groups by 1,725, 1,950, and 2,053 persons on the respective dates show a decline in distance reactions as follows, 2.14, 2.12, and 2.09. While these decreases may seem to some persons to be too small to be mentioned, yet they take on significance when the total number of distance reactions that is represented by each arithmetic mean is considered, namely, 48,500, 58,500, and 61,590, respectively.

In tabulating the data given by the 134 Jewish members of the 2,053 respondents in 1956, it was found that they, like other races, place themselves at the head or near the head of the nearness pole of the distance figures, but that they placed the other races in pretty much the same order as all the respondents placed them. The scores for the Russians and the Czechs were closer to the farness pole than those given by the entire group of respondents. However, the arithmetic mean of the scores given the thirty races by the Jewish respondents was 2.04, a figure representing more nearness on the whole than that shown by the total number of subjects. The sample of Jewish participants was not large enough to draw anything more than a preliminary notation.

19. In tabulating the Scales that were completed by the 218 Negro members of the panel, it was found that they naturally put themselves at the head of the nearness pole. Next in point of nearness came the English, Canadians, and Americans (U. S. white) but the distance reactions to these groups were greater than those expressed by the total number of 2,053 respondents. It is of interest to note that the Negro respondents placed Americans (U. S. white) near the top of the nearness end of the distance scale. Reasons advanced were (1) "we have white friends to whom we feel close because they treat us like humans," (2) "we'd rather belong to white America than to any other country," (3) "we aspire to achieve what white people have achieved here in the United States even if they do discriminate against us." Also in the nearness third of the Negro reactions are other races in the following order, French, American Indians, Spanish, Chinese, Mexican Americans, and Italians.

In the middle third of the thirty races, the Negroes placed in order the Filipinos, Japanese Americans, Indians from India, and Mexicans, but at a less distance score than was given these groups by the total number of respondents. In the third section the greatest distance scores were given by the Negroes to the Czechs, Poles, Japanese, Koreans, Turks, with the Russians being assigned the greatest distance. The arithmetic mean of the distance reactions given all thirty races by the Negroes is 2.32, which is higher than that given the thirty races by all 2,053 respondents. Interviews indicate that the higher distance score is related to the discrimination which many Negroes received at the hands of lighter colored people. It may be added that the data concerning Negro racial reactions come from four different areas, that is, from two areas in the South, from one area in the Border region, and from one area in the North. However, the N is not large enough to claim for it any final conclusions.

The foregoing data suggest a number of hypotheses. 1. Racial distances decrease very gradually, if at all, when embedded in deep-seated sentiments and traditions.

2. In the case of a given race social distances may increase suddenly and extensively toward another race when situations develop that arouse an awareness of insecurity, a sense of fear, a loss of status caused by the latter race.

3. As peoples become better informed about one another, social distances tend to decrease gradually between them, unless unequal competition develops that arouses insecurity, fear, loss of status.

4. A people feels nearer to another people of similar culture patterns and backgrounds than to other peoples unless serious competition of some kind occurs between them.

5. The reactions of some members of a people may become more friendly and the reactions of other members of the same people may become more unfriendly at the same time, and hence the arithmetic mean by itself of the total number of race reactions may not reveal any change in race relations.

6. The use of a social distance scale needs to be supplemented by depth interviewing involving a widespread sampling of the subjects in order to obtain related experiences and, more important, the explanations of the reactions to the given experiences.

7. Questionnaires are useful for obtaining reports of experiences that precede racial reactions, but are not penetrating enough as a rule to locate the reasons why people react as they do in their racial experiences.

8. A racial distance scale is useful in measuring the amount of racial reactions, in making comparisons of racial reactions, and in locating changes in racial reactions, while depth interviewing in particular is important in locating the reasons for racial reactions and for the changes that occur in them.

9. The rank order of social distance ratings gives an indication of the social status accorded each of the racial groups.

ETHNIC DISTANCE SCALE (1st edition 1925; 9th, 1954) E. S. Bogardus
(Ethnic is used here largely in the cultural sense.)

1. In order to keep Scale anonymous, do not sign name, but give yourself as much freedom as possible; use only check marks.
2. Please give your first feeling reactions in every case.
3. Give your feeling reactions to each ethnic group in terms of the chief picture or stereotype you have of entire group. Mark each group even if you do not know it.
4. Check as many of seven columns in each case as your feelings dictate.
5. Work as rapidly as possible.

	1 Would marry into group	2 Would have as close friends	3 Would have as next door neighbors	4 Would work in same office	5 Have as speaking acquaintances only	6 Have as visitors only to my nation	7 Would debar from my nation
Armenians							
Americans (U.S.white)							
Canadians							
Chinese							
Czechs							
English							
Filipinos							
Finns							
French							
Germans							
Greeks							
Hollanders							
Indians (American)							
Indians (of India)							
Irish							

1. Please remember to give your first feeling reactions for every group.
2. Remember to give feeling reactions to your chief picture of each group as a whole.
3. Also, to check as many columns for each group as you can, and to work rapidly.

Italians							
Japanese							
Japanese Americans							
Jews							
Koreans							
Mexicans							
Mexican Americans							
Negroes							
Norwegians							
Poles							
Russians							
Scots							
Spanish							
Swedish							
Turks							

Please check. (1) Your ethnic backgrounds: Caucasian___, Mongoloid___, Negro___.
(2) Your religious backgrounds: R. Catholic___, Jewish___, Protestant___, Other___.
(3) Rural backgrounds___, urban backgrounds___. (4) Sex: male___, female___.
(5) Education: 8th grade___, high school grad.___, 2 yrs. coll.___, coll. grad___, postgrad. work___.
(6) Age: under 15___, 15 to 30___, 31 to 50___, 50 or over___.
(7) Occupation: none___, student___, housewife___, unskilled worker___, skilled___, clerical or secretarial___, managerial___, executive___, professional___.
(8) Annual income: none___, under $2500___, $2500 to $5000___, over $5000___.

PACIFIC SOCIOLOGICAL NEWS

University of California, Berkeley. Reinhard Bendix, newly appointed chairman of the department, has received the 1958 annual MacIver award for the best sociological work of the year, *Work and Authority in Industry.* Charles Y. Glock, professor of sociology and director of the Bureau of Applied Social Research at Columbia University, has accepted an appointment as professor of sociology and director of the newly established Center for Survey Research. Ernest Greenwood, now professor in the School of Social Welfare, is conducting research on social work as a profession and has recently completed a study of the careers of a sample of social workers. Judson T. Landis, professor of family sociology in the Department of Home Economics has been elected to the General Council of the International Union of Family Organizations. He has returned to Berkeley after teaching at the University of Alaska. Jack London, associate professor in the School of Education, served as a faculty fellow in the Summer Institute of Social Gerontology at the University of Connecticut. Anselm Strauss, assistant professor of sociology at the University of Chicago, has been appointed as an associate professor of sociology in the School of Nursing of the University of California. Clark E. Vincent, assistant professor of family sociology in the Department of Home Economics, has completed a study of *Unwed Mothers* which will be published shortly.

Oregon State College. William A. Foster, Jr., a recent Ph.D. in rural sociology at Cornell University, joined the staff as an assistant professor. Frank L. Parks, associate professor of sociology, taught at the University of Colorado School of Education during the summer. Hans H. Plambeck, professor of sociology, is a member of a college-wide coordinating committee for a comprehensive two-year study of the human and natural resources of the Warm Springs Indian Reservation.

Stanford University. Takeyoshi Kawashima, professor of sociology at Tokyo University, has been appointed visiting professor of sociology for the coming academic year. Dr. Kawashima will offer courses on Japanese family and society, areas in which he has published seven books. Charles Drekmeier, who is receiving his Ph.D. in social science from Harvard University, has been appointed assistant professor of sociology. He will give courses in political sociology and social thought. The department has received a grant from the Russell Sage Foundation to plan, in collaboration with the Stanford Medical School, a teaching and research program in medical sociology. Edmund H. Volkart, executive head of the Department of Sociology, and Thomas Gonda, executive head of the Department of Psychiatry, are directing the project. Robert A. Ellis, assistant professor of sociology, has received a grant-in-aid from the Society for the Investigation of Human Ecology to initiate a study of social differences in the academic performance of college undergraduates. David Mechanic and Leslie C. Waldo have received Public Health Service research fellowships from the National Institute of Mental Health. Alex Clarke has received a William Randolph and Dora Haynes Foundation Fellowship.

Pomona College. Professor Alvin H. Scaff has been re-elected editor of the *Alpha Kappa Deltan* of the national sociology honor society, Alpha Kappa Delta.

Professor Emeritus Ray Baber has returned from a two-year membership on the faculty of International Christian University, Tokyo, where his time was divided between teaching and research in sociology.

SOCIAL PROBLEMS AND WELFARE

TORNADOES OVER TEXAS. By Harry Estill Moore. Austin: University of Texas Press, 1958, pp. xxiii+334.

What happens when a community is struck by disaster? Civic leaders and social scientists seeking answers to this question will want to turn to a study of two Texas cities that were struck by tornadoes in 1953.

A research team under the direction of Harry Moore of the University of Texas spent more than a year collecting data by interview and study of records. The results include comparisons between the immediate rescue operations and the later and longer process of rehabilitation; between Waco, where the worst damage was in the business district, and San Angelo, where a residential district and school were struck; and between reactions in the different income, racial, and age groups.

The scantiness of previous research in this field and the need for haste in collecting the data precluded rigorous testing of the many hypotheses formulated in the course of the study. On the other hand, insight is provided into such problems as why the Red Cross was unpopular in spite of the large-scale aid it provided. BRUCE M. PRINGLE

Southern Methodist University

MODERN COURTSHIP AND MARRIAGE. By E. E. LeMasters. New York: The Macmillan Company, 1957, pp. xxvii+619.

The book aims to assist students in becoming oriented to societal problems related to modern courtship and marriage as well as to aid them in their own personal adjustment, and to present a more complete analysis of the American courtship system than is found in other texts in this area. Theoretically, the analysis is oriented toward "functionalism." The data have been drawn from a wide range of sources and from the author's own experience as a teacher of marriage and family courses and as a family case worker. After the introductory section on "perspectives," the main divisions of the text deal with "the American courtship system" and "marriage in modern society."

The American marriage system is monogamous and semipatriarchal, but the courtship system is of a romantic type, leaving the young people much on their own. Courtship is competitive, youth-centered, flexible, democratic, and involves a progressive commitment process. If the process is not altered by a variety of circumstances and conditions, it involves the following steps or stages: group and random dating, going steady, engagement, and marriage. Going steady seems to be the preferred dating status. After marriage, some of the conditions and problems include the delicate matters of marital and sexual adjustment, money matters, religion, child-rearing, and not too infrequently marital failure. These and other phases of courtship and marriage are discussed with candor and documented to indicate the basic findings. The suggested references are selective, designed to aid students in further study. On the whole, this is one of the better texts on courtship and marriage.

M.H.N.

ENRICHING FAMILY LIFE: THROUGH HOME, SCHOOL, AND COMMUNITY. By Bess B. Lane. Washington, D.C.: Public Affairs Press, 1958, pp. xiv+121.

The main purpose of this book is to provide information of value to parents and parent study groups. One of the basic assumptions is that parents can be of great help to one another. The material was derived chiefly from parents and is transmitted to other parents who may benefit from the experiences related in the book. Questions for study and bibliographies for further study are added.

M.H.N.

PRINCIPLES OF COOPERATION. Second Revised Edition. By Emory S. Bogardus. Chicago: The Cooperative League, 1958, pp. 77.

In this revised edition (first published in 1952) a number of factual points are brought up to date and recognition is taken of new developments in the world cooperative movement. Revisions have been made throughout the book in order to facilitate an understanding of the seven basic principles on which cooperatives operate. These principles, characteristic of cooperatives in practically all democratic countries of the world, are discussed in terms of the following concepts: democracy, voluntarism, autonomy, equity, mutuality, universality, and evolution. Special attention is given to educational techniques for developing cooperatives, which are described as representing "the private property system and free enterprise in their finest expressions." This analysis of cooperatives merits close scrutiny by individuals interested in the principles of cooperative action from either an academic or a practical point of view.

WOODROW W. SCOTT
George Pepperdine College

GOVERNMENT AND SOCIAL WELFARE. By Wayne Vasey. New York: Henry Holt and Company, 1958, pp. 506.

The author, dean of the Graduate School of Social Work at Rutgers University, describes in this volume the respective roles of federal, state, and local governments in providing welfare services. He has brought together, in concise and readable style, a knowledge and understanding gained both from his own rich direct personal experience in local, state, and federal welfare administration and from his experience in teaching this subject.

The book is divided into three parts: Background, Programs, and Organization. The first deals with the scope of needs and services, describing the philosophical base for the assumption of responsibility by government for social welfare programs. While some attention is directed toward the relationship of governmental and voluntary services, it is regrettably brief, leaving only the purpose of providing some perspective on the total welfare picture.

The second part describes the social insurances, the public assistance programs, and other programs such as Child Welfare Services, Mental Health Programs, Correctional Programs. This section is particularly valuable. The naturally complex material is presented with a clarity that makes it of special importance in undergraduate curricula of social welfare; the illustrations contained in the first two parts of the volume are useful in emphasizing points of importance so that the ordinarily complicated legal provisions of the programs assume a simplicity that is very desirable in teaching those being exposed for the first time to learning about this essential and intricate segment of our society.

Like the two companion parts, the third, concerned with organization, structure, and relationships of agencies established on a federal or state or local basis, is presented with a quality of chatty simplicity that contributes to its value as a tool in undergraduate education. The selected references that appear at the end of each chapter are a further aid.

FRANCES LOMAS FELDMAN
School of Social Work,
University of Southern California

THE AGED IN AMERICAN SOCIETY. By Joseph T. Drake. New York: The Ronald Press Company, 1958, pp. ix+431.

This is an excellent college textbook on gerontology. In the first of five parts the author traces the evolution of mores relating to the aged from a primitive agrarian society to our present urban-industrial organization. He shows how improved medical care and improved living conditions have increased the proportion of the aged, creating a minority problem to which society is giving belated adjustment. In the second part he discusses the difficulties of the aged in remaining employed or in finding new jobs. Part three takes up economic needs of the aged. Plans of federal, state, and private agencies to meet these needs are presented in detail. The fourth part is devoted to a study of physical and mental illness of the aged and problems of rehabilitation, retraining, and psychological adjustment. The last part of the book stresses the rapidly increasing concern of society for the aged and the attention being given to their housing, recreation, general comfort, and to the study of their problems.

The most noteworthy quality of the book is the fact that the author looks upon an aged person as a human being rather than as a statistic. Quoting the classic four wishes of Thomas he says: "Every person has a need for security, recognition, response, and experience. These needs vary —but if they are not satisfied in some measure, the person becomes maladjusted emotionally." The value of the book is enhanced by the inclusion of thirteen pages of bibliography.

JOHN B. GRIFFING
American International Association

TREATMENT OF THE CHILD IN EMOTIONAL CONFLICT. By Hyman S. Lippman, M.D. New York: The McGraw-Hill Book Company, 1956, pp. x+298.

In his treatment of children having an emotional problem the author recognizes four types of such children: (1) the child whose abnormal behavior cannot be controlled by parents or teachers, (2) the neurotic child who is constantly in trouble, (3) the child suffering from emotional conflict, (4) the unstable and immature child.

A section of the book is devoted to each of these types and its subdivisions. Among the more unusual forms of conflict encountered were the child with school phobia, the overprotected child, the narcissistic child, and the effeminate child. Each is given profound discussion, and case studies are used to illuminate the problem and the difficulties involved.

The background and prior experiences of children as portrayed throw much light on causes of conflict and difficulty. Children who have remained in institutions several years are found to be markedly narcissistic. The unsocialized child is too often the victim of an unwelcome or an unhappy home or of inconsiderate and temperamental parents.

The author agrees with the conclusion reached by Anna Freud's Seminar in Vienna, "that a well-trained, intelligent, non-medical person is qualified to treat neurotically conflicted children." Social workers are now entering the field of direct therapy for such children, but this is a task which requires training not only as a social worker but as a therapist as well. Such workers are now needed in all social agencies concerned with the welfare of children.

The book takes a forward step in insisting that the workers must understand the problems of the family and also know the community. No longer can the treatment of a child be attempted apart from the environmental conditions in which he lives. The child with emotional conflicts should be treated by a psychiatric team consisting of the case worker, the clinical psychologist, the child psychiatrist, and the group therapist.

G.B.M.

THE ACADEMIC MARKETPLACE. By Theodore Caplow and Reece J. McGee. New York: Basic Books, Inc., 1958, pp. 262.

This book represents the first major effort to analyze university teaching as an occupation. The researchers selected nine universities (unnamed) and investigated the facts surrounding all professorial vacancies and replacements which occurred in the liberal arts departments during the academic years 1954-55 and 1955-56. Some 237 vacancies were listed for the nine institutions. The research team interviewed some 215 chairmen and 162 peers of the professors who vacated their positions. Most of the interviews reflected some of the basic dynamics involved in academic mobility.

Significant findings of the work center on how the vacancies occur, how performance is evaluated, the strategy of getting offers and counter offers, procedures of recruitment, patterns of choice, who does the active recruitment, and some thoughtful recommendations concerning termination of faculty contracts and faculty recruitment. The median age of professors when they leave for new positions is as follows: 34, assistant professor; 42, associate professor; and 57, for a full professor. It appears that most faculty men leave, not because of higher salaries elsewhere, but because of personal problems and personal relations. Some of the quotations appear to be sociological gems. The book is interesting, perhaps a little too interesting for some rigorous methodologists.

E.C.M.

COOPERATIVE HOUSING MANUAL. **Steps to Cooperative Housing in Nova Scotia. By Joe Laben. Antigonish, Nova Scotia: Extension Department, St. Francis Xavier University, 1958, pp. 84.**

A remarkable fact about this manual is that it is written by a man who has worked in coal mines for twenty-five years. The ambition of this coal miner was awakened by the stimulating ideas of Father J. J. Tompkins, who told him and others that they could build and own their homes if they wanted to badly enough, even though at first they lacked money and the know-how.

Joe Laben has been a cooperative housing expert for twenty years, since he and ten other miners built Tompkinville (with help from Mary Arnold), a housing project of eleven homes. "Joe" has supervised about seventy other similar cooperative projects. This booklet gives the practical details for carrying through to completion a cooperative housing project. Ten to fourteen is considered to be the best number of families to join together in building their homes cooperatively. Study group meetings each week for several months are considered essential for success in entering on a cooperative housing project. This booklet is far more important than its modest claims and detailed specifications would seem to indicate.

E.S.B.

CHILDREN OF THE KIBBUTZ. By Melford E. Spire. Cambridge, Massachusetts: Harvard University Press, 1958, pp. xx+500.

This book represents a study of a collective agricultural settlement (Kibbutz) in Israel. The Kibbutz practices comprehensive collective living, communal ownership, and cooperative enterprise. More than three hundred such settlements are scattered over the country. They are welcomed as an experiment in collective enterprise and the achievement of brotherhood. Money is rejected by them as a medium of exchange, the profit motive has been eliminated as a stimulus to production, and the distribution of goods is determined by the principle of "from each according to his ability, to each according to his needs."

The field work for this book, carried out by the author and his wife, required participation by the two in the work and social life of the group studied.

According to the Kibbutz plan, children are removed soon after birth to small cottages and cared for by nurses and other attendants. Parents may daily visit their children, but the nurse assumes virtually all the functions and duties of the parents. After completing the first grade, the children from seven to twelve move into the grammar school. Here they live as in earlier years in bisexual dormitories.

All courses in the humanities and social services are taught in the light of Marxism (p. 257). Many of the activities of the children are expected to result in socialized behavior without deliberate control by nurses and other workers. The techniques of social control are various, but the abdication of authority by the teachers is a frequent occurrence.

At the age of twelve the children enter the combined junior-senior high school, and activities and training suitable to these older children are carried on.

Part VI deals especially with the sabras, adult individuals who have graduated from the Kibbutz but are continuing as functionary members of the organization. Although they exhibit a high degree of cultural conformity, serious problems of emotional adjustment remain. The program of socialization, in spite of certain indications of insecurity, has yielded an efficient, productive, and functioning adult.

Appendix B is most valuable in that it outlines the five-grade curriculum of the Kibbutz high school.

The author wisely hesitates to generalize results because his observations relate to the activities of a single Kibbutz only. Further study is contemplated.

G.B.M.

FACT BOOK ON COOPERATIVES WITH 1957-1958 DEVELOPMENTS. Chicago: The Cooperative League of the USA, 1958, pp. 56.

This new edition brings the major facts about the cooperative movement in the United States up to date. Special attention is given to the new developments of consumer cooperatives, of farm marketing cooperatives, of national cooperative organizations; and to the ways in which co-ops pay all the kinds of taxes that other forms of business do. Thirty-five photographs enliven the pages, and a list of many other publications of the Cooperative League adds to the usefulness of this *Fact Book*.

E.S.B.

SOCIAL PROBLEMS AND SOCIAL ACTION. By Mary F. Walsh and Paul H. Furfey. New York: Prentice-Hall, Inc., 1958, pp. xiv+465.

In this volume written by two professors of sociology of the Catholic University of America, the major social problems considered relate to mental care and mental health, the American family, the juvenile delinquent, the adult criminal, intergroup problems (prejudice and racial minorities), the American economy, the subproletariat (the lower-lower class), and war. Each of these problems is carefully tested "in the light of actual, contemporary conditions" and of "the whole social situation" in which it occurs.

A unique chapter is the one on "America's Balance Sheet," in which the authors indicate "some characteristics of American society" which "actually generate social problems," and, on the other hand, suggest other characteristics which aid in controlling the conditions that create problems. Another special feature of the book is a "bibliographical essay" at the close of each chapter, which in an informal way cites and evaluates important current literature pertaining to the subjects of the given chapters.

The authors state the position of the Catholic Church regarding the solution of social problems in terms of "charity" and "social action," which are concepts with specific Catholic meanings. The treatment of social problems throughout the book is consistent with the special meaning of these concepts. More space might have been given to the city as a social problem, to the use of leisure, to immigration and refugee problems, to international relations as a social problem, although of course a limitation has to be established and choices made regarding the main emphasis.

E.S.B.

EGO PSYCHOLOGY AND DYNAMIC CASEWORK. Papers from the Smith College School for Social Work. Edited by Howard J. Parad. New York: Family Service Association of America, 1958, pp. 282.

Written under the aegis of the Smith College School for Social Work, the nineteen papers by social workers, psychiatrists, and social scientists included in this volume propose "to examine the impact of ego psychology on casework practice" and to relate casework theory to new developments in the social sciences. As indicated in the Introduction, "the reader will find in these pages a series of interrelated inquiries into the dynamics of personality and the technical problems of casework treatment." The book does not pretend to offer a definitive statement of casework theory, but is rather "an exploration into the subtleties of diagnosis and treatment, with consideration of ways in which the understanding of ego phenomena can be effectively applied in helping relationships." The papers have been organized into three sections: (1) Ego Psychology and Casework Theory; (2) Selected Applications in Casework Practice; and (3) Toward New Knowledge for Practice.

In the first section such distinguished social work educators as Gordon Hamilton, Florence Hollis, and the late Annette Garrett discuss the contributions of psychoanalytic thought (notably the theories of Sigmund Freud) to casework theory and method, and the later contributions of Anna Freud to the social worker's understanding of ego functioning. The application of ego psychology to casework practice is seen as an important modern trend, influencing the caseworker's thinking and activity with reference to the worker-client relationship, personality diagnosis, and treatment objectives and methods.

In the second section several psychiatrists and social workers discuss the dynamics and treatment involved in a few specific case situations, making application of ego psychology concepts in the presentations.

The third section includes articles by social workers, psychiatrists, and social scientists discussing opportunities and problems in social work and clinical research, and ways of furthering interdisciplinary collaboration and the productive use of social science materials in social work. Of particular interest to social scientists will be Herman Stein's paper on "Social Science in Social Work Practice and Education."

Ego Psychology and Dynamic Casework will appeal primarily to the social work audience for which it was written, since it deals in social work terminology with casework practice. The psychological orientation is Freudian, and the ego psychology discussed stems from Anna Freud's theories concerning the ego's patterns of adaptation and ways (conscious and unconscious) of coping with life's daily problems and stresses. While the book's emphasis is an application of a particular psychological theory of personality to a particular professional helping method, the material should hold interest for all disciplines concerned with the nature of man and the nature of therapy. The authors all stress the importance of a *psychosocial* approach in thinking about and dealing with people—an approach that sees the "person in the situation" and hence makes use of both psychological and social science theories. The book adheres to its central purpose in presenting the impact of ego psychology on social work, but also (albeit briefly) considers the relevance to social work practice of theoretical advances in the social as well as the behavioral sciences.

LOLA G. SELBY
School of Social Work,
University of Southern California

TEACH THEM TO LIVE: A Study of Education in English Prisons. By Frances Banks. New York: International Universities Press, Inc., 1958, pp. xxiv+287.

In all that has been written about prisons and prison life, only a few references deal with the growth of educational programs in prisons. This is one of the most important aspects of rehabilitation of prisoners. The historical growth of prison education is briefly traced. This is followed by discussions of students and conditions; education as therapy; education for culture, recreation, and vocation; the means of study, including libraries, study rooms, and correspondence courses; the place of education in prisons for women; and the problems associated with staffing for education, especially the qualifications and training of staff members and the integration of education with the total program in prisons. The book is packed with information and ideas. Possibly the greatest development in the training of prisoners has been the establishment of the open prison system. The therapeutic approach, including group as well as individual therapy, has been used to good advantage. Vocational training, work experience while in prison, education for leisure and recreation (drama groups, art classes, hobbies and handicrafts, and physical culture), the provision of library facilities, and other educational developments in prisons are described in considerable detail. It is evident from the emphasis and material used in the book that the author is a passionate believer in providing better education for prisoners.

M.H.N.

DRUG ADDICTION: PHYSIOLOGICAL, PSYCHOLOGICAL, AND SOCIOLOGICAL ASPECTS. By D. P. Ausubel. New York: Random House, 1958, pp. vii+126.

This small volume constitutes a compact treatise on the problem of drug addiction, the physiological and psychological effects of opiates, the psychological and social characteristics of opiate addiction, elements of treatment and prognosis, addiction to nonopiate drugs (marihuana, barbiturates, cocaine, and benzedrine), and the prevention of drug addiction. The effects of opiates on the users are described in considerable detail. The author recognizes the difficulties in classifying drug addicts and in ascertaining the causal factors. He thinks that the most defensible classification in the light of available evidence includes three main types: "primary addiction, in which opiates have specific adjustive value for particular personality defects; symptomatic addiction, in which the use of opiates has no particular adjustive value and is only an incidental symptom of behavior disorder; and reactive addiction, in which drug use is a transitory developmental phenomenon in essentially normal individuals influenced by distorted peer group norms" (p. 39). Clinical studies show that over one half of the addicts are in the first group, i.e., they are primary addicts. They suffer from various types of personality disorders or inadequacies and they are the most difficult to cure. The author feels that Lindesmith's habit theory of opiate addiction, with the emphasis on the withdrawal-distress factor, and Becker's similar explanation of the genesis of marihuana use are inadequate, chiefly on the ground that they do not account for the factors of personality predispositions, which he regards as most important. However, the author does not stress sufficiently the sociological factors involved in drug addictions.

In dealing with the problem of drug addiction, various methods of treatment and preventive measures are described. It is evident from the studies of the treatment of addicts that much research is needed before an adequate program of control can be put into operation. Pharmacological research in the prevention of narcotic addiction does not offer much hope for the discovery of an effective analgesic. Research along psychological, psychiatric, and sociological lines seems to be more fruitful. "Perhaps the most important of the research tasks is the definitive identification through controlled longitudinal studies of the personality factors that predispose addiction and affect prognosis and the outcome of therapy" (p. 119). Other research problems include the influence of cultural tolerance and group pressures in the various stages of drug addiction, the conditions under which relapses occur, and the relative efficacy of different forms of therapy.

M.H.N.

FAMILY RELATIONSHIPS AND DELINQUENT BEHAVIOR. By F. Ivan Nye. New York: John Wiley & Sons, Inc., 1958, pp. xvii+168.

Recognizing that there are disproportionate numbers of delinquent children from broken homes in reformatories and training schools, the author used noninstitutionalized school groups to ascertain the forms and extent of deviant behavior and the possible relationship of the family to the various types of behavior patterns. After a brief discussion of the various frames of reference that have been used to study delinquent behavior, the methodology and general framework of the present study are described. The family structure in relation to delinquent behavior is analyzed, especially the socioeconomic status, size, composition (broken-unbroken), ethnic backgrounds, and affiliations outside the family; legally and psychologically broken homes; employed mothers; and spatial mobility. The final and more extensive part of the study deals with parent-adolescent relationships as these affect delinquent behavior. The acceptance-rejection matrix, the problems of discipline and punishment, freedom and responsibility, family recreation, parental disposition and character, value agreement, money matters, information, and advice are discussed. The descriptive and analytical material on parent-child relationships treats delinquent behavior as a variable rather than an attribute.

The sample included both delinquents and nondelinquents in three small Washington towns (population 10,000 to 30,000) and additional data for comparative purposes. "Two basic, related problems were encountered in the collection of the research data. First, it was necessary to create research instruments which would measure delinquent behavior, parental rejection, attitudes toward discipline, freedom, money distribution, parental interaction, and other variables in family interaction" (p. 11). The next problem was to secure reliable data from the respondents. The delinquency scale included a list of 23 items. Anonymous questionnaires were administered in classrooms of grades 9 to 12. Both the size of the sample and the careful administration of the questionnaires provided a fairly adequate basis for measuring the family relationships in relation to delinquency. Interviews with a sample of parents would have provided a check on the answers given by the boys and girls studied. The questionnaire method presents a cross-sectional rather than a developmental picture of the subjects studied. However, the care with which the data were gathered and analyzed obviated some of the methodological difficulties.

It is not possible to review the basic findings. Most of the book is devoted to a summary of the findings, which are compared with the findings of other studies. The behavior patterns of the "most delinquent" and the "least delinquent" are compared. The study represents a significant contribution to the family in relation to delinquent behavior and the extent of delinquency in the age groups studied. M.H.N.

THE CO-OPERATIVE MOVEMENT IN INDONESIA. By Mohammad Hatta, Vice-President, Republic of Indonesia, 1945-1956. With an Introduction by Roesli Rahim, Head of the Cooperative Service. Edited by George McT. Kahim. Ithaca: Cornell University Press, 1957, pp. xxxiv+121.

This volume records the remarkable progress that cooperatives have made in Indonesia in the past few years, considering all the handicaps that they have had. It also portrays the tremendous need for their further development and extension. A far-reaching comprehension of the principles of cooperatives is shown in the addresses on cooperation given by former Vice-President Hatta, and also by Mr. Rahim in the Preface.

The Government of Indonesia considers cooperatives "a means, even a basic principle, for the reconstruction of the economy in Indonesia," and has established a Cooperative Service Department in the Ministry of Economic Affairs. A total of 7,700 cooperatives with a combined membership of 1,180,000 is considered only a beginning of what is needed. The government regards the establishment of cooperatives as "an ideal means for providing practical training in the economic field, the safest way for forming national capital, and at the same time a means for animating the initiative of the peasant and strengthening his self-respect." Cooperatives develop both solidarity and individuality. It is highly significant that important government leaders in Southeast Asia present the significance of cooperatives as clearly as do Mr. Hatta and Mr. Rahim. E.S.B.

THE ROLE OF FACTORING IN MODERN BUSINESS FINANCE. By Clyde William Phelps. Baltimore: Education Division, Commercial Credit Company, 1956, pp. 70.

What is factoring? The author says, "Modern factoring involves a continuing agreement under which a financing institution assumes the credit and collection function for its client, purchases his receivables as they arise without recourse to him for credit losses, and, because of these relationships, performs other auxiliary functions for its client." This definition suggests the range of analysis undertaken in this monograph.

The idea of factoring is not new, yet the growing importance of its functions in the modern economy is not generally known or realized. Currently about 4 billion dollars of financing assistance is being supplied to American business firms annually through the factoring of open accounts receivable, and other factoring functions are becoming increasingly important. Of special significance to economists and sociologists is the author's explanation of factoring as a social institution which needs to be understood in terms of its methods, policies, and functions.

J.E.N.

PEOPLES AND CULTURE

SINHALESE VILLAGE. By Bryce Ryan. Coral Gables, Florida: University of Miami Press, 1958, pp. x+229.

This book consists of a part of the findings of a broad research project of Ceylon Village Society, which was conducted by the staff of the Sociology Department of the University of Ceylon, during the period of 1948-52. Pelpola, the specific subject of the book, a village of about four hundred households, is located in the Low Country of Ceylon, the most urbanized section of the island. This community was chosen as a sample of village culture undergoing change in that area, and one might say that it is also a "sample" of Sinhalese culture in general. Since one of the main objects of the study was to analyze cultural change taking place in Ceylon Village Society, the frame of reference had to be Sinhalese folk culture. The study included community structure, economic activities, familial and kinship relationships, religion, and social stratification. These are described and analyzed from the standpoint of change, that is, transition from sacred to secular society. Historical, statistical, descriptive, and comparative approaches were used in collecting and analyzing the materials.

The reviewer, who is familiar with Bulgarian peasant society, was much impressed by a number of striking similarities in Sinhalese and old Bulgarian village culture, especially so because the two cultures are far apart geographically. In the reviewer's opinion, this book is an important contribution to our knowledge of folk cultures that are in the process of change.

LOUIS PETROFF
Southern Illinois University

DESEGREGATION: SOME PROPOSITIONS AND RESEARCH SUGGESTIONS. Prepared by Edward A. Suchman, John P. Dean, and Robin M. Williams, Jr. New York: Anti-Defamation League of B'nai B'rith, 1958, pp. 128.

This treatise summarizes comprehensively the relevant knowledge concerning desegregation and presents a number of promising implications of such knowledge for the actual course of desegregation in the United States. The authors are cautious in purporting what seem to be the principles and facts uncovered by the behavioral sciences of pertinence to the process of desegregation. They are aware that a great deal more research needs to be undertaken before the "level of confidence" in specific action programs can approach anything like complete endorsement. Most of the basic ideas and suggestions for research in this area emerge from some seven years of intensive work undertaken by the Cornell Studies in Intergroup Relations. The work is unusually well organized and is a gold mine for dissertation topics. E.C.M.

FROM COMMUNITY TO METROPOLIS. A Biography of São Paulo, Brazil. By Richard M. Morse. Gainesville: University of Florida Press, 1958, pp. xxiii+341.

This is a thoroughgoing treatise by a historian of the development of a metropolitan center that was founded in 1554 by the Jesuits in a region remote from Western civilization and in an infertile land area. For years it grew very little, but, beginning about 1890, its growth made phenomenal strides. Today its population exceeds 3,000,000, and the maximum has not yet been attained. This amazing population increase finds its basis in part in a coffee-growing boom, a cattle-raising hinterland, an impetus due to railroad connections with Rio de Janeiro and with the port city of Santos, a marked industrial development, a relatively large immigration from Italy and a smaller amount of immigration from Japan.

The city's energy is doubtless due to a considerable degree to the nature of the Italian immigrants, who came from north Italy and who possessed the industrious traits characteristic of the German immigrants who have contributed so much to the growth of certain regions in the United States. A great deal remains to be done sociologically in completing this biography of a city. E.S.B.

THE POPULATION AHEAD. Edited by Roy G. Francis. Minneapolis: University of Minnesota Press, 1958, pp. x + 160.

Population studies are necessarily concerned with numbers, but the papers making up this symposium are also directing attention to the qualities that will prove desirable in the numbers we breed, both on the physiological and on the cultural side. These papers are notably moderate in their citation of statistics as such, while emphasizing the probable consequences of demographic change if the present trends are continued. From this standpoint, the papers of timely interest include the following: A Generation of Demographic Change, by Pascal K. Whelpton; Optimum Rates of Population Growth, by Frederick Osborn; The Man-Land Ratio, by Jan O. M. Broek; and The Equilibrium Population, by Edward S. Deevey. Other population factors presented are essential to round out the symposium, such as the implications of minimum subsistence for an explosive increase in population, the genetic future of man, and cultural aspects of the population problem. The symposium as a whole will prove to be valuable for courses in population and particularly refreshing for its style of interpretation. J.E.N.

WEST OF THE GREAT DIVIDE. NORWEGIAN MIGRATION TO THE PACIFIC COAST, 1847-1893. By Kenneth O. Bjork. Northfield, Minn.: Norwegian-American Historical Association, 1958, pp. 671.

In this historical narrative Professor Bjork recounts, with exceptional sympathy and insight, the Norwegian immigration into the region of the United States which is "West of the Great Divide"—tracing the Norwegian pioneers into California in the days of the gold rush, into the Mormon West, Washington Territory and Oregon, and in certain sections of the Rockies. The people depicted were hardy and venturesome, engaged in mining, farming, fishing, shipbuilding, and other activities according to their talents. They were a religious people and established not only their traditional Lutheran church but other Protestant denominations; these developed in response to social and psychological differences among them which were concealed under a cloak of theological conflict.

Personal letters, anecdotes, leadership factors, and other glimpses of Norwegian motivation lend human interest to the story. The author's perspective is broad, Norwegian western migration being dealt with as a movement, and the book is commendable as a major contribution to immigrant and western history. J.E.N.

MISSIONARIES, CHINESE, AND DIPLOMATS. The Protestant Missionary Movement in China, 1890-1952. By Paul A. Varg. Princeton, New Jersey: Princeton University Press, 1958, pp. xii+335.

This is a historical study of the American Protestant missionary movement in China, with emphasis on the attitudes of the missionaries and their home church toward the Chinese people and what they conceive to be the central purposes of missionary work. Viewing religion as a phase of culture, the author discusses the changing religious emphases in America through the years as reflected in the attitudes of the missionaries. He is especially critical of the early missionaries who were afire with evangelical zeal but short in sociological perspective, who looked upon the Chinese as depraved heathens (pp. 18, 114 ff.), and who "made war on the whole Chinese value system" (p. 35).

The facts are well documented, and the style of writing is very readable. The data are gleaned from the files of the Department of State and the Missionary Research Library, from the letters and reports of missionaries on their work and on conditions in China, and from the writings of Chinese and American writers. Missionary work has not been more successful, the author points out, not only because of its early reliance on "unequal treaties" and privileges associated with imperialism, not only because the missionaries lived in walled compounds symbolic of their isolation from the stream of social life in the land they tried to serve, but because it failed to provide a program to solve the political and economic problems with which the Chinese were much more concerned than with the saving of souls (pp. 319 ff.). In his conclusion, he makes an interesting attempt to apply the lesson learned from missionary work to the larger problem of U.S. policy and U.S. aid to the lesser developed countries. While the missionaries were concerned with narrow evangelism, the American government was concerned with commerce and failed to see the significance of the Chinese revolution. In contrast, "the Soviet Union sacrificed the petty advantages of commerce in order to win the larger battle" (p. 322).

Though critical, the book is not unsympathetic to the missionary movement. Credit is given to liberal-minded and farsighted missionaries who tried to map out a larger program of social significance, but "the great majority of missionaries did not go along; they side-stepped political and economic issues" (p. 320).

THEODORE CHEN

A BLACK CIVILIZATION. A Social Study of an Australian Tribe. Revised Edition. By W. Lloyd Warner. New York: Harper and Brothers, 1958, pp. xx+618.

This study has, since its first publication in 1937, ranked as one of the best concerning Australian natives, and it is fortunate that a revised edition is now available. The tribe studied is the Murngin, located in Arnhem Land in Northern Australia. These natives belong to the aboriginal Australoid race found throughout Australia—not Mongoloid, Negroid, or Caucasian, but a variant group which seems to be a blend of various features of the white and black races. They have a Stone Age culture, their technical development falling between the Old and New Stone ages.

Warner deals at length with the social structure and supernaturalism of these tropical Australian people. The family and kinship structure is one of the most intensely organized known to anthropologists, and the age grading structure is basic in their social grouping in general. Institutionalized aspects of their warfare are dealt with at length, also their practice of magic and medicine, and their totemism which is uniquely significant in Australian native life. There are nine appendices which constitute an important part of the book. Besides a few illustrations, there are sixteen charts to delineate the complex kinship and group organizations. J.E.N.

HUMAN TYPES. An Introduction to Social Anthropology. By Raymond Firth. New York: The New American Library of World Literature, 1958, pp. 176.

In this new paperback "Mentor Book," the author, who is professor of anthropology, University of London, revises an older work, and gives "the main problems discussed and conclusions reached in modern social anthropology." This is an up-to-date, well-balanced, concise, and important treatise of such themes as racial traits and mental difference, work and wealth of primitive communities, principles of social structure, the regulation of conduct, reason and unreason in human beliefs, and anthropology in modern life. A selected list of readings and eight plates, chiefly of primitive people, are appended in this handy, compact document. A.R.R.

THE DISPLACED PERSON AND THE SOCIAL AGENCY. A Study of the Casework Process in Its Relation to Immigrant Adjustment. By David Crystal. Rochester, New York: United Hias Service and the Jewish Social Service Bureau of Rochester, 1958, pp. 182.

A displaced person in this study is defined as a person who has been forced by war or subsequent circumstances to flee from his homeland. He has no government or society which would welcome him home and has to seek a new way of life. In many cases he is stateless.

The study involves 182 clients arriving at a given casework agency where a research design was set up to test three hypotheses, two of which seem to have been well supported by the results. The first of these findings indicates that those displaced persons "who seemed to be most relaxed and least threatened in their initial contact with the agency" are "the same people who constructively use the social services and require these services for the briefest period." The second finding shows that "as hostility toward the services of the agency fails to diminish in intensity," so economic dependency of the subjects persists. E.S.B.

CLINICAL STUDIES IN CULTURE CONFLICT. Edited by Georgene Seward. New York: The Ronald Press Company, 1958, pp. xvii+598.

It is not easy to make socioclinical problems concrete, but to this end the editor has collected case studies from professional colleagues in psychology, psychiatry, anthropology, and from the social worker; the volume is commendable for its contribution in an important area of conflict analysis. The patients who have suffered conflicts associated with ethnic minority status, which is the factor on which attention is focused, include the Negro, the American Indian, the Mexican-American, the Puerto Rican, the Filipino, the Japanese, and the Jew. The diagnosis in each case is remarkably thorough and objective from early childhood onward, and specific findings in response to clinical tests in current practice round out the report in each case. The compilation shows the great importance of culture conflict in psychopathology. The emphasis of the book is diagnostic. J.E.N.

WHITE MAN, LISTEN! By Richard Wright. Garden City, New York: Doubleday and Company, 1957, pp. 190.

This group of revised lectures deals first with a series of attitudes of white and colored people in thinking about each other as expressed in special terms, such as "frog perspective," the suspicion of stupidity, negative loyalty, flight into the past. In the second part the theme is "tradition and industrialization." Through industrialization white men have tried "to harness the body of colored mankind into personal service." Racism was introduced for the colored people and profits for the whites, but, says the author, "freedom is indivisible." White men aimed "to save the souls of a billion or so heathens and to receive the material blessings of God while doing so."

The third part presents a variety of sample quotations from the literature of the Negro in the United States, and what "some of that writing means, how it came to be written, what relationship it had to its time, and what it means to us today." He meets these aims forcefully. The fourth and concluding section gives a kind of social case history of how Ghana came to be born; in fact, it is a type of leadership case history, for it deals extensively with Nkrumah, his role in "The Secret Circle," the struggle to free the people from British domination and the problems involved in warding off the efforts of the "black bourgeois leaders of the United Gold Coast Convention" who didn't want independence for their country. This part of the book tells how six black men, organized in The Secret Circle, "unarmed and penniless," lead the way in "establishing a nation of their own in the teeth of British opposition and the stagnant traditions of their own people." As to be expected from the author of *Native Son,* this book, although disconnected, above all else is forthright. E.S.B.

SOCIAL THEORY AND RESEARCH

THE DYNAMIC OF PLANNED CHANGE. A Comparative Study of Principles and Techniques. By Ronald Lippitt, Jeanne Watson, and Bruce Westley. New York: Harcourt, Brace and Company, 1958, pp. xi+312.

Personal and social aspirations for change seem to emerge from such trends as the fact that man seizes new opportunities to use or modify natural resources and to adjust to changes in environmental situations. Throughout the book the authors focus discussions upon four types of somewhat overlapping dynamic systems, which they call "levels of problem-solving efforts." These are (1) internal personality factors; (2) group aspects, especially small group systems; (3) the large organizations or systems which comprise the community; and (4) the community, defined politically and ecologically, as a dynamic system which is made up of interacting subparts. Planned change, the types of client systems, and the role of professional change agents are examined.

The objectives of the study include a comparative analysis of the ways of defining problems and methods, an exploration of the general framework within which the wide variety of techniques and orientations could be conceptualized, a survey of types of research undertakings which seem to contribute directly to the theory of planned change, and to derive from the comparative study of principles and techniques ideas about the training of students in the behavioral sciences and to prepare professional agents of change. Selected illustrations of the work done by several agents of change proceeding upon similar assumptions about what is causing trouble for their clients or client systems and how to help them move toward a more desirable state of affairs provide concrete material. This is followed by a more abstract analysis of the processes of planned change, including the motivation of the client system, various aspects of the change agent's role, and special phases of planned change. The remainder of the book is devoted to such problems as the initiation of planned change, working toward change, problems of research, and the scientific and professional training of the agents of change.

Even though this book is obviously designed to aid those who are interested in the practical aspects of planned change and how to produce and direct it, the discussions in part are theoretical and somewhat formal in nature. Except for the sources indicated in the bibliography, to which references are made in the text of the book, the source material apparently is somewhat limited.

M.H.N.

SURVEY METHODS IN SOCIAL INVESTIGATION. By C. A. Moser. New York: The Macmillan Company, 1958, pp. 352.

Students of methodology in the behavioral sciences will find this work a rewarding review of the principal problems faced by the researcher in developing a research design and in completing the task. Many of the ideas and techniques discussed in this book were developed over a number of years when the author was lecturing at the London School of Economics. The following topics are discussed: defining the problem, preparing questionnaires, selecting the sample, collecting the responses, tabulating the responses, and presenting the finished product for publication. An unusually strong section is devoted to the difficult problem of sampling, and to the common errors to be avoided in sample selection. The book is characterized by clarity of exposition and maturity of point of view.

E.C.M.

THE PARADOX OF PROGRESSIVE THOUGHT. By David W. Noble. Minneapolis: University of Minnesota Press, 1958, pp. viii+272.

This book presents what historian Noble chooses to call a "climate of opinion" held by nine progressive-minded social philosophers in many of their writings from 1880 through 1920. The nine—Herbert Croly, James Mark Baldwin, Charles H. Cooley, F. H. Johnson, H. D. Lloyd, Richard T. Ely, Simon Patten, Thorstein Veblen, and Walter Rauschenbusch—all expounded in their writings some phases of the liberal tradition in America and were attempting to define and delineate social progress. Underlying his exposition of much of their thought, Noble examines the thought and influence of Carl L. Becker, who "believed that he and his contemporaries shared the faith in a rational world developing irresistibly along the course of progress." The writers are shown to have believed in the legacy of progress, with man having power to alter his own institutions.

Croly of *New Republic* fame held that social science could demonstrate that man was social and society cooperative in nature; Cooley averred that society moved onward and upward by the formulation of ever higher ideals; Ely thought that reason and science would reveal the sociological laws of progress and bring about a social utopia; Patten postulated a material world that man could transcend and control; Rauschenbusch could state that God had provided the inspiration for men to visualize the completed outline of heaven on earth. Such were some of the reflections of these men on social progress in an era which came to an end after the first World War. The paradox of progressive thought lies in the postulation of "total freedom accompanied by total uniformity as a basis of the completed commonwealth which would be the Kingdom of God on earth." Now, one asks the question: Is there any chance of man ever becoming so nearly perfect that he will be able to insure constant progress? The author states that Becker's final admonition is that consideration must be paid to "the constant humanity of man throughout time."

M.J.V.

AMERICA AS A CIVILIZATION. Life and Thought in the United States Today. By Max Lerner. New York: Simon and Schuster, 1957, pp. xiv +1036.

This truly magnificent book analyzes and interprets American life as completely as one could ever expect in a 1,000-page volume. The reader acquires a conception of American culture as a whole, and yet countless details stand out clearly. The volume has a tremendous scope, every chapter and section integral to the development of American civilization from its beginnings to its present form.

Beginning with the American cultural heritage, the author goes on to describe the American population and its habitat; the rise of machine culture, capitalist economy and business; the political system with its unique features; the open-class society with its class and caste aspects; the general life cycle of the American, and other characteristics of American culture in its ascendancy. The nature of American thought is stressed in religious and secular terms as an influence in the arts, in literature, and in mass media of communication. Finally, America is interpreted as a world power; the American world image is contrasted with the world's image of America.

Every chapter is rich in detail, readable, and intensely interesting. American civilization is seen in its making, its growth, and just as it is today—a remarkable blending of America's past and present.

J.E.N.

MOTIVES IN FANTASY, ACTION, AND SOCIETY. **Edited by John W. Atkinson. Princeton: D. Van Nostrand Company, Inc., 1958, pp. xv+873.**

Well-conceived and nicely organized, this book offers forty-six articles pertaining to the development of a valid method for measuring or assessing human motivation "through the content of thematic apperceptive stories and other kinds of imaginative thought." In selecting the readings, the editor states that he had in mind an integrating theme in his search for the method, namely, that a trio of virtues must be present—validity, flexibility, and generality. Those interested in motivational theory will find in the recorded research projects many vitally interesting factors, such as the effects of motivation on the content of imaginative thought, detailed manuals for content analysis of imaginative protocols producing indices of the strength of such motives as achievement, affiliation, and power, the arousal of motivation and its influence on behavior in certain situations. Sociologists are likely to be concerned with Parts IV and V which deal with the social origins of human motives and with motivation and society. The selected articles embrace many research projects and their findings in such particular areas as sex, fear, achievement, anxiety, status, and stratification. The appendices provide detailed scoring materials for assessing the achievement motive. Research students may well find the reports suggestive for further experimentation. M.J.V.

MEDICAL SOCIOLOGY. Theory, Scope and Method. By Norman G. Hawkins. Springfield, Illinois: Charles C. Thomas, 1958, pp. xx+290.

Doctor Hawkins presents a definition, a theoretical framework, a sampling of the areas of interest, and pertinent methods of study, relevant to medical sociology, as a guide to sociologists, students, and teachers in the health sciences, to help foster principles of cultural organization, definition, and specialization in this field.This is done with acknowledgement of inevitable changes in form, structure, and limitations of the field, and is not intended to be exhaustive. This book is not light reading, and assumes a good grounding in introductory sciences and an acquaintance with statistics. It consistently blends sociological, statistical, and biological terminology into one frame of reference.

Chapter One presents a historical sketch of medical sociology with the ultimate emphasis on the assertion that there is wide agreement among the people associated with the field that medical sociology is distinct from social medicine, but is, instead, a professional approach to social epidemiology, to the study of cultural factors and social relations in connection with physical and mental illnesses, and to the social principles in medical organization and treatment.

The theoretical framework of the book attempts to embrace the chemical, physical, psychological, and cultural organizations of human life, with emphasis especially on a consistent interdisciplinary balance, on the social, emotional, and cultural elements of health and sickness, on the process of breakdown, pathology, and recovery as a unity, and on providing a common ground for epidemiology and ecology, social etiology, and the analysis of health service organizations.

A medical sociologist is here viewed as a scientist, not a technician; a generalist who can conscientiously learn from specialists of other disciplines. Efforts are made to suggest some requirements and thoughts relevant to the role and status of the medical sociologist as a scientist. This book of necessity leaves much to be desired, which is largely the fruit of its being provocative, assertive, and ambitious—a much-needed step forward, demanding more to follow. RICHARD A. NIES

EDUARD C. LINDEMAN AND SOCIAL WORK PHILOSOPHY. By Gisela Konopka. Minneapolis: University of Minnesota Press, 1958, pp. 220.

This effort to assemble material about a man who was a leader in social work during a formative period, and to analyze his thought and writing, provides much interesting and useful information. Eduard C.

Lindeman was a self-made educator. He entered Michigan State College at the age of 21 without a high school diploma and was graduated five years later with high honors. Throughout his life he gave evidence of great capacity for independent thinking and hard work. His major career was as a teacher of social philosophy on the faculty of the New York School of Social Work from 1924 to 1949. But his writing and participation in a wide range of social movements were an integral part of his activities throughout his life. His interest in philosophy was an outgrowth of his early concern about religion and its expression in Christian socialism, and of his association with the many leaders of social thought around the time of the first World War, such as John Dewey, Herbert Crowley and associates, Mary Parker Follet, and others.

Part I gives biographical data and background material which affected Lindeman's thought. Part II introduces the author's interpretation of social work "goals and values" prior to 1924 and, against this backdrop, discussion of Lindeman's contribution to and understanding of group and community process and values, as he developed them to the time of his death in 1953. His ability to grow and change was found in the incorporation into his philosophy of precepts and values from religion, democracy, and mental hygiene, blended into a related whole. In Part III, Mrs. Konopka undertakes her own statement of an "Integration of Value, Method, and Knowledge." A comprehensive bibliography concludes the book.

Mrs. Konopka, who is a well-known social work author and teacher at the University of Minnesota, wrote the book as her doctoral dissertation at the New York School of Social Work, Columbia University. This probably accounts for some unevenness and injection of what seems occasionally to be extraneous material. The style is sometimes informal. On the whole, however, Mrs. Konopka's book will serve a useful purpose in acquainting students with the contribution of a man whose thinking was often in advance of his times. ARLIEN JOHNSON

VALUES IN CULTURE AND CLASSROOM. By H. Otto Dahlke. New York: Harper and Brothers, 1958, pp. vii+572.

This is a useful book for the teacher and student teacher. It is a cultural approach to education. The style is easy and flowing; the tables, charts, and other illustrations clarify the author's points of view.

The book is divided into five parts. In the Introduction, the author defines the meaning of culture—a design for living that has three aspects:

instrumental, regulative, and directive. He discusses the school in relation to the structural elements of a society, the school as a group, the school as a group among groups, and the informal social relations that exist within the school as well as their influence upon the general aspects of education.

In the next section, the sociocultural context of education and the school is discussed at length, including a historical development of public education in the United States, the American values that shape its growth, the legal order in relation to education, and the community context of the school.

Education is also acquired through the structure and organization of the school. Modern or obsolete buildings and equipment, ceremonial occasions, teaching techniques, types of control are significant in the educational process which takes place within the school. The composition of the school population is another factor—social classes, nonwhite groups, the maladjusted and unpopular pupil, the problems that bother children and teen-agers.

Other areas of education in relation to the thesis of the book are considered: training and selection of teachers; types of school organization; special interests, controversy, attacks upon the school; legal controls regarding secularism, religion, and segregation.

The book ends in a general summary and evaluation of the "dilemma of our culture in terms of incompatible principles"—the principle of sovereignty versus the principle of natural rights. In a time of national crisis the former is likely to be in force; in a time of peace the latter is likely to prevail. Therefore, the hope of the future lies in a reinterpretation of these two sets of principles by society and the schools in order to bring forth "an era of genuine fulfillment of human potentialities."

CECIL EVVA LARSEN

THE CRIMINAL MIND: A STUDY OF COMMUNICATION BETWEEN THE CRIMINAL LAW AND PSYCHIATRY. By Philip Q. Roche. New York: Farrar, Straus and Cudahy, 1958, pp. vi+299.

Dr. Roche's book won the fifth Isaac Ray Award of the American Psychiatric Association. It is a study of the problem of communication between criminal law and psychiatry. Conflicts between the two realms have their roots in the difference in conceptional models and in the language employed in the approach to the criminal mind. The sharpest conflicts occur when law as a moral system and psychiatry as a beginning scientific discipline are brought together in the criminal courtroom.

After general discussions of the mid-20th century setting of American criminal law and the meaning of mental illness, the author describes the criminal law and psychiatry in action during the pretrial, criminal trial, and posttrial phases. In these chapters (III, IV, and V), concrete cases are presented. As examples of the pretrial phase, the cases of "The College Boy" and "The Cleric" are described in detail, indicating the complexity of the problem of unraveling the variables that may play a part in criminal behavior. The examination of criminal trial cases reveals the greatest differences in the legal and psychiatric approaches in analyzing the conditions of crime. The posttrial case is analyzed from the point of view of the treatment process.

One of the conclusions of the author is that the function of a psychiatrist in criminal justice needs to be reassessed. He proposes that the functions of psychiatry be removed from the public (trial) phase of investigation and that they be enlarged in the pretrial and posttrial phases. The book is restricted to a discussion of the place of psychiatry in criminal justice. Other sciences, including sociology, have an important contribution to make in the investigation process. M.H.N.

SOCIOLOGY. Second Edition. By Leonard Broom and Philip Selznick. Evanston, Illinois: Row, Peterson and Company, 1958, pp. 661.

The second edition of this successful introductory text in sociology has been improved in a number of important ways: (1) a substantial proportion of the facts are brought up to date (especially true of data cited in tables, graphs, and statistics in the text), (2) a definitive statement of the thinking of George Herbert Mead on the social significance of the self is made available, (3) the chapter on Social Organization now contains a concise discussion on the nature of social roles, and, finally, the style has been improved to attain greater clarity of meaning and ease of reading.

Perhaps the chief advantage of this text is that it takes a few major concepts and provides a strong framework for organizing the essential facts and findings of sociology, which are now approaching the encyclopedic in range. Students ought to gain the habit through the use of this book, and similar books with built-in frames of reference, of thinking in terms of a few major sociological concepts. The essence of sociology is becoming a blend of a way of gathering social facts and a way of looking at these social facts. This text does a splendid job of providing the intellectual tools for the apprentice sociologist. E.C.M.

THE PSYCHOLOGY OF RELIGION. An Introduction to Religious Experience and Behavior. By Walter Houston Clark. New York: The Macmillan Company, 1958, pp. xii+485.

The purpose of this book is to provide an up-to-date, comprehensive treatment of the field of the psychology of religion. Part I is devoted to orientation and the definition of religion. Part II analyzes religious growth from childhood through adolescence and youth to maturity. Doubt and conflict are explained functionally; healthy-mindedness and suffering are evaluated as roads to religious growth; conversion and faith are interpreted as psychological aspects of religion. In Part III special attention is given to mysticism and to the roles of the prophet, priest, and the intellectual—topics which have heretofore received scant attention in psychologies of religion. The nature of prayer and worship and the relation of religion to abnormal psychology and psychotherapy are discussed in more traditional manner. Thus it appears that this new text offers an excellent approach and plan for a course on the psychology of religion. The bibliography is extensive and study aids are included at the end of the volume. J.E.N.

SAMPLING OPINIONS. An Analysis of Survey Procedures. By Frederick F. Stephan and Philip J. McCarthy. New York: John Wiley & Sons, Inc., 1958, pp. xvi+451.

The authors of this book would be justified if they changed the subtitle to read "A Comprehensive Analysis of Survey Procedure." The subject matter provides extensive coverage and its treatment is intelligible. This latter characteristic is nowadays unfortunately all too rare, since so many writers in the field seem to elaborate esoteric approaches in order, perhaps, to conceal from outsiders and initiates a suspicion that all social interaction might not reduce to statistical relationships. At a time when the hangers-on of mathematics have assumed such a hieratic pose, it is refreshing to read the following on page xv of the Preface: "They [statisticians] should not, however, overlook the fact that there are in this field important elements of the sampling problem which have not yet been treated adequately by mathematical theory and which seem to offer very serious difficulties to anyone seeking at this time to treat them mathematically." Some overly zealous toilers in the field of microstatistics might well heed this admonition.

The book is divided into three parts. The first is an analysis of survey operations intended to describe and explain for readers of opinion studies the various sampling methods used. The second part associates the methods with data accumulated from actual studies made by the authors and others. This, in the reviewer's opinion, is the outstanding section of the book, since the authors demonstrate both the strengths and the weaknesses of available sampling techniques and discuss research plans for developing competent interpretative processes. The third covers problems connected with the creation of survey designs. It is, on the whole, a practical treatment of the steps to be taken to begin, carry out, and conclude a survey. After a reading of this material the student cannot say that he has not been forewarned of the many obstacles likely to be encountered on the road to research.

HAROLD T. DIEHL
Los Angeles State College

THE SOCIOLOGY OF AMERICAN LIFE. An Introductory Analysis. By Harold Hoffsommer. Englewood Cliffs, New Jersey: Prentice-Hall, Inc., 1958, pp. xi+628.

This textbook is designed to supply the freshman or sophomore with a full perspective of American life and also to introduce him to the science of sociology. Those two purposes blend into an excellent analytical and descriptive portrayal of American society as the sociologist sees it. Readings have been skillfully placed at the end of each of the twenty chapters to supplement the material written by the author. This volume contains many attractive charts, graphs, and illustrations as well as excellent bibliographies and a large assortment of suggested projects which may be conducted by students in connection with major topics. The discussion possesses clarity, and the author has taken care to define and explain technical terms.

This book is divided into four parts. Part I treats of immigration, cultural backgrounds, and assimilation, population characteristics, the westward movement, rural-urban migration, and the suburban movement. Part II discusses rural locality groups, urban and suburban communities, and social differences in the United States. Part III deals with institutions and pays special attention to familial, religious, educational, economic, and political institutions in American society. Part IV covers social interaction, communication, American culture, personality and the group, and the nature of social change in America. Well written throughout and with the definitive purposes logically pursued, this book merits a favorable reception.

T. C. KEEDY, JR.
San Jose State College

SOCIAL FICTION

SEIDMAN AND SON. A Novel by Elick Moll. New York: G. P. Putnam's Sons, 1958, pp. 288.

Novelist Elick Moll has chosen to tell this delightfully droll and humorous story in the form of a monologue delivered by Morris Seidman, a New York Seventh Avenue garment manufacturer whose insight into the panorama of living in these days is gifted with both vision and prevision. Capturing and captivating a male writer sitting on a bench in New York's Central Park, Morris, like the Ancient Mariner, tells his story—the story of his wife Sophie and her psychoanalytic adventures, their teen-age daughter Jenny, their son Harold just home from Korea, and his sister Bessie with a constant ear on the telephone, to say nothing of some of his employees, especially his designer, the temperamental Miss Youssem, and his beautiful young model, Marie. Harold has upset the family by returning from Korea with some ideas of reforming the socio-economic system which has done so well by his father, who as an immigrant has worked himself to the top of the ladder in the garment business. The novelist in a most subtle and telling manner manages to defend the economic folkways and mores of the system and to expose some of the nonsense of ill-advised leftist reformers. Morris has enjoyed every step on the way up and has had a keen eye on every eventful situation. Part of the joy in reading Morris' own account of his family and business life comes from the entertaining way in which he uses the King's English. The Jewish family life is portrayed in an unforgettable manner, reminiscent of such other stories as "I Remember Mama," "Life with Father," and even the old stage success "Potash and Perlmutter." This is a novel that is magnificently entertaining and yet gifted with a bundle of social wisdom. M.J.V.

Sociology and Social Research

AN INTERNATIONAL JOURNAL

Articles in Forthcoming Issues . . .

January-February and later

A Theory of Cultural Change .... OTAKAR MACHOTA
Sociological Contributions of Znaniecki .... THEODORE ABEL
Status and Social Tropism .... E. C. McDONAGH
Ethnic Prejudice and Social Class .... A. L. ROSENBLUM
Division of Labor Among Communal Groups .... HENRY ZENTNER
Attitudes Toward the Family .... PANOS D. BARDIS
Computers and Social Research .... E. F. BORGATTA
Empathy in the Dating Situation .... R. L. STEWART AND G. M. VERNON
Social Distance Scales and Stratification .... F. R. WESTIE
Group Processes and Prohibition .... NORMAN JACKSON AND M. SHERIF
Self-Tattooing Among Delinquents .... JOHN H. BURMA
Occupations of Sociology Majors .... MARGARET L. HELBRICK
Changing Attitudes in China .... THEODORE AND WEN-HUI CHEN
Lower Levels of Industrial Leadership .... AMITAI ETZIONI
Social Influence on Children .... R. G. HUNT AND V. SYNNERDAHL
Job Satisfaction and Leisure .. A. T. W. MATTHEWS AND B. ABU-LABAN
A Note on British Health Service .... J. B. MONTAGUE, JR.
Administrative Role in Desegregation .... R. J. DWYER
Social Work and Sociology .... JOSEPH W. EATON

Articles in Preceding Issue . . .

September-October 1958

American Culture Themes ...... WILLIAM TORRENCE AND PAUL MEADOWS
Labor Under Review: 1957 .... MELVIN J. VINCENT
Concerning Marriage and
Family Life .... V. A. CHRISTOPHERSON AND J. WALTERS
Social Class in Philadelphia Methodism .... FREDERICK A. SHIPPEY
Art and Communication .... BRUCE A. WATSON
Anomie and Religious Orthodoxy .... T. C. KEEDY, JR.
Direction of Sociological Research .... EMORY S. BOGARDUS

Sociology and Social . . . Research . . .

AN INTERNATIONAL JOURNAL

Social Influence Among Children 171
R. G. HUNT AND V. SYNNERDAHL

Attitudes Toward Parents in China . . . 175
THEODORE H. E. AND WEN-HUI CHEN

Administrative Role in Desegregation . . 183
ROBERT J. DWYER

Job Satisfaction and Leisure Time . . . 189
A. T. V. MATTHEWS AND B. ABU-LABAN

Social Work and Sociology 197
JOSEPH W. EATON

British National Health Service 205
JOEL B. MONTAGUE, JR.

Lower Levels of Industrial Leadership . . 209
AMITAI ETZIONI

Mannheim and Systematic Sociology . . . 213
EMORY S. BOGARDUS

Social Problems and Welfare 218 Peoples and Culture . . . 225
Social Theory and Research 230

VOL. 43 JANUARY-FEBRUARY 1959 No. 3
YEARLY SUBSCRIPTION, $3.50 SINGLE COPIES, 70 CENTS

Sociology and Social Research

AN INTERNATIONAL JOURNAL

PUBLISHED BIMONTHLY AT THE UNIVERSITY OF SOUTHERN CALIFORNIA
UNIVERSITY PARK, LOS ANGELES 7, CALIFORNIA

YEARLY SUBSCRIPTION, $3.50 SINGLE COPIES, 70¢

Entered as second-class matter March 31, 1936, at the post office at Los Angeles, California, under the act of March 3, 1879.

Contributed materials which appear in *Sociology and Social Research* do not necessarily express the opinion or the policy of the editorial staff and publisher.

Articles published in this journal are indexed in *The International Index to Periodicals*, and abstracted in *Sociological Abstracts* and *Psychological Abstracts*.

PUBLISHED BY

UNIVERSITY OF SOUTHERN CALIFORNIA PRESS

UNIVERSITY PARK LOS ANGELES 7, CALIFORNIA

SOCIOLOGY AND SOCIAL RESEARCH
January-February 1958

SOCIAL INFLUENCE AMONG KINDERGARTEN CHILDREN
AN EXPERIMENTAL NOTE

RAYMOND G. HUNT
University of Buffalo

VONDA SYNNERDAHL
Buffalo Public Schools

Although a very considerable literature has accumulated dealing with various facets of social influence, the examination of developmental aspects of this problem area has not kept pace. This is all the more surprising, since what investigations have been reported indicate that exploration of this field may prove a fruitful source of hypotheses concerning important features of the psychology of childhood, as well as the phenomenon in question.

The present study was an exploratory investigation of the operation of social influence processes among a small group of kindergarten children. Its main reference point was provided by the extensive work of Berenda.[1] Using the experimental procedure devised by Asch, this investigator studied responses to social pressure among children ranging in age from 7 through 13, drawn from grades 2 through 7, and covering a fair range of intelligence.

Berenda found a tendency for younger children (7 through 9) to follow the group more frequently than did older children (10 through 13). While she reports that the younger children seemed to show less personal involvement in the experiment, Berenda felt they exhibited greater dependence upon the group. As a result, they tended to be more susceptible to influence by social pressures arising within the group.

Berenda's data suggest susceptibility to social influence to be some decreasing function of age. Whether this is true, and, if so, the precise nature of the function, is unknown.

[1] Ruth W. Berenda, *The Influence of the Group on the Judgments of Children* (New York: Kings Crown Press, 1950).

It was felt that the present investigation could help to shed some light upon this problem by its extension to a group which is both younger and at a beginning step in its integration into group functioning.

Procedure. The general procedure developed by Asch[2] was used, though a number of liberties were taken with it. The writers felt this to be more or less justified, since they were more interested, at this point, in general qualitative aspects of the children's performance than in precise quantitative analysis.

One of the more important modifications in the Asch procedure was the method of having "stooges" give incorrect responses on all trials. This made for an easier task for the young confederates and minimized variations in their performance. It might be noted in passing that, like Berenda, the present experimenters found the younger "stooges" to have some difficulty in giving incorrect answers.

A group of ten kindergarten children (all from the same class) served as subjects. They ranged in age from 5 to 6 years, were about evenly distributed among the two sexes, and were unselected as to I.Q. Three children from the same class served as the "instructed majority,"[3] the experimenter being the classroom teacher.

Subjects judged the lengths of lines as per the Asch procedure in two series of nine judgments each for a total of 18 judgments. In general, the instructed confederates functioned efficiently and followed instructions surprisingly well.

Each child was instructed to do his best to give correct answers and appeared to cooperate fully. In fact, the children seemed to enjoy the "game," many of them asking when they could play it again.

Results. As was noted above, only general findings will be reported without extensive quantitative analysis. This seems dictated by the small N coupled with the difficulty in producing a fully standardized experimental situation.

The median number of "yielding" responses was one with a range of 0 to 8 (of a possible 18). None of the children followed the group on all trials, while four (40 per cent) followed the group on none of the trials.[4]

---

[2] S. E. Asch, "Effects of Group Pressure upon the Modification and Distortion of Judgments." In G. E. Swanson, T. M. Newcomb, and E. L. Hartley, eds., *Readings in Social Psychology.* Rev. ed. (New York: Henry Holt and Company, 1952), pp. 2-11.

[3] The "instructed majority," or "stooges," were confederates of the experimenter and had been instructed prior to the experiment in the responses which they were to give.

[4] The "group" here refers to the "instructed majority" or "stooges" who formed the group context in which each critical group functioned.

Of a total of 180 judgments, only 21 (12 per cent) were in the direction of the group judgment. Five judgments (3 per cent) were incorrect but not consistent with the group judgments, while 154 responses (85 per cent) were correct.

Qualitative aspects of the performance of these children are consistent with the above findings. While the children were cooperative and interested, they were (in general) hardly aware of any "pressure." They gave their own judgments and regarded the "stooges" as curiosities who were obviously wrong. ,

One example can serve to characterize the attitude of the critical subjects. After several judgments had been made, on all of which the "stooges" gave incorrect judgments, one critical subject turned to the nearest stooge and said, "Listen to me, I'll tell you the right ones." Yet only one subject (a female) appeared to have any inkling that the other children had been coached.

Discussion. It is evident from the above results that the children employed in the present study were but little influenced by the social pressures ostensibly developed in the experimental situation. In fact, it seems safe to say of these children that, for the most part, there actually was no "social pressure." It is quite apparent, as is probably well known, that so-called social pressure does not arise from the group per se, but from an interaction between the individual and the group.

The present findings contrast with those of Berenda. It would appear that sensitivity to social pressure, or even perception of social pressure, does not bear a simple relationship to age. It may be, as Duncker[5] suggests of still younger children, that the awareness of the five- to six-year-old of social contingencies is simply not wide enough to permit this sort of social influence.

On the other hand, it may be that the socialization of the kindergarten child has not progressed to the point of developing the kinds of group orientations which characterize the slightly older child. Perhaps he just hasn't been in school long enough.

Of course, there is nothing to preclude the operation of both of these factors and/or still others. In any event, further and more extensive analysis, from a developmental perspective, of both the operation of social influence and the "meanings" attached to group participation seems called for.

---

[5] K. Duncker, "Experimental Modifications of Children's Food Preferences Through Social Suggestion," *Journal of Abnormal and Social Psychology*, 33:489-507.

Summary. A group of ten five- to six-year-old kindergarten children participated in an Asch-type social influence experiment. The children exhibited very little tendency to go along with the group judgments and, in fact, seemed hardly aware of any "social pressure," even though they were cooperative and interested in the experiment.

CHANGING ATTITUDES TOWARD PARENTS IN COMMUNIST CHINA

THEODORE HSI-EN CHEN
AND
WEN-HUI C. CHEN
University of Southern California

Since the establishment of the Communist regime in China, important changes have taken place in its political, economic, social, and cultural policies. In social ethics and morals, the present Communist policy is in many ways different from that of a few years ago. The marriage law, which was introduced in 1950, has been given new interpretations in the light of changed conditions. Family relationships which the Communist attempted to foster a few years ago are no longer favored today. The nature of the changes that have taken place in recent years is clearly reflected in the attitudes toward parents. Five or six years ago, the Chinese Communists were encouraging young people to turn against their parents. Today, an opposite trend is in evidence.

The Communists talk much of the need of a "new morality" in China or what they call "Communist morality." The essence of this "new morality" is that the individual must surrender completely to the group, to the "revolution," and to the Party and state. Loyalty to the state (which, in turn, is directed by the Communist Party) must supersede all other loyalties. Since a major obstacle to this all-embracing loyalty was the traditional family loyalty of the Chinese, the Communists set out a few years ago to break the old family ties and to ridicule the traditional loyalties as vestiges of feudal society. In the name of democracy and freedom, children were taught to rebel against their parents, and in the name of patriotism or the revolutionary cause, young people were encouraged to leave their homes and family ties to take up "revolutionary tasks" at places far away from the home.

An important phase of the effort to uproot the old family loyalties was a campaign against parental respect and filial piety. This campaign later proved to be more successful than the Communists intended. To destroy the old was easy, but to build a new positive morality was not so simple. The attack on filial piety resulted in complete neglect of the parents. The attitude of young people toward their parents underwent a radical change. The long-accepted responsibility of supporting and caring for aged parents was now rejected. Even helpless and invalid parents were left without care. The result was the birth of a new social problem which was inimical to the stability which the Communists wanted to achieve when they began to consolidate their power. Neglected and unwanted aged people wandered in the streets. Some found that the only way out was to commit suicide. Fathers were reported to have jumped into rivers, old grandmothers leaped to their death.[1] Many old people were reported to have said: "Communism is good in many ways but the way it treats the old people is not good at all."[2]

The situation became so serious that the Communists found it necessary to inaugurate a campaign to emphasize the respect and support of parents. From October 1956 to the early part of 1957, the Chinese Communist press and periodicals abounded in articles exhorting young people to love and support their parents. The articles censured the younger generation for maltreatment and cruelty toward their parents. It is evident, however, that nonsupport of parents is a social problem which the Communists have brought upon themselves. Neglect of parents is the result of changes originally encouraged by the Communists. The following are some of the significant changes.

1. *Attack on filial piety.* The Communists have condemned filial piety as "feudalistic" and as "excess baggage" to be discarded. The views of the leftist writer Lu Hsun are widely quoted and have had a great influence in Communist China. Lu ridiculed the long-revered Chinese classic known as "Twenty-four Examples of Filial Piety." He attacked "filial piety" as inhumane behavior. As a result of this influence, the "progressive" came to look upon filial piety as feudalistic. Consequently, some of the young people today do not respond readily to the recent compaign to reinstill parental respect. They ask why they should be criticized for neglecting filial piety when they are only fighting against the outmoded practices of feudal society.[3]

2. *The class struggle and the conflict between generations.* The "class struggle" is one of the central concepts of the Communist revolution. In the city, the Communists incited the workers to struggle against their employers, while in the countryside, they organized the peasants to engage in a "bitter struggle" against the rich peasants and landlord class.

---

[1] Yu Yuan-fang, "Tsung'hsiao' t'an tao tsen-yang tui-tai fu-mu" (Filial piety and how to treat parents), *Chung-Kuo Ch'ing-Nien* (Chinese Youth, Peking semimonthly), 1956:21, November 1, 1956, pp. 5-7.

[2] "Chan-yang fu-mu shih tzu-nu ti tse-jen" (Supporting parents is the responsibility of sons and daughters), editorial, *Chung-Kuo Ch'ing-Nien Pao* (Chinese Youth Journal, a Peking daily), November 30, 1956.

[3] Chueh Tsai, "Ai fu-mu" (Love parents), *Jen Min Jih Pao* (People's Daily, official organ of the Chinese Communist Party), December 24, 1956.

In the home, "struggle" was waged by the children against their parents and by wives against husbands. Conflict between the older and the younger generation was freely utilized as an instrument of the Communist family revolution. In the Communist scheme of things, the older generation is often cast in the role of oppressor and the younger generation in the position of the oppressed. The frustrated daughter-in-law, the widowed daughter-in-law not permitted to marry again, and the maltreated reared-daughter-in-law[4] were publicized as examples of feudal oppression and were encouraged to rise in opposition to their oppressors, to "spit out bitterness" and to pour out their "grievances." The Communists offered to give them "support" and an opportunity for "fansheng" (literally, a "turning-over," which means, actually, a new life). In short, the Communist ideology of "class struggle," when applied to the family, resulted in conflict instead of harmony between generations.

3. *Mutual spying at home and denunciation of parents for the sake of "righteousness."* The Communist secret police and espionage system, powerful as they are, could not penetrate the home and the "sleeping chamber." To extend and reinforce their control, the Communists utilized the children to spy on their parents and wives on their husbands. Mutual surveillance within the family circle was exalted as glorious service for the cause of the revolution. This method was extensively used in the campaign for the suppression of counterrevolutionaries and the "three-anti" and "five-anti" campaigns of 1952. During these campaigns children were asked not only to watch the thought and behavior of their parents but to report their findings to the Party organization and the Communist authorities.[5] In the schools as well as the youth organizations the children were taught to spy on their parents and to report any reprehensible behavior observed. Needless to say, the denunciation of parents or other family members for the good of the state is a form of behavior diametrically opposed to the old Chinese mores which sanctioned the cooperation of family members in concealing each other's faults instead of washing "dirty laundry" in public. Nevertheless, by utilizing children in espionage against their parents, the Communists succeeded in uncovering many "crimes against the state," and the guilty parties were punished for the good of the revolutionary cause. At the same time,

---

[4] The term "reared-daughter-in-law" refers to a baby girl adopted into a family to be brought up and later married to a son to become a daughter-in-law.

[5] Wen-hui Chen, *The Family Revolution in Communist China* (Alabama: Human Resources Research Institute, 1955), p. 31. See also Wen-hui Chen, *Wartime "Mass" Campaigns in Communist China* (Alabama: Human Resources Research Institute, 1955), Chaps. II, VII, VIII.

mutual surveillance within the family and the denunciation of family members for the "revolutionary" cause resulted in mutual suspicion and distrust within the family and encouraged young people to be cruel and harsh toward the parents. Moreover, the Communist way tended to encourage rebellion instead of obedience on the part of the children.

4. *Ideological struggle.* In the Communist "ideological struggle," an appeal was made to "progressive youth" to help change the feudal and reactionary ideology of their elders. The younger generation became the teachers, while the older generation must humble themselves to learn from youth. This enabled the younger people to gain the upper hand over the older generation and to discard the old ideology of revering and following the examples of the old. Many children came to look down upon their parents.

5. *Nonsupport of "enemy parents."* In Canton there was a Communist youth whose father was a landlord and was executed as a "village despot." Having been reared in the Communist ideology, this young man made no protest because his father had been exposed as an "enemy of the people." He bravely assumed the support of his mother and younger sister. In doing this, however, he met with the official disapproval of his youth organization. He was censured for his uncertain "class stand" as shown in his continued relationship with the "landlord class."

The children of the landlord class, the bourgeoisie, and the counterrevolutionary class were asked to sever all relationships with their families in order to prove their unmistakable stand on the side of the "people." Since the differentiation between "friends" and "enemy" (though all important to the class-conscious Communists) is not such a simple matter when applied to family relationships, the punishment of those who support members of the landlord and counterrevolutionary classes tends to induce people to resort to the safe way of refusing to give any support at all to relatives and the older generation.

6. *The abolition of private property.* Under the old system of private ownership of property, many old people were in charge of their life savings and all family property handed down by previous generations. Since they held the purse strings of the family, they naturally enjoyed the status and authority that went with financial control. In recent years, however, the Chinese Communists have steadily pushed the program of socialism and moved toward the abolition of private property. In the city, the capitalists have become employees of state-controlled enterprises, and, even before the "socialist transformation" of their enterprises, business people had lost most of their assets through confiscatory

fines, taxes, and levies. In the countryside, not only have the landlords been divested of their holdings, but even the ordinary peasants have surrendered their newly acquired land to the cooperatives and collectives. As a result of this change, the older generation have lost the power and authority which went with the control of family property and assets. The propertyless old people have been put at the mercy of the younger generation, who feel free to treat the aged in any manner they like.

7. *Pay according to work.* When the means of production and distribution are owned and operated by the state, all able-bodied persons work for state-owned enterprises and get paid according to their work. Eventually, in a Communist society, those who do not work will not be fed. Although Communist China has not arrived at this stage of development, the Chinese Communists are definitely moving in the direction of abolishing remuneration for property ownership and paying individuals according to their work. To be sure, the state theoretically takes care of the old people who are not able to work. At the same time, the new ideology creates an atmosphere in which those who cannot work are looked upon as the parasites of society. Accordingly, there is a tendency for able-bodied children to consider their aged parents as impediments to progress who live on the sweat and blood of their children.

8. *Public care of the aged.* In theory, the Communists advocate public care of the aged and disabled. The socialist state is supposed to establish homes for the aged so that those who are left without means of support can depend on the state for security. At present some of the big agricultural cooperatives have adopted the slogan of "five guarantees," which provide their members with the five necessities of life: namely, food, clothing, fuel, education, and funeral expenses. Some cooperatives have added medical care and shelter to the list.[6] In theory, individuals are guaranteed a minimum standard of living, and the responsibility of caring for the aged and disabled is transferred from the family to the cooperatives. When the system of "five guarantees" was proclaimed in some of the agricultural cooperatives, young people quickly repudiated their responsibility for the care of their parents and asked their parents to turn to the cooperatives for support.[7] Unfortunately, many cooperatives which aroused the hopes of their members with high-sounding theory did not have the material resources to care for the aged and the disabled. Thus, the old people were left without any means of support.

---

[6] *Jen Min Jih Pao*, November 15, 1956.
[7] Editorial, *Chung-Kuo Ch'ing-Nien Pao*, November 30, 1956.

After a few years of Communist control and indoctrination, the relationships in the Chinese family underwent a great change. Evidently, the young people went much farther than the Communists wanted them to. The repudiation of responsibility not only caused much suffering on the part of the old people but also brought along a marked degree of social disorganization. To bring order out of chaos, a campaign was launched to reinculcate parental respect and to emphasize the duty of parental care. Cruelty to parents is now condemned as incompatible with "Communist morality."

What are the reasons for the change of policy on the part of the Chinese Communists? A few are here briefly examined. In the first place, a revolution always begins with a destructive phase and must in time move on to the constructive stage. The generation conflict was utilized by the Communists for a political purpose. After seven years, the Communist revolution had come to the stage where the need of consolidation and stabilization was greater than the need of destroying the old. From a period of social disorganization, the Communists wanted to move on to a new stage of social reorganization.

The Communists now want to recapture the support of the older generation. While utilizing the young generation, the Communists lost the support of the older generation, who not only suffered personal damage as a result of the new changes but grieved to see the old traditions and morals discarded and ridiculed. In the past, the Communists depended on adolescent youth as a major source of support. Now, concerned with the stabilization of their regime, they want the support of the whole population.

The Communists have been alarmed by the "lack of discipline" of youth. Reliance on youth for revolutionary activities has given the young people a feeling of self-importance and resulted in unrestrained behavior and the misinterpretation of freedom as unbridled license. Juvenile delinquency has increased.[8] Sexual laxity has become more common, with boys and girls engaging in multiple sexual relationships.[9] There is also a tendency for boys and girls to marry quickly and divorce easily. In schools, the teachers find that the students do not submit to discipline. They do not study hard, and they ignore the school regulations.

It is obvious that unrestrained "freedom" could not be permitted in a Communist state. The Communists set store by collective living and

---

[8] *Jen Min Jih Pao*, November 27, 1956; *Hsin Kuan Ch'a* (New Observation, a Peking semimonthly), 1956:24, December 16, 1956, p. 8.

[9] *Jen Min Jih Pao*, November 15, 1956; *Chung-Kuo Ch'ing Nien Pao*, August 30, 1956.

expect all individuals to submit to the group and the authority of the "organization."[10] Alarmed by the spread of rebelliousness on the part of youth, the Communists started a new campaign to emphasize discipline and obedience to authority. In the schools, the authority of the teacher was reasserted. In the home, parental responsibility for the education of youth was now given a new sanction. This means more authority on the part of the parents and more parental respect on the part of the young. The campaign for a partial return to the old pattern of relations with parents is in line with the general trend to curb youthful licentiousness and to enforce a stricter control over youth.

Finally, one of the most important reasons for launching the new campaign is the inability of the Chinese Communist state to support its aged population at this time. Ideologically the Communist state is supposed to establish homes for the aged, but this is easier said than done. Rarely, some large cooperatives have operated homes for the aged; but, by and large, the state still does not have the resources to care for the aged population. Consequently it is still necessary to have the family take care of the aged. This viewpoint is well expressed by a writer for *Chinese Youth*, who said: "When children fail to support their parents, they are in practice shifting this responsibility to society or the nation. In doing this, they are undoubtedly doing harm to socialist construction and will at the same time create serious social problems."[11]

Another writer presented statistical figures to support his arguments. He said: "According to the 1953 census, there were 64,000,000 men over sixty and women over fifty. If the government has to support all these people with even a small sum, say $50 per year for each person, the total cost to the government will come to $3,200,000,000. This sum is greater than the total 1955 expenditure for welfare and education and is more than 10 per cent of the total expenditures of the nation according to the budget of 1956. If the system of the state care of the aged is adopted, it will plunge the nation into deep financial troubles and cause serious interference with the development of socialistic reconstruction."[12]

The campaign to repair the damage created by the earlier Communist attack on the loyalties and obligations of old "feudal" society gathered

---

[10] The term "organization" in Communist China means the Party organization which exercises all-powerful control over individuals.

[11] "Chien-li kao-shang ti kung-ch'an chu-yi lung-li kuan-hsi" (Build up high Communist ethical relationships), *Chung-Kuo Ch'ing Nien*, 1956:24, December 16, 1956, p. 14.

[12] Chi-Ya, "Kuan-yu 'Chan-yang fu-mu' chi ko wen-t'i ti ta pien" (A few arguments and answers concerning the support of parents), *Chung-Kuo Ch'ing Nien*, 1957:2, January 16, 1957, p. 26.

momentum in the latter part of 1956. Newspaper and magazine articles preached the virtue of parental care and respect. Members of youth organizations were asked to set good examples for the nation. Many arguments were put forth to show the necessity of taking good care of parents. Parental love is now extolled as beautiful and deserving of continued gratitude on the part of the children. Youth are told to love their parents because they will be the parents of tomorrow. It is also argued that old people are often helpful at home. Young people are exhorted not only to feed and clothe the old people but to love and respect them in order to make them happy.

Nevertheless, the new Communist morality does not permit any family loyalty to overshadow loyalty to the state or the revolutionary cause. One should love one's parents, but one should love the "people" or the state even more. After the campaign for parental love was launched, some cadres thought that it would now be appropriate to ask to be assigned to tasks in the home town so as to be able to take better care of parents or to get a leave to visit their parents. Their requests were rejected by the Party authorities. A Party leader explains the official position as follows:

> When *Chinese Youth* criticized young people for slighting and non-support of parents, it was asking young people to accord respect and support to parents on the *condition that there is no interference with the interests of the state*. . . . A revolutionary cadre must put the interests of the state above all; he must yield to the needs of his revolutionary work and accept the assignments of the Party organization. When we advocate love of family and care of parents, we do not mean to go back to the feudalistic way of putting family interests above national interests.[13]

In short, Chinese youth are asked to love and support their parents if such behavior works to the advantage of the state. But if there is a conflict between love for parents and love for the state or between family devotion and the Communist revolution, the state and the Party have definite priority over the parents.

---

[13] "Tai-feng fu-mu pu neng wei-fan kuo-chia li-i" (Care for parents should not conflict with the interests of the state), *Chung-Kuo Ch'ing Nien*, 1957:4, February 16, 1957, p. 8. [Italics not in the original.]

THE ADMINISTRATIVE ROLE IN DESEGREGATION

ROBERT J. DWYER
Idaho State College

The purpose of this paper is to describe some patterns of administrative policy and the role of the administrator in public school desegregation in a border state. The report is based upon a study of seven school systems in central Missouri, conducted during the year 1955-56. The communities where these schools were located ranged in population from 3,000 to 30,000. In no school did the Negro student enrollment exceed 10 per cent of the total student body.

There was little uniformity in approaching the problem of desegregation. The direction of the administrative action was largely determined by the extent and nature of the opposition and by the preliminary steps taken by the school board and the superintendent. The following patterns were observed in the process leading up to the decision to desegregate:

1. The decision to desegregate was made by the school board and the superintendent and announced in the local press. This occurred in a community where the climate of opinion was relatively favorable and where there had been little opposition overtly expressed. The superintendent enjoyed the confidence of the community and was accustomed to making policy decisions on other matters without consulting parents or other groups. This superintendent expressed his conviction that this was the only effective approach to desegregation. He stated:

> This thing is coming and whether anyone likes it or not, the thing to do is to go right ahead with integration. I don't ask people if it is all right. That would give them something to object to. If I am hesitant and uncertain, the people will hesitate and it is just giving them a chance to say "No." Don't give them a chance, is what I say. Just go ahead and take positive steps.

2. The decision to desegregate was made after inviting parents and other adult members of the community to participate in meetings and preliminary discussions or to serve on investigating committees. In one such case there were numerous meetings of both Negroes and whites, with eventual agreement on a desegregation program only after the use of the Negro school building by white students was hotly debated and a decision made to abandon the building. In another case the superintendent encountered indifference on the part of parents when he scheduled meetings of P.T.A. groups for the purpose of exploring the problems of desegregation.

3. A third pattern was observed in one school system where community opposition to the change was extensive and was expressed in threats of violence and a cross-burning incident. In this case there was disagreement among school board members, vacillation by the school superintendent, and a reluctance in the community to take any action at all. There was an announced decision to desegregate. The order was rescinded and finally, as a matter of economic expedience and for the lack of an alternative, the decision to desegregate was once more announced. Meetings of irate parents continued, however, and the policy makers indicated that they would entertain any feasible plan to avoid desegregation. The status of the Negro students remained in doubt until the opening day of the new term, when it was apparent that they would attend the previously all-white school or not attend school at all.

Although the course of desegregation in any community depends much upon public sentiment and the degree of opposition by the prosegregation forces, some communities are in a state of "indifferent equilibrium"[1] with regard to race relations. That is, there are no extremes of opinion and the issue could be decided one way just as easily as another. When this is the case, a firm, unhesitating stand by the school board and the superintendent seems the most effective approach and sets the stage for a less troublesome administration of the program, once it is put into effect.

In the school systems studied, the tendency was toward segmental, gradual desegregation, rather than an immediate and complete change-over from the segregated to the mixed pattern. The form which desegregation took in each school system was dependent upon such factors as available space and number of Negro students at each grade level, availability of still-segregated schools which would accept nonresident students, the cost of operating a transportation system for such Negro students, and the attitudes of parents of children at the various grade levels.

In some instances immediate desegregation on a particular grade level would seriously overcrowd existing facilities and hamper the teaching program. The result is the postponement of desegregation until adequate facilities can be built, but this can, and often does, serve as a device to make the postponement indefinite; some communities will tolerate over-crowded conditions which already exist and inadequate equipment for their white children rather than construct a building which will serve a mixed student body. In five of the school systems studied, this appeared

[1] Gunnar Myrdal, *An American Dilemma* (New York: Harper and Brothers, 1944), p. 392; and MacIver, *The More Perfect Union* (New York: The Macmillan Company, 1948), p. 58.

as a factor in avoiding the desegregation of the elementary schools.

If another school system will accept nonresident Negro students either on a segregated or desegregated basis, this offers an alternative to desegregation in any community wishing to evade the issue. This possibility led school officials in systems which were already desegregated to adopt a policy whereby only their resident Negroes were eligible for enrollment. They did not want to be swamped with other communities' Negroes, and indicated that it was only just that all should "suffer" equally. In one case where the Negro students were accepted in another system's segregated school, the transportation cost was considered prohibitive and the idea abandoned.

The greatest opposition in all communities came from the parent-group, and particularly from parents of elementary school children. There was no opportunity to interview parents, but school administrators, teachers, and students who were questioned explained it in terms of fear of intermarriage. In their opinion, parents believe that the small children will become accustomed to participating on an equal basis with Negro children throughout their most formative years and that by the time they reach high school they will fully accept Negroes. The ultimate outcome of this, they argue, is dating and marriage across race lines. On the other hand, they know that the high-school-age child has been conditioned in the segregated community to the point where he is fully conscious of the prohibitions regarding "social" interaction and will be capable of handling a desegregated school situation without going "too far." In other words, although there is less student-resistance and more *real* integration among the younger children, the prevailing pattern is to desegregate on the secondary level, where there is assurance that there will *not* be complete integration. If a community is extremely reluctant to desegregate, a minimum program may be put into effect which includes only the grade levels where there are few Negroes involved. In one such case of "symbolic" desegregation, eight Negro students on the junior and senior levels of high school were physically present in the mixed school, but there was serious doubt that they participated in any organized school activities, including classroom work.

The following designs were observed in the administration of desegregation programs in the school systems studied: (a) Three years of high school, desegregated; junior high school in same building, segregated; elementary school, segregated. Plans to desegregate the junior high school "in a year or two," and to desegregate the elementary school, "if funds can be raised for a new building." Negro high school students have a choice of attending the desegregated school or an all-Negro school in another town. (b) High school and junior high school in same building, desegregated; kindergarten desegregated, but other grades in same elementary school building, segregated. No plan to desegregate these elementary grades. (c) Desegregation on all levels, but retention of Negro school and faculty. Students have a choice of attending desegregated or segregated school. (Largest Negro enrollment is in desegregated junior high school. Only six high school students, all girls, enrolled in the high school. Some schools had no Negro students, as a result of residential segregation in the city.) (d) Desegregation on all levels with elimination of Negro school and dismissal of Negro faculty. (e) Desegregation of junior and senior levels in high school. No plan to extend the program.

Another aspect of administrative policy concerns the status of Negro students within each school. In general, the superintendent indicated the broad outlines of policy for the school system, and the principal of each school evaluated each situation as it arose in terms of parental pressures, community mores, and his own attitudes toward intermingling of the races. Policies were fluid as administrators, teachers, and students were constantly defining and redefining situations. There were no clues as to the appropriateness of new desegregated relationships nor was there any necessary carry-over of a definition from one type of interaction to another. In general, the more formal, organized activities were considered appropriate for mixed groups, but informal, intimate associations were avoided. This was particularly true of situations which are symbolic of status, such as eating and dancing. Official policies in all the school systems provided for rather full participation of Negro students in all activities. The actual patterns which emerged were due to a great extent to the attitudes of individual administrators. A principal could either *permit* a situation or he could actively encourage intermingling of Negroes and whites.

In all the schools students were registered by name, with no mention of race. Students were seated in classrooms in alphabetical order or permitted to choose their own seats. There were restrictive policies with regard to lunchrooms, toilets, drinking fountains, gymnasium or shower facilities. Negro students and parents attended assemblies, athletic events, and plays as members of nonsegregated audiences. Negro students attended dances in all but one school, but in no instance was there mixed dancing. Intimate contact across race lines was avoided by tacit agreement of students in both groups, although it was stated policy in one school that Negro students present form their own group for square or circle dances. If too few in number, they were to remain off the floor during the dance. In the one school where Negroes did not attend dances there was no official prohibition, but a background of near-violence and racial tension in the community served to discourage their participation. In the same school Negro students were permitted to use lunchroom facilities, but elected to eat as a segregated group in a vacant classroom. In none of the schools did Negro students participate in drama activities. Administrators and teachers interviewed admitted that they were not excluded by official policy, but could not conceive of a Negro student in any but a stereotypical Negro role.

The administrator's own attitudes toward desegregation may be favorable, unfavorable, or indifferent, but desegregation is a controversial issue, and most administrators see a desegregation program in their school systems as the onset of "trouble." Lacking tenure in most instances, and beset by the pressures and demands of many groups, it is not surprising that the administrator is cautious, conservative, even fearful. If community feelings have been relatively mild, or if he is supported in a desegregation program by a prestigeful element in the community, he may actively encourage the integration of Negro students. But if there is a vocal prosegregation group and community antagonism toward the change, the administrator may make a positive statement of policy and then discourage Negro students from participation in school activities.

The reluctance of school administrators to sanction research on the desegregation process within their schools is a major problem. If permission to make the study is finally granted, there are often specific restrictions, and cooperation may be withdrawn at any time. In one school the investigator may not contact parents, in another he may interview white students but not Negro, and in still another he is limited to interviews with the superintendent and principals. The administrator defines his job as that of "keeping the peace" and avoiding trouble. The following statements of administrators illustrate their attitude toward controversy.

Things are going smoothly. I'm afraid of any publicity that may be attached to it (the desegregation study). Maybe nothing would happen if you talked about it in town or interviewed students, but why take the chance?

Things are going along well now. We had some trouble at first, so why take a chance on stirring things up again?

Parents are beginning to believe that their children are used as guinea pigs by the University in all these research studies, and they resent it.

A school superintendent has so many problems, not only this type but all kinds, that he just doesn't want to take the chance of creating another problem.

It is better to let sleeping dogs lie. I'm not sure this is the time to make such a study. Maybe in a few years. It is working so well now that I just don't want to mention the issue. I would rather that you did not question students, especially Negro students. It puts them on the spot. We want as little publicity as possible. There has been plenty of opposition. I'm not sure about your getting a questionnaire out to parents. If these questions were to get into the hands of the wrong people, that is, those who are against integration, it would give them something to get hold of again, and there's no telling what they might do with it. I'd hate to see you fan those fires again.

You see, as an administrator, I have to keep the peace. Peace has to be maintained in a school. You can't have tension of any kind. You can do all kinds of good things for these people (parents) and they just figure it is your job. But just let something happen . . . there can't be anything controversial and that's that. That's my job.

In his study of hospitals in a Midwestern metropolitan area, Peter New observed that each piece of institutional research seems to introduce new types of tactical problems. As in the desegregation study, the cooperation of hospital administrators was sometimes withdrawn after the initial interviews.[2]

Time is an important factor in the integration process, and tensions tend to decrease after the initial year of desegregation. Thus, the outlook for greater administrative cooperation in future desegregation research is more promising. Meanwhile, social scientists may have to be content with limited objectives in their study of the early stages of desegregation.

The administrator is the crucial figure in any desegregation program. If he possesses qualities of leadership, takes firm and direct action in the early stages, and has the support of the community, he can be a positive force in the movement toward integration. If, on the other hand, he is overly cautious and fearful, he may be instrumental in creating conditions which are conducive to tension and conflict. In the absence of strong community feelings or when feelings are ill-defined, the administrator has a unique opportunity to determine and implement a policy within the school which may be instrumental in breaking down barriers to intercommunication of Negroes and whites in the community.

---

[2] Peter Kong-Ming New, "Tactical Problems in Institutional Research," a paper presented at the Midwest Sociological Society Annual Meeting, Des Moines, Iowa, April 4-6, 1957.

JOB SATISFACTION AND LEISURE-TIME ACTIVITY
IN A RESTRICTIVE ENVIRONMENT[1]

A. T. V. MATTHEWS*
AND
BAHA ABU-LABAN**
Bureau of Social Science Research,
Washington, D.C.

Interest in leisure-time pursuits as a distinct category of social life has received increasing attention in recent years.[2] Aside from attempts to discern differential activity patterns according to social class, however, research efforts designed to explore the implications of leisure for other areas of human activity have been few in number.[3]

The notion that hobbies and other recreational activities contribute to the well-being of every individual is generally accepted. Implications are that such activity contributes to the effectiveness of a worker, and consequently it is not unusual today to find large businesses that support recreational programs for their employees. It would seem, therefore, that organizations which are located in isolated or inclement environments would do well to look to the recreational needs of their employees.

This paper reports an attempt to explore the relationship of job satisfaction to the leisure-time activity of a group of professionals working in a restrictive environment. The professionals were a group of male primary school teachers who had come from Egypt, Iraq, Jordan, Lebanon, Palestine, and Syria to work temporarily in Kuwait. This small desert sheikdom which lies on the Persian gulf just south of Iraq has experienced a rapid rise in wealth since the discovery of its great oil resources

---

*Associate, Bureau of Social Science Research, Inc.
**Research assistant, University of Washington.

[1] This study was conducted under the direction of the senior author while he was assistant professor of sociology at the American University of Beirut. For a more extended discussion of recreation in Kuwait, see the junior author's unpublished master's dissertation, "Relationship of Recreation to Job Satisfaction: A Study of Teachers in Kuwait," American University of Beirut, 1956.

[2] Stimulation for a number of these studies appears to stem from the activities of the Center for the Study of Leisure at the University of Chicago, *American Journal of Sociology,* LXII (May 1957); entire issue is devoted to this substantive area.

[3] Some examples of the latter are the following: Bartlett S. Atwood and E. H. Shideler, "Social Participation and Juvenile Delinquency," *Sociology and Social Research,* 18: 436-41; Jean Ogden Cavanaugh, "Relation of Recreation to Personality Adjustment," *Journal of Social Psychology,* 15: 63-74; Joshua A. Fishman, "Degree of Bilingualism in a Yiddish School and Leisure Time Activities," *Journal of Social Psychology,* 36: 155-65.

ten years ago. Lacking trained personnel, Kuwait has attracted foreign specialists by paying a salary two to three times that obtainable in the professionals' home countries. Though the city of Kuwait has a population estimated at more than 300,000 and is a modern large-scale version of a Western boom town, still its public recreational facilities are severely limited compared with other Arab capitals.[4]

Design of Research. Delineation of the concepts of leisure-time activity and job satisfaction was the initial step in designing the research operation. Recreational activity performed during leisure time was taken as equivalent to leisure-time activity. Recreation was defined as "any activity pursued during leisure, either individual or collective, that is free and pleasureful, having its own immediate appeal, not impelled by a delayed reward beyond itself or by any immediate necessity."[5] Leisure time was taken to be "the time we are free from the more obvious and formal duties which a paid job or other obligatory occupation imposes on us."[6] No established referent for the other central concept—job satisfaction—was discovered. For purposes of the study it was broadly defined as that feeling of elation or "worth-whileness" which an individual secured in the process of his participation in and identification with a particular occupational position. (It will be noted that this definition brings the concept very close to that of "morale.")

From a series of hypotheses three basic ones were selected for testing. Hypothesis 1: There exists a positive relationship between the extent of leisure-time activity and the degree of job satisfaction. The feeling was that the man who was busy in recreational activities would find his work in the restrictive environment more tolerable than the man who was relatively inactive. Hypothesis 2: The degree of job satisfaction is negatively related to the number of desired, but unavailable activities. This is an extension of the previous hypothesis and is related to the concept of relative deprivation. It emphasizes that the greater the desire for unavailable types of activities, the greater the dissatisfaction with the job. Hypothesis 3: The degree of job satisfaction is related differentially to the type of leisure-time activity engaged in. Here the question of the context in which activity takes place was of foremost importance. Also the notion that different leisure pursuits might be sought by the satisfied

[4] For all practical purposes the city of Kuwait is Kuwait. The only other significant community is that of Ahmadi, where the British maintain a colony in connection with their exploitation of the oil resources of the area.

[5] Henry Pratt Fairchild, ed., *Dictionary of Sociology* (New York: Philosophical Library, 1944), pp. 251-52.

[6] G. A. Lundberg, M. Komarovsky, and M. A. McInerny, *Leisure* (New York: Columbia University Press, 1934), p. 2.

than by the unsatisfied was of interest.

A proportional stratified random sample of 50 per cent of the foreign male primary school teachers working in the city of Kuwait was chosen for the study. The size of the sample (209 subjects) was determined in accordance with the minimal requirements for a simple multivariate analysis involving two or possibly three variables. With the aid of a table of random numbers the interviewees were selected from two alphabetical lists of "newcomers" and "old-timers." The sample was found to be reasonably adequate, having a coefficient of variation of less than 10 per cent.

Data collection involved the use of an interview schedule. It was initially prepared in English and then translated into simplified classical Arabic. Respondents were required to indicate the extent and nature of their leisure-time pursuits on a check list containing forty-two activities (with provision for adding others). Further, a series of questions designed to elicit their degree of job satisfaction were administered, and also inquiry was made to secure background information. The schedule was pretested in December 1955, revised, and administered to the selected teachers by the junior author of this paper in the spring of 1956. Responses were coded and entered on summary sheets for purposes of analysis.

Findings. To secure some measure of job satisfaction was the salient initial task of analysis. From the responses to five of the questions it was possible by using the Cornell technique to construct a Guttman scale having a .944 coefficient of reproducibility.[7] On the basis of the five items six scale types emerged. Those in type one were considered to have "high" satisfaction, those in types two and three, "medium" satisfaction, and those in types four, five, and six, "low" satisfaction. The assignment here was on an arbitrary basis, taking into consideration primarily the requirements for construction of contingency tables. Thus the groups were divided into units as close to equal as practicable (high, medium, and low: 23, 43, and 34 per cent respectively).

Seventy-eight different recreational pursuits were reported for the group of teachers. The rank of the leisure-time activities engaged in by

[7] The questions involved together with the proportion of their replies judged favorable are as follows: Would you encourage other teachers like yourself to come to Kuwait? (87 per cent); In general, how satisfied would you say you are with teaching here in Kuwait? (81 per cent); How much concerned is the administration with the well-being of teachers here in Kuwait? (68 per cent); Would you like to teach in Kuwait permanently if you were given the chance? (52 per cent); How do you compare teaching as a profession with other jobs? (33 per cent).

one quarter or more of the male teachers in Kuwait is given in the following statement in parentheses and the name of the activity is followed by its frequency of adherents—209 possible—as follows: (1) reading, 200; (2) visiting with friends, 188; (3) listening to radio programs and music, 187; (4) attending lectures, 185; (5) attending films, 161; (6) picnics, 156; (7) spectator at sports, 142; (8) walking, 140; (9) writing, 111; (10) backgammon, 110; (11) going to exhibitions, 106; (12) ping-pong, 94; (13) attending parties or night gatherings, 84; (14) sitting at coffeehouses, 83; (15) swimming, 79; (16) attending plays, 78; (17) playing cards, 75; (18) sitting and/or daydreaming, 68; (19) photography, 68; (20) attending a club, 65; (21) playing with children, 57; (22) badminton, 56; (23) car drives, 56; (24) body building, 55.

The range in number of activities in which an individual teacher participated was from 1 to 32 with the mean being 15 and the median and mode 14 and 13 respectively. Inquiry as to the amount of activity rather than simple variety revealed a range of from 1 to 26 pursuits engaged in *once a week or oftener*. Here the mean was 9, while the median and mode were both 8.

Concerning the desired but unavailable activities, we found the range to be from 1 to 11 with the mean, median, and mode being 6, 3, and 3 respectively. The most frequently desired but unavailable activity—movies—was the choice of slightly over one fourth of the teachers. The rank of the unavailable leisure-time activities desired by one tenth or more of the male teachers in Kuwait with their frequency of adherents—209 possible—is as follows: (1) attending movies, 58; (2) visiting public gardens, 54; (3) dating young ladies, 44; (4) picnicking, 43; (5) attending a club, 37; (6) wenching, 37; (7) sitting at modern cafes, 34; (8) attending cabarets, 29; (9) attending plays, 29; (10) having mixed parties, 26; (11) swimming, 24; (12) having cocktail parties, 20.

For simplicity in analysis the frequency of leisure-time activities was divided into three parts (multivariate analysis). Assuming an essentially normal distribution, the attempt was made to have the middle group contain two thirds of the respondents (approximating one standard deviation each direction from the mean) and the two extremes one sixth each. These units of participation in combination with the units of job satisfaction formed ninefold property space tables.

Beginning with the relationship of job satisfaction to variety of activity, cross tabulation indicated that there was a significant fluctuation in the response. The cutting marks for the categories of variety of activity were as follows: limited, 9 or fewer; moderate, 10 to 19; and extensive, 20 or more. The distribution of the cases of low satisfaction (79 cases) among these categories of activity was 15, 62, and 23 per cent respectively. For the medium satisfaction group (90) it was 9, 72, and 19 per cent, and for the teachers with high satisfaction (48) the distribution was 33, 56, and 11 per cent. The table's chi-square of 15.02 was significant at the 1 per cent level. The modal frequencies viewed from the standpoint of participation gave a hint of a trend with the low satisfaction group having the slightly largest proportion of highly active persons, the medium satisfaction group the largest proportion of moderately active, and the highly satisfied the largest proportion of teachers most limited in activity.

By tying the respondents down to those activities in which they engaged once a week or more, it appeared that an index of the extent of leisure-time activity could be secured. Thus, in this alternative cross tabulation greater stress was put on the amount rather than simply on the variety. Here again a significant relationship was indicated. But this time a very definite trend between leisure activity and job satisfaction was discernible. It was, however, a negative correlation—the greater the participation, the less the satisfaction.

With the introduction of a time element, the cutting points for the activity categories became 5 or fewer for the limited, 6 to 13 for the moderates, and 14 or more for the extensive unit. The distribution of the cases of low satisfaction (71 cases) among these new categories of activity was 8, 72, and 20 per cent respectively. For the medium satisfaction group of teachers (90) it was 15, 68, and 17 per cent, and for those with high satisfaction (48) the distribution was 34, 58, and 8 per cent. A chi-square of 13.77 obtained, which again was significant at the 1 per cent level.

When inspection was made of the relationship between desire for unavailable activities and extent of job satisfaction, it appeared that the result was consistent with the previous findings. But in this case the trend was not so clear and the correlation dropped to the 10 per cent level of significance.

For the analysis of the relationship between job satisfaction and desired but unavailable activities, the activity categories were as follows: limited, 1 or none; moderate, 2 to 4; and extensive, 5 or more. Cases of low satisfaction (71) were distributed among the activity categories in the amounts of 15, 58, and 27 per cent respectively. The medium satisfaction group (90) was 28, 45, and 27 per cent, and the teachers with high satisfaction (48) had a distribution of 35, 50, and 15 per cent. The total distribution was characterized by a chi-square of only 8.29.

Other than the variety, amount, and desire for leisure-time activities, the nature of the activities themselves was thought to be important. It was felt that participation in leisure-time pursuits by oneself might have different consequences than taking part in group activities. To explore this idea the respondents were classified into three categories: those participating in a majority of their activities with a group of other persons, those having a majority of activities in which they participated alone, and those who had an equal division of group and individual activities. Inquiry as to the importance of this aspect of participation was not as revealing as hoped for. Only a slight suggestion of a negative trend for the group-oriented participants and a slight positive trend for those with a balanced record resulted.

The distribution of the cases of low satisfaction (79) among the balanced, individual, and group categories was 9, 18, and 73 per cent respectively. For the medium satisfaction group (90) it was 11, 20, and 69 per cent, and for the highly satisfied teachers (48) it was 25, 15, and 60 per cent. The chi-square of 7.67 was significant at the 20 per cent level.

Further consideration suggested that perhaps simply participating in a leisure-time activity with a group was not sufficiently focused. After all, it was possible for an individual to pursue relatively independent activities, while at the same time being in the presence of a group (a "lonely crowd" type). A comparison made of the most frequent leisure pursuits of the respondents having high and low satisfaction ruled out the applicability of the more common typologies of recreation: commercial versus noncommercial and spectator versus nonspectator. However, the analysis did suggest that a classification based on the extent of participation in activities emphasizing communication might be fruitful. This was done, but no significant difference in response resulted with respect to job satisfaction.

Discussion. The over-all picture of the findings which bear on the extent of leisure-time activity seems to refute our initial hypothesis. While the relationship between job satisfaction and participation is established, its direction is negative rather than positive—the higher the satisfaction, the fewer the number of activities. The results which indicate support for the second hypothesis seem to suggest that action and desire are expressions of a common factor. Thus a man who is very active is likely to desire even greater variety of activity. It may be that his awareness of possibilities is greater than that of the relatively inactive person.

The negative relationship between job satisfaction and recreation may be interpreted as indicating that the highly satisfied man devotes his leisure time to job-oriented activities, if any, rather than to engaging in recreational pursuits. In contrast, the teacher who is low in job satisfaction may look upon his occupation as a means of securing the wherewithal to enjoy leisure-time activities. Such an interpretation lends itself to the bipolar typology of "job-oriented" versus "leisure-oriented" person.

An alternative approach to this negative correlation, and one that might take us further along the road toward scientific theory, is that dissatisfaction is a stimulus to activity. From this standpoint, the greater a man's dissatisfaction, the greater will be his motivation to participate in other, hopefully, more rewarding activities. On the other hand, the man who is well satisfied may feel little or no compulsion toward leisure-time activity beyond what minimal obligations to friends and colleagues require.

Attempts to test the third hypothesis, which related job satisfaction to type of activity, were not very fruitful. While there was some indication that the teacher who was low in satisfaction was more likely to prefer group activities than his colleague who was highly satisfied, still the difference was not great. To suggest that the dissatisfied person seeks a group where he may "blow off steam" must be countered with the fact that for many group activities irrelevant discussion destroys the play. It may be that just what a man does in his leisure time is not so significant as the fact of his desire to do something or other.

There are at least three factors that seem likely to affect the relationship between job satisfaction and leisure-time activity. First, the amount of free time which a person has available may be important. A man with much leisure time may be more adversely affected in outlook by a dearth of recreational activities than one with little or no time.[8] This may explain the cases of low job satisfaction which have a limited amount of leisure-time activity. Closely related to this is the factor of marital status. Thus a single teacher having fewer demands upon his nonworking time than a married one may be more responsive to conditions in the recreational sphere—may simply be able to engage in more

---

8 This notion suggested to the authors by Capt. Norman A. Hilmar, social psychologist at Walter Reed Army Institute of Research, is a finding from an unpublished study of recreation among military personnel which he directed.

activities. Finally, the length of time a person resides in a restrictive environment seems likely to affect his response patterns both satisfactionwise and recreationwise. We hope to examine the consequences of these conditional variables for the basic relationship in a subsequent paper.

Conclusion. The growing tendency toward decentralization of industry for reasons of convenience or security is resulting in the establishment of working communities in isolated areas often characterized by inclement or even hostile physical environments. Certainly Siberia, the wilds of Idaho, and the Great Arabian Desert leave much to be desired for modern social living. Whether or not plans for these new communities should include provisions for recreation is not answered by this research. What has been indicated is that in such a restrictive environment men do engage in leisure-time activities and that those who are dissatisfied with their jobs tend to be more active in these pursuits than those who are relatively satisfied.

The study has been made in a non-Western cultural area, and the reliability of the empirical relationship which emerged would benefit substantially from replication in other cultural areas. Also a longitudinal study over time might give considerable insight into the manner in which an increasingly dissatisfied person responds recreationwise.

It appears that this substantive finding is focused on a potentially significant relationship. Consequently, an attempt to place it in a theoretical scheme before further investigation would seem prudent. Such an operation should enable us to anticipate other ramifications of the relationship and to direct research efforts toward the testing of theoretically relevant variables.

THE RELEVANCY OF SOCIAL WORK FOR SOCIOLOGY

JOSEPH W. EATON
University of California at Los Angeles

COMMON ORIGIN

Miss Helen Culver, a schoolteacher who turned realtor and became a millionaire in later life, gave Jane Addams most of the Hull House Settlement physical plant and furnished William I. Thomas with $50,000 to produce the monumental study of the *Polish Peasant in Europe and America.*[1] Both wanted to do something about the problems of adjustment of immigrants. Jane Addams and her collaborators were concerned with social action. She transmitted her experiences to social workers in the School of Social Service Administration at the University of Chicago. William I. Thomas had his sights on social study. He taught in the Department of Sociology at the University of Chicago. Thus, two of the pioneer professional accomplishments in social work and in sociology were melioristic siblings, nurtured from a common purse.[2]

There was a time in 1865 when social work, penology, and other helping professions were unified in the American Social Science Association.[3] It was the common organizational ancestor of such practice groups as the National Conference of Social Work, the American Prison Association, and the National Child Welfare Committee. It also was the predecessor of the American Sociological Society, the American Statistical Association, and the American Economic Society.

THE EMERGENCE OF PROFESSIONAL AUTONOMY

The American Social Science Association died in 1909, a victim of the need of its component special interests to develop by organizing autonomous disciplines. Most of the graduate schools of social work

[1] William I. Thomas and Florian Znaniecki, *The Polish Peasant in Europe and America* (Boston: Richard C. Badger, 1918-20), Vol. I-V (reprinted by New York: Alfred Knopf Publishing Co., 1927).

[2] These related movements of action and of study grew up to exhibit symptoms typical of "sibling rivalry." The Chicago-trained sociologists and social workers, many of whom became leaders in their respective fields, learned to work in separate compartments almost hermetically sealed against academic collaboration. Their common values, objectives, and nurture were rarely acknowledged. But both worked energetically on inseparable problems of observation and interpretation of social data.

[3] L. L. and Jessie Bernard, *Origins of American Sociology* (New York: Thomas Crowell Co., 1943), pp. 527-607.

were nurtured by the university's Department of Sociology before acquiring academic autonomy. Undergraduate curricula of social work are still frequently combined with sociology. But social work educators have become increasingly insistent on jurisdictional separateness.

Social work is concerned with a broad spectrum of services that defy any neat definition of functions. It is more than a profession. It also is a social institution.[4] It emerged in agencies, public and private, that served the needs of the lower classes, the impoverished, the ill and unloved. It is still carried on almost exclusively in agencies, but the functions of those with professional training are heavily concentrated on work with the emotionally troubled.

Social work is, perhaps, the most inclusive of the helping professions. Its professional jurisdiction is shared in part by many other occupations that are also concerned with the application of scientific and "common sense" knowledge to social-psychological problems.[5] For example, its role and functions overlap those of clinical psychology, psychiatry, the ministry, and the law. But each of these other professions, as Helen Wright suggests, limits its services to a more narrowly defined segment of practice, "the psychiatrist to the emotional, the physician to the physical, the clergyman to the spiritual, and the lawyer to the legal involvement."[6] In actual practice, however, these distinctions are far less readily maintained than they are asserted in theory.

All the helping professions draw from a common area of knowledge that might best be described as the *behavior sciences*. The core of this relatively new academic "label" encompasses most of the concerns of such traditional disciplines as psychology, social psychology, sociology, anthropology, economics, and political science. As we move toward its periphery, no sharp boundaries can be drawn. There are common frontiers with biology and medicine, with the physical sciences and mathematics, and with the humanities. The concept of *behavioral sciences* is not a faddish substitute of a new term for others that are familiar and with which we feel comfortable. Its emergence is symptomatic of the recognition that the study of man cannot be done well within the limits

---

[4] Arthur Hillman, *Sociology and Social Work* (Washington, D.C.: Public Affairs Press, 1956), has made a good description and analysis of the institutional nature of the profession.

[5] Joseph W. Eaton, "Whence and Whither Social Work: A Sociological Analysis," *Social Work*, 1: 11-26; "Regulations of Psychological Counseling and Psychotherapy," *Columbia University Law Review*, Vol. 51, No. 4, April 1951.

[6] Helen R. Wright, "The Professional Curriculum of the Future," *Social Service Review*, 25:466-76.

of any one of the traditionally defined social science fields. A multidisciplinary approach is needed, and new terminology is the result.

RESURGENCE OF COMMUNICATION

In spite of the historical and functional relatedness of the two occupational jurisdictions—sociology and social work—their interaction has been characterized by many communication barriers. It is still somewhat fashionable among "pure" science-oriented sociologists to be stereotypically disdainful of social workers and ignorant about what they do. Conversely, "sociology" and "sociological" are occasionally used as epithets by social workers. The breakdown in intellectual communication between the students of social problems and those who wanted to ameliorate them through social work became most pronounced, as Ruth Faith Carrier has so well documented,[7] after social work practitioners discovered the relevancy of psychoanalytic theory to their practice in the early 1930's.

These manifestations of jurisdictional hostility are on the decline. Social work practitioners and educators are rediscovering the crucial significance of sociology for their work, a trend evident in many contemporary social work writings.[8] Anyone who is functioning as a participant observer in the subcultural milieu of both professional sociology

---

[7] Ruth Faith Carrier, *The Relationship Between the Social Sciences and Social Work from 1920-1952* (Ann Arbor: University of Michigan Press, 1952) (master's thesis).

[8] Herman D. Stein, "Social Science in Social Work Practice and Education," *Social Casework*, 36:147-55.

Alfred J. Kahn, "The Nature of Social Work Knowledge," in Cora Kasius, ed., *New Directions in Social Work* (New York: Harper and Brothers, 1954); "Sociology and Social Work: Challenge and Invitation," *Social Problems*, 4:220-28.

Ernest Greenwood, "Social Science and Social Work: A Theory of Their Relationship," *Social Service Review*, 29:20-33.

Robert C. Angell, "A Research Basis for Welfare Practice," *The Social Welfare Forum* (New York: Columbia University Press, 1954).

Robin M. Williams, Jr., "Application of Research to Practice in Intergroup Relations," *American Sociological Review*, 18:78-83.

Grace L. Coyle, "New Insights Available to the Social Worker from the Social Sciences," *The Social Service Review*, 26:289-304.

Werner W. Boehm, "Social Work and the Social Sciences," *Journal of Psychiatric Social Work*, 21:4-8.

Elizabeth G. Herzog, "What Social Casework Wants of Social Science Research," *American Sociological Review*, 16:68-73.

Henry Maas, "Collaboration Between Social Work and the Social Sciences," *Social Work Journal*, 31:104-09.

Herbert H. Stroup, "The Contribution of Anthropology to Social Work Education," *Social Casework*, 31:189-94.

H. David Kirk, "Social Science and Social Work: Issues Genuine and Spurious." Address to the Canadian Conference on Social Work (June 1958).

and social work will find considerable intellectual readiness in social work circles to look to sociology and sociologists for help in meeting unresolved problems of practice and of education for social welfare. Sociological concepts like role, reference group, status, and community are part of the professional vocabulary of practitioners and are applied in the description and analysis of what they do. To illustrate, sociologists, with and sometimes without social work professional training, are on the faculties of many schools of social work. Doctoral programs in social work are closely related in several universities to the graduate offerings of the behavioral science departments. Among a good many social work practitioners and educators, there is a tendency to ascribe to sociology more potentiality for providing answers than can be delivered.

SOCIAL WORK'S APPLIED SOCIOLOGY FUNCTIONS

This resurgent flirtation between social work and sociology has been rather one-sided. The significance of social work for academic sociology, while never denied in theory, is far less widely acknowledged. Only occasionally is it analyzed in sociological writings, textbooks, and course offerings.[9] Urban sociology, marriage and community studies, though relevant to much that social workers do, are usually reported upon without much attention to their significance for problems that must be acted upon by practitioners.

The relevancy of social work experiences to sociology is particularly obvious in the social disorganization-reorganization area, in courses often taught by sociologists under the label of *social problems*. The consequences of war, unemployment, migration, and other social crises for peoples, groups, and communities are important social work tasks. The same can be said about more individualized symptoms of social-psychological stress, including behavior disorders, economic indigency, sex deviancy, and divorce. Yet how many sociology majors will learn in their department's courses how social workers function in these fields? Many will be ignorant of the fact that there is a relevant social work literature.

Social work practice also makes contributions to the knowledge of social theory. While these contributions rarely come to be stated ex-

[9] Alvin W. Gouldner, "Explorations in Applied Social Science," *Social Problems*, 3:169-81.

Olive M. Stone, "What Can Social Case Work Contribute to the Social Sciences?" *American Sociological Review*, 15:66-73.

R. M. MacIver, *The Contribution of Sociology to Social Work* (New York: Columbia University Press, 1931).

plicitly, they arise from the fact that social practitioners test theory in the pursuit of their work. For example, oversimplified theoretical models, such as economic determinism or psychological determinism, have been popular among practitioners from time to time, but their inadequacy was demonstrated when they were applied. In the 1930's practitioners sensed quickly that money was neither the root of all evil nor the salvation of all ills. They found it necessary to become interested in power factors, so crucial in lobbying for social legislation. They discovered that many impoverished clients could not attain self-sufficiency merely with economic support. The difficulties experienced when caseworkers attempted to meet the emotional problems of their clients from "purely" economic and/or psychological approaches did much to further the present rediscovery by social workers of the field of social psychology—of role theory and the situational approach. The realities of life have forced most practitioners monistically concerned with economic or psychoanalytic aspects of casework to modify their work to bring about change in the environment in which their clients live.

Social workers have also given concrete institutional expression to one of the central theories of the sociology of knowledge: Human perception and ideas are influenced by the social system in which they arise, its economic conditions, its value system, and other cultural and psychological considerations. The social work institution of *supervision* is rationalized on the basis of this theory that knowledge should be viewed in its situational context. Supervision is provided, in all agencies with good professional standards, not only for the fledgling practitioner, but also for those with considerable experience. The supervisor assumes the role of a watchdog against the undue projection of a practitioner's personal needs, social values, or past experience when working with clients, groups, and communities.

Social workers are practitioners of *social change.* This label is appropriate even for those who approach their work primarily in psychological terms. The psychiatric bias they profess is far more preached than it is practiced. Most caseworkers do more than therapeutic counseling. They help clients to change their environment. They may find them jobs, get a homemaker to care for children, or recommend that Johnny join a Cub Scout troop at the settlement house. Group workers lead friendship and activity groups. Community organization workers are active in neighborhood planning. They also plan and coordinate social services in the community. These diverse social work practitioners may have forgotten much about the content of the academic sociology courses which nearly all of them have been exposed to. But they apply much of what sociologists teach. And they do more than that. Through experience they acquire new knowledge. Their hunches about social problems and services, if generalized and communicated, could be used by sociologists to formulate worth-while research and to improve the quality of their teaching.

SOCIAL WELFARE SOCIOLOGY

Present and future social workers constitute perhaps the largest group of direct consumers of sociological knowledge. Probably more sociology majors enter social work practice than any other single occupation. Some take social work jobs without further study beyond the bachelor's degree, particularly in the field of public welfare. Others obtain a master's degree in one of the 59 graduate schools of social work. Several dozens are now enrolled in social work studies in one of the 12 doctoral level programs.[10] Education, formal and informal, is highly prized in the profession. This fact is further indicated by the large number of in-service programs and institutes conducted by social work agencies for their staff.

Academic sociologists have shown little interest in this professional social system of social practice. There are course offerings in a variety of institutional fields of specialization such as industrial sociology, medical sociology, criminology, the family. But social welfare sociology is not yet a definite part of the academic structure of the field. This lack is all the more surprising if one considers that approximately $20,000,000,000 were devoted in 1950 to public and private social service activities in the United States. Public health officials, juvenile judges, and employment interviewers, to mention only a few of these occupations, are also in the business of providing social practice services. There were approximately 100,000 persons engaged in activities defined by the census as social work. There are many more times that many individuals engaged in the welfare institutional network, the exact number depending upon one's operational definition of the field of social welfare.

The reasons for the undeveloped status of social welfare sociology would be an interesting subject of investigation. The social mobility

[10] In 1955, 76 students were enrolled in school of social work programs beyond the master's level. Most of these were interested chiefly in the "third year" program, a primarily clinically oriented experience of post-master's graduate education. Others, however, are planning to complete the requirements necessary for a degree of Doctor of Social Work or Ph.D. Council on Social Work Education, *Statistics on Social Work Education, November 1, 1955 and Academic Year 1954-55* (New York, Council on Social Work Education, 1956).

strivings of the field of sociology may have much to do with why in recent decades many academicians have avoided contact with activities of an ameliorative nature. Even when this is done in a research capacity, the "practical" aspect is viewed by some as a threat to the self-image of being a "pure scientist." Sociology graduate students have been more often attracted to fields of sociological specialization involving the more prestigeful institutions, such as medicine and industry, than the study of the culture of social work and those other professions which devote most of their attention to serving the needs of the poor, the handicapped, the intellectually limited, and the economically indigent.

The profession of social work stands to sociology (and the other behavioral sciences) in a relationship like that of medicine to bacteriology, biochemistry, and biophysics. But there is considerable uncertainty in the thinking of social work educators and practitioners about the use of the body of knowledge transmitted to them in sociology courses.

One reason may be that a hypothesis formulated in a sociologist's mind is viewed by the social worker as a guide to decision making. When so used, it will affect real people in something more than an academic fashion. This leads to questions of just how valid these theories are.

The probability of nonapplicability of a theoretical formulation to a particular category of cases can be expressed neatly in the statistician's coefficient of nondetermination. But it has much more personal significance for the practitioner. He looks for a theory in which he can have clinical confidence. To the academician uncertainty and error are an invitation to do more research; to the practitioner, they are a worry. The unsophisticated degree of assurance with which psychoanalytic theories have sometimes been propounded was therefore much more reassuring than alternate social-psychological formulations presented academically with the intellectual modesty becoming to their tentativeness.

Yet this alone is probably no adequate explanation of why it is that so many social caseworkers, after years of undergraduate tutelage by sociologists, have ignored in their subsequent appreciation of the ideas of Sigmund Freud the relevancy to their work of the contributions of men like Charles H. Cooley and Max Weber. There is need for academic introspection of how sociologists communicate their ideas in textbooks and in their classrooms![11]

---

[11] Thomas D. Eliot made an investigation of the question of how sociology is taught more than three decades ago, but his observations and suggestions are still timely and relevant. See Thomas D. Eliot, "The Social Worker's Criticisms of Undergraduate Sociology," *The Journal of Social Forces*, 2:506-12; "Has Sociology a Contribution to the Equipment of the Social Worker?" Papers and Proceedings of the American Sociological Society, 16:231-37; "Sociology as a Pre-Vocational Subject: The Verdict of Sixty Social Workers," *The American Journal of Sociology*, 29:726-46.

CONCLUSION

Social workers aim to apply much of what sociologists suspect to be approximately valid on the basis of their theories and their research data. But the practitioners are also called upon to function beyond the known boundary of scientific knowledge. In meeting this role, they often discover hunches that will be the basis for advancement in knowledge whenever they are put to test. In other words, social workers furnish sociologists with a laboratory of social action, thought, and feeling. This is not always readily accessible, but there are enough instances of successful completion of research investigations of social practice problems by sociologists and others to support the following conclusions: Discoveries in the relatively "basic" behavior sciences can come about on the basis of examination of questions raised by practitioners and the hunches formulated by them from their experience.

A PROBLEM OF REMUNERATION OF THE BRITISH NATIONAL HEALTH SERVICE

A Supplementary Note to Mangold's Paper*

JOEL B. MONTAGUE, JR.
State College of Washington

Mangold's paper, it seemed to me, was an accurate report on the National Health Service and some of its social implications. There is one aspect of the scheme which always comes up in discussions of socialized medicine that I think should be further explored. That is: What about the financial remuneration of doctors? In my own thinking, these pecuniary aspects of the program are not of primary importance, but in the minds of many—particularly doctors—they seem to be of utmost pertinence. In England the pay of the doctors has recently been of concern to both the profession and the government.

The English doctors' dispute with the government about remuneration was being carried on at the time we were last in England (February to August 1957), and I made some effort to understand the situation. I talked with both general practitioners and administrators and read newspapers and journals. The *British Medical Journal* reviewed the history of remuneration under the National Health Service in an article in the issue of April 6, 1957. Much of the following information is taken from that source.

In 1946: Aneurin Bevan, the Minister of Health, in preparation for inaugurating the National Health Service, appointed a committee, the function of which was to make recommendations on remuneration of general practitioners, consultants, and specialists. This committee was known as the Spens Committee. It made two reports, one in 1946 and one in 1948. In these reports, the committee made recommendations as to the proper levels of pay for the two branches of the profession and was concerned also with maintaining levels of remuneration in the future, which were to be set after taking into consideration the value of money, that is, real purchasing power at the time. These recommendations were accepted by the doctors and by the existing Labour government as the basis upon which the profession entered the National Health Service. The legal status of the Spens report is still in question.

March 1952: After adjudication by Mr. Justice Danckwerts, which gave effect to the Spens Committee's recommendations for general practi-

*George B. Mangold, "Social Aspects of the British National Health Service," *Sociology and Social Research*, 42:92-98, November-December 1957.

tioners (taking into account the change in value of money from 1939), a "betterment award" of 100 per cent was made, above the 1939 levels. The Minister of Health accepted the award as just, but pointed out that there was no justification for any assumption that such a raise represented an appropriate standard of remuneration for all professionals in the country.

By 1954, all three branches of the profession—general practitioners, consultants and specialists, and hospital staff—had received comparable salary increases.

June 1956: The profession submitted notice of intention to request increases in salary according to the Spens Committee agreement. The Minister of Health and the government (now Conservative) took the view that the remuneration of the medical profession, like that of others, must be determined from time to time in the light of all relevant circumstances, and that in the present circumstances they would not feel justified in giving consideration to any increase in medical remuneration. The doctors considered that the Spens Committee report, which had been accepted by the government, represented a contractual obligation to the profession. The government denied this, and charges were made in Parliament that the medical profession was trying to isolate itself from the effects of inflation which were felt by other working groups.

January 1957: Mr. D. Vosper was appointed Minister of Health. The doctors pressed the new Minister for a 24 per cent raise, which had been arrived at in keeping with the Spens report. The Minister announced that a Royal Commission would be set up to review medical and dental remuneration. The doctors did not consider a Royal Commission to be the proper agency to consider their claims and suggested that some form of arbitration be used to settle the dispute. In February, the General Medical Services Committee of the BMA recommended the resignation of general practitioners from the National Health Service if the government did not agree to "immediate and satisfactory settlement of claim or, alternatively, arbitration." This recommendation was later endorsed by the British Medical Association Council and, in addition, they resolved not to cooperate with the Royal Commission.

In April 1957, Mr. Macmillan announced that the government had decided to grant an increase of 5 per cent to all doctors and dentists. The doctors called this an arbitrary decision without previous consultation with representatives of the profession which, in accordance with the Spens report, it was obliged to do. Also they maintained that the cost of living had gone up by 24 per cent since the previous adjustment. They recommended that the 5 per cent increase be placed in a "suspense account" and reiterated their desire for arbitration. However, after the Royal Commission had issued a statement on how it intended to proceed, the doctors changed their minds and decided that they would give evidence before the Royal Commission. The profession was not, of course, obliged to accept its decision. Also at this point the British Medical Association set up a committee to conduct an over-all study of the National Health Service with the aim of "eradicating those faults of the present system which cause dissatisfaction to the public . . .," not to do away with it.

June 1957: At a special representative meeting of the British Medical Association, the position of cooperating with the Royal Commission was confirmed, and withdrawal from the National Health Service was deferred.

July 16, 1957: At the British Medical Association's annual representative meeting, a "draft plan" was drawn up which was to be submitted later to the BMA Study Committee mentioned above. The draft proposed certain changes in method of payment, instituting charges for some medicines, and modifications in administration of the program. In presenting the draft to the meeting, Dr. H. H. D. Sutherland stressed its tentative nature and that the public interest was uppermost. He said that no significant changes in the National Health Service were expected in the next five to ten years.

It should be clear that the doctors did not attack the National Health Service; much less did they suggest its abolition. The fundamental rightness of the present system of administering health services has not been questioned. Socialized medicine is accepted by both the public and the doctors as the only morally and socially justifiable way to administer medical services in a civilized society. The doctors' threat to walk out of the National Health Service was effective only because of the existing consensus in the country in wanting the service to continue without interruption. A request for a raise in pay is not a demand for the abolition of the employing agency.

Although I followed the problem with considerable interest, I would not like to make a judgment as to whether or not the request for higher pay was justified. It may be pointed out, however, that the English doctors' income compares very favorably with that of other professionals in Britain.

In the National Health Service[1] a doctor is remunerated by a capita-

[1] Ninety-eight per cent of the general practitioners, 94 per cent of the dentists, and nearly all pharmacists are participating in the NHS. See *Health Services in Britain* (London: H. M. Stationery Office, 1957), pp. 7-8.

tion payment for each patient registered with him. In 1957, the payment was 17 shillings a year with an additional 10 shillings for every patient within the range of 501 to 1,500 on the doctor's list, plus special allowances for travel, for practicing in "less desirable locations," plus interest-free loans for acquiring premises for group practice, etc.[2] (There are different rates for specialists and other personnel.) The average doctor has 2,200 people on his rolls,[3] which means that he receives approximately 2,370 pounds a year ($6,636). Less than 1 per cent of employed persons in England receive over 2,000 pounds a year.[4] A general practitioner may have a maximum of 3,500 patients on his rolls, in which case his income would be approximately 3,475 pounds ($10,000) a year.[5]

"The starting salaries in many professional and technical careers are often in the range of 350 to 500 pounds a year. . .Most of the senior posts in business, the professions and the Civil Service are in the range of from 1,000 to 5,000 pounds a year."[6]

---

2 *Ibid.*, p. 14.
3 *Ibid.*, p. 13.
4 *Britain, An Official Handbook* (London: H. M. Stationery Office, 1956), p. 273.
5 *Health Services in Britain*, p. 14.
6 *Britain, An Official Handbook*, pp. 272, 273.

LOWER LEVELS OF LEADERSHIP IN INDUSTRY

AMITAI ETZIONI
University of California, Berkeley

The distinction between formal and informal organization may serve to delineate the sources of motivation for accepting or rejecting the role-expectations of an organizational structure. Leadership plays a major role in recruiting identification with the organization's objectives, regulations, and directions. Most studies in the field focus on the lower level of leadership, the foreman, who is considered the direct bridge between formal and informal organization. These studies are mainly concerned with the conditions under which organizational demands are accepted and participants experience satisfaction or deprivation.

I

What is meant by leadership in an organizational context is often not clearly defined. Many studies agree that leadership is a social relationship and not a personality characteristic. It is situational in the sense that a person may be a leader in one situation and not in another. But is leadership in organizations a role-characteristic independent of the incumbent? Some studies seem to imply that every foreman is a leader if he has authority, i.e., if his orders are legitimate to the workers. Although this is a matter of definition, we suggest that it is more fruitful to distinguish leadership from a role which carries authority (foreman, army officer).[1] While authority can be rational and external, accepted leadership always includes an emotional commitment to the personality of the leader.[2] Thus a foreman may have authority but no leadership, his orders being accepted for motives other than a personal commitment to him. This may have no apparent consequences in the ordinary industrial situation. But in crisis situations (e.g., fire, strike) and/or situations of rapid change, when orders outside the specific delimited area of authority have to be given and accepted, only the leader will be followed, while orders of the regular authority holder will be disregarded.

II

If this distinction between leadership and authority is accepted, an intriguing substantive question arises: Does every organization need low

---

[1] *Cf.* R. Bierstedt, "The Problem of Authority" in M. Berger, T. Abel, C. H. Page (ed.), *Freedom and Control in Modern Society* (Toronto: D. Van Nostrand Company, 1954), pp. 67-81.

[2] In psychological terms one could claim that the relationship between leader and follower includes some elements of identification.

level leadership in order to function? The answer depends on the nature of the organization. The more diffuse its goals and requirements are, the more personal commitment it needs, and therefore the more leadership is required. The more specific its objectives and demands, the less leadership is required. In organizations with specific goals, acceptance of regulations and directions may be based on external needs of the actor which are satisfied through complying with the organizational requirements. A worker may fulfill his organizational role in order to earn a living and derive his psychological rewards for conformity to the factory rules and orders, from his family and his status in the community. Authority may also be accepted on cultural grounds, earlier socialization, etc., without personal commitment to the holder-of-authority in the formal structure.

Economic organizations, e.g., industry, are relatively specific organizations compared with most political parties and religious movements. Economic organizations themselves can be classified from this point of view. It seems that at least the more specific industries can do without eliciting identification by relying on external motivation and rational legitimation. Foremen in industry may be authority holders without possessing any leadership characteristics. We must learn under what conditions they become leaders. To assume that every authority holder is a leader is unwarranted by the existing data[3] and makes the connotation of the term "leader" too broad.

III

Some industries, for reasons only partially understood, seem to require recruitment of identification with the organization as an internal source of motivation, since external sources are insufficient. Both formal and informal leadership are considered important factors in this process. It is not clear how the informal organization, when it exists, is linked to the formal organization. Does the authority holder take upon himself the role of leader of the informal group, or are these two mutually exclusive roles?

The Michigan studies seem to suggest that both roles can be combined.[4] A foreman may be *production oriented*: he emphasizes quality and quantity of performance, acceptance of orders, is not interested in

---

[3] In the initial stage of the process of change described by E. Jaques in *The Changing Culture of a Factory*, no signs of leadership can be recognized in the various authority holders, but orders are still followed and regulations are accepted.

[4] See Daniel Katz, N. Maccoby, G. Gurin, L. G. Floor, *Productivity, Supervision and Morale Among Railroad Workers* (Ann Arbor: University of Michigan Press, Institute for Social Research, 1950), Part I.

workers beyond their organizational roles, and would rather work than supervise. In short, a production-oriented foreman is an authority holder but not a leader. On the other hand, a foreman may be *human relations oriented*: he is interested in the workers' personalities, in guiding them, and in building a positive human relationship. Thus he attempts to create a personal commitment of the workers toward himself which means that the foreman attempts to become a leader. Whether this attempt is successful or not depends on many psychological and sociological conditions which cannot be discussed here. Thus there seem to be three alternatives: an authority holder without leadership (production-oriented foreman); an authority holder with leadership (some human-relation-oriented foreman), often referred to as a formal leader; and a leader without a position of authority, an informal leader.

Can the formal leader be the only leader of the informal group or must he work through an informal leader? The Harvard studies of Bales and his colleagues, when applied to our problem, seem to suggest that two leaders are needed, as in most cases one person will not be able to carry out both roles.[5] The two roles require different psychological characteristics and are to some degree contradictory in the very attitudes and actions they demand. The instrumental leader (who comes close to the formal leader) and the expressive leader (who is quite similar to the informal leader) are usually two different people. "Giving ideas" and "guiding" usually do not coincide with being well liked. A leader who puts on the group pressure to achieve more and better performance creates at the same time some amount of rejection and hostility toward himself. Therefore, the roles of tension releasing and increasing solidarity in the group are almost inevitably left to some other actor. Since the foreman, if a leader at all, tends to be an instrumental leader, some other actor, perhaps an elderly worker, will carry out the expressive role of the informal leader.[6] This problem concerning the possible relationships between the authority holder and the informal leader has practical implications for the human relations instructor and counselor who guide the foreman. Should the foreman strive to fulfill the role of the leader of the informal group or leave it to a worker, who has no authority position, and strive to be accepted by the group and supported by its informal leader?

---

[5] See T. Parsons, R. F. Bales, and E. A. Shils, *Working Papers in the Theory of Action* (Glencoe: The Free Press, 1953), pp. 111-61.

[6] In this context a reversal of roles, where the formal leader is primarily expressive and the informal leader takes a primarily instrumental role, is quite unlikely.

The last problem to be discussed here is the pattern of the relationship between the two roles in those cases where they are separated. The relations may vary all the way from a coalition between the foreman and the informal leader to constant collisions between them. Directions given by foremen can be differentiated among (1) those which are given directly to the workers without prior consultation with or "informing" the informal leader, (2) those which "require" such consultation, and (3) those which are given indirectly, i.e., "told" to the informal leader to transfer to the group. The balance of rejection and acceptance has to be more carefully studied. Some rejections of orders by the informal leader are functional for the maintenance of the pattern of acceptance in toto. Too much subordination of the informal leader by the foreman and too much acceptance by the informal leader may undermine the following of the informal leader and in some cases leave room for the emergence of a leader more ready to reject the foreman's directions.[7]

Further analysis of the dynamic relations between the foreman and the informal leader must be complicated by introducing the roles of the steward and business agent. Are they formal or informal leaders from the point of view of the industry? How do they influence the dynamics of the relationship discussed above? Are there more than two basic types (mutually exclusive) of leadership? These are only a few of the questions which need further study in order to understand better the lower levels of leadership in industry in particular and in organizational structures in general.

[7] This is the main point of tension in the political structure of the classroom in "Blackboard Jungle."

MANNHEIM AND SYSTEMATIC SOCIOLOGY

EMORY S. BOGARDUS
University of Southern California

In *Systematic Sociology*, which has been published posthumously and edited by ten of his research students, Karl Mannheim stresses the need for a framework within which sociological research can be efficiently conducted.[1] He aimed to bring about a synthesis between theoretical and empirical methods within an adequate universe of thought. He would have these two types of procedure develop together with each offering stimuli and balance to the other. To this end he attempted, with a measure of success, to construct a synthetic system of thought to which theory and experiment would mutually contribute.

Mannheim believed that the special field of sociology is found in the forms and processes of "human living together." In a larger sense, sociology describes "one by one the main factors of this living together" that may be found in every kind of society, beginning with primitive groups and coming down to and including all current social groupings.[2] Sociology proceeds, not haphazardly, but in a systematic manner, from simple to complex classifications and from casual and transient social contacts to the permanent "frame-groups" within which, as a rule, social contacts take place and which to a degree condition their expressions.

In addition to the study of the causes and results of all social grouping, sociology gives attention to the historical variations within the same social grouping, as for example in the family, and searches for the common features as distinguished from the special features.[3] Then, sociology considers ways in which the different social factors interact and offset one another in a given society during a given period of time, for example, how commerce and industry affect government in a particular society. Human living together is an all-comprehensive social process. Some of the subprocesses that Mannheim emphasizes will now be reviewed.

1. *Distancing.* Distancing is defined as "rendering something remote."[4] It signifies either a higher or a lower status "which limits the concept of social distance to what the present writer has defined as ver-

---

[1] Edited by J. S. Eros and W. A. C. Stewart (New York: Philosophical Library, 1958).
[2] *Ibid.*, pp. 1 ff.
[3] *Ibid.*, p. 2.
[4] *Ibid.*, pp. 47 ff.

tical distance,"[5] and which ignores the important social field of horizontal distances. Distancing is viewed by Mannheim as being essential to "the persistence and continuity of an authoritarian civilization." On the other hand, the more democratic a society, the less the distancing.

The simplest form of distancing results in "fear distance," which, as in the case of animals, is based on relative strength. Fear distance leads to other types of distance, such as "power distance," which in turn leads to "the hierarchy of social rank" and, it may be added, to a "power elite,"[6] who operate behind the social scene and may influence or control the elected representatives of the people in a democracy.

One of the main functions of distancing is to maintain a social hierarchy (that is, by distance of the vertical type). Sophisticated procedures of dress, manners, conventions "can serve to keep up distance between the ruling groups and the subjected ones."[7] The same purpose is further achieved by limiting or excluding social relations, such as forbidding intermarriage.

"Existential distancing" refers to the closeness or remoteness between the personal selves of two persons, as distinguished from the distancing effected by acts of a social nature.[8] Existential distancing and social distancing "usually act simultaneously," but democracy "as a rule tends to diminish social distance and uncover the purely existential relationships" between persons.

"Self distancing" involves a separating of peripheral aspects of the self from the inner core of the self. It means that distance is created within the self. Mannheim puts this type of ambivalence in a somewhat startling way when he says, "an individual can be near or far from his own essential being, in the same way as he can be near or far from the essence of another person."[9]

2. *Individualization.* By individualization, Mannheim means making "the individual more or less independent of his group and to create in him a self-consciousness of his own."[10] This process is not carried through "solely by the individual himself" and is not primarily a mental or spiritual process which is being spread through the prevailing ideas of a time or place.

---

[5] E. S. Bogardus, "Social Distance and Its Applications," *Sociology and Social Research*, XXII:470.

[6] C. Wright Mills, *The Power Elite* (New York: Oxford University Press, 1956).

[7] Mannheim, *op. cit.*, pp. 52, 53.

[8] *Ibid.*, p. 54.

[9] *Ibid.*

[10] *Ibid.*, pp. 65 ff.

Four main aspects of individualization are indicated as follows: (1) a process of "becoming different from other people," (2) developing new forms of self-awareness, such as "becoming aware of one's unique and specific character" and developing a new kind "of self evaluation or organization of the self," (3) individualizing one's wishes regarding external objects, and (4) a deepening of one's self or extending "the inner dimensions of self."[11]

Individualization may result from isolation, e.g., Beethoven's deafness (organic isolation) forced him "to live in exile," as he once said. The organic type of individualization, as distinguished from the physical type, may lead to special forms of behavior, such as "shyness, distrust, inferiority or superiority feelings, and pedantry."[12] Privacy is a form of isolation in which "man withdraws part of his inner self from public control."[13]

3. *Integration.* Integration is a major social process, for it makes living together possible. The term is the core concept in Mannheim's systematization of sociology. Around it all other concepts are organized.

Integration accounts for all types of grouping in society. It explains organized groups which are characterized by (1) a relative persistence, (2) an organizational structure with a division of functions, (3) traditional ways of doing and thinking, (4) certain norms or standards, (5) ideas about the functions of the group and its relations to other groups, (6) a collective interest, (7) a power elite, and (8) typical tensions as well as typical "repressive and discharging agencies."[14] Then, there are groups with a loose structure, such as a crowd and a public. The latter is defined as "an integration of many people not based on personal interaction but on reactions to the same stimuli" that arise without the members "necessarily being physically near to one another."[15] Moreover, there are special kinds of grouping, such as the dyad and triad, in which there are differences in personal behavior according to the number of the persons in the group.

Integration is also expressed in the form of social classes. A social class is a stable group which is "more a layer than a group," and which is formed of people who have "chances of similar experience." When vertical mobility from one class to another is stopped by "institutionalized regulations," the result is ranks or classes. Class consciousness is an

[11] *Ibid.*, p. 66.
[12] *Ibid.*, p. 59.
[13] *Ibid.*, p. 61.
[14] *Ibid.*, pp. 109, 110.
[15] *Ibid.*, pp. 103 ff.

awareness of "the similarity of social chances" and "an emotional tie" connected with this intraclass relationship.[16]

An extreme form of integration is monopoly, which "means the limiting of the chances of success prevailing in a given social scope of action to a certain limited number of people."[17] The members of a closed group, such as a monopoly or caste, tend to behave differently from members of an open group. They grow narrow-minded and intolerant and "hostile to anything which does not fit into the framework of their prejudices."[18]

An important integrating activity is cooperation, which arises in part from survival needs and in part from a recognition of advantages to be obtained by it. People may cooperate in order to compete. They may cooperate to fight. However, the priority of cooperation over competition is not recognized by Mannheim.[19]

Cooperation may be "simple collaboration" or may develop an elaborate division of labor, or it may reach "a division of professions." In a division of labor, the activities of one person or group find completion in the work of another person or group. It becomes "the strongest kind of social integration."[20] A division of professions is one of the most specialized types of cooperation.

4. *Competition.* There are forces in society which "compel people to act against one another" as well as to act together. One result is competition, which Mannheim defines as "a kind of a peaceful striving of several individuals or groups for the same good."[21] Competition may be psychological and create inferiority feelings which "make the individual active" or which paralyze him. Free competition can be abused and become "a tool of negative selection." In order to maintain fair play, free competition must "always be accompanied by certain binding rules and accepted standards."[22]

Competition leads to selection, and competition and selection "decide which human types, which standards, which thought patterns will be dominant in a given society."[23] Intensive selection may result in "the segregation of the weak," as in the case of slum dwellers. The segregated group becomes isolated and "unfolds its own mentality."

5. *Other Concepts and Conclusions.* Although social distance, individualization, integration, and competition receive major attention in

---

16 *Ibid.*, pp. 120 ff.
17 *Ibid.*, p. 83.
18 *Ibid.*
19 E. S. Bogardus, *Principles of Cooperation* (Chicago: The Cooperative League, 1958), p. 1.
20 Mannheim, *op. cit.*, pp. 93, 98.
21 *Ibid.*, pp. 76 ff.
22 *Ibid.*, p. 80.
23 *Ibid.*, p. 88.

the *Systematic Sociology*, other concepts are discussed, such as social conflict, social control, and social value. Mannheim contends that class struggles leading to social control by the proletariat are "not inevitable." They are "only a tendency" and "not the only form of transformation of society." There are other factors besides material production that lead to social change, such as increased nationalism and the concentration of people in metropolitan centers.[24] Mannheim does not believe that class struggles are inevitable, for through social reforms and the removal of those agencies that hamper normal evolution, class struggle can be made unnecessary.[25] Class struggle is not "a dogmatic necessity."

Social controls are a representative of authority, having objective expression in customs and laws and personal expression through the ability and prestige of leaders. Leaders are persons who exercise authority because of personality and not because of the office they represent.

Social values are not abstract entities but aspects of social processes and of "the valuating object or of the group for which they are valid."[26] Value is acquired "in the context of a certain activity, through performing a desired function."

Systematic Sociology is organized on the belief that there is a basic unity in the development of society. This unity functions in an all-comprehensive social and cultural process of living together. Had Mannheim lived longer than the age of fifty-four, he doubtless would have made substantial additions to his sociological system, which is unevenly but significantly developed.

---

24 H. L. Vilensky and C. N. Lebeaux, *Industrial Society and Social Welfare* (New York: Russell Sage Foundation, 1958).

25 Mannheim, *op. cit.*, p. 145.

26 *Ibid.*, pp. 131 ff.

SOCIAL PROBLEMS AND WELFARE

WHY MARRIAGES GO WRONG: HAZARDS TO MARRIAGE AND HOW TO OVERCOME THEM. By James H. S. Bossard and Eleanor S. Boll. New York: The Ronald Press Company, 1958, pp. xi+224.

This book was written primarily for the guidance of those about to marry or already married, but the authors are also concerned with the importance of marriage in modern society. Instead of using numerous statistics and citing many references, the authors have drawn on many case histories from their long experience in dealing with this subject. The social pressures that lead to overemphasis on romance, to marriage at an early age, and to the use of marriage to serve individual rather than family ends are emphasized. Americans are the most married people in the world, but also the most divorced, at least insofar as total numbers are concerned. Several countries have had higher divorce rates.

The discussion starts with the emphasis on marriage as a serious business and on the way to understand marital and family problems. Then there are discussions of courtship and dating as preludes to marriage, romance, marrying one's own kind, the best age for marriage, individual rights versus family responsibility, marriage in an open-class system, parenthood, the family as a group; and the final question raised is: "What do we really think about marriage and family life problems?" On the whole, the book is thought-provoking, stimulating, and interesting reading, with many practical aids and suggestions for happy marriage and the avoidance of marital pitfalls. M.H.N.

CHRISTIANITY AND WORLD ISSUES. By T. B. Maston. New York: The Macmillan Company, 1957, pp. ix+374.

This might be called a book in applied sociology, although the author doubtless would prefer to call it "a work in applied Christian ethics." It is comprehensive in scope, dealing with the family and its future; races and racial tensions; economic life and problems; the sources, programs, strengths, and weaknesses of communism; the church and state; war and the Christian conscience; the world in crisis; and the relation of Christianity to world transformation.

The book is well documented, and the pros and cons of various solutions to problems are presented; the acquaintance with religious, economic, and sociological viewpoints is extensive. The discussions are intended for the use of teachers, preachers, and church workers in general. The tone is fair-minded and constructive. A.R.R.

THE GUILTY AND THE INNOCENT. By William Bixley. New York: Philosophical Library, Inc., 1957, pp. 176.

William Bixley was for fifty years a supervisory official of the Central Criminal Court of London, better known as the "Old Bailey." An account of the history of this criminal court from the time of the Romans, remarks about famous trials, and the author's personal observations of trials comprise the contents of his book, *The Guilty and the Innocent.* The material, sufficiently startling in itself, permits his succinct style.

Mr. Bixley's stories include a recounting of a variety of types of crimes committed, but he himself seems unsure of the reasons which bring men to commit the crimes. He presents the facts of the cases, is assured that justice is done in court, but he stops there. Any reasoning as to why or how, or what can be done to rehabilitate the criminal, is only brief and vague. He makes only a short observation about the change he has seen in the men and women who have passed through the courts. "When I first went to work there was a very definite criminal class. . . . Today, even in proportion to the increase in population crime is not much more serious than it used to be, but the criminal is part of every class in society" (pp. 172-73).

One of the eleven chapters is devoted to a history of the "Old Bailey." This is followed by nine chapters describing some of the famous cases and trials in its history, and a brief concluding chapter. This short volume is interesting and easy reading, but for more than background material and the subjective observations of one man, the sociologist will have to look elsewhere.

HENRY L. MANNHEIM
Arizona State College

SOCIAL WORK IN THE AMERICAN TRADITION. By Nathan E. Cohen. New York: The Dryden Press, 1958, pp. x+404.

The purpose of this book is to aid in the integration of the objectives, principles, services, and method of social work through a historical analysis of the development of social work in the United States in six periods of time from colonial days to the present. The analysis deals with American history in terms of "internal" and "external" factors. "Internal factors" refer to the social, economic, political, and scientific climate of the period.

Over the years social work found a methodology and a two-pronged approach growing out of two types of humanitarian influences, the giving of charity and the reshaping of the environment. The two-pronged approach included a concern for the adjustment and development of the individual toward more "satisfying human relations" and for the "improving of the social institutions" within which the individual functions. Thus social work is concerned with the individual, the social institutions within which he functions, and the relationship between these two factors. The three primary methods for accomplishing these objectives are casework, group work, and community organization. Basic to all three methods are the understanding and the use of the "relationship." The development of social work theory, the evolution of the principles of social work, the practice of it, and its goals are well presented in this book.

WOODROW W. SCOTT
George Pepperdine College

HANDBOOK OF CO-ED TEEN ACTIVITIES. By Edythe and David DeMarche. New York: Association Press, 1958, pp. xxv+640.

As the title indicates, the major portion of the book deals with material for teen-age recreation activities at home and anywhere teen-agers may gather. The book is replete with practical suggestions and descriptions for leading activities in a wide variety of fields, including parties, dances, sports and games, beach and pool fun, music, reading, traveling, and hobbies. Six full chapters are crammed with "fun-how" on giving memorable parties. More than a thousand things to do during leisure are described. This is an invaluable book for parents and adult leaders, but the authors stress that teen-agers should be left largely to do their own planning. Material is also included to help adults to understand the adolescent group as well as to assist young people to enjoy socially maturing good times together. Nineteen pages of bibliographical material are included to assist those who desire to explore further the different types of teen-age activities.

M.H.N.

THE OLDER WORKER IN INDUSTRY. A Study of the Attitudes of Industrial Workers toward Aging and Retirement. By G. Hamilton Crook and Martin Heinstein. Berkeley: Institute of Industrial Relations, University of California, 1958, pp. vi+143.

With the set of procedures employed by the investigators and appearing in the several appendices, this study of the attitudes of industrial workers toward aging and retirement is valuable for indicating the necessity of developing some sound measures for testing and measuring physiological age as compared with chronological age. The sample survey included 846 industrial workers in the San Francisco and Los

Angeles areas during 1952-54. It embraced a comparison between a group averaging 35-40 years of age and one averaging 55-60, with about one third of the older group being 60 or more. Both male and female workers were included, although the males outnumbered the females. These came from twenty-seven different industrial firms. Are older people physically and mentally slow? Are they accident prone? Are they self-centered and demanding? The study aimed to test the credibility of these questions and to ascertain what the workers thought about aging and retirement and whether or not they had made adequate preparations for retiring.

Some findings are as follows: (1) Older workers display a reasonable degree of confidence toward the process of aging. (2) The closer the approach to retirement, the less workers want to think about it. (3) Older workers generally are less inclined to favor compulsory retirement. (4) Some of the older workers have continued to turn in high work performance ratings, suggesting perhaps that those who continue to work after 65 are in better health than those who have left the labor force. The findings have implications for the necessity of a review of retirement policies. M.J.V.

JUVENILE DELINQUENCY. Edited by Joseph S. Roucek. New York: Philosophical Library, Inc., 1958, pp. xiv+370.

A flood of publications has appeared during recent years dealing with the problem of juvenile delinquency. The need for a systematic analysis of the widely scattered material has been recognized for a long while. Attempts have been made to systematize divergent yet related views and approaches to the subject. The present work represents a survey of the various phases of the subject by fourteen writers in the field.

The dimensions of the problem are indicated by a discussion of the diverse definitions of delinquency and the estimates of the extent of the problem in the United States as compared with selected countries of Europe and Asia. Special consideration is given to the legal aspects of juvenile delinquency. Proposals are presented for legal reform in delinquency legislation.

The major part of the book is devoted to discussions of "the search for causes." The biological, psychiatric, and sociological approaches are described and compared; and special chapters deal with the educational, economic, and mass media aspects of the subject. These are chiefly critiques of the various theories, approaches, and the major findings. Even though certain generalizations may be made on the basis of the current state of knowledge, as is done in the various articles on causation, it is apparent that no systematic and definitive statement of basic causes of juvenile delinquency is possible. The specialized studies have contributed important information, but the findings of the various types of studies and approaches are not sufficiently integrated to make a comprehensive analysis possible. The need for a more definitive typology has been recognized for some time. The concept "juvenile delinquency" as generally described includes such heterogeneous behavior patterns that adequate theories of delinquency causation can hardly be developed empirically. The subgroups of delinquents need to be differentiated and studied objectively.

The final section deals with international trends in juvenile delinquency, indicating that youth problems are to be found around the world. The publications of the United Nations have indicated world trends. M.H.N.

SLAVERY. By C. W. W. Grenidge. New York: The Macmillan Company, 1958, pp. 235.

It will surprise many of the readers of this book to learn about the large amount of slavery that still exists in the world. Among the different forms are chattel slavery, slave trading, debt-bondage, peonage, sale of women into marriage, and slavelike adoption of children. The antislavery movement is reviewed, the work of the Anti-Slavery Society in England is described, the actions of the United Nations and of the League of Nations are canvassed, and a concluding chapter deals with "What Remains to Be Done." The total discussion is set within the concept of personal freedom. The important sociopsychical effects of slavery upon the subjects are not taken up in this factual and historical treatise. E.S.B.

HAWTHORNE REVISITED. *Management and the Worker*, Its Critics, and Developments in Human Relations in Industry. By Henry A. Landsberger. Ithaca, New York: Cornell University, 1958, pp. x+119.

In this summary and analysis of *Management and the Worker* and of its proponents and critics the stated purposes are: first, to show that many of the criticisms leveled against Elton Mayo do not apply to *Management and the Worker*; second, to review briefly the contents of the book. The author points out the following misconceptions: (1) that the counseling program was a minor part of the Hawthorne Studies, (2) that the authors explicitly place no faith in the efficacy of training supervisors in human relations skills, (3) that the authors explicitly state that managers as well as workers are moved by sentiments, (4) that neither group is thought of as irrational because they have sentiments, and (5) that the prime motive for the formation of the bank wiring group was the desire of the group to resist change.

The review of *Management and the Worker* states that Roethlisberger and Dickson did present data that stimulated many specialists to make further studies and focused on (a) the effect of the situation on individual attitudes and (b) the effect of attitudes on subsequent individual behavior. The positive effects of this book, according to Landsberger, were (1) showing that empirical research within industry and organizations in general was possible, (2) broadening and changing the subdiscipline of industrial psychology, and (3) touching upon most of the problem areas into which the field of human relations is now entering. Any person interested in industrial sociology will gain considerable information about the Hawthorne Studies by carefully considering the analysis made by the author.

WOODROW W. SCOTT
George Pepperdine College

SUCCESS IN MARRIAGE: HOW TO MAKE THE MOST OF YOUR MARRIAGE. By David R. Mace. Nashville, Tennessee: Abingdon Press, 1958, pp. xx+158.

As the title indicates, this book is intended as a practical guide to successful marriage. The material is divided into four parts. Young people who are looking toward marriage should consider the five basic principles of choosing, preparing, adjusting, sharing, and maturing. Many married couples face no serious problems, but others may be confronted with problems pertaining to sex, money, work, in-laws, and parenthood. There are also difficult partners to live with, such as the "frigid" wife, the silent husband, the nagging wife, the unfaithful husband, and the aging wife. Jealousy, religious differences, wandering affection, childlessness, and gradual drifting apart may cause perplexing problems.

In discussing the principles and problems, the author presents excerpts from cases drawn from his long years of experience as a marriage counselor. Few sources are given and the discussions of the various topics are brief and concise. The major objective is to discuss the problems of almost every married couple, not only of those with serious difficulties, and to provide practical helps in dealing with those problems.

M.H.N.

STATISTICS OF FARMER COOPERATIVES, 1955-56. By Anne L. Gessner. Washington, D.C.: Farmer Cooperative Service, U.S. Department of Agriculture, 1958, pp. 73.

In this report it is stated that the members in the farmer cooperatives in the United States, according to the latest survey, have reached a grand total of 7,730,000, and the number continues to increase. The total gross volume of business done by them in 1955-56 exceeded twelve billion dollars. The number of farmer cooperatives remains about the same, but the average size of the cooperative societies has increased from 250 in 1926 to 783 in 1956. Minnesota and Wisconsin occupy first and second places, respectively, in the number of cooperatives. The farm products that utilize cooperative methods are headed by grain and followed by dairy products, cotton, livestock, and poultry products, in that order. It would seem that farmers are finding cooperatives an outstanding method for safeguarding free enterprise. E.S.B.

THE PRISON COMMUNITY. By Donald Clemmer. New York: Rinehart and Company, Inc., 1958, pp. xii+341.

Even though this book is a reissue of the one originally published in 1940, the descriptive and analytical material has pertinence for the understanding of prison life today. In analyzing the structure and relationships of prison life, the writer is concerned with social processes rather than with matters of administration and management. The discussions deal with the composition of the prison population, the organization of the penitentiary, the social groups and relationships within the prison, leadership and social control aspects, rules and the dominant group, leisure and recreation, sexual patterns, social significance of labor, and the way the prison culture tends to determine personal attitudes. The author had no special hypotheses to test and from the methodological standpoint the study has shortcomings; but as a description of prison culture, based on many years of experience as a worker in prisons, the book not only is interesting but represents a valuable contribution to our knowledge of prison life. M.H.N.

PEOPLES AND CULTURE

FRENCH WEST AFRICA. By Virginia Thomson and Richard Adloff. Stanford: Stanford University Press, 1958, pp. 626.

This is virtually a handbook on many phases of life in French West Africa—political, economic, rural and urban, industry and labor, social and religious—and gives important insight into the problems of the natives.

STRIDE TOWARD FREEDOM, THE MONTGOMERY STORY. By Martin Luther King, Jr. New York: Harper and Brothers, 1958, pp. 235.

Like the famous Martin Luther of the sixteenth century days who was drawn into a momentous protest against certain injustices of his day, the author of this book was drawn into a deep-seated protest against certain injustices of a modern day. His description of a local protest movement, of which he was the courageous and the most important leader, is strikingly effective, and is bound to have world-wide repercussions wherever there are people who have suffered from unfair treatment at the hands of their fellows.

The book is more than the account of a protest movement and more than an autobiographical account of a relatively young man who, because of heroic leadership of his people in one local community, has suddenly become a world figure. It tells how one who had studied the works of Borden P. Bowne, Hegel, Jeremy Bentham, Thomas Hobbes, John Locke, Reinhold Niebuhr, Nietzsche, Rousseau, and Alfred Whitehead had accepted some of the teachings of each of these profound scholars and also had rejected some of the ideas of each one. Stage by stage he was pulled into a concrete practical situation full of political, social, legal problems, and therein demonstrated his deep Christian faith with reference to holding fast, despite desperate threats against his life, to the principle of nonviolent resistance. Gandhi could not have asked more of Martin Luther King, Jr., than the latter has done. If anyone is in doubt about what nonviolent resistance can do when personified by thousands of people laboring under a sense of injustice to the point where "they can take no more," let him read this book. Here is described a nonviolent resistance that actively resisted in terms of Christian love, without answering violence with violence or hatred with hatred.

E.S.B.

THE CHANGING SOCIAL STRUCTURE OF ENGLAND AND WALES: 1871-1951. By David C. Marsh. New York: The Humanities Press, 1958, pp. xiv+266.

This book provides a cautious quantitative description of changes in the composition, distribution, and differentiation of the population of England and Wales between 1871 and 1951. Basing his material primarily on decennial census data, the author describes variations in growth of population; in urban-rural population distribution; in family size and structure; in geographical, industrial, and occupational population distribution; in associational membership (trade unions, cooperatives, political parties, and religious organizations); in the distribution of wealth (income and property); and in patterns of social problems (morbidity, mortality, crime, and punishment).

The author is well versed in the limits and possibilities of his source material. He has set for himself the limited and useful task of describing some rather fundamental trends. Hence, while no attempt is made to relate or explain these trends, and facts are often left "to speak for themselves," the book does provide an excellent chronicle of apparently significant social changes. In addition, it is an adequate and authoritative guide to the primary sources of social statistics of England and Wales.

D.C.M.

DESEGREGATION: RESISTANCE AND READINESS. By Melvin M. Tumin. With Eleven Graduate Assistants. Princeton: Princeton University Press, 1958, pp. xvii+270.

This study began as "an education venture" of training graduate students "in methods of research in the social sciences" but ended in "a systematic analysis of attitudes toward Negroes and toward desegregation of the public schools." The study was made by choosing by the random sampling method 287 adult white residents of Guilford County, North Carolina. The experiments were conducted so as to find out how differences in education affect attitudes toward Negroes, how occupational status and mobility affect such attitudes, and how exposure to mass media influence these attitudes. Two types of portraits are drawn, one "of the kind of person who is most ready for desegregation and the other of those who are most resistant."

Space does not permit a presentation of all the interesting experimental designs that were developed and used. An unusual definition of readiness for desegregation is given, namely, "to be unwilling to resist the Supreme Court order to desegregate." Resistance to desegregation is explained as "to be willing to do any or several things to prevent desegregation, ranging from amending the United States Constitution to the use of force, if necessary."

Among the findings are these: (1) "A combination of high status, high income, high education, and high exposure" to mass media is "powerful" in its "influence on readiness for desegregation and in the development of a more favorable image of the Negro." (2) Readiness for desegregation is found in people having "the widest perspective on themselves and their communities, and the deepest sense of stake in the community-in-process." This study was carefully conducted and caution is expressed regarding the findings. Similar studies in other communities are needed as bases for comparison. E.S.B.

GAMES OF THE ORIENT: KOREA, CHINA, JAPAN. By Stuart Chapin. Rutland, Vermont, and Tokyo, Japan: Charles E. Tuttle Company, 1958, pp. 177.

A book first published in 1895, this volume is enlarged and covers Oriental counterparts of American games as well as various "quaint and imaginative" games of the Eastern world. The book is extensively illustrated by 135 "figures in text" and 22 Korean plates.

NEITHER BLACK NOR WHITE. By Wilma Dykeman and James Stokely. New York: Rinehart & Company, 1958, pp. 371.

In this book a married couple report on what would seem to be journeys into nearly every community in the Southern states. They are Southerners who have had widespread success in gathering firsthand reports and comments on how people in all walks of life and of all descriptions, both white and colored, feel about race relations. The interview materials are very extensive but admit of generalization only with a great deal of caution. The authors refrain from stating forthright conclusions but leave their interview types of source materials to speak for themselves.

The interview data seem to suggest a number of observations, as follows: (1) There is an increasing lack of free communication between whites and colored people. (2) It is better to talk about doing away with discrimination in schools than about integration. (3) To the whites integration means mixing the races, and mixing the races suggests miscegenation. (4) It is difficult for white people in the South today to take a moderate position regarding desegregation; it is difficult to discuss race relations even with one's friends. (5) A white person who publicly favors integration is *persona non grata.* If in business, he loses trade; and if in a profession, he will lose clients and experience social ostracism. (6) It is easiest to integrate where about 10 to 15 per cent of the population are colored and hardest where they predominate, or where there are few Negroes. (7) Certain white sections of the South are being coerced into social relationships that they do not want. (8) Negroes who are better educated and better trained in labor skills are migrating from the South, leaving the South with a weakened labor force and with a surplus of lower-class colored people. (9) Negroes who fought for our country on foreign soil during World War II and in Korea want to know how long it will be before they will have civil rights at home. (10) White people who are not extremists for or against integration are largely nonvocal. (11) Negroes who become "belligerent" or "upstage" hinder their cause. (12) Dollars are not segregated. Because of the present racial conflict, there is a slowdown in industry, and new industry and money are slow about moving into conflict regions. These are but a few of the generalizations which are suggested by the interviews that are reported in this book. E.S.B.

THE OLDER POPULATION OF THE UNITED STATES. A Volume in the Census Monograph Series. By Henry D. Sheldon and Clark Tibbitts. New York: John Wiley & Sons, Inc., 1958, pp. xiii+223.

There is a wealth of information in the United States Census Reports, but few persons have time or skill to dig it out. The Social Research Council, in close cooperation with the Bureau of the Census, is now providing interpretation of these abstract statistics through a series of monographs related to particular fields of interest, by specialists in those fields. This book is the fifth such monograph. Dr. Sheldon, a former professor of sociology now chief of Demographic Statistics of the Bureau, has written the core of the book, with aid in applying the data to the problems of the aged by Clark Tibbitts of the United States Department of Health, Education, and Welfare.

Drawing upon census data, the authors portray the growth of the problem of the aged through extension of the life span, and the increase in both numbers and proportion of those 65 years and older. They show the parts played by epochs of diminishing human fertility such as the depression, followed by an increased rate of reproduction in the decade of World War II. The ebb and flow of immigration are considered. The marked geographic differences are discussed, such as the concentration of the aged in Florida and in some of the older suburbs of California. Much attention is given to the diminishing participation of the aged in the labor force and the relation of age to employment in different occupations. The shifting mores of family living, with the breakup of the large family into small independent units and the relation of these facts to housing, income, and living conditions, are discussed.

It is regrettable, since much of the information is based upon records up to 1950, that the monograph could not have been published sooner. The authors have made up for this lack in part by frequently quoting recent studies by other agencies. An excellent appendix presents additional statistics relating to the respective chapters of the book.

JOHN B. GRIFFING
American International Association

MIGRATION AND ECONOMIC DEVELOPMENT IN RHODE ISLAND. By Kurt B. Mayer and Sidney Goldstein. Providence, Rhode Island: Brown University Press, 1958, pp. 64.

Migration statistics are presented in order to "contribute to our understanding of the interrelations between the changes of Rhode Island's population, its social structure, and its economic growth."

EAST TO WEST. By Arnold J. Toynbee. New York: Oxford University Press, 1958, pp. xii+243.

This book contains the weekly articles that the author wrote for *The Observer* regarding his observations on "a journey round the world" from April 28, 1956, to August 3, 1957. He notes that for this seventeen months trip he gave a year and a half to planning the details. The journey included the land of the Incas, New Zealand and Australia, the Philippines, Japan, and various countries on the Asian continent.

A large share of the observations involves, first, geographic descriptions and then, more extensively, historical references to the vast range of conflict and struggle of peoples, such as those of India, Assyria, Iran, Palestine, Saudi Arabia. He tried to avoid the capital cities of countries and sought out the rural communities, for "even today, the countryside still remains the real world," and "every capital city is more or less unrepresentative." Modernization "standardizes urban life on Western lines." It is these offhand observations that give this book its charm.

E.S.B.

MADE IN ICELAND. By Grace Blaisdell Golden. New York: Alfred A. Knopf, 1958, pp. vii+165.

In this Borzoi book "for young people" the author has done an artistic piece of writing about the life of the people of Iceland, with their intriguing history of over a thousand years. She tells how these people, inhabiting an island of volcanic origin close to the Arctic Circle, have built up a modern civilization with some accomplishments surpassing those of larger and better known countries.

After describing briefly such aspects of Icelandic life as their sagas, their New World explorations, their parliamentary government, their farming and fishing, the author specializes in Icelandic wood carving, goldsmithing, weaving, and needle arts. Her appreciation of Iceland is summed up in the justly deserved evaluation: "Today Iceland occupies a strategic spot on the map and bids fair to become a very important member of the world's family of nations." E.S.B.

SOCIAL THEORY AND RESEARCH

EDUCATION IN SOCIETY: READINGS. By Bernard N. Meltzer, Harry R. Doby, and Philip M. Smith. New York: Thomas Y. Crowell Company, 1958, pp. v+495.

This book of readings includes selections from a wide variety of authors in sociology, education, and related fields. The book is divided into ten parts, each dealing with various aspects of a certain area of educational sociology. Various authors define educational sociology and outline its scope and perspective. They discuss the cultural setting of education and the problems that arise because of cultural change. In indicating the significance of the school as an agency of socialization and social control, they point to the dangers involved in restrictions upon academic freedom and the effect of political control of textbooks and teachers. Other selections examine the relationships that exist between the school and the community, the role of the teacher in the community, and the class structure in the school. Attention is directed to the social factors in the learning process, such as social climate in the classroom, types of teaching approaches, and classroom discipline.

The book closes with a section dealing with controversial issues that plague the educational world: the "progressive education" issue, desegregation, religious instruction in the public schools, and the current educational crisis. CECIL EVVA LARSEN

THE PSYCHOLOGY OF INTERPERSONAL RELATIONS. By Fritz Heider. New York: John Wiley & Sons, Inc., 1958, pp. ix+322.

Is there a system hidden in our thinking about interpersonal relations, and can this system be uncovered? Professor Heider does his best to answer these questions in the affirmative by offering "suggestions for the construction of a language that will allow" the representation "of a great number of interpersonal relations, discriminated by conventional language in such way that their place in a general system will become clearer." These suggestions may be utilized in building a "conceptual framework suitable to some of the problems" in the field. As he uses the term "interpersonal relations," it refers to the relations between a few, usually two, persons, and his discussions center on the person as the basic unit of the investigation dealing with that person "represented as standing in relation to and interacting with another person." Holding that common sense contains much psychological theory, Heider begins with simple illustrations of the behavior of two interacting persons in his "arrival at a description of the implicit theoretical models of perception, action, motivation, sentiments, and norms." By focusing attention on an analysis of interpersonal behavior in terms of some of the basic elements involved, the book offers some good materials for a better understanding of such behavior and provides "work notes towards a pretheory of interpersonal relations." These work notes at least may provide good stimuli for testing the worthiness of the author's construction of constant symbolic notations with which to make a scientific assessment of interpersonal relations. M.J.V.

THE SOCIOLOGY OF RELIGION. By Thomas Ford Hoult. New York: The Dryden Press, 1958, pp. xii+436.

Among recently published books on the sociology of religion, this one offers a structure and scope which may prove useful for the guidance and organization of courses offered in colleges. The book is essentially an extended outline of a sociological approach to the study of religion. The four major parts of the text may be indicated as follows: I, Basic Theoretical Considerations; II, Religion as a Social Institution; III, Religion and Other Major Social Institutions—including the family, political, economic, stratification systems, education, and science as institutions; and IV, Summary and Conclusions. An appendix features brief historical surveys of religions of the world, viz., Hinduism, Jainism, Buddhism, Taoism, Confucianism, Shintoism, Zoroastrianism, Judaism, Christianity, and Mohammedanism. J.E.N.

CLUES TO SUICIDE. Edited by Edwin S. Shneidman and Norman L. Farberow. Foreword by Karl A. Menninger. New York: McGraw-Hill Book Company, Inc., 1957, pp. xii+227.

This book, which is an outgrowth of a Western Psychological Association symposium on the psychology of suicide, is divided into two parts. The first consists of nine papers which briefly summarize current theories and researches on suicidal behavior. The emphasis here, as might be expected, is psychological, with the ideas of Freud, Menninger, and Zilboorg receiving major attention. Yet the effort is not a parochial one. The writers are cognizant of other points of view, and three of the papers are specifically devoted to nonpsychological factors in suicide. Henry and Short provide a synopsis of their theoretical position that suicide is the consequence of frustrations immanent in the status system. An interesting social-psychological analysis of the relationship between suicide and Catholicism is made by Ferracuti, an Italian doctor; Helen Silving, a professor of law, explores the often overlooked legal implications of suicidal behavior. The nine papers in the second part of the book deal with clinical considerations involved in treating the suicidal person. While this section may appear to be outside the realm of sociology, it should not be ignored by the sociological audience. Here are found some interesting case materials and some very frank and provocative comments by the practitioners concerning the difficulties they encounter in communicating with this type of patient (i.e., effectively taking the attitude of the suicidal person). Despite many weaknesses, this is a book which will serve as a useful and readable reference for sociological students of deviant behavior.

ROBERT ELLIS
Stanford University

THE STUDY OF LEADERSHIP. Edited by C. G. Browne and Thomas S. Cahn. Danville, Illinois: The Interstate Printers and Publishers, Inc., 1958, pp. xi+487.

In this volume two psychologists have joined their efforts in producing an interesting and important book of readings on the subject of leadership. This has been a long-neglected field, as far as an appropriate and convenient set of readings is concerned. A total of 51 carefully selected and happily abridged readings are assembled under headings such as approaches to leadership, the trait-situation orientation, observation and participant evaluation methods, leadership criteria, social perception and personality dynamics of leaders, behavior of leaders, leaders and followers, and training of leaders. Well-known contributors include Ralph

M. Stogdill, Helen M. Jennings, Raymond B. Cattell, Theodore Newcomb, Kurt Lewin, Ronald Lippitt, Carroll L. Shartle, and F. J. Roethlisberger.

The selections cut across a number of areas of leadership, and the materials are drawn from both psychologists and sociologists. Leadership is not looked upon as "a set of attributes, but rather as a group of variables describing interactions among group members." The publisher and the editors have produced a commendable document. E.S.B.

SOCIOLOGICAL THEORY. A Book of Readings. Edited by Lewis A. Coser and Bernard Rosenberg. New York: The Macmillan Company, 1957, pp. xiii+578.

Characterized by an excellent selection of readings pertaining to various aspects of sociological theory, this book focuses attention upon a series of concepts which have been utilized in the field of sociology to account for uniformities of behavior. Fortunately, the editors have had in mind through their selectivity of concepts ("the variables between which empirical relationships are to be sought"), and the included discussions about them, the empirical investigations which have been induced or suggested for the future. Thus, they have pursued, as it were, "lines of investigation programmatically stated by the founders of our science." Specific comment may be made here on the introductory chapter, "Definition of the Field,"—definitely a superior exposition.

The readings are arranged under three major headings: General Concepts, Self-Other Concepts, and Structural Concepts. Under the first are placed readings dealing with culture, interaction, social control, power and authority, and cohesion and conflict. These selections are gleaned from such writers as Tylor, Malinowski, Kluckhohn, Simmel, Weber, Marx, and Durkheim. The second heading displays such writers as Thomas, Znaniecki, MacIver, and Mead, who devote themselves to the social situation, groups, and role-taking. The structural group concepts include among others the primary group, status, class, structure and function, and the sociology of knowledge. Some of these readings have been culled from Faris, Shils, Merton, and Hughes. The readings have been formally introduced with lucid explanations for orientation. The book as a whole is meritorious and built upon the idea that "theory is an indispensable part of the scientific enterprise." Furthermore, it is one which could be placed with great profit in the hands of those engaging in social research. M.J.V.

STATISTICAL ABSTRACT OF THE UNITED STATES, 1958. 79th Annual Edition. Prepared under the direction of Edwin D. Goldfield, Chief, Statistical Reports Division. Washington, D.C.: Bureau of the Census, United States Department of Commerce, 1958, pp. xxxiv+1040.

The *Statistical Abstract* has been published since 1878 and is a standard summary of statistics on the social, economic, and political organization of the United States. It serves as a convenient volume for statistical reference and as a guide to other statistical publications and sources. The current volume has 1,197 tables and 42 charts. A 44-page alphabetical subject index and a 40-page bibliography of sources of statistical data enhance its usefulness. More than 60 tables are new. They include such subjects as recreational activities, research and development in the natural sciences, homicides and suicides, child adoption, and the contribution of the United States to international organizations.

Over a half million facts are recorded in concise form. Of special interest to sociologists are the sections on population, vital statistics, immigration and emigration, education, law enforcement, parks and recreation, labor force and employment, income and expenditures, social insurance and welfare services, communications, housing, and comparative international statistics. Governmental and economic data have wide applications.

The population of the United States continues to grow, having reached an estimated total of 170,562,000 by March 1, 1958. From 1940 to 1957 the population pyramid has changed considerably, with a wider base (age brackets to age 15), slight losses in the age group 15-24, and some gains in all other age brackets. The total births for 1957 reached an all-time high of 4,254,000 (a total of 4,301,000, if births are adjusted for underregistration) and the rate was 25.0 per 1,000 population. But the number of deaths increased by 71,524 over 1956, reaching a total of 1,636,000 and a rate of 9.6 per 1,000. Marriages declined slightly, but divorces increased slightly, after an almost continuous decline since 1946. The total divorces for 1957 was 382,000 as compared with 377,000 in 1956. The number of physicians, dentists, and nurses increased steadily, as did health services. The school enrollment, ages 5 to 34, reached a total of 41,166,000, an increase of nearly eleven million since 1950. The crime rate increased, with a total of 2,796,400 major crimes known to the police, according to the Uniform Crime Reports of the Federal Bureau of Investigation. On the other hand, recreation facilities and participation in recreation activities are steadily on the increase. For instance, visitors to areas administered by the National Park Service totaled 68,016,000 in 1957, nearly twice the number of visitors in 1950 and ten times the number of visitors in 1943. Over 60,957,000 persons visited areas administered by National Forest Service. These are only a few of the numerous types of data contained in the 1958 edition of the *Statistical Abstract*. M.H.N.

THE SEIZURE OF POLITICAL POWER IN A CENTURY OF REVOLUTIONS. By Feliks Gross. New York: Philosophical Library, 1958, pp. xxx+398.

Two types of violent transfer of power are discussed in this study: revolution from above and revolution from below. Revolution from above is a seizure of power by a group of armed men, at the very top of the social structure, while revolution from the bottom is largely the result of social disorganization, unrest, and of class struggle. The Russian Revolution of 1905 and 1917 and the French Revolution of 1848 were revolutions from below. The Latin-American revolutions are typical of revolution from above.

The focus of this study is on the pattern of actions and the major types of revolution. Attention is concentrated on the Russian revolutionary movement, though the empirical case studies cover coups and revolutions in Latin America, Egypt, China, Italy, Germany, France, and other countries. J.E.N.

SOCIALISM AND SAINT-SIMON. By Emile Durkheim. Edited by Alvin W. Gouldner and translated by Charlotte Sattler. Yellow Springs: Antioch Press, 1958, pp. xxix+240.

The editor points out the importance of considering the historical antecedents of present-day thinking; otherwise, we may get an exaggerated impression of current thought, and we may be setting an example for future writers to ignore what we of the present day may be contributing to social thought.

The editor indicates how Durkheim followed in the footsteps of August Comte and yet disagreed with him at certain important points. For example, Comte emphasized social consensus, while Durkheim held that too much social cohesion will lead to disorganization and hinder progress. In other words, the *status quo* can be stifling.

Durkheim responded to the theories of Saint-Simon by developing an extensive analysis of socialism as given in this book. As Marcel Mauss states in the "Introduction to the First Edition," Durkheim considered socialism from "a purely scientific point of view," that is, "without prejudice and without taking sides." He never became a socialist and reacted against "certain features of this movement: its violent nature, its class character," and its "political and even politician-like tone." He desired change not for one part of society but for "the benefit of the whole of society." The book contributes to a better understanding, not only of Durkheim, but also of Comte and Saint-Simon, and leaves the reader free "to cut and choose" as he pleases. E.S.B.

METHODS OF RESEARCH IN THE BEHAVIORAL SCIENCES. By Thomas C. McCormick and Roy G. Francis. New York: Harper and Brothers, 1958, pp. xii+244.

Often graduate students in sociology when undertaking their first serious researches feel the need for friendly counsel on some of the methodological aspects of their projects. At the same time, jealously aware of their maturing abilities, they may be reluctant to reveal to their professors through questions just how much they have failed to learn in their courses. This book, *Methods of Research in the Behavioral Sciences,* should go a long way toward meeting the needs of most sociology students for such methodological counsel.

Methods of Research in the Behavioral Sciences is not a handbook of social research nor is it a dictionary of statistical techniques. Rather, it is a brief review of the most commonly encountered methodological considerations in social research, rounded out with learned commentaries and suggested sources of further information. The plan of the book approximates the order in which the student becomes aware of the problems involved. A brief chapter on the theoretical aspects of research is followed by chapters on choosing a problem, designing a study, and using the library and personal documents. Four more chapters then discuss measurement, surveys, sampling, tabulations, and tests. A final chapter discusses the preparation of a report and the possibilities of its publication.

It should be noted that the title of the book somewhat overstates its case. Anthropologists and psychologists will not find much methodology in the book that is not clearly *sociological* or at the most *social research.* Nevertheless, the book should prove invaluable not only to graduate students of sociology but also to all those social science students who need a review of methodology in order to appreciate more fully the methods and statistics reflected in current journal articles.

JOHN F. CROWTHER
Compton College

HUMAN POTENTIALITIES. By Gardner Murphy. New York: Basic Books, Inc., 1958, pp. x+340.

Over one hundred years ago, August Comte attempted to reveal to man his power to control, through scientific knowledge, the paths to a well-being of all societies. In this book, psychologist Gardner Murphy essays a similar task but with a wealth of far more knowledge about man's scientific achievements than it was possible for Comte to entertain. In short, the task is simply worded as follows: revealing how "thoughtful men and women define the various kinds of future societies and the various kinds of individual lives which are realistically possible, and make conscious and voluntary choices," for the purpose of supreme realization of themselves as social human beings.

Despite the crises of the present—social, economic, political—in which men find themselves, and which are loaded with hundreds of uncertainties, the point is made that the discovery "of our own identity, belief in ourselves and in the use of the intellectual weapons of a democratic society—a science-minded and technology-minded society—can strengthen those moral, intellectual, and social devices without which, in a world such as this, there is no strength at all." Is there any chance for discovering "especially through the ways of science and the intellectual children of science, a new kind of human living?" For answer, the author begins to examine and analyze three kinds of human nature, the first, "a rich amalgam of instinctual drive, effort to understand, and general learning ability," the second, "organized around symbols and values" capable of being shared over regions of space and time, and the third, that which involves a spirit of intellectual adventure, a living curiosity culminating in a demand for and a discovery of man's greatest potentialities.

Three parts of the book are occupied with excellent elaborations of these three kinds of human nature, while the fourth part discusses self-directed change. The book concludes with the general subject, "Man and World," and ends with a fine essay on the human natures of the future. Daring to end on an optimistic note, Murphy avers that "if we cannot make rapid gains in the control of conflict, there will be no human future," but if we can, "the future extension of scientific and esthetic interest, together with the evolution of greater capacity for satisfaction in relations between people. . . will define a widening theater for the development of new potentialities." Summary: challenging, stimulating, enriching. M.J.V.

DIE SKEPTISCHE GENERATION. Eine Soziologie der deutschen Jugend. By Helmut Schelsky. Duesseldorf, Germany: Eugen Diederichs Verlag, 1958, pp. 523.

One of Germany's foremost sociologists of the younger generation writes an analysis of German youth in encyclopedic length and depth. According to Schelsky, there are many sociological *Schichten* (layers) of the youth problem, such as the meaning of youth for society and the meaning of society for youth. He describes between these two "social horizons." It seems that Schelsky develops the theme of the "skeptical" youth from the interrelationship of today's *Jugendbewegung* (Youth Organization), the youth's political subdivisions of political parties, and the *zeitgeschichtlichen Phasen einer Verhaltensgestalt der deutschen Jugend* (contemporary phases of behaviorism of German youth). While the first part of the book is devoted to theory of the interrelationship between youth and society in general, the second and third parts deal with environmental and social "forces" imposed on, or imposed by, youth in Germany. Today's role of youth in the family, its authority, tension, and *Ersatz*, the role of youth on the labor market including apprenticeship, and *Wander- und Meisterjahre* (years of wandering and mastery of skill), sex differences and discriminations on the job, recreation and sociability are discussed. The book closes with fascinating descriptions of, and comparisons with, pre-World War II conditions of youth's attitudes toward politics, morals and morale, youth organizations, education, religion, and the state. The volume, all told, aims to present the *Uebergang* (transition) of youth from one era to another and youth's skepticism toward all and "old" ideologies. HANS A. ILLING

FREE SOCIETY AND MORAL CRISIS. By Robert Cooley Angell. Ann Arbor: The University of Michigan Press, 1958, pp. ix+252.

This essay deals with moral and social integration in a free society. Among the problems of a technical society such as ours, emphasis is placed on the hazards to which disintegrated sections of its cities expose the life of youth. It becomes apparent that the pluralism of our culture prevents the simple integration of individual life which more homogeneous societies achieve. A characteristic of the author's analysis is his emphasis on moralization in preference to socialization as fundamental in the diagnosis of individual and group deviants or delinquents, and achieving for them social and moral integration. J.E.N.

THE ROLE OF THE SOCIAL SCIENCES IN DESEGREGATION: A SYMPOSIUM. New York: Anti-Defamation League of B'nai B'rith, 1958, pp. 48.

This collection of papers is full of meaty suggestions. Martin Deutsch writes on "Some Perspectives on Desegregation Research"; Setsuko Matsunaga Nishi, on "Some Problems and Prospects for Research on the Function of Churches and Religion in the Desegregation Issue"; Robert T. Bower, on the "Role of Opinion Research in Desegregation"; Melvin M. Tumin, on "Some Problems for Sociological Research in Desegregation"; Bonita H. Valien on the "Role of the Social Sciences in the Desegregation Process" (St. Louis and Clinton as case studies). These and other papers suggest to advanced sociology students many important problems for research. An underlying contention is that sociologists as citizens have a responsibility to do something about the findings of such research. E.S.B.

INTRODUCTORY SOCIOLOGY. By Paul H. Landis. New York: The Ronald Press Company, 1958, pp. xl+726.

Many textbooks have been published for introductory courses in sociology. To add a new one requires some justification for its publication. It should have some uniqueness in organization, emphasis, presentation of subject matter, and appeal. The author attempted to "make sociology a vital subject in the student's experience" because of a conviction that the "introductory course should be one of the most humanizing influences in the college curriculum." With this in mind, the book begins with the concept of culture, which the author feels is usually fresh and revealing to the student. This is followed by discussions of society (groups in interaction); social structure and its operations; personality and its problems in a group context (the self and society); social control, disorganization, and planning; and the basic social institutions.

The forty chapters indicate the comprehensiveness of the treatment, even though some of the chapters are only a few pages in length. The material is presented concisely and in a readable and understandable manner, with numerous illustrations and practical applications. A minimum of statistical material is used. Ample use is made of graphic aids. Each chapter has a summary, questions for discussion and review, sourcebook readings, and selected readings. Certain sourcebooks are referred to repeatedly. The definitions of terms are made an integral part of the descriptive material, and most of them are either illustrated or related to practical situations that students can easily understand.

Some of the best sections are those that deal with culture, society, and social structure. The section on social institutions is fairly comprehensive, except that recreation institutions are omitted. Less satisfactory are the discussions of social disorganization and personality factors. Discussions of such subjects as population factors, collective behavior, and social problems are found in various sections and are not presented in an integrated manner. It is obvious that an author must make choices in selecting the topics to emphasize and the material to be included. There is as yet no agreement about the basic content of an introductory text in sociology. On the whole, the textbook by Landis is one of the most satisfactory attempts to cover the basic material and to present it in an appealing manner. M.H.N.

SOCIOLOGY. Joseph H. Fichter. Chicago: The University of Chicago Press, 1957, pp. 427.

Sociology, by Joseph H. Fichter, is an introductory text for the beginning student in sociology. It is, however, a sociological work and not a preliminary to the study of sociology. Concentration has been focused upon the fundamentals of sociological science and no attempt has been made to extend into related fields of study.

The text is divided into three sections: I. Person and Society, II. Patterns and Culture, and III. Culture and Society. The first section begins with the minimum unit of society, the social person, and evolves to the total society. Part II starts with the basic component of culture, the culture pattern, and evolves to the total culture. The third section analyzes the manner in which society and culture and their components are intertwined throughout the entire sociocultural system.

Discussion questions and bibliography are provided after each chapter. Particularly noteworthy are the series of "original readings" which each chapter contains. These readings discuss various American phenomena pertinent to, and illustrative of, the principles and generalizations contained in the chapter; for example, the chapter on social categories includes discussion of such topics as class consciousness of Americans, the shifting Negro category, and categories reached by advertisers.

Sociology is a clear and objective presentation of the basic concepts of sociology. It should prove useful both to the student and to the serious general reader. Joseph Fichter is a Catholic priest, but, as he states in his foreword, fundamentals are presented without moralizing from any particular ethical point of view. BILLYANNA NILAND

EDUCATION ON THE AGING. A Selected Annotated Bibliography. By Betty Arnett Ward. Washington, D.C.: U.S. Department of Health, Education, and Welfare, 1958, pp. 145.

This document of over 700 annotated references to educational programs and activities treating of "vital, purposeful living during the years of later maturity" does not deal with social, recreational, or economic aspects of aging. Master's theses and doctor's dissertations are not cited. The materials suggest several propositions, such as (1) education "is a lifelong process," (2) individual differences "are more marked among adults than among children and youth," (3) foundations for education in later life "should be laid in early childhood and youth."

E.S.B.

PERSONALITY. An Interdisciplinary Approach. By Louis P. Thorpe and Allen M. Schmuller. New York: D. Van Nostrand Company, Inc., 1958, pp. v+368.

This well-conceived and finely written book on the subject of personality reviews and evaluates "some of the propositions on the foundations and determinants of personality in an attempt to discover the principles and laws governing personality formation and development and point to the more fruitful lines of study designed to fill in the gaps of our knowledge." After a brief introduction, it begins as it should with a well-founded discussion of the biological basis of personality, including some attention to genetic origins, endocrine functioning, motivation, and the affective factors. Based upon a "patterned eclecticism," the authors have taken full advantage of the findings of some of the more important researches in personality gathered from a variety of disciplines. These are presented with due relevancy in the text. Some are centered upon personality development in its relationship to environment and its cultural determinants. Needed attention has been given to the major contributions of psychoanalysis.

A good contribution may be found in the chapter entitled The Organization of Personality, in which the various frames of reference—traits, attitudes, factors, and dimensions—are presented, while the research experiments dealing with these are subjected to review and criticism. The book concludes with an excellent chapter on the interdisciplinary necessity for arriving at what is called a "closed theory of personality," a theory which will probably need to recognize and scientifically demonstrate that personality arrives as a result of a total process involving the interaction of the individual with all of life's experiences. M.J.V.

KULTUR OG FRED. PITIRIM A. SOROKINS SOSIALE OG HISTORISKE FILOSOFI. By Johanne Reutz Gjermoe. Oslo: Olaf Norlis Forlag, 1957, pp. 192.

This interpretation of Sorokin's social and historical philosophy is virtually a selective digest of his views on culture and peace, as revealed in his publications up to 1954. Among the principal subjects developed by the author are cultural systems, the significance of art, morals, and lawmaking in the crisis of our age, social conduct or behavior, and a more extended section dealing with war and revolution.

J.E.N.

AN INTRODUCTION TO SOCIOLOGY. By Gladys Sellew, Rev. Paul Hanley Furfey, and Rev. William T. Gaugham. New York: Harper and Brothers, 1958, pp. xxvii+598.

Introductory textbooks in sociology are becoming quite numerous. There must be some justification for a new book in this field. The authors have two groups of students in mind: those who take only one or two courses in sociology for its general cultural value and those who intend to major in sociology and perhaps go on to professional work in the field. Another reason given is that it is frankly and intentionally a Catholic treatment, but the authors do not substitute "pious generalities for the facts of empirical science." Sociology deals with human group behavior, but it touches on moral issues and religious truths. In such instances the Catholic position is stated.

The book is divided into six main parts, dealing with an introductory section on sociology as a study of society, followed by sections on culture, man's social nature, social interaction (social processes), social organization and structure (social institutions), and population and community factors. The discussion of social disorganization and of social problems is limited.

The subject matter is systematically organized, clearly stated, and written for students rather than for professional sociologists. Statistical and other dated material is kept to a minimum. Each chapter begins with an outline, which is repeated in the chapter, and closes with a concise summary, a limited number of questions and topics for discussion, and a selected bibliography. Other than a series of thirty-two well-chosen pictures, there are few graphic aids or other special helps to learning. Chapter Four on Briefs of Books and Articles Illustrating Certain Phases of Social Organization is an exception. It consists of readings about various contemporary societies, which are used as a basis for much of the discussion in the ensuing chapters. More of such reference material would have added to the value of the book.

The authors stress what, in their opinion, are the newer trends in the study of sociology: greater cooperation with other sciences, especially other social sciences, increasing emphasis on the sociology of childhood, and a more precise concept of environment. M.H.N.

SOCIOLOGY AND THE FIELD OF EDUCATION. **By Orville G. Brim, Jr. New York: Russell Sage Foundation, 1958, pp. 93.**

In this document which was prepared for the American Sociological Society, the author reviews the "basic research studies of the institution of education which have employed the concepts and theories of sociology," and he "seeks also to indicate those areas of study which have been neglected by sociologists." The concluding chapter "considers the roles which the sociologist has taken, and potentially could take, so as to further his contributions to education through theory and research."

The subjects that are treated include the aims of education; the allocation of materials; the allocation of personnel, both educators and students; the roles of both educators and students; and the functions of education. Each of these subjects is treated in terms (1) of the work done, (2) of accumulated resources, and (3) of a projection into developmental planning. About 100 basic references are treated in this manner and are included in a classified bibliography. This booklet will be useful in a number of ways, not the least important of which are the many pertinent suggestions that it makes to graduate students in sociology who wish to do advanced research in what may be called the sociology of education. E.S.B.

PSYCHOLOGICAL STRESS. **By Irving L. Janis. New York: John Wiley & Sons, Inc., 1958, pp. xiv+439.**

The author, a psychologist who was trained at the New York Psychoanalytic Institute, states that his "primary purpose" in writing *Psychological Stress*, "is to highlight the theoretical implications" of data revealing the dynamics of adjustment to objectively dangerous life situations. The particular form of stress chosen for study is surgery.

The first part of the volume presents a detailed account of the reactions to surgery of a patient whom the author was treating as part of a psychoanalytic research project at Yale University. A number of heuristic hypotheses were derived from the depth material of this analysis before and after her hospitalization.

In the second part of the book, which is concerned with behavioral studies, there is an effort to discover the factors that play a major role in increasing or decreasing postoperative fear and anger. A series of thirty patients randomly selected from the surgical ward of a general community hospital provide the chief source of evidence. The relationships between preoperative and postoperative attitudes were validated by a follow-up questionnaire survey of 149 Yale undergraduates who had recently undergone surgery. The results indicate that those who react with a moderate degree of anticipatory fear are less likely to have a history of psychoneurotic disorder than individuals at either extreme of the fear continuum. The need for adequate psychological preparation for stress, through the "work" of realistic worry, is emphasized.

In conclusion, Janis points up the importance not only of replicating his study of surgical trauma, but also of checking his hypotheses in other types of situations involving external threat. In his opinion, research in the area of objective danger could profitably be extended and adapted to subcultures of ethnic, social-class, religious, and national origin.

Despite certain serious methodological flaws concerning which the author is commendably apologetic, *Psychological Stress* fulfills his expectation of making a significant contribution to the theory of stress. The many social implications make Janis's book well worth reading not only by psychologists and psychiatrists but by other behavioral scientists as well.

GEORGENE H. SEWARD
Department of Psychology,
University of Southern California

THE STRUCTURE OF FREEDOM. By Christian Bay. Stanford: Stanford University Press, 1958, pp. xii+419.

For ages men have struggled with the idea of freedom, attempting to define its significance as applied to society and to the individual. From earliest times social thought has concerned itself with the themes of either service to or manipulation of people. In this book the author undertakes a thoroughgoing inquiry into the heart of the matter about freedom and succeeds in producing a work that should prove to be a most effective reference for a timely topic. At the outset he indicates that the recent demand for the services of the behavioral scientists "has been in connection with leading or manipulating people." His present purpose is linked with an opposite demand, producing "insights into human behavior" so that they may be employed "in the service of sheltering the growth of individuality and freedom in modern society."

The Introduction is concerned with a brief discussion of the present types of obstacles which restrain the development of modern man in Western civilization: namely, defensiveness, limiting psychological freedom; coercive actions limiting social freedom; and limitations on potential freedom or freedom from manipulation. The major portions of the book are devoted to demonstrating how far modern psychology may be brought to bear light upon those freedoms which mean self-expression (psychological), those that refer to the relative absence of perceived external pressures on the individual (social), and those referring to the "relative absence of unperceived restraints upon individual behavior" (potential).

In the quest for maximal freedom, which Bay considers equally desirable for all, the most difficult empirical problem arises, how to determine "the criteria for compatibles between various freedom values for the same individual and between various freedom demands of different individuals." In the final chapter on policies toward freedom, some necessitous limitations are discussed, one such being that cultural and educational matters should be under the jurisdiction of those who have a strong concern for these questions. Here, it may appear to some readers that Bay's policy preferences on the attainment of maximal freedom smack of bias and that he has departed from scientific appraisal. However, his discussions, especially on freedom, restraint, and power, are provocative, always stimulating, always enlightening. M.J.V.

CRIME AND INSANITY. Edited by Richard W. Nice. New York: Philosophical Library, Inc., 1958, pp. xiii+280.

The chief question discussed in this book is: When shall a man be held legally insane and thus escape the penalty dealt out to other normal criminals? Twelve experts in jurisprudence, psychology, prison psychiatry, education, and sociology discuss various aspects of the problem. The term "insanity" has a legal rather than a psychiatric connotation. Schizophrenia, paranoia, and related forms of mental disorders usually come under the legal designation of insane. The various authors discuss the principles of punishment, irresistible impulse and criminal responsibility, the differential association theory and forms of compulsive crime, psychiatric and sociological variations in the analysis and interpretation of the criminal act, the various applications of the legal designation of "not guilty by reason of insanity," the conflict between law and medicine in judicial practice, the pros and cons of the NcNaghten and Durham rules, the functions of psychiatrists and psychologists in courts and in prisons, and the "Model Penal Code" formulated by the American Law Institute.

A questionnaire sent to over three hundred psychiatrists of the American Psychiatric Association included the question: "Do you believe the right and wrong concept as promulgated by the McNaghten case is satisfactory?" Only 12 per cent stated that it was satisfactory, 79 per cent believed it unsatisfactory, and the others were not certain. One of the main reasons for not endorsing the right-wrong test is that it lacks scientific reliability. It is difficult to determine the existence or nonexistence of an individual's ability to know right from wrong at the time the crime is committed. M.H.N.

EMOTIONAL DYNAMICS AND GROUP CULTURE. By Dorothy Stock and Herbert A. Thelen. New York: New York University Press for the National Training Laboratories, 1958, pp. xviii+296.

The National Training Laboratories, a section of the National Educational Association, engages itself in research in, and application of, social science in certain particular areas of human relationships. In this book may be found the reports of a research program with a psychiatric approach to the group-as-an-organism, meaning the consideration of "emotional phenomena as central objects of direct study," and viewing "the group as a system whose properties would depend upon the network of interaction among its members." Guiding the research program, five postulates and nine propositions emanating from them were formulated to guide the experimental investigation. Several of these propositions have to do with what psychiatric therapist W. R. Bion has termed two different modes of group life: "emotionality"—characterized by high feelings, disorder, contagion—and "work"—characterized by sobriety, orderliness, and reflection.

Much use is made of his term "valency," defined by him as "a capacity for instantaneous and involuntary combination of one individual with another, for sharing and acting on a basic assumption." Combining with others implies the capacity of individuals to support or cooperate with other group members in furthering or moving away from group objectives or group culture. The training groups studied were designed to help "members improve their understanding of group operations and of their own feelings and behaviors in group situations." Some of the findings are obvious, but in the Preface an apology for this is made in advance. The obvious may be confirmed by research, but doors are opened to new ideas. M.J.V.

Sociology and Social Research
AN INTERNATIONAL JOURNAL

Articles in Forthcoming Issues . . .

March-April and later

Measuring Marriage Satisfaction .... NATHAN HURVITZ
Social Problems in Pakistan .... JOHN E. OWEN
Attitudes of Teen-agers .... T. B. JOHANNIS, JR., AND JAMES ROLLINS
Political Participation Among Orientals (Hawaii) .... G. YAMAMOTO
Groups Versus the Individual .... F. T. CARLTON
Reappraisal of Comte's Sociology .... RUSSELL MIDDLETON
Bilingualism in Hawaii .... NORMAN MELLER
Sociology of Alfred Weber .... RUDOLF HEBERLE
A Theory of Social Change .... OTAKAR MACHOTKA
Sociological Contributions of Znaniecki .... THEODORE ABEL
Status and Social Tropism .... E. C. MCDONAGH
Ethnic Prejudice and Social Class .... A. L. ROSENBLUM
Division of Labor Among Communal Groups .... HENRY ZENTNER
Attitudes Toward the Family .... PANOS D. BARDIS
Social Distance Scales and Stratification .... F. R. WESTIE
Computers and Social Research .... E. F. BORGATTA AND J. ROBBIN
Group Processes and Prohibition .... NORMAN JACKSON AND M. SHERIF
Self-Tattooing Among Delinquents .... JOHN H. BURMA
Occupations of Sociology Majors .... MARGARET L. HELBRICK
Empathy in the Dating Situation .... R. L. STEWART AND G. M. VERNON

Articles in Preceding Issue . . .

November-December 1958

The Concept of the Group .... MARIE L. BORGATTA
Areas for Research in Leisure .... MARTIN H. NEUMEYER
Teaching Sociology by Radio and Television .... THOMAS F. HOULT
Teaching Sociology via Television .... MARVIN B. SUSSMAN
Teaching Sociology by Means of Television .... R. A. SCHERMERHORN
Measuring Group Opinion .... L. K. NORTHWOOD
Economic Motivation in Ethnic Relations .... RALPH R. IRELAND
Racial Distance Changes in the United States .... EMORY S. BOGARDUS

Sociology and Social
. . . Research . . .

AN INTERNATIONAL JOURNAL

Social Distance Scales 251
FRANK R. WESTIE

High Speed Computers in Social Research 259
E. F. BORGATTA AND J. ROBBIN

Group Processes and Prohibition 265
NORMAN JACKMAN AND MUZAFER SHERIF

Ethnic Prejudice and Social Class 272
A. L. ROSENBLUM

Occupations of Sociology Majors 276
MARGARET L. HELBRICH

Correlates of Empathy in Dating 279
R. L. STEWART AND G. M. VERNON

Racial Reactions by Regions 286
EMORY S. BOGARDUS

Pacific Sociological News 291

Peoples and Culture . . . 292
Social Problems and Welfare 296
Social Theory and Research 302
Other Publications Received 320

VOL. 43 MARCH-APRIL 1959 No. 4

YEARLY SUBSCRIPTION, $3.50 SINGLE COPIES, 70 CENTS

Sociology and Social Research

AN INTERNATIONAL JOURNAL

PUBLISHED BIMONTHLY AT THE UNIVERSITY OF SOUTHERN CALIFORNIA
UNIVERSITY PARK, LOS ANGELES 7, CALIFORNIA

YEARLY SUBSCRIPTION, $3.50 SINGLE COPIES, 70¢

Entered as second-class matter March 31, 1936, at the post office at Los Angeles, California, under the act of March 3, 1879.

Contributed materials which appear in *Sociology and Social Research* do not necessarily express the opinion or the policy of the editorial staff and publisher.

Articles published in this journal are indexed in *The International Index to Periodicals*, and abstracted in *Sociological Abstracts* and *Psychological Abstracts*.

PUBLISHED BY

UNIVERSITY OF SOUTHERN CALIFORNIA PRESS

UNIVERSITY PARK LOS ANGELES 7, CALIFORNIA

SOCIOLOGY AND SOCIAL RESEARCH
March-April 1959

SOCIAL DISTANCE SCALES
A Tool for the Study of Stratification*

FRANK R. WESTIE
Indiana University

The concept of social distance has been used almost exclusively as a tool for the study of intergroup relations. Thus the phenomenon itself has come to be identified by many sociologists as being an intergroup relations phenomenon. It may very well be, however, that social distance scales are equally well suited to the study of social stratification in general, apart from an intergroup relations context.

Social classes on the local community level are, in the final analysis, groups of people who interact selectively according to status characteristics which they share, believe they share, or "would" share. Social distance, on the other hand, is a concept which describes the degree to which one would admit another to certain spheres of interaction; thus social distance scales are, in effect, measures of selective interaction. What is it, ultimately, that separates the members of one social class from another, if not social distance—social distance with the same meaning it was originally given by Bogardus?

One might ask: If social classes do exist on the local level as selective interaction systems, why not simply observe such interaction systems directly? Why use scales at all? As is well known, Warner and a few others have done precisely that. It is also well known, perhaps, that the making and recording of such observations is extremely difficult, time consuming, and expensive. In fact, the reason W. L. Warner developed his Index of Status Characteristics[1] (a socioeconomic status index) and related it, through correlation, to Evaluated Participation (an index of

*The observations made in this paper are to a large extent an unanticipated outgrowth of a research program dealing with the nature and genesis of intergroup prejudices in groups and individuals. Support of this program by the Social Science Research Council is gratefully acknowledged.

[1] W. L. Warner, M. Meeker, and K. Eels, *Social Class in America* (Chicago: Social Research Association, Inc., 1949).

selective interaction along class lines) was in order to use the former, Index of Status Characteristics, to estimate where a person stood on Evaluated Participation without going through the laborious process of establishing such participation through direct observation. Social distance scales of the types described here can be used to determine one's selective interaction preferences in the realm of social class, without going through the arduous labor of direct observation and without making the risky inferences required in estimating selective interaction from socioeconomic status characteristics. For example, it is doubtful that the relationship between Index of Status Characteristics and Evaluated Participation is the same for communities of different sizes.

The social distance scale originally developed by Bogardus for hierarchizing various ethnic groups would not be appropriate for the study of stratification. The type of scale we propose below (and which we have been using in our research) breaks general social distance down into more specific subdimensions in terms of the kind of interaction involved. Moreover, in the kind of adaptation of the Bogardus Scale that we propose, subjects are asked to indicate the degree of distance they would prefer (or, conversely, the degree of intimacy they would permit) with persons of various status characteristics, such as occupation, education, economic status.

As stated above, one of the reasons why social distance scales have not been used for the study of social distance within the majority group is that such scales have been regarded, in effect, as devices for assessing relative degrees of prejudice toward ethnic outgroups. Because they were designed for this purpose, they have not lent themselves to direct employment in the study of stratification. Although the same is true in the case of the scales we have been using in our intergroup relations research program, we have found, however, that they do discriminate among the interaction preferences of persons of differing class attitudes. One of our scales, the Interpersonal Social Distance Scale, is presented by way of illustration:

I BELIEVE I WOULD BE WILLING TO HAVE "A"
(attitude object, i.e., person with specified status characteristics)

	Strongly agree	Agree	Undecided	Disagree	Strongly disagree
1. as a close, personal friend					
2. as a dinner guest in my home					
3. as a person I might often visit with					

4. as an acquaintance
5. as someone to say hello to
6. as someone I might see on the street

Although this scale has many inadequacies as a tool for the study of selective interaction preferences along class lines, it may be regarded as a prototype of the kind of scale that needs to be developed for this purpose. Among other changes, there should be more items on the intimate end of the scale with smaller degrees of intimacy separating these intimate items. Moreover, the range should be reduced on the end of the scale implying greatest distance. Obviously, items 4, 5, and 6, though quite discriminatory in a race relations context, are of doubtful utility in a social class setting.

The Study of the "Stratification Potential" of a Population Through the Identification of Psychological Class-Types. One application of social distance techniques to the area of stratification would be in the study of the susceptibility of a given population to stratification. This susceptibility, which we might call a society's "stratification potential," would be analyzed, not in terms of whether the members of the group *do* interact selectively according to status attributes of one another, but, rather, in terms of what they *would* do in the way of selective interaction, given the future social and economic circumstances which would provide the opportunity. What would their preferences be, not simply as regards their interactions with members of obvious out-groups, but particularly with regard to interactions with persons of various status attributes within their own societal or communal group?

Despite the fact that the shape the individual personality takes in any society is to a large extent a consequence of culture, the fact remains that the characteristic psychological orientations of individuals in a society are not a perfect reflection of current culture or "cultures" or of prevailing social and economic circumstances. Often "psychologies" of individuals, and especially ideologies, are more understandable in terms of their relation to past social and economic characteristics of the society rather than in terms of present characteristics. This would seem to be especially true of rapidly changing modern societies. This being the case, the prediction of stratification trends would seem to be more than a purely sociological or purely economic problem. It is also a problem of social psychology. For example, we might attempt to predict the future course of stratification in America by analyzing trends in productivity, economic surplus, income distribution, education distribution, etc., but such predictions would be severely limited if they did not take into account social-psychological trends which often bear an enigmatic relationship to these more crucially societal trends.

There comes to mind here the essentially psychological distinction elaborated by MacIver and Page[2] between corporate class consciousness (essentially the "class-view" that identifies one's personal welfare with that of his class and vice versa) and competitive class feeling (the class-view wherein one has an awareness, albeit vague and inaccurate at times, of his place in the class structure, but where he is always ready and willing to leave his class for higher, greener pastures). Predictions of the future of stratification in America which fail to take into account the phenomenon of competitive class feeling are likely to be no better than those of Marx, who, we might add, also failed to consider this psychological variable except as a one-to-one reflection of the individual's position in the class structure.

Social distance scales would be particularly useful for establishing the relative prevalence of such psychological types. Although there is some evidence that corporate class consciousness tends to be found at the apex and occasionally at the bottom of the class pyramid in America, an individual's psychological class-type cannot be determined simply through the determination of his socioeconomic or his social class position. We frequently encounter factory workers with a more typically middle-class outlook in their competitive class consciousness, and occasionally upper-class persons with ideologies more appropriate, theoretically, for persons lower in the structure.

Social distance scales adapted to the measurement of distance between persons of varying status characteristics would permit the determination of whether a particular individual is *upward-oriented* in his interaction preferences, and hence competitively class conscious, or equal-oriented (or "loyal"), and hence corporately class conscious. The relative prevalence of corporate class consciousness as opposed to competitive class feeling would be a crucial datum in any analysis of the stratification potential of a given population.

Social Distance Differentials and Selective Interaction. Another way in which social distance scales may be useful in the area of stratification is in the study of "*social distance differentials.*" This concept, coined by Bogardus, very succinctly describes a basic social phenomenon. The concept refers to the difference between the social distance the subject would

---

[2] R. M. MacIver and Charles H. Page, *Society, An Introductory Analysis*, pp. 359 ff.

accord the object and that which the object would accord the subject. It is epitomized in the question: "Is he as good a friend of mine as I am a friend of his?" or "Is he less friendly to me than I am to him?" To use Bogardus' own definition, "The social distance differential is the difference in the favorable or unfavorable reaction of persons to each other, of persons and groups to each other, and of two groups to each other."[3]

In the study of stratification, the application of this concept and measures of the same would involve the measurement of the social distance differential between persons of different occupation, education, family background, etc. In a society that is, in general, competitively class conscious, we do find that there are a number of kinds of social interactions which a person would not indulge in with a person of lower-class status than himself, while, at the same time, the person of lower status would agree to these same interactions with the person of higher status. Of course, the same is true also as regards the interactions between groups. The Moose lodge might be quite ready to entertain the Elks, but the Elks may not be very anxious to entertain the Moose. In the stratification context, one might refer to the social distance differential as a "selective interaction differential."

The Study of Social Class Ideology. In the social distance scales we have a convenient tool for studying the relationship between a person's ideology regarding social class and his interaction preferences along class lines. When, as in the case of many studies, persons are asked to indicate what social classes they belong to, many Americans, before finally checking "middle class," protest that we really do not have classes in America.

When, on the other hand, through the use of social distance scales, we study people's class attitudes by asking them whom they would interact with, that is, with what kinds of people of what kinds of occupation, economic position, education, family background, etc., and to what extent and in what kinds of social situations, then we may very well get at the extent to which the individual in question would, by his own behavior, actually perpetuate the existence of social classes in his community and his nation, regardless of his response to the general symbol, "social class." We have a situation here very much akin to that where people were asked whether or not they favored socialism. The vast majority responded by saying "no," but when their responses to specific issues regarding government ownership and control of particular enter-

[3] Cf. Emory S. Bogardus, "The Social Distance Differential," *Sociology and Social Research*, XXXII: 882-87.

prises and activities were called for, the majority turned out to favor socialistic measures. Social distance scales may well be useful for determining the extent to which the American people, who may be described as finding the idea, or at least the symbol, of social class unpleasant, actually do, or would, given the opportunity, behave in ways which create and perpetuate stratification.

In the research program currently under way, we have been using social distance scales along with a number of other devices to investigate a number of relationships between stratification and race prejudice. Despite the fact that our primary purpose in this research has been the determination of factors contributing to the development of race prejudice in groups and individuals, our indirect technique of measuring prejudice required that we measure the attitudes of whites toward whites of varying status as well as toward Negroes of varying status. Unfortunately, because our primary purpose was the measurement of prejudice, a rather large number of our scale items were meaningful only in a race relations context rather than in an interclass relations context. Some of the items did, however, have relevance for interclass relations, and these provided us with the kind of impressionistic knowledge regarding stratification among whites.

Despite these limitations, we did come across a number of white people who indicated a marked preference for interaction with higher status whites. For example, many persons of middle- and upper-class status indicated not simply a preference for higher status persons as neighbors, friends, fellow members of their organizations, etc., but rather expressed an unwillingness to have persons of lower occupational status as neighbors, friends, etc. Thus, through the use of social distance scales, we found some degree of class selectivity among whites responding to whites of various occupational statuses.

One social distance scale was designed to tap the subject's degree of aversion to the attitude object because of imputed physical characteristics of the object. Although such a scale as this is more meaningful in a race relations context, we did find *some* whites who evidenced physical aversion to *some* occupational types among whites. One item which our respondents found particularly irritating and which, *a priori*, one would assume to be undiscriminating in a study of the attitudes of any class of respondents toward any social category, was the following: "I believe I would be willing to have (*person in a particular occupation*) use the same towel that I use." The characteristic response to this statement (an item which our judges rated as indicating extreme intimacy of a physical sort) was "I wouldn't want anyone to use my towel, regardless of his personal characteristics." In fact, responses of this kind were frequent even among people living in slums where one towel per person is hardly the characteristic pattern. One woman, whose house and person looked as if they hadn't been exposed to soap and water for ages, replied: "I don't think I'd want *anyone* to use my towel." The significant point, however, is that, though most people didn't want anyone to use their towel, *some* people did say it was all right with them for *some* higher status occupational types to use the towel they used. The stereotypically clean physician was the most frequent object of such largesse.

Although, as we have indicated, scales of the type presented above do discriminate between at least some persons of differing class attitudes, they have certain conspicuous shortcomings for this purpose. The following considerations would have to be taken into account in any attempt to study social stratification through the use of social distance scales:

1. "General" social distance has to be broken down into more specific subdimensions. Unlike kinds of interaction should not be assumed to be scalable on the same continuum. Unidimensionality in each scale with regard to type of interaction would, of course, contribute to increased scalability. We are more likely to know just what it was we measured.

Some dimensions which might possibly be explored are interpersonal interaction, involving intimate socializing on a friendship basis; family relationships, concerning degrees of closeness of connection through marriage; business relationships; interactions involving trust; public interactions where the status of the participants is known; and physical aversion. There are many other possible dimensions of interactions besides these.

2. The items on the intimate end of the scale ought to be extremely sensitive; there should be very small intervals between each item. This means that the scales ought to be perhaps at least twice as long as the six-item scale presented above. The first item ought to refer to situations implying the greatest possible degree of intimacy. For example, in an adaptation of the Interpersonal Distance Scale, items might be added referring to marriage, courtship, dating, entertaining in intimate groups drawn from one's most significant reference groups, etc. The scale presented achieved considerable variation in response of whites according to occupational characteristics of the attitude object, when the objects were Negroes-in-occupations. It was considerably less discriminating, however, where the respondents were white and the attitude objects were whites-in-occupations.

3. The attitude objects should be persons whose status is varied according to occupation, education, income, and other class-related characteristics. The effect of these many status variables on response could be assessed through the repetition of the items with a different status attribute attached to the object person in each repetition. On the other hand, perhaps a better technique would be to see how the various socioeconomic status attributes *in combination* affect the selective interaction response. This could be done through the use of paragraphs preceding each presentation of a scale in which a person of X occupation, X education, X income, etc., is described. The respondent would be asked about the kinds of interaction he would be willing to indulge in with the "person described above." In a later repetition of the same scale, the same subject would be asked about his preferences regarding a person of X occupation, X education, and Y income. Through such rotation of the various significant socioeconomic status characteristics of the attitude objects, an assessment could be made of the relative power of particular status variables in determining selective interaction.

This might well be the most important contribution to be made through the application of social distance scales to the study of stratification. The question of what the relationship is between one's particular socioeconomic attributes and his position in the class system is one of the most important questions in the area of stratification, but it is also one of the most poorly answered. Warner and his associates, through the most arduous labor, have provided sociologists with answers based on systematic, empirical evidence. But this evidence has been derived from studies of smaller communities. To do in a metropolitan community what Warner and his associates have done in smaller communities would be prohibitively expensive in a society that isn't likely to channel hundreds of thousands of dollars into social research, and least of all into research into its social class system.

The study of interaction preferences through the use of social distance scales would obviously be an inadequate substitute for direct observations of actual interactions. Such devices might, however, if properly constructed and applied, provide sociology with knowledge that is at least superior to the knowledge we now have of the relationship between socioeconomic status and social class in the urban community.

SOME IMPLICATIONS OF HIGH SPEED COMPUTERS FOR THE METHODOLOGY OF SOCIAL RESEARCH[1]

E. F. BORGATTA
AND
J. ROBBIN
Russell Sage Foundation

Science often seems to limp instead of gallop because there isn't a smooth sequence from conceptual scheme through method to the reality of operation. The researcher may become lost in inappropriate speculation at the start; he may attempt to formulate "theory" on facts that are tenuous; he may be too restrictive in the questions he wishes to ask to permit the answers to be perceived with relevance to the body of knowledge for the field; or he may not key his thinking to a level that is productive of appropriate research questions. In terms of the last possibility, he may not be sufficiently aware of the methods and techniques and the scope of operation these permit.

Sociology and psychology are both relatively new sciences, and so are their tools, including statistics. In the early history of these sciences, even the empiricist often operated largely upon the basis of intuition in judging the reliability of his findings, or on more demanding tests of replication than might be necessary with present inferential methods. The development of statistical methods associated with measurement has greatly facilitated the techniques of handling data, particularly because they permit reduction of certain kinds of procedures to arbitrary and routine ones. It is in this particular instance that the advent of punched card and other electronic computing equipment has made its major contribution to social research. With machine procedures, the scope of data-handling techniques has been broadened while eliminating much of the toil and susceptibility to error that formerly plagued the researcher.

Sociology and psychology have not yet felt the full impact of the advances made possible by these machines that can be instructed to perform, at great speed, any technique encountered in regard to data handling. What makes this even more impressive is that each technique is easily generalized. An efficient machine program is completely versatile

[1] Revised version of a paper presented at a symposium on Applications of High Speed Computers to the Study of Human Behavior, April 26, 1958, The Laboratory of Social Relations, Harvard University.

in regard to changes in parameters of problem size, scale and format of input, and so on. For example, with the same program, it is possible to intercorrelate a matrix of 250 variables with 1,000 observations on each, or do a single correlation with 3 observations. To appreciate the full significance of high-speed computing techniques, in their power as a data-handling tool and the implications for the methodology of research that this power holds, some specific information about the machines and the tasks that they are able to perform is necessary.

The Machines and What They Do. There has been an extremely rapid evolution of computing resources over the past ten years. This has resulted in the overlapping of available facilities in regard to size, cost, and complexity. The researcher is faced more often with the problem of choosing the most appropriate machine for the job rather than determining limits for his work. The most far-reaching improvement in the development of digital computers came with the superseding of the wired (punch board) program by the internally stored program machine. In the former, the programmer is forced to limit his computation to a finite sequence of arithmetic and logical operations that are determined by actually completing the circuitry of machine components on the control panel with plugged wires. In the latter, however, control over the sequence of operations is achieved by a symbolic numerical language that the machine interprets and is stored in the machine "memory" along with the data. As opposed to the wired program system, these internally stored instructions may be modified at the origin or in the course of a computation by the same means used for the treatment of the data. That is, the program may be operated upon like ordinary numbers.

The internally stored program machines are characterized by greatly increased logical facility. The wired program machines are well adapted to small one-shot jobs, and today they are commonly used as auxiliary machines in handling the input and output of the large-scale digital machines. Many of the procedures now programmed for the internally stored program machines were formerly set up for the wired ones, though much more limited in scope and requiring a great deal more time and labor for completion. For example, the tabulators, IBM 405, 402-3, and 407, and small wired program computers such as the 602-A, 604, 607, 608, and Card-Programmed Calculator, as well as the programmable keyboard computers, the IBM 610, or the Burroughs E-101, are available for tasks such as accumulating distributions, tests of significance, analysis of variance, and so on. With stringent limitations, and with the time and endurance needed for the basic card handling, even matrices of product-moment correlations and small factor analyses may be performed on these machines.

One plug-board machine that has not been obsoleted by the internally stored program computer, however, is the IBM 101, a high-speed counter sorter with a printing device. Being designed for purely logical rather than digital operations, the 101 is well adapted to processing that examines the distribution of items and deals with the counting of unique combinations, thus being especially adaptable to use with qualitative variables. It may be used to determine correlation by cross tabulation, printing scattergrams, and providing input for such coefficients as Flanagan's Coefficient, phi, or the tetrachoric r through the two-by-two table. The 101 is used with great efficiency for routine procedures of scaling corresponding to Guttman scales, Likert scales, or common item analysis.[2]

The vast implications for social research, however, become apparent in the use of the large-scale internally stored program digital computers. One of these machines that is relatively low in cost and available to the researcher in most academic communities in the country at this time and that possesses most of the attributes of the largest computers is the IBM 650, a magnetic drum data-processing machine. As a technical definition of the IBM 650, it is a serial stored-program, modified single-address, biquinary digital computer possessing 20,000 decimal digits of storage arrayed in 2,000 registers or "words" of ten digits each, with sign, as magnetized spots on a metal drum revolving at 12,500 revolutions per minute.

The IBM 650 has been operated in the field for about two years, and many standard operations and computing systems, as well as aids to programming, are readily available. Programs exist for "t" tests, contingency tables, curve-fitting and regression equations, the analysis of variance and covariance, extensive matrices of product-moment correlations, partial correlations, factor analysis by the centroid and principal components methods, and rotations of factors to orthogonal and oblique structure, as well as many other general and special purpose computations applicable to the handling of social data. The above computations, it goes without saying, may be performed with only a small fraction of the time and effort heretofore necessary, and their scope is limited only by the storage capacity and basic execution time of the machine.

---

[2] Edgar F. Borgatta, "Cumulative Scaling as a Routine Procedure on the IBM 101," *Sociometry*, 20: 317-25 (1957).

A typical job for the basic IBM 650 might run as follows: 40 items are given as scores having a range from 0 to 9, and the data consist of the responses of 100 subjects to these items. It would be possible to intercorrelate this matrix, factor analyze it by the complete centroid technique, and then to rotate the factor matrix to an approximate orthogonal simple structure (quadrimax solution) in a period of about three hours, assuming that there are only 8 factors that are worth retaining for rotation. Incidentally, if the same job were put on the larger IBM 704 in accordance with its factor of 30 to 1 in increased execution time over the IBM 650, it would be accomplished in about 20 minutes.

Methodological Implications. It is easy to give concrete illustrations of how research is influenced by the availability of these data-processing techniques. For example, if one is concerned with describing a given class of situations, he will examine all the known studies in the area, and all of the generalizations he can locate pertinent to it. It would not be sociology or psychology if he found that there was only a single and firm theory that existed in the area, so it can hardly be said that the person will be hypothesis testing. He will be concerned with *exploring* a given problem situation. Thus, he will not want just to ask a single question and test the hypothesis, and then reject or not reject the hypothesis. Rather, what he will want to do is to find out if certain hunches that he has are in accord with the empirical data. But, above and beyond this, he is interested in locating any information that will help to predict his criterion, that will help to explain or take into account any additional variance in regard to the phenomenon that is the focus of his attention. Instead of asking a few questions, then, the researcher is more likely to want to ask all possible questions that seem to be relevant. Doing this is not, as some people like to suggest, avoiding thinking. Rather, this is, indeed, saying that one thinks when it is appropriate to think, and this is not in the absence of knowledge. One is actually avoiding speculation and inviting discovery.

The task becomes one of empirical description, and this essentially is what is required in order to formulate theory, if one minimally defines theory as empirically based generalization. It would be nice, of course, if the researcher would also make provision for independent replication of his descriptive generalizations. At this point, however, the researcher is *not* forced to neglect questions that he would like to ask because he would have no feasible technique for examining the data. With computers at hand, he is encouraged, rather, to ask all relevant questions. Essentially he is searching in the realm of the unknown. He is asking questions on the chance that if he locates some significant variation, it may give him a clue toward being able to explain the phenomenon that concerns him. At one time this kind of procedure in social science would have been a luxury. Today it is a luxury only as it poses problems of getting the data.

In a typical analysis of the type with which we have been concerned, suppose we gathered data for 75 items that represent one class of data—say, ratings that members of a given type of group make of each other. These can then be intercorrelated and the matrix examined to remove all items that correlate with no others, and to cluster and organize at a preliminary and intuitive level those that remain. From these remaining items may be selected representative items; that is, some identical or apparently identical items may be eliminated, thus reducing the matrix still further and providing a parsimony of definition. Suppose that the resulting matrix involves 35 items. This matrix may now be factor analyzed in order to get a better knowledge of the organization of the content that is involved. From this analysis, the researchers might conclude that there are two very substantial kinds of content in the ratings, and three lesser contents, and they may be named. If the contents tend to be represented in the population of items in a correlated way, this information is also available to the researchers.

It may be that at this point the researchers would want to develop five tests to represent these contents, or possibly even more tests to represent the five contents, and use these in conjunction with other measures or in attempts to predict behavior in terms of other measures. It may also be that the researchers will become concerned with the question of what the meanings of these measures are in terms of other classes of situations, and thus they may replicate their study and attempt to find the stability of the factorial structure that they have uncovered in their initial study. The point, however, is that if the researcher wishes to have a measure of "assertive behavior" in interaction as measured by the responses of subjects to each other, he can find this measure in terms of all measures that he can conceive of as existing in this class of interpersonal rating phenomena. If he at some later point wanted to know what the relationship of assertiveness was to aggressiveness, because of something that he found of interest in the literature, he could at this point return to his initial analyses and find out what the factorial structure of aggressiveness is according to these five factors located. Now, we do not want to elaborate this kind of procedure too far, because it requires certain assumptive bases to be able to understand all that is involved. What we emphasize, however, is that it becomes routine procedure for researchers to develop their tests in a factor context, so that essentially the question of analyzing all measures of a given class in order to use one or several in a particular study becomes the rule rather than the rare and wonderful exception.

The most important implication to be drawn from this discussion is that the advent of high speed computers serves to free the scientist rather than to restrict him, as is sometimes suggested by those who see the machines as holding the researchers to particular techniques and presumably to asking only certain kinds of questions. The high speed data-processing procedures allow the research scientist to do any of the operations that he has done that involve numbers with greater speed, precision, and with a knowledge that he can do almost anything that he can bring to the computers. This knowledge should encourage the researcher to become more thorough in his search for important relationships by allowing him to examine data more rapidly and according to any arbitrary standards that may be set. At the same time, it does require that if the scientist is to be master of his research he should understand the processes involved, their assumptions, and their limitations in practical application and in terms of relative investment of resources. Avenues for training for social scientists in this direction need to be expanded to include not only the subject matter of statistics and methodology courses, but also an opportunity to become acquainted with computing facilities.

GROUP PROCESSES AND COMMUNICATION ON THE PROHIBITION ISSUE*

NORMAN JACKMAN
AND
MUZAFER SHERIF
The Institute of Group Relations, University of Oklahoma

This paper touches upon the background of the present prohibition issue in a "dry" state, the groups involved, the impact of functionally related organizations, stereotypes of "wets" and "drys," interpretations of pressure tactics used by the in-group and the adversary, and briefly upon factors emerging under prevailing conditions. It is intended to serve as the starting point for a social-psychological study of wet and dry groups and their communications.

Oklahoma is the only state in the nation which completely bans the production and sale of spiritous liquor. Five attempts at repeal of the prohibition clause in the state constitution since the statehood referendum of 1907 and one attempt, in 1957, to restrict the sale of 3.2 beer, have failed.

The Referendum as a Focal Issue. The prohibition issue in Oklahoma reaches a climax every few years in a popular referendum. An approaching referendum serves as a focal point of interest for members of the groups concerned with the issue. When the issue touches the motives or interests of individuals, or group pressures are brought to bear on them, the uncommitted and unconcerned are forced to make decisions and so declare themselves. Lines are sharpened among community organizations as they tend to cluster about the poles of wetness or dryness. During this process groups may be torn by internal dissension.

After a prohibition referendum has been decided by popular vote, stereotypes of opposing groups which developed prior to voting are strengthened. Of course, an overwhelming victory destroys the opposition, but if decisions are close, as they have been in the past, the aspirations of victorious organizations are raised, while those of the losers are temporarily lowered. Thus, after the continued defeat of repeal measures, Oklahoma drys submitted a measure for local option which would

---

*Paper read on program "Studies in Group Process and Social Judgment," arranged by the Institute of Group Relations, University of Oklahoma, at the annual meeting of the Southwestern Social Science Association, Dallas, Texas, April 4, 1958.

have prohibited in various counties even the sale of 3.2 beer. Another referendum for the repeal of the prohibition clause is expected in the near future, following the defeat of the local option measure.

In-group and Intergroup Ties. The norms of wet and dry groups are those traditions, values, and definitions which are accepted by members as intrinsically right and proper. They serve as guides for the conduct of members as they interact with one another, with members of opposing groups, and within the wider community. These norms are subject to change over time as the composition of groups changes and as new social, economic, and political factors develop.

Since most individuals belong to many associations and organizations, conflicts among divergent norms may occur. For example, some members of church sects with militant prohibitionist orientations depend for their livelihoods on the brewery industry. Because of status aspirations, others with strong dry motivations will attend functions where liquor is served. Furthermore, groups with diametrically opposed norms may find themselves aligned on the prohibition issue. Thus, dry organizations are embarrassed by a common interest they share with bootleggers.

The common norms of organizations concerned with the prohibition issue cause them to unite in the pursuit of their aims and goals. The most effective organizations are those which pursue the single goal of prohibition, or its repeal. Thus, the liquor industry and the brewers, on the one hand, and the United Drys and the Woman's Christian Temperance Union, on the other, function as leading organizations in the pursuit of their respective aims. Of course, the tendency of organizations to guard jealously their autonomy creates intergroup conflicts among organizations sharing common norms. For example, the anti-Saloon League was hostile to the Prohibition Party during the eighties and nineties of the last century because the former endorsed candidates of both major parties who were supporters of the dry cause. The Prohibition Party split the vote by entering their own candidates.[1]

Today in Oklahoma the United Drys and the W.C.T.U. work very closely with most Protestant sects. They recruit members through the established churches' recreational and educational organizations, and those of their leaders who are ordained ministers preach the gospel of total abstinence from the pulpit.[2] Conversely, the liquor interests enlist the support of business organizations, community service clubs, and labor unions.

---

[1] Cf. Peter Odegard, *Pressure Politics* (New York: Columbia University Press, 1928), p. 83.

[2] The evidence for this statement, and following statements not otherwise cited, is found in our interviews with members of wet and dry organizations.

Pressure Tactics. Prohibition has been largely a rural movement from the beginning. Charles Merz[3] has pointed out that only thirteen states had attempted total prohibition before the Eighteenth Amendment to the Constitution was adopted in 1920. These states covered more than a third of the area of the United States, but held only one seventh of its population.

The prohibition movement remains largely a rural movement, as do the Protestant groups from which it draws its strength. As Odegard has noted,[4] the rural church is the principal center of social life and reflects such rural values as hostility toward the metropolis and toward the foreigner. Actually, the rural church is not a monolithic entity. Hostility toward urbanites and support of moral reform are strongest in the more fundamentalistic Protestant groups: the Baptists, the Methodists, the Assembly of God Church, and the Christian Church. Other Protestant groups, Catholics, and Jews represent a more sophisticated segment of the population and reflect the more tolerant drinking habits of their congregations. As organized groups they do not actively participate in the dry movement, though a small minority of their congregations belong to such organizations as the United Drys and the W.C.T.U.

The wet movement is spearheaded by distillers and, in the case of beer referendums, by brewers, who mobilize support during a campaign from business and service organizations, veterans' organizations, and political groups. Groups with the single goal of fighting dry legislation arise and are active for the duration of the campaign, after which they dissolve.

Traditional and Emergent Factors. The norms and values of opposing groups in the present prohibition issue in Oklahoma are based on the traditions of the movement as it developed nationally during the nineteenth century. From a study of the W.C.T.U., Joseph Gusfield[5] concluded that this group has not changed its doctrine in order to preserve its organization, though the characteristics of its membership have changed. In its statement of aims when it organized in 1874, the W.C.T.U. stressed Christianity and abstinence.[6] In the February 1958 issue of *The Christian Patriot*, the Reverend John Coleman, D.D., Ph.D., professor emeritus of political science, Geneva College, wrote that

[3] Charles Merz, *The Dry Decade* (Garden City, New York: Doubleday, Doran and Company, Inc., 1932), pp. 22-23.

[4] *Op. cit.*, p. 30.

[5] Joseph Gusfield, "Social Structure and Moral Reform: A Study of the Woman's Christian Temperance Union," *American Journal of Sociology*, 61: 221-32, November 1955.

[6] Odegard, *op. cit.*, p. 38.

the Woman's Christian Temperance Union has two aims: it is a society that seeks universal personal total abstinence and the adoption of local, state, and national prohibition, and secondly, the exaltation of the Lord Jesus Christ and personal acceptance of him as Saviour and King.[7]

The values and tactics of the dry movement may be summarized as follows: (1) the consumption of alcoholic beverages is evil and should be prohibited by law, (2) those who advocate the production and consumption of alcoholic beverages are evil, misled, sick, or foreigners, and (3) they are more powerful politically and financially, but "God is on our side and the Truth shall prevail," through education, political pressure, and the mobilization of religious organizations.

The values and tactics of the wet resistance to prohibition may be summarized as follows: (1) drinking is a matter of personal decision, and the Constitution of the United States guarantees every man the right of his personal decision in matters not affecting the general welfare, (2) the liquor traffic is a legitimate business and, under laissez-faire capitalism, should not be the subject of special legislation, (3) facts prove that the free production and consumption of alcoholic beverages reduces crime, contempt for the law, alcoholism, and taxation, and (4) these values shall be implemented through advertising, political pressure, and the mobilization of business and service organizations.

In-Group and Out-Group Stereotypes. Both wet and dry groups standardize judgment of their members and of the adversary. In-group members view themselves as reasonable men who simply advocate that which any honest, right-thinking person must recognize as truth. On the other hand, they view their adversaries in an equally stereotypic manner, but as polar opposites. As Sherif and Sherif have indicated, "stereotypes can be taken as one index of social distance,"[8] which develops out of the history of groups in conflict over divergent interests. Here we can present only a small sample of stereotypic statements from several periods of wet-dry conflict.

As with all in-groups following diametrically opposite goals, drys and wets have standardized favorable stereotypes in regard to their values and goals and unfavorable stereotypes for the adversary. Prior to national prohibition, established in 1920, the enemies of total abstinence were viewed as un-American foreigners and greedy corrupters for profit of all that was fine, Christian, and democratic in this country. At the

[7] John Coleman [n.t.], *The Christian Patriot*, 14: 4, February 1958.

[8] Muzafer Sherif and Carolyn Sherif, *An Outline of Social Psychology* (New York: Harper and Brothers, 1956), p. 653.

same time, dry organizations constantly presented a picture of their members as representative of all that was good, righteous, and patriotic. They identified themselves with God and Christianity.[9]

Wet groups viewed their opponents as "canting hypocrites and jesuitical grafters,"[10] and themselves as representatives of hard-working, child-rearing, honest immigrants.

Since the repeal of national prohibition in 1933, dry forces have generally been on the defensive. Values regarding social drinking have changed under increased urbanization and industrialization. Gusfield noted the occupations of the husbands of local W.C.T.U. leaders in thirty-eight cities in five states from 1885 to 1950. Using this factor as an index of socioeconomic status, he concluded that there has been a steady decrease in skilled and professional groups within the prohibition movement. The awareness of this shift is recognized by present W.C.T.U. members whom Gusfield interviewed.

Recent Interviews. Interviews recently conducted among members of both wet and dry groups in Oklahoma substantiate Gusfield's findings and point to a number of other factors. The factor of revenue is of increasing importance, particularly since the beginning of the present recession which has cut deeply into state tax revenues needed for the development of schools, highways, and aid to the needy. In this initial interviewing we were concerned with members' stereotypes of themselves and of the adversary and the tactics of organizations mobilized over the issue of prohibition.

The stereotypic attitude of drys toward their opponents is illustrated by the statement of the chairman of a county United Drys group: "The leading proponents of repeal. . .are conniving, cheap and petty. They are misguided through satanic influence."

On the other hand, the stereotypic attitude of wets toward their adversary is illustrated by the statement of an editor of a newspaper advocating repeal: "There is a lot of pyhocrisy which is illustrated by some people who teach Sunday School on Sunday and at other times use a complete bar in their basement for parties. . . . They drink wet and vote dry."

In contrast to this statement, the local leader of a United Drys unit declared that many politicians "vote dry and drink wet." The same

---

[9] Cf. Odegard and Merz, *op. cit., passim.* Also Luke Ebersole, *Church Lobbying in the Nation's Capital* (New York: The Macmillan Company, 1951); Wayne B. Wheeler, "The Inside Story of Prohibition," *The New York Times* (March 29, 1926); *The Anti-Saloon Year-Book* (1909-1931).

[10] Odegard, *op. cit.*, p. 147.

pattern of behavior is attributed by each group to the adversary.

The attitude of the drys toward themselves is illustrated by the statement of a former leader of a W.C.T.U. unit: "Of course ours is a Christian organization. Being on the side of the Christian people, we take the Bible as our guide."

The attitude of wets toward themselves is illustrated by a man who was formerly active in politics and in dry organizations: "I am more or less objective about it. Liquor means little to me, but I realize that the law enforcement of prohibition is costing a great deal of money and will have little effect on illegal activities concerning liquor. A pretense at law enforcement creates an attitude of contempt."

These indications of stereotypes of the out-group are pertinent to results of an earlier study of communication on the prohibition issue carried out in Oklahoma during the year following the most recent referendum on repeal, and recently reported by Hovland, Harvey, and Sherif.[11] In that study it was found that a communication presenting a strongly antiprohibition or a proprohibition position was viewed by listeners with opposing stands on the issue as "propagandistic" and "unfair." Exposure to communication from the opposite camp usually resulted in individuals remaining unchanged in their stands and strengthened in their values. The persons influenced by strongly proprohibition or antiprohibition communication were those who took a moderate or noncommittal position on the issue. On the other hand, a communication presenting a moderate position on prohibition, in this case a moderately wet stand, was judged by persons committed to a definitely wet and dry stand as being more divergent from their own stands than it actually was. Thus drys regarded the moderate communication as quite prorepeal, while wets displaced the position of the moderate communication toward the dry position.

These findings are substantiated in recent interviews of wet and dry leaders. Neutral individuals tend to be displaced toward the opposition. This judgmental tendency is exemplified in the response of a W.C.T.U. leader toward a clergyman who remains noncommittal on the prohibition issue. The W.C.T.U. leader stated: "X is wet; he favors package houses."

A clergyman, who is also a leader of a county unit of the United Drys, felt that the failure of some clergymen to preach total abstinence from the pulpit indicated their complete abdication of the ministerial

[11] Carl I. Hovland, O. J. Harvey, and Muzafer Sherif, "Assimilation and Contrast Effects in Reactions to Communication and Attitude Change," *Journal of Abnormal and Social Psychology*, 55:244-52, September 1957.

role. "In the ministry indolence, complacency, indifference, and so forth, is taking its toll. It hurts me to see among my own brethren what has developed. You'll find it in your own profession. There are professors who do the minimum and simply get by and draw their salaries."

The tactics of both groups are roughly the same. They attempt to mobilize a following through organizational appeals, they bring pressure to bear on legislators through lobbies, and they seek to gain the vote of the uncommitted voter through the media of mass communication and direct advertising.

Each group, however, pictures the tactics of the opposing group as unfair. Drys accuse wets of buying votes, frightening voters with false propaganda, and seducing voters by pouring immense sums of money into propaganda. The belief that wets spend millions of dollars on a campaign was stated by a dry leader as follows: "The breweries can invest a million dollars, because they will make it back in beer profits. After an election they are out several millions, but this isn't as hard on them as the several thousand the United Drys are out."

The tactics wets impute to their opponents also include the charge of corruption through bribery. A political candidate running for office on a repeal ticket told one of our interviewers that "the bootleggers. . . are donating to the professional drys. One dealer donated five thousand dollars to a Tulsa organization. Some of the others who are fighting repeal are paid religious drys in Oklahoma."

Conclusion. The projected research is intended to be a study of pressure groups utilizing the wet and dry issue as a paradigm, bringing into focus the factors mentioned above. Specifically, the plan is the investigation of the following problems: (1) In-group and out-group stereotypes, (2) stereotypes related to the organizational patterns of the groups involved, (3) pressure group tactics and their evaluation in terms of in-group and out-group values, stereotypes and goals, and (4) the effects on the above of newly emerging situations and factors in economic, social, and organizational life.

A combination of methods will be utilized which will include participant observation, interviews, in-group and out-group stereotypic ratings, and specially arranged experimental situations.

ETHNIC PREJUDICE AS RELATED TO SOCIAL CLASS AND RELIGIOSITY*

ABRAHAM L. ROSENBLUM
Graduate Student,
University of Southern California

Recently, much attention has been given to prejudice phenomena. Studies in this field usually emphasize prejudice directed toward a minority group on the part of a majority group.[1] This study was undertaken to ascertain the extent of prejudice toward selected ethnic groups on the part of respondents belonging themselves to specific ethnic groups and religious denominations.

This study also considers the variables of social class affiliation and religiosity and their relationships to the ethnic prejudice phenomena and attitudes toward leadership. It is hypothesized that there exist differential attitudes of prejudice toward ethnic groups and toward types of leadership on the part of the different social strata in society.[2]

Procedure. A questionnaire was constructed by the writer with the view in mind that it would reveal differential attitudes of ethnic prejudice on the part of different segments of the population. The survey contained twenty-two questions with multiple-choice answers, with question 20 being broken down into subquestions with multiple-choice answers. This questionnaire was designed to reveal ethnic prejudices and attitudes toward "authoritarian" and "democratic" leadership. This survey was mailed to a 25 per cent systematic random sample selected from three church membership lists of "Pine City," California: Episcopalian, Jewish, and Presbyterian. The numbers of questionnaires mailed were as follows: Episcopalian, 75; Jewish, 71; and Presbyterian, 68—

---

*This report is a condensed version of a study which won the 1958 Emory S. Bogardus Social Research Award, sponsored by the Alpha Kappa Delta Chapter of the University of Southern California.

[1] For a brief description of types and causes of discrimination, see Marie Jahoda, *et al.*, "Discrimination and Prejudice," in *Research Methods in Social Relations* (New York: The Dryden Press, 1955), "Appendix B," pp. 364-80; see also D. Robinson and S. Rhode, "A Public Opinion Study of Anti-Semitism in New York City," *American Sociological Review*, 10:511-15; Kurt Lewin, R. Lippit, and R. K. White, "Patterns of Aggressive Behavior in Experimentally Created 'Social Climates,'" *Journal of Social Psychology*, 10:271-99.

[2] For a discussion on leadership attitudes see William J. MacKinnon and Richard Centers, "Authoritarianism and Urban Stratification," *American Journal of Sociology*, 61:610-20; Richard Christie and J. Garcia, "Subcultural Variations in the Authoritarian Personality," *Journal of Abnormal and Social Psychology*, 46:457-69.

a total of 214. Total returns received were 178, of which 6 returns were not tabulated for reasons of incompleteness, including one respondent who objected to the term "social class." The percentage of returns was 83. This study is based on the returns of 64 Episcopalian, 54 Jewish, and 54 Presbyterian respondents.

After these data were tabulated, a comparison of the following criteria was made: (1) degree of ethnic prejudice and social class identification, (2) degree of prejudice and frequency of church attendance, (3) class affiliation and intensity of prejudice, (4) degree of prejudice and range of authoritarian-democratic attitudes toward leadership, (5) range of authoritarian-democratic attitudes toward leadership and class self-identification, (6) class self-identification and attitudes toward President Eisenhower's leadership.

A scale purporting to measure the degree of prejudice was constructed and subjected to the judgment of advanced graduate students at the University of Southern California. The weighted items from no prejudice to extreme prejudice toward ethnic groups are therefore based on the consensus of these judges. A test of the reliability of this scale was also made by the split-half technique and realized a Pearsonian r of .78. The weighted numbers were given according to the answers of the respondents to the questionnaire, and scales amenable to measurement were constructed.[3]

Social class affiliation was measured by self-identification according to a modified Centers' type question.[4] The question posed was: "Some social scientists have found that in the United States people designate themselves as belonging to four major social classes: Upper, middle, working, and lower. On the basis of these findings in which class do you belong? Upper—Middle—Working—Lower." In the final analysis, we considered a trichotomy of social classes: Upper, Middle, and Lower. The designation of "working" is included in the term "lower." We can assume reliability of correlation with the socioeconomic scales of Hollingshead, Warner, and/or the North-Hatt scale, since studies correlating results of these scales and the self-identification approach show a high correlation.[5]

The scale of "religiosity" and "nonreligiosity" was determined by the frequency of church attendance. When a respondent stated that he at-

---

[3] Copies of the scales will be furnished by the writer upon request.

[4] Cf. Richard Centers, *The Psychology of Social Classes* (Princeton: Princeton University Press, 1949).

[5] See, for example, J. Kahl and A. J. Davis, "A Comparison of Indexes of Socio-Economic Status," *American Sociological Review*, 20:317-25.

tends church once a week, twice a month, or once a month, he was considered operationally "religious." If he stated his church attendance to be less than once a month he was considered "nonreligious."

The frequency of church attendance, then, is taken to mean degree of religiosity. We realize that attendance may not be the sole or the best criterion for religiosity. One may attend religious service every week and have other than religious motivation for this behavior. Another one may actually not attend church and basically be a religious person. It would, in this instance, be a matter of definition of what is meant by *religiosity*. However, a person attending church regularly, regardless of his motivation, whether out of curiosity regarding the sermon or for social reasons, is bound to be affected by its religious atmosphere; something will "rub off" on him. For our purpose in measuring this variable, we operationally define *religiosity* by the variable of church attendance.

The statistical results were computed by means of percentages and subjected to chi-square analyses.[6]

Findings. The findings of the study are as follows:[7]

1. The findings in this study support the assumption at the outset that "Pine City" is a predominantly middle-class locale. The majority of the respondents, 69.1 per cent, declared themselves to belong in the middle class.

2. There is no significant statistical relation between prejudice toward ethnic groups and different church affiliations. The percentages of prejudice and nonprejudice are almost equally divided among the three church membership groups (Episcopalian, Jewish, and Presbyterian).

3. Prejudice is definitely related to social class identification, i.e., the higher one's social class status identification, the more likely he is to be prejudiced toward ethnic groups. The percentage of prejudiced persons among the various social groups as revealed in this study are 83.3 per cent, 70.6 per cent, and 14.6 per cent for upper, middle, and lower classes, respectively.

4. There are more ethnic prejudice attitudes in respondents who attend church less than once a month, seldom, or never than those attending church regularly—every week, twice a month, or once every month. The percentage of prejudice for those who attend church more regularly up to and including once a month is 51.3 per cent, while for those of lesser attendance it is 72.7 per cent.

---

[6] Copies of the tables will be furnished by the writer upon request. The tables have been omitted for space reasons.

[7] All of the chi-square statistics are significant at the 1 per cent level.

5. It was found that attitudes of authoritarianism in the context of this study follow the U-shaped curve. More of upper-class and lower-class respondents than middle-class respondents have "authoritarian" attitudes, 83.3 per cent and 70.7 per cent, respectively; only 37.9 per cent of the middle-class respondents displayed "authoritarian" tendencies.

6. The positive answers to President Eisenhower's leadership also follows a U-shaped curve. Of the respondents, 83.3 per cent of the upper, 48.9 per cent of the middle, and 73.2 per cent of the lower classes declared themselves for the President "as a good leader."

7. These findings indicate that the "democratic" type of individuals[8] shows less ethnic prejudice than the "authoritarian" type.[9] The percentage of the democratic type respondents who display attitudes of ethnic prejudice is 44.5 per cent, while 75.0 per cent of the authoritarian types display attitudes of ethnic prejudice.

8. It was first assumed that the more religious a person is (since he would be more likely to accept the religious leader's authority), the greater would be his tendency to accept "authoritarian" leadership. This study reveals the opposite. The majority of religious respondents, 58.1 per cent, display democratic tendencies, while of the nonreligious respondents, only 36.3 per cent have democratic tendencies and 63.7 per cent display "autocratic" tendencies.

9. The democratic-authoritarian attitude on the part of the Episcopalian, Jewish, and Presbyterian respondents seems to follow the general trend. Since the majority of respondents seem to designate themselves as middle class, they have the highest majority of democratic tendencies. The percentage of preferences to accept the "democratic type of leadership" as operationally defined in this preliminary study reveals the following distributions: the Episcopal group, 28.1 per cent; the Jewish group, 72.2 per cent; and the Presbyterian group, 57.5 per cent.

10. A table of the percentage of the intensity of prejudice for the upper, middle, and lower classes was also computed. Here only the respondents were considered who scored on the prejudice side of the scale. The number of this group is 100. A new dichotomy of "some prejudice" and "very prejudiced" was formed. Here again the trend follows the U-shaped curve. The percentages of "very prejudiced" respondents are high on each end: 80.0 per cent for the upper and 83.3 per cent for the lower class, while the middle-class respondents scored only 4.8 per cent for the "very prejudiced."

[8] The "democratic" type of individual is operationally defined here according to the answers to question 20 of the questionnaire.

[9] The "authoritarian" type is operationally defined here according to the answers to the questionnaire.

OCCUPATIONS OF SOCIOLOGY MAJORS
A Selected Group

MARGARET L. HELBRICH
University of Pittsburgh

The purpose of this study was the discovery of the areas and fields of employment of a selected group of sociology majors. It should be pointed out that most of the graduates in this study had some additional education beyond the A.B. degree or additional training after graduation. Analysis of the data revealed that most students who received additional education took graduate work in sociology or social work.

This study is concerned with the occupations of a selected group of seventy-eight sociology majors who were graduated from the University of Pittsburgh between 1946 and 1950 with an A.B. degree. The questionnaire method was used in obtaining the data.

Thirty-nine male former sociology majors were included in this study. Each of the male respondents reported that he had been employed at some time since graduation from the University of Pittsburgh, and with few exceptions each reported that he had been employed in several full-time jobs since graduation.

The leading occupational categories in which these male former sociology majors reported having been employed are social work, sales, clerking, teaching, ministry, and social research. Twenty-one males reported having been employed at some time as social workers, eight as salesmen, seven as clerks, five as college teachers, five as ministers, three as social researchers, and the remaining in miscellaneous occupational categories with not more than two individuals in any one category.

A few statements can be made concerning occupational mobility within the categories in which most of these male former sociology majors have been employed. For the purpose of this study, "occupational mobility" may be defined as any change from one area or field of employment to another, or an advancement or demotion in the same field or area of employment. It should be pointed out that occupational mobility was rather difficult to determine because not much time had elapsed since the members of this group had graduated from the University of Pittsburgh.

Social workers tend to remain in social work, even though they may change their place of employment. Only three of the twenty-one male former sociology majors who were employed as social workers at the time they answered the questionnaire had been employed in other fields. Of these three, one had been a college teacher who later returned to social work, one had been a home and school visitor, and one had been a salesman. Of the total of eight salesmen, two had been employed in other jobs: one had been a salesman and one a machine operator. The other six remained salesmen.

The clerks, seven in number, show an interesting pattern of occupational mobility. Only two of the seven remained clerks. The other five were later employed in the following occupations: foreman, industrial representative, job analyst, timekeeper, and construction supervisor.

The five college teachers show the following pattern of occupational mobility. Three of these teachers have changed their jobs: one is in social research, one is in social work, and one is in the Army. The two who are presently employed as college teachers of sociology reported that they were associated at some time with social research. In the case of the five ministers, two reported their positions as pastor and two as assistant pastor; one had been a secretary, the only one of the five ministers reporting previous employment.

A total of thirty-nine questionnaires were received from female former sociology majors. Several of these female respondents reported that they were married immediately after graduation and never had a full-time job for which they received an income. Each of the other female former sociology majors reported that she had been employed in one or several full-time jobs since graduation.

Analysis of the data showed that there are three leading occupational categories among the members of this group. Twenty-seven are housewives, eighteen have been employed as social workers, and seven have been secretaries. Others are employed in miscellaneous occupational categories with not more than two individuals in any one category.

A few statements can be made concerning occupational mobility in the occupational category of female social worker. As was the case with the male former sociology majors in this study, there seems to be a tendency for this group of female social workers to remain in this occupation. Of the eighteen females employed as social workers, only two have gone into another field of employment: one is now employed as a librarian and one as a saleswoman. Analysis of the data revealed that there is little occupational mobility among this group of secretaries, only one of the seven reporting previous employment, and she had been a clerk; one is now a college teacher, and five remained secretaries.

Summary. A comparison of the occupations of this group of graduates shows that, excluding the housewives, the leading occupational category among both the male and female former sociology majors in this study is social work. Other occupational choices of both male and female sociology majors include social worker, salesman or saleswoman, secretary, clerk, and college teacher.

The findings of this study concerning the occupations of sociology majors are in agreement with the findings of other studies. According to a study of sociology majors made by Alexander[1] in 1948, the leading occupational categories of male sociology majors were social work, teaching, personnel work and labor relations, business, ministry, and research, in that order. This seems to indicate that the occupations of male sociology majors have changed little in the past few years.

Likewise, a study of sociology majors by E. S. Bogardus[2] in 1941 revealed that more sociology majors were employed in social work than in all other occupations combined. Teaching sociology in college also ranked, as did ministry and marriage.

An informal survey of the college bulletins of a number of leading departments of sociology revealed the following statements of objectives of training in sociology: (1) to prepare the individual for better citizenship; (2) to provide for an understanding of the nature of culture, social institutions, and groups; (3) to prepare the individual for advanced sociological study; (4) to provide a prerequisite for vocations and professions such as social work, research, teaching, and the ministry.

A conclusion from the present study might be that these objectives are being realized and that the understanding of culture and social relations acquired by sociology majors, while it is not specific occupational training, is useful in qualifying them for the occupations they have been found to enter.

---

[1] Walter Alexander, Jr., "Occupational Interests of Sociology Majors," *American Sociological Review*, 13: 758-63.

[2] E. S. Bogardus, "Why Major in Sociology?" *Sociology and Social Research*, 26: 154-63.

FOUR CORRELATES OF EMPATHY IN THE DATING SITUATION

ROBERT L. STEWART
AND
GLENN M. VERNON
Central Michigan College

Almost every conceivable social act involves the complex process of imaginatively putting oneself into the place of the other or others in a social situation and attempting to structure the situation and one's role within it as the other does. This empathizing helps to determine what action one will take in a particular situation. For this reason, the empathic process has a crucial influence upon the outcome of any social interaction. Our research, a part of which is reported here, has been designed to explore this process at the empirical level.

At the outset of this research we hypothesized—on the basis of the theoretical insights of such individuals as Mead, Dewey, and Kuhn—that empathy emerges from the interplay of two general factors: (1) that which is brought to the situation by the individual and (2) the characteristics of the situation. This is contrary to the view of empathy as a trait or a capacity.

We have explored this hypothesis by studying the dating experiences of college students. Our sample was composed of 104 persons or 52 couples enrolled in college during the 1955-56 school year. All respondents were volunteers. The respondents were not informed that we were interested in empathy but were told only that they were participating in a study of dating. This structuring was supported by the nature of the questions appearing on the questionnaire.

While 52 couples provided a sufficiently large sample for initial exploration, we recognize that the sample was seriously deficient in at least one important aspect. This deficiency is related to the use of volunteers, rather than a random sample of students, and to the fact that role taking may be related to the volunteering process. It is well known that this method draws together an unrepresentative portion of the universe. Consequently, our findings cannot be considered to be representative of any larger group. However, we feel that the findings can be utilized to understand some factors associated with the empathic process in situations similar to that studied.

Our respondents were couples who completed a questionnaire with reference to a specific recent date. Two types of information were secured in the two-part questionnaire from both the young man and the girl concerning fourteen areas of this date: (1) the respondent's satisfaction in each of the fourteen areas; (2) the respondent's guess of the satisfaction felt by his partner in each area.

The measure of empathy was derived by determining how closely the respondent's guess of his or her partner's satisfaction coincided with the satisfaction actually reported by the partner. Thus, we could determine how well each individual was able to transpose himself into the thinking and feeling of his or her partner in fourteen areas of the situation. If the guessed satisfaction coincided with the stated satisfaction, empathy was at a maximum. Any deviation of the guessed satisfaction from the stated satisfaction was determined and stated as the deviation score. Thus, empathy was measured in terms of the size of the deviation score —the higher the deviation, the lower the empathy. The total deviation score for each individual was computed by adding the plus and the minus deviations irrespective of signs.

The following items from the questionnaire illustrate the technique. These items were answered by both individuals. No. 14. Check one of the following statements which best describes how you felt about the means of the transportation used on the date: (1) I was very satisfied, (2) I was satisfied, (3) I was neutral, (4) I was unsatisfied, (5) I was very unsatisfied. No. 28. Check one of the following statements which best describes how you thought your partner felt about the means of transportation used for the date: (1) I was very satisfied, (2) I was satisfied, (3) I was neutral, (4) I was unsatisfied, (5) I was very unsatisfied. These items appeared in different sections of the questionnaire.

The scoring weights were assigned according to the Likert Method. These scores were then utilized to obtain the measure of empathy—the deviation score. Thus, if a young man guessed that his partner was "neutral," whereas she had actually indicated that she was "very satisfied," *his* deviation score would be a minus two. Likewise, if the girl guessed that her partner was "very satisfied," whereas he had indicated that he was "neutral," *her* deviation score would be plus two. A deviation score as high as minus or plus four was possible for each item, with a possible total deviation score of 56.

Dating areas included in the study were feelings about the following: (1) going with the person dated when the arrangements for the date were made, (2) time set for the beginning of the date, (3) kind of date, (4) amount of money spent, (5) means of transportation used, (6) individual's own dating manners while on the date, (7) partner's dating manners while on the date, (8) the decisions made while on the date, (9) physical intimacies which did occur on the date, (10) how far the individual went (physical intimacies) while on the date, (11) amount of time spent on the date, (12) going on another date with the individual, and (13) over-all satisfaction with the date.

Our analysis of these data has provided general support for our original hypothesis as to the emergent nature of empathy. Previously published findings from this study have indicated that empathy is associated with the following three interrelated factors: (1) involvement with the dating partner, (2) whether or not the individuals have dated each other previously, (3) frequency of dating the same individual. We found further that when the involvement factor was controlled, there was no association between amount of dating and empathy, indicating that frequent daters are not better empathizers unless they are also highly involved with their partners.[1]

This article presents additional data bearing on the original hypothesis and reports our findings as to the relationship between empathy and (1) satisfaction with the dating experience, (2) type of date, (3) leadership, (4) self-conception.

Concerning the relationship between dating satisfaction and empathy, it was hypothesized that high satisfaction would be associated with high empathy scores. We obtained our measure of satisfaction by adding the scoring weights for each of the eleven items pertaining directly to satisfaction, according to the Likert Method. The corrected chi-square (Yates) observed was significant at the .05 level.[2] The data indicate that high empathy is associated with high satisfaction. Since satisfaction on the date is something which emerges during the process of dating, and since there is this observed association between satisfaction and empathy, this finding provides further support for our thesis.

The observed association between empathy and satisfaction can be interpreted in the following manner. There appears to be a reciprocal influence here—satisfaction leads to empathy and empathy leads to satisfaction. Individuals who are satisfied with the dating experience are probably more relaxed and at ease—a condition which may contrib-

---

[1] Glenn M. Vernon and Robert L. Stewart, "Empathy as a Process in the Dating Situation," *American Sociological Review*, 22: 48-52.

[2] Corrected with Yates formula. See Margaret Jarman Hagood and Daniel O. Price, *Statistics for Sociologists* (New York: Henry Holt and Company, 1952), p. 370. This correction was used in all chi-square analysis.

ute to high empathy. Likewise, being able to take the role of the other successfully makes social relations move along more smoothly and thus contributes to greater satisfaction.

With respect to the association between empathy and the type of date, the following observations and interpretations were made. Dating is an experience which has many different expressions. For instance, a date to attend a basketball game is considerably different from a date for a formal dance. If the empathy level were significantly higher for the group engaging in one type of dating experience than for the group engaging in a different type of date, this would support the premise that empathy is of an emergent nature, since empathy would *vary* with the situation—not the individual.

Such an association was found in our study. However, this finding is somewhat tenuous, since some of the cells of our contingency table were too small for adequate statistical treatment and no logical rationale for combining categories was apparent.

However, an interpretation of the differences that were observed is suggested by comparing "coke" dates and dinner dates. Empathy was greater for the dinner date group than for the coke date group. Since a dinner date is generally defined as being of greater importance than a coke date, we might assume that the dater would be likely to select as a partner someone with whom good relationships had already been established—one with whom satisfactory empathic experiences had occurred. On the other hand, a coke date is generally more casual and less expensive, and the outcome is not as important to the individual as in the case of a dinner date. Consequently, a dater may be more willing to use this type of date for trying out an untested relationship. It would seem, then, that some dates are used for tested relationships, and that the daters thereby reap the rewards of previously developed empathy; while other dates are used for testing relationships, that is, to see if empathy can be developed. This, again, emphasizes the relationship between the situational factors and the level of empathy.

Additional evidence concerning the nature of empathy was secured by relating dating empathy to campus leadership. If empathy were a quality which an individual carried with him in the same degree from situation to situation, the high empathy individuals in our sample should also be high empathy individuals in other situations. If, however, individual factors do not determine empathy but rather *contribute* to empathy in interaction with situational factors, then it would follow that high empathy individuals in our group may not evidence high empathy in another group. Our data permitted us to test this association.

Research by Chowdery and Newcomb has indicated that "leaders of a group are significantly superior to non-leaders and isolates in their ability to judge group opinion on familiar and relevant issues."[3] In other words, leaders were found to evidence greater empathy than nonleaders and isolates. From this we could assume that those of our sample who were leaders in the various campus organizations would be high empathy individuals in such groups. Granting this assumption, it would then be possible to see whether or not campus leaders were concentrated among the group of high dating empathizers.

Our study finds no significant concentration of campus leaders in the high empathy group. This finding, then, provides additional support to the hypothesis that empathy is processual in nature.

The last check of association to be reported here is that between empathy and self-conception. Theoretically the self-conception is an essential variable in the empathic process. The substance of this process involves imaginatively putting one's *self* into the place of the other. Therefore, it is logical to presume that the nature of the self should be related to the success with which this process is carried out. For this reason an initial attempt was made to determine what associations might be observed between the self-conception and the empathic process in the dating situation.

The Kuhn-MacPartland Twenty-Statements Test, the TST, was used as the instrument for making observations of the self.[4] This test has the following form:

In the spaces provided below please give twenty different statements in answer to the question "Who am I?" Give these answers as if you were giving them to yourself, not somebody else. Write fairly rapidly, for the time is limited.

Twenty numbered blank lines follow these instructions. Typical responses to this instrument are "I am a student," "housewife," "girl," "happy," "conceited," "five feet six inches tall." Frequently the "I am" is omitted and merely single words or identifying phrases are listed.

Several different measures have been derived from the TST. However, so far in this research we have been concerned only with the scale

---

[3] Kamla Chowdery and Theodore M. Newcomb, "The Relative Abilities of Leaders and Nonleaders to Estimate Opinions of Their Own Groups," in A. Paul Hare, Edgar F. Borgatta, and Robert F. Bales (editors), *Small Groups* (New York: Alfred A. Knopf, 1955), pp. 235-45.

[4] Manford H. Kuhn and Thomas S. MacPartland, "An Empirical Investigation of Self-Attitudes," *American Sociological Review*, 19: 68-76.

of locus.[5] Briefly, the locus scale is a measure of the kind of attachments people have to the major elements in the social structure of their society. This scale is obtained by analyzing the responses made to the TST in terms of two categories: one a consensual category, that is, responses which have a generally agreed-upon meaning; and a nonconsensual category, that is, a class of responses which have no clearly understood meaning. The characteristics of the responses are such that they produce a satisfactory Guttman scale if the consensual statements are placed in one category and if "no responses" are combined with nonconsensual statements and placed in the second category.

The scale score obtained by this procedure is the locus score. The corrected chi-square obtained was significant at the .05 level. This indicates that the persons with the medium locus scores have the greatest proportion of high empathy scores, with the ratio of good to poor empathizers being three to one. Individuals falling into the high locus category most often are poor empathizers at a ratio of better than two to one. At the low locus end of the scale the high and low empathizers are about equally divided.

While the interpretation of such exploratory findings is hazardous, the following is suggested as a possible explanation. The locus score is a reflection of the degree to which a person is effectively anchored in the main (consensually agreed to) culture. Thus, persons with high locus scores might be described as having achieved stable identification by, and in terms of, the larger culture. As a result, such persons may find less motivation to take the role of the other (to empathize) as they know who they are and what they are going to do, and they are proud of it. If high locus score can be interpreted as reflecting a lack of concern with taking the role of the other, this could explain the general inaccuracy of high locus respondents in the empathic process.

On the other hand, persons with middle locus scores, because they are less strongly attached to the larger culture and perhaps less clearly defined in their own eyes, may have a greater desire to take the other fellow into account. This would help explain the greater accuracy of the middle locus respondents.

However, it was observed that the respondents with the low locus scores were not as frequently accurate as the middle locus respondents. This could be due to the fact that at least a minimum amount of clear

[5] A complete description of the means of arriving at the locus score is given in Thomas S. MacPartland, *The Self and Social Structure: An Empirical Approach* (Iowa City: State University of Iowa Library, 1953), p. 147, Ph.D. dissertation, microfilm.

anchorage in the main culture is necessary to empathize efficiently and consistently.

From this exploratory analysis it is clear that there is an association between empathy and the self-conception as measured by the TST. If in subsequent research any support can be provided for the admittedly tenuous interpretations of these data, a significant addition to the understanding of the empathic process may be provided. It should be noted here, however, that to some extent this interpretation is contrary to the general view of empathy as an emergent, for there is the suggestion that clarity of self-conception, which is an individual factor, accompanies high empathy.

In summary, then, we can say that the observed association between these four factors and empathy gives further support to the hypothesis that empathy is processual in nature. Clearly, there are now good reasons for exploring this hypothesis in a larger setting and with respect to different situations.

RACIAL REACTIONS BY REGIONS

EMORY S. BOGARDUS
University of Southern California

One of the special studies resulting from the racial distance research made by the writer in 1956 was reported under the title of "Racial Distance Changes in the United States."[1] These data included the racial reactions of persons most of whom were from 18 to 35 years of age, about half being college students and the other half being employed professionally while taking one or more postgraduate courses. The subjects were about equally divided between the two sexes.

Of the 2,053 persons from whom reactions of a racial nature were obtained, 88 per cent were Caucasian, 11 per cent Negro, and 1 per cent Mongolian in background, but all 100 per cent were native-born citizens, with no exceptions as far as ascertained. When the racial reactions were tabulated according to the regions of the United States, interesting results were observed and are reported in the accompanying table. The United States was divided into four regions as follows: northeast, south, north middle, and Pacific west. The N for each of the four regions was as follows: northeast, 424; south, 524; north middle, 487; and Pacific west, 613. The data from eight different sources in each of the four regions and the arithmetic means of all the reactions for each region were used as bases of comparisons, so that the limited differences in the N's for the four regions were neutralized.

It will be seen that while comparisons were made of the reactions of the respondents from the four regions by arithmetic means, the N nevertheless was not large enough to serve as a basis for generalizations except in a tentative way. In order to make the N large enough to be adequately representative, it would have to be increased several times. It also needs to be remembered that the N refers to members of a given age group, and not to people above 35 or 40 years of age; and that it pertains to persons in college or with a college education in certain fields chiefly of a social science nature. The findings, therefore, will be stated in the form of hypotheses, or statements to be tested further before anyone draws any final conclusions from them.

The arithmetic mean of the reactions of the 424 participants from the "northeast" region was 2.06, and included the area from Maine to Pennsylvania. The arithmetic mean of the 524 participants from the "south" was 2.40, and included the states from North Carolina and Florida to Texas. The arithmetic mean for the 487 participants from

[1] *Sociology and Social Research,* 43: 127-35.

the "northmiddle" region was 1.958, and included the area from Michigan to Minnesota and Nebraska. The arithmetic mean of the 613 participants from the "Pacific west" was 1.97, and included the area from Washington to California. Some other regional division of the United States might have been made, but this one had reasonable merits. In any such division there would always be border states between any two regions.

In examining the arithmetic means it will be noted (1) that when the scores favor the nearness pole in one of the four regions, they also favor that pole in the other three regions, and likewise when the score indicates farness in one region, a similar farness is likely to be found in the other regions as well. While there are variations from region to region in which distance is shown in the various races, yet similarity in distance reactions is more to be noted than dissimilarity. Two exceptions are noticeable above others, that is, with reference to reactions toward the Russians and the Poles. Interview data throw some light on these last-mentioned results. Some respondents in all four regions reacted toward Russians as people and some toward them as Communists, and some experienced both types of reactions and reacted in favor of what seemed to them to be the more important way to view the Russians. In three of the four regions, the nearness scores for Russians as people offset to a greater or less degree the farness scores given the Russians as Communists in the given region, but in the region designated as "south" in this study there were more persons who reacted to Russians as Communists (farness) than as people (nearness), and hence the greater distance given the Russians in the "south" than in the other regions. The interview materials indicate that a similar bifurcation of attitudes occurred in the "south" regarding reactions to the Poles.

(2) The difference in the distance reactions between the region with the lowest arithmetic mean, the "northeast" with a score of 1.958, and the region with the highest, the "south" with a score of 2.40, was .442. The other regions fell in between these two. The higher distance reaction in the "south" was higher, not for all races, but for particular ones, such as the Chinese, Czechs, Germans, Koreans, Poles, Russians. But it was not higher for the Negroes because many Negro respondents were in the "south" and kept down the score of racial reactions toward the Negroes.

(3) The differences in the social distance reactions in different regions are related to the nature of the acquaintance of the people in each region with each one of the thirty races. (a) Sometimes the distance score runs high if there is little firsthand knowledge of a given race and if the hearsay reports are unfavorable. (b) Sometimes the distance reactions are great toward a race in a region because low economic-level

and low cultural-level representatives of that race who live in the given region cause firsthand experiences to be unfavorable. (c) The distance reactions run high in any region toward a particular race where the group in control, whether in the majority or in the minority, feels that it is in danger of losing status or control because of competition of any kind from the given race.

(4) Another hypothesis may be stated to the effect that less racial distance develops in those communities where few traditions are tied in deeply with local life. A sort of free-for-all attitude prevails with reference to races. Conversely, the stronger the traditions in an established locality, the greater the opposition to any racial group that seems to be forging ahead to the point where the established *status quo* is endangered. Since traditions have the support of sentiment, such sentiment is easily aroused in defense of endangered traditions; it cannot be easily overcome by argument or persuasion; it resents the use of force and even of law.

(5) Another hypothesis that may be advanced for testing is that less distance is expressed in those communities where incoming races have gradually arrived over a period of time and whose members are slowly climbing out of the lower economic levels. By their gradualness they do not arouse opposition because of their "invasion," and they are likely to be viewed as people who are deserving rather than as people who are demanding their "rights." Conversely, low economic-level races who "invade" a community suddenly in numbers arouse insecurity and fear. In fact, races of any economic level who enter a community suddenly and in numbers arouse racial farness reactions, because of a fear of the loss of status and power and of rumors that the community will be "taken over" by usurpers.

(6) A related hypothesis is: Lesser racial distances are expressed in those communities where the established residents (who perhaps were "invaders" themselves at one time) feel little or no anticipated economic or social competition from the newcomers, or where their sympathies for the newcomers have been aroused by persecution that the newcomers have received elsewhere.

(7) Any minority group is likely to feel expressions of racial farness if its members rise rapidly in the economic, social, or political fields and seem to be ready to assume local control, especially if rumormongers magnify the danger and prey upon the fears of those in power.

(8) Any minority group that is in control in a community views askance any stirring activity on the part of a majority group that is not in control as being a threat to its possible shaky social position. A majority group in control may become antagonistic toward an unusually active minority acting as a group.

RACIAL REACTIONS BY REGIONS (Total N 2048) (Spring, 1956)

	Northeast (N 424)	*South* (N 524)	*North Middle* (N 487)	*Pacific West* (N 613)	*Difference between high and low*
1. American (U.S. white)	1.09	1.23	1.07	1.03	.20
2. Armenians	2.34	2.47	2.36	2.15	.32
3. Canadians	1.17	1.28	1.16	1.12	.16
4. Chinese	2.54	2.84	2.51	2.59	.33
5. Czechs	2.09	2.78	1.89	1.90	.49
6. English	1.22	1.43	1.19	1.17	.26
7. Filipinos	2.45	2.58	2.42	2.52	.16
8. Finns	1.78	2.15	1.75	1.66	.49
9. French	1.47	1.73	1.41	1.32	.41
10. Germans	1.62	2.09	1.45	1.33	.76
11. Greeks	2.12	2.46	2.05	1.80	.66
12. Hollanders	1.65	2.13	1.43	1.44	.30
13. Indians, American	2.44	2.31	2.32	2.32	.13
14. Indians from India	2.72	2.96	2.76	2.76	.24
15. Irish	1.77	1.87	1.42	1.29	.58
16. Italians	1.81	2.29	1.81	1.68	.61
17. Japanese	2.71	2.88	2.59	2.77	.29
18. Japanese Americans	2.40	2.57	2.16	2.23	.41
19. Jews	1.75	2.18	2.02	2.12	.43
20. Koreans	2.87	3.09	2.63	2.75	.46

	Northeast (N 424)	*South* (N 524)	*North Middle* (N 487)	*Pacific West* (N 613)	*Difference between high and low*
21. Mexicans	2.77	2.99	2.75	2.72	.27
22. Mexican Americans	2.50	2.70	2.49	2.49	.21
23. Negroes	2.53	2.74	2.80	2.89	.36
24. Norwegians	1.67	2.26	1.39	1.37	.89
25. Poles	2.04	2.79	1.77	1.74	1.05
26. Russians	2.32	3.68	2.32	2.19	1.49
27. Scots	1.63	1.97	1.41	1.39	.58
28. Spanish	2.08	2.33	2.00	1.97	.46
29. Swedish	1.64	2.02	1.36	1.34	.68
30. Turks	2.62	3.14	2.46	2.48	.68
Arithmetic means of 61,590 reactions	2.06	2.40	1.96	1.97	.44

PACIFIC SOCIOLOGICAL NEWS

University of California at Los Angeles. Donald R. Cressey, chairman of the department, has been elected president of the Pacific Sociological Society for 1959-60. Associate Professor Wendell Bell will be on leave in the 1959 Spring Semester to continue studies on political change, leadership, and social mobility in Jamaica under the final year of his three-year Social Science Research Council Faculty Research Fellowship. Assistant Professor Oscar Grusky has been awarded a Ford Foundation Faculty Fellowship in Social Science and Business for 1959-60. Assistant Professor Richard Hill is directing a research project designed to evaluate adult education programs, under a grant from the Ford Foundation Fund for Adult Education. Professor Franz Adler from the University of Arkansas is serving as lecturer in sociology in 1958-59, replacing Professor Svend Riemer, who is on sabbatical leave to conduct research on housing in Europe.

University of Idaho. Shortly before the Fall Semester, Dr. Alfred W. Bowers suffered a heart attack. Dr. Wayne M. Wellman taught the classes scheduled for Dr. Bowers. Dr. Mhyra S. Minnis will again conduct a tour to Europe during the coming summer. Dr. Minnis is interested particularly in European communities. Dr. Harry C. Harmsworth is planning a two-week workshop in social gerontology (June 15-26) on the Idaho campus.

University of Oregon. Dr. Joel V. Berreman has gone on half-time status with the department for two years in order to serve as research associate with the Oregon Study of Rehabilitation of Mental Hospital Patients. Dr. Robert Dubin has been appointed research professor of sociology. Walter T. Martin was visiting lecturer in rural sociology and sociology during the Summer Session at the University of Wisconsin. New additions to the department include Dr. Harry Alpert, professor of sociology and dean of the Graduate School. Dr. Lionel S. Wishneff joins the staff as an assistant professor.

Portland State College. Dr. John James, professor of sociology, is continuing on part-time leave during 1958-59 while serving as research director, Oregon Study of Rehabilitation of Mental Hospital Patients. Dr. Charles Brant, assistant professor of anthropology, served as consultant to the Department of Psychiatry, University of Utah School of Medicine, in early January, concerning integration of the behavioral sciences with the activities of that department. Mr. Frederic Chino, assistant professor of sociology, was a consultant to the Oregon Study of Rehabilitation of Mental Hospital Patients during the summer of 1958.

Dr. Warren Kalbach, in September 1958, accepted a joint appointment as assistant professor of sociology and director of the Oregon Board of Census. Dr. Charles Frantz, assistant professor of anthropology and sociology, is on leave during 1958-59. He is spending the year in Southern Rhodesia conducting research in race relations and teaching at the University College of Rhodesia and Nyasaland.

University of Southern California. Dr. Arnold Rose, professor of sociology from the University of Minnesota, will be visiting professor during the coming Summer Session. He will teach a graduate course in research methods and a course in race relations. Dr. Reed Powell, Harvard Graduate School of Business Administration, will serve as visiting professor during the Postsession. Dr. Powell will teach courses in industrial sociology and social change. Professor Harvey Locke is on sabbatical leave during the Spring Semester. Mr. Peter Geiser, of San Fernando State College, successfully passed the preliminary examinations recently for the Ph.D.

PEOPLES AND CULTURE

IN SEARCH OF IDENTITY: THE JAPANESE OVERSEAS SCHOLAR IN AMERICA AND JAPAN. By John W. Bennett, Herbert Passin, and Robert K. McKnight. Minneapolis: The University of Minnesota Press, 1958, pp. x+369.

This readable book is the fourth monograph resulting from a project sponsored by the Social Science Research Council's Committee on Cross-Cultural Education. The authors, all of whom have had considerable binational experience, utilized case studies, participant observation, questionnaires, depth interviews, and TAT and other tests to obtain data on Japanese students who have studied in universities in the United States.

There were three objectives in the research: "first, to study the . . . American-educated student in the historical context of the modernization of Japanese society and Japan's cultural relations with the United States; second, to describe and portray the experiences of the individual Japanese student on the American campus and back home in Japan; and third, to analyze the processes of adjustment of the type-case of the Japanese student to differing cultural environments."

As a result of the nation's modernization trends, Japanese students who have studied abroad have been confronted with such issues as Western culture versus the Orient's, democracy vis-a-vis autocracy, and individualism versus collectivism. To the individuals who have returned from an educational experience in another country, such issues have led to a search for identity. It is the authors' conviction, on the basis of this research and studies of other nationalities in the Social Science Research Council program, that the "tendency to equate the nation and the individual in the search for identity is widespread and forms a major problem of intercultural relations in the modern world."

Perhaps a more adequate sample and a larger N would have given the study greater validity. But even as it is, the keen insight which the authors brought to the research and the thoroughness of their inquiry make this an outstanding work. The appendixes and bibliography contain valuable material, and the study as a whole contributes substantially to a better understanding of the complex processes of intercultural experiences.

I. ROGER YOSHINO
University of Arizona

A TIME TO SPEAK. By Michael Scott. New York: Doubleday & Company, Inc., 1958, pp. 358.

In this vividly written book, the author tells how he grew up in the slums of Southampton, where his father was an Anglican clergyman, and how he became interested in championing the welfare of oppressed peoples, even of those in faraway South Africa. After becoming convinced that communism does not hold the solution of the problems of unjustly treated peoples, Michael Scott became an exponent in word and deed of the Gandhi principle of *satyagraha,* sometimes referred to as passive resistance but which is much more, namely, a "way of life" that substitutes love for hate and peaceful protest, even at the expense of going to jail, for violence, as an active call for the just dealing of man with man.

The author demonstrated his courage in South Africa in accepting arrest and a jail sentence as protests against oppression in a land where "policies of race supremacy" are used to "impose legal or artificial handicaps on the African people on the grounds of race." He later succeeded in presenting, against great odds, the cause of the Heroro people in South West Africa before the United Nations. Only love, he insists, can break through "the vicious circle of hate and counter-hate." The time is coming when "the United Nations will have to face the question of color or race discrimination as one of the fundamental issues for the future of civilization." Deprivation of justice because of color anywhere in the world creates a chain reaction which will "inevitably lead to an explosion if injustice remains irremediable by constitutional means." A short review cannot adequately present the dynamic appeal of this book.

E.S.B.

JORDAN, ITS PEOPLE, ITS SOCIETY, ITS CULTURE. By George L. Harris and collaborators. New York: Grove Press, Inc., 1958, pp. 246.

This is the second volume in the new "Survey of World Culture Series" (the first was on Poland; the next will deal with Algeria, and then comes one on China). In the pages of this book, a succinct, factual account will be found about such aspects of Jordan as historical setting, geography and population, ethnic groups and languages, social organization, religions, diffusion and control of information, industrial development, public health, the family, art and intellectual life, politics and national attitudes, and values and patterns of living.

The integrating factors in Jordanian life are religion (Islam), language (Arabic), and the rule of a national government. The hindrances to integration are found in the threefold division of the population into Bedouin nomads (200,000), village cultivators of the soil (800,000), and urban dwellers (400,000). These groups are divided by differences in social values, outlook on life, expectations, reactions to national government. There is another chasm, that dividing the west or Palestinian Jordanians from the East Bank people; the former are more Westernized and advanced, while the latter live more largely in their past, that is, in traditions. The emotional reactions toward the Israeli republic rise to a "passionate intensity" that would destroy Israel. Communist forces are at work undermining the influences of the West. Social change is taking place throughout Jordan and the future of this new nation is uncertain. A.R.R.

BIRTH AND REBIRTH. The Religious Meanings of Initiation in Human Culture. By Mircea Eliade. Translated from the French by W. R. Trask. New York: Harper and Brothers, 1958, pp. 175.

In these essays, originally given as the Haskell Lectures at the University of Chicago, initiation ceremonies from those of earliest tribes to those of higher religions are reviewed. Initiation ceremonies are considered in part as introducing the young to their culture heritage by impressive ceremonies of the older generation.

INTERNAL MIGRATION IN THE UNITED STATES. 1940-1957: A List of References. By G. L. Wilber and J. S. Bang. State College, Mississippi: Mississippi State University, Agricultural Experiment Station, 1958, pp. 52.

A total of 602 references are given, classified according to such topics as trends and population redistribution, rural-urban migration, urban area migration, migratory workers, characteristics of migrants, selectivity of migrants, ethnic groups, and planning and policies.

THE PEOPLE OF SHIP STREET. By Madeline Kerr. New York: The Humanities Press, 1958, pp. vii+215.

The People of Ship Street is a study of some nigh-dwellers in a Liverpool slum. The first three quarters of the book is devoted to a superior but nevertheless conventional social-anthropological "community" study. The fourteenth and fifteenth chapters then report the results of Rorschach and Lowenfeld Mosaic tests given to the children of Ship Street. The remainder of the book presents some general statements about subculture and personality in Ship Street, about basic personality and social organization, and some resulting hypotheses which have clear-cut and pertinent implications for a theory of personality.

Professor Kerr documents the role of the "Mum" in this matricentric, matrilocal, matriarchal subsociety and concludes, after considering the findings of several other scholars, that "it seems as if poor working-class conditions do tend to result in a dominant female." Frequent comparisons with an earlier study which she made of a Jamaican subsociety, as well as with studies by Kardiner, Mead, and others, help to remind the reader that he is dealing with something more relevant to sociological theory than the mere history of some anonymous persons in a unique society. From the case studies and the projection tests, Kerr infers relationships between role deprivation, intellectual development, emotional disturbance, and personality nonintegration that constitute engaging hypotheses about how the social environment functions in the development of personality.

This book is an example of the way in which an empirical study using clinical and case techniques can be interrelated with theory in a utilitarian as well as a scholarly way. The research design is commendable. New and important aspects of culture-personality theory are disclosed.

THOMAS ELY LASSWELL
Grinnell College

AFRICAN NOTEBOOK. By Albert Schweitzer. Translated by Mrs. C. E. B. Russell. Bloomington: Indiana University Press, 1958, pp. 144.

In this "Midland Book," the world-famous Schweitzer delves into the traditions and customs of the Negro peoples who live in the Lamberene region of west Africa, and produces many fascinating anecdotes of native practices and viewpoints. Numerous interpretations of and comments on the behavior of the natives are included.

The natives spend so much energy and time in rowing upstream and downstream in order to meet the necessities of life that they cannot understand how white men can spend hours and days in the practice of rowing, just to enter a boat race. The reasons why white men will work long hours day after day and week after week the year around seem strange to them, accustomed as they are to freedom from disciplined and regular daily toil. To them, white men seem characterized by "impetuous rudeness." These natives are surprised to find that white men make even animals, horses, for example, work regularly for them. While bound by taboos and magic, and lacking a sense of the sacredness that has been attached by the whites to property, the natives have much in their nature "that is good and valuable." Although not socially minded in the broad sense, the native exhibits a noteworthy kindheartedness in a personal sense. These anecdotes and interpretations throw considerable new light on the psychology and sociology of the natives of the Lamberene region of Africa. E.S.B.

SOCIAL PROBLEMS AND WELFARE

INTERNATIONAL REVIEW OF CRIMINAL POLICY. New York: United Nations, Publication No. 11 (January 1957), pp. 187.

The symbols of the United Nations documents are composed of capital letters combined with figures. The material is printed in three languages—English, French, and Spanish.

The main articles in the current issue deal with "Aspects of and Trends in the Treatment of Young Adult Offenders," by the Secretariat of the United Nations, and "Trends in Sweden in the Treatment of Youthful Offenders Who Have Reached the Age of Eighteen but Are Not Yet Twenty-one," by Karl Schlyter. The remainder of the volume contains information received from correspondents, new legislation pertaining to offenders and their treatment in various countries, and an extended bibliography of 1,099 titles. Besides the valuable information contained in the articles and the reports, one of the most important services rendered by the United Nations in publishing the various issues of the *Review* is the compilation of the publications on crime and delinquency throughout the world. The bibliography in the current issue covers chiefly the publications during 1956 and to a lesser extent the 1955 publications. M.H.N.

DER MENSCH UND DAS KINO. A Sociological Examination. By Edgar Morin. Stuttgart, Germany: Ernst Klett Verlag, 1958, pp. 248.

This monograph aims to examine the multifold experiences resulting from the effects of frequenting movie theaters. The *Umformung* (transcendence) of the cinema in relation to society, the spirit (*Seele*) and magic of the motion picture, its dynamics, symbols, words, and music, and participation in cinematic production are thoroughly analyzed. Daily, the author feels, the motion pictures *ueberfluten die Leere und Langeweile des modernen Menschen* (permeate the emptiness and boredom of modern man), and modern man comes to accept the "reality" of the pictures rather than the reality of his daily life. Sociology and social psychology will have to come to grips with the author's theory of "photographic realism," as he defines "realism."

HANS A. ILLING

THE EXPLODING METROPOLIS. By the Editors of *Fortune*. New York: Doubleday & Company, Inc., 1958, pp. 193.

"This book is by people who like cities." With these words William H. Whyte, Jr., initiates this highly readable polemic concerning some facets of urban life. Taken as a whole, this compilation of articles—which appeared in recent issues of *Fortune*—consists of a critique of those (Whyte says most) city planners who apparently do *not* like cities and a plea for popular active participation in urban planning. Presumably this plea is directed to *Fortune* readers.

This is a "problems" book. There are articles on the problems of urban and regional planning, metropolitan government, and urban renewal. And there are some suggested solutions or directions toward the solution of these problems—Jane Jacobs' discussion of "Downtown Is for People" provides some thoughtful directives. These articles are assisted by cityscape paintings—unfortunately reproduced in black and white—and several small studies. These studies include surveys of the characteristics of "high rise" and "low rise" apartment dwellers, opinions of the attitudes of these occupants about housing, surveys of commuter transportation costs, commuter attitudes toward transportation costs, and commuter views of possible forms of mass transportation. These studies suffer from popularization. There is scant concern with presenting the details of methodology, sampling, tests of significance, and other information ordinarily expected of serious social research. Technical appendixes or footnotes of technical details would have greatly strengthened this material.

One small section of the book deals with an evaluation of "which are America's best run cities." Cities with an estimated population of over 500,000 are more or less subjectively ranked according to such attributes as public health programs, traffic engineering, air-pollution control, recreation, etc. Here as elsewhere the book would have greatly benefited from a review of pertinent sociological writings. For example, Angell's work on the moral integration of American cities is neglected in the evaluation of cities, as is Ogburn's analysis in the discussion of the ecological importance of public transportation. In fact, this "study of the assault on urbanism and how our cities can resist it" incorporates scarcely a single major idea, concept, study, or finding from urban sociology. Typically, "urbanism" is discussed without definition, sans Wirth, sans Simmel. D.C.M.

THE SOCIAL WELFARE FORUM, 1958. Official Proceedings, Eighty-fifth Annual Forum, National Conference on Social Welfare, Chicago, May 11-16, 1958. Published for the National Conference by Columbia University Press, New York, 1958, pp. xiv+311.

The presidential address by Eveline M. Burns deals with the current responsibilities of social workers and is entitled "Social Work Is Our Commitment." Eighteen other major papers are included. In these, social work is related to the family, community development, welfare financing, social work administration. Especially significant are the papers on "Effecting change through social group work," "An assessment of social action," "Change through group experience," and "The bridge between social work and the social sciences." In the last-mentioned paper the author, Grace Coyle, points out how at the beginning of the present century social work and the social sciences began to draw apart as independent developments took place. Social work specialized in becoming "a profession providing social services" and developing "expert practitioners," and the social sciences engaged in refining their concepts, developing special theories and "appropriate research techniques."

Within the last ten years a rapprochement between social work and the behavior sciences has been taking place, with social work schools increasing the amount of social science materials in their curricula and collaborating more with social scientists in social work research. Social work thinking is also making more and more use of the concept of culture. A hindrance in this larger development is the fact that the social sciences engage in abstract generalizations and unfamiliar terminology. Another hindrance in this connection is the lack of integration among the social sciences themselves, so that it is difficult to know what new concepts to accept and what not to accept.

Throughout the group of papers in this volume there is still an evident lack of a philosophy of social work. A system of social values within which social work practitioners could view their activities would give new life to one of the most significant professions. E.S.B.

SOZIALE SCHICHTUNG UND SOZIALER WANDEL IN EINER INDUSTRIEGEMEINDE. Eine Soziologische Untersuchung der Stadt Euskirchen. By Renate Mayntz. Stuttgart, Germany: Ferdinand Enke Verlag, pp. ix+281.

In its seven chapters the book aims to "divide" the city into several social strata, examining the length of residence of the inhabitants, their desire for migration within the city limits, the types of neighborhood, the various *soziale Schichten* (social strata), as the censor, the city administration, and the populace itself see them, and the distribution of the populace among these strata. The author sees a *soziale Mobilitaet* (social mobility) among the people, particularly among, and according to, the levels of education. A valuable chapter discusses the intrasocial and intrapsychic interactions between the various strata, and the *soziale Distanz* according to the loyalty of a certain occupation or occupations, a loyalty stronger than the common bond of people of the given city, the size of which is approximately that of Pomona, California.

HANS A. ILLING

COMMUNITY ORGANIZATION 1958. Papers presented at the 85th Annual Forum of the National Conference on Social Welfare. New York: Columbia University Press, 1958, pp. ix+139.

The thirteen papers selected include a variety of subjects, with the authors representing both voluntary and public welfare agencies. The first article was written by the former Commissioner of Social Security, Department of Health, Education and Welfare of the United States.

The interrelationship between American social welfare and international affairs is significant. Besides, the far-flung welfare services are demonstrated in the fact that the United States is "paying insurance benefits to about 67,000 persons living in over 90 countries." In addition, the United States is a participant in many international conferences dealing with such subjects as family, child welfare, education, health, and agriculture. The author points out the basic principle that "community development usually begins with a different emphasis in different countries."

Other papers consider rural development and the family in the changing cities. One article on "Issues in Social Planning" sets up one of the weaknesses in community organization: "Social problems are seldom if ever considered on a community-wide basis. The focus is agency- rather than community-centered."

Special problems discussed include "Racial Integration in the Nation's Capital," "The Special Youth Program Approach to Chronic Problem Families," and "State Programming for the Mentally Deficient." "Community Organization in Public Administration" advocates the appointment of citizen boards and advisory committees in public welfare services, both in their central and their district offices. The trend to substitute United Funds for the earlier community chests is made clear.

Two articles are given over to research: "Social Work Research in the Future" and "Motivation Research." One question is raised which calls forth different answers: Can the social worker become a social scientist? No longer can the social worker deal glibly with terms from the social sciences. He needs a broad training and an ability to analyze and synthesize social theory and practice. This book may well be read by workers in both voluntary and public service, and it has much to offer any person devoting himself to any of the social sciences.

B.A.MCC.

JUGENDLICHE IN DER BERUFSBEWAEHRUNG. Reported by Wilhelm Hagen, Hans Thomae, Ernst Mansfeld, and Franz Josef Mathey. Stuttgart, Germany: Georg Thieme Verlag, 1958, pp. viii+179.

Four scientists—two of them public health officials and two sociologists—corroborated their findings regarding the development of maturity and *Berufsbewaehrung* (vocational success) among juveniles, examining the relationship of vocational choice and success, personality and achievement on the job, and the family in its relation to the successful achievements of the adolescent and postadolescent individual. Many tables provide the reader with insight into young people who come from intact families, as opposed to those who come from broken families; yet in both, the intact as well as the broken families, the graphs show that the developmental career of the youngster can be favorable or unfavorable. For other factors have to be taken into account, such as "predominantly inner or outer motivation," phases of physical and psychological development, and a "special diagnosis of development during puberty." Numerous case histories illustrate this useful book, which is based on three methods: the medical (physical handicaps and injuries, anthropometric measures, etc.), the psychological (tests, impressions, surveys, etc.), and the sociological (statements of parents and collaterals).

HANS A. ILLING

PROCEEDINGS OF THE 21ST BIENNIAL CONGRESS OF THE CO-OPERATIVE LEAGUE OF THE U.S.A. Held in Minneapolis, September 1958.

A fairly complete picture of the speeches, discussions, and actions of this Congress is presented in this document. It includes the addresses of Murray Lincoln and Jerry Voorhis, president and executive secretary, respectively, of The Cooperative League, as well as other cooperative leaders. It is contended that cooperatives should not engage in partisan activities but should act "within all parties." A major emphasis of the Congress was the need for greater cooperation among all cooperatives, so as (1) to obtain more capital, (2) to achieve greater legislative strength, (3) to improve the public relations of cooperatives, (4) to do more research work and to share more research data, (5) to reconcile producer and consumer differences. Emphasis was placed on developing large cooperative shopping centers so as "to handle seventy-five per cent of the items which seventy-five per cent of the people need."

The need for cooperative education was made clear by survey facts indicating that people generally do not understand that cooperatives are forms of private enterprise that make state ownership unnecessary in many fields, how they defeat communistic tendencies, and how they supplement political democracy with economic democracy. A weakness of the Congress was that inadequate consideration was given to improved and both intensive and extensive methods of specific educational programs for cooperatives.

E.S.B.

PREGNANCY, BIRTH AND ABORTION. By Paul H. Gebhard, W. B. Pomeroy, C. E. Martin, and Cornelia V. Christenson. New York: Harper and Brothers and Paul B. Hoeber, 1958, pp. xiii+282.

This book emanates from the Institute for Sex Research, founded by Alfred C. Kinsey. While the two earlier books dealt with "sexual behavior per se," this volume presents data concerning the reproductive consequences of a part of such behavior. Based on a sample of 5,293 white nonprison females, 572 Negro nonprison females, 309 Negro women interviewed in prison, and 900 white women interviewed in prison, the book presents extensive data "on conceptions among unmarried females and the prevalence of induced illegal abortion among both married and unmarried females in this country." The presentation is relevant to the problem and forthright throughout. The sample is not representative of all the persons in the United States in the categories involved, and hence the results as given are subject to the danger of being quoted as though they were truly representative. Brief notes are added concerning abortion problems in several other countries. The social implications of this study "must of necessity be left to others who are specialists in the various fields of the social sciences."

A.R.R.

SOCIAL THEORY AND RESEARCH

PARTICIPATION IN UNION LOCALS. By Arnold S. Tannenbaum and Robert L. Kahn. Evanston, Illinois: Row, Peterson and Company, 1958, pp. xii+275.

This book appears as a report of one of the studies conducted by the Organizational Behavior Program of the Survey Research Center of the University of Michigan. The particular research project was centered around the members and leaders of four unidentified local labor unions. Its principal objective was to ascertain "the extent to which members involve themselves in and devote energy to the operation of the local union." Two basic problems guided the inquiry, namely, the nature of the active union member as contrasted with the inactive one and the nature of the active union as compared with the inactive one. The research design as carried out gives a definitely clear picture of the locals studied, as well as much of the background and nature of their memberships. Nicely revealed are the functioning of the locals, their relationships with management, motivation of union leadership, as well as some good reporting upon the personalities, goals, and attitudes of union members. The active union member, as one might suspect, is one with a high level of energy, enabling him to give a great deal of time to participation in union affairs. He is a "repository of union values and norms." The active union commands an emotional allegiance from its membership which shows more cohesion than is found in the inactive union. It has skilled and effective leadership. The active union has more visible signs of control at work, these emanating from the membership or from the officers in combination with membership. One of the most profitable chapters deals with the social-psychological implications of the organizational control structure. Herein may be found the various aspects of the controls exercised in locals. The whole study is most commendable.

M.J.V.

ORGANIZATIONS. By Mames G. March and Herbert A. Simon, with collaboration of Harold Guetzkow. New York: John Wiley & Sons, Inc., 1958, pp. xii+262.

The twentieth century has yielded much literature about human relations in industry, with little attention to its organization into a comprehensive, theoretical framework. In attempting to correct this shortcoming, the authors have surveyed an extensive number of publications—chiefly from industrial psychology and sociology, economics, and political science—and have organized the theoretical materials into a form suitable for analysis and the empirical testing of hypotheses.

Theories of organization behavior are classified into three general "models." Model one, developed during the first quarter of the twentieth century and typified by Taylor's studies in scientific management, regarded the employee as essentially an instrument or physiological automaton. In model two theories, which characterized the second quarter of the century, the employee was seen as a human being, with feelings and emotions. Both of these approaches, however, fail to account for humans as "adaptive, reasoning beings," capable of making rational responses to the multifold, differentiated, and often unanticipated stimuli of an organization milieu. The more current model three theories attempt to supplement previous models by greater emphasis upon cognitive factors.

The book's contextual organization is carefully and logically arranged. The style is concise and undoubtedly quite abstract to the professionally unsophisticated reader. A more liberal use of illustrative materials probably would have made the book more adaptable to a wider audience.

The authors have, nevertheless, accomplished their purpose well in bringing into a single framework, for study and evaluation, the varied theories of organization behavior. The book is a valuable contribution, and should be welcomed by behavioral scientists in industrial and organization relations.

HARRY C. HARMSWORTH
University of Idaho

SOZIALE VORURTEILE. Ein Problem der Persoenlichkeit der Kultur und Gesellschaft (A Problem of the Personality in Culture and Society). By Peter Heintz. Cologne, Germany: Verlag fuer Politik und Wirtschaft, 1958, pp. 218.

Prejudices (*Vorurteile*) are classified by the author in three connections: social prejudices appear in society when they contrast with prevailing situations and when they are planned under false premises; prejudices also appear when one's own image as well as the "other" image are at odds with each other (the author cites as examples our Negro problem, the "great" number of our Indian tribes, and the "emancipation" of women); and finally, prejudices make their appearance whenever there are clearly visible differentiations within the in-group, which are expressed by corresponding stereotypes. The author leans heavily on Nathan Ackerman and Mary Jahoda. The monograph, as a whole, is designed to make a first attempt at examining this problem in Germany, since the author unequivocally credits America as the first and only country which has examined this problem in terms of "modern empiricism."

HANS A. ILLING

THE PORTABLE VEBLEN. Edited by Max Lerner. New York: The Viking Press, 1958, pp. 632.

An Introduction of 52 pages by the editor gives a critical evaluation of the works of Veblen and explains the bases for making the choices of materials. Veblen is referred to as "the most creative mind American social thought has produced." Reference is made to "his slow acid style that corroded the sanctities." Weaknesses and blind spots in his system of thought are noted. His dynamism was limited to the economic, and he seemed "to care little about any values outside the technological."

The book gives about the first half of Veblen's *The Theory of the Leisure Class* and excerpts from nine of the other ten books by Veblen. In making the selections for a "portable," the editor aimed "to give a sense of Veblen's variety, flavor, power; to do justice to his academic economic and social theory, but to give the greater emphasis on social institutions and current practices." The editor has fulfilled his aims well, and most readers will find their favorite Veblenian passages in this compact and convenient book. "Further Reading on Veblen" gives a valuable list of five biographical references and 32 critical articles and books, with a special accolade for Dorfman's *Thorstein Veblen and His America.* E.S.B.

STATISTICS IN THE MAKING. By Mary L. Mark. Columbus, Ohio: Ohio State University Press, 1958, pp. vii+436.

The aim of this book is to "acquaint beginners with the fundamentals of production procedures in their logical, technical, and administrative aspects." Since students of the social sciences and specialized types of social administration are often faced with the task of gathering and interpreting data, they need to acquire a knowledge of how to collect, describe, translate, and present empirical evidence. Although this text confines its coverage to one research pattern—the survey or census based upon the interview or questionnaire methods—it includes a good propaedeutical treatment of the logical design of inquiry, the common types of sampling, tabulation procedures, techniques of storage, and the construction of statistical tables. No attempt is made, however, to demonstrate the ways in which data can be converted into probability values for the purpose of making inferences. For information concerning this step the reader is referred to a well-selected reference list.

Statistics in the Making should, if supplemented by an adequate statistics text, meet the requirements of an elementary class in social research. The chapters covering the schedule, the interview, the questionnaire, and the punch card are particularly well done. Unlike those authors whose lack of practice in the field has inclined them to an all too academic preoccupation with what scientific research ought to be like, Mary L. Mark has here presented, out of the wealth of her experience, a realistic account of the subject. An awareness that, once the researcher is "on the road," he will in effect have to realize the best union of expediency and principle under the circumstances goes far to promote the anticipation of many problems that the inexperienced could not imagine. This is, in the best sense, an imaginative book.

HAROLD T. DIEHL
Los Angeles State College

POLITICAL POWER AND SOCIAL THEORY. By Barrington Moore, Jr. Cambridge: Harvard University Press, 1958, pp. xi+215.

Six studies or essays comprise this attempt to analyze political power and repression in modern society. In the first the author sets out to discover the ways in which some groups or individuals exercise domination over others. He suggests that there are three principal types of situations serving to initiate an active search for power and its centralization. These are (1) new sets of activities demanding central coordination, (2) shock or internal decay producing a movement for the forced integration of society around new or partially new patterns of behavior, (3) situations in which rulers of a loosely organized system gradually expand their control over the system.

The second study deals with the rise of totalitarian elements in preindustrial societies and cites historical evidence associated with Stalinist Russia and Nazi Germany with analogues taken from the nonliterate societies of China and India and a side excursion into the situation of Calvin at Geneva. The final study discusses conformity in industrial society. Is conformity wholly bad? What would society be without conformity? One conclusion that is offered suggests that not all forms of behavior can be tolerated and that some elements of repression must be involved. Throughout the essays there are suggested the limitations of social science empiricism in dealing with the issues involved.

M.J.V.

WHAT MAKES ACTS RIGHT? By Archie J. Bahm. Boston: The Christopher Publishing House, 1958, pp. 207.

The author sets forth thirteen reasons that have been and are being advanced for justifying behavioral actions: (1) they are "customary," (2) the "group approves them," (3) they are "legal," (4) they are "according to contract," (5) they are "successful," (6) conscience calls for them, (7) some authority "commands them," (8) they lead to "self-realization," (9) they have "good results," (10) they have good results "for others," (11) good results for one's self, (12) good results for "the best people," and (13) good results for "the greatest number." The strong and weak aspects of each of these points are summarized.

The author also gives his list of "qualifications of a good theory of right action," and suggests that the list should (1) be self-consistent, (2) be consistent "with the facts of common sense," (3) be adequate for all kinds of right action, (4) provide for moral progress, (5) be workable, (6) have more advantages and fewer disadvantages than "other theories of right action," and (7) provide for wrong and "ethically neutral acts." These categories will provide the experimentally minded with a number of important hypotheses to be tested.

E.S.B.

THE POLITICS OF DESPAIR. By Hadley Cantril. New York: Basic Books, Inc., 1958, pp. xv+269.

"In order to understand the behavior of any group of people, we must so project ourselves into their state of mind that we get a sense and a feel of the patterns of assumptions, aspirations, hopes, frustrations, and anxieties which together compose the psychological reality world in which they live." The significance of the meaning of this statement forms the construct on which Cantril has built the purposive research undertaking related in this rewarding book. The problem involved: finding out why the protest voters in France and Italy vote the Communist ticket when they themselves are not members of the party. According to Cantril, Communism is the most important mass movement of our time, the greatest heresy of our age, the greatest force opposing the established order, the greatest influence tending to promote division and dissension. The method: interviews with well-informed people in France and Italy to note what they thought were the reasons for the heavy Communist vote; large-scale interviews of industrial workers and case studies of Communist sympathizers; designing and testing approaches that might affect the state of mind of voters; and reinterviewing, after the Hungarian uprising, some of those whose life stories had been obtained earlier. The time: November-December 1955, January 1956, and October-November 1956. Some findings about the protest voters: they desire to experience what they sense is potentially available outside but which they cannot secure because of, as they see it, "The System," "The State," "The Ruling Class," "The Government"; the most effective way for them to show resentment is to vote Communist. Conclusion: "Only when the protest voter begins to experience in his own life the psychological consequences of new value symbols which he can accept. . .will the abstractions he now blames for his troubles really become insignificant, really lose their reality." This research, probing into the minds of those interviewed, results in establishing the fact that those who wish to preserve the West must understand and comprehend the aspirations and values of the masses who seem to want any change that will provide relief from their frustrations and anxieties. M.J.V.

DIE LEHRE DER GESELLSCHAFT. Ein Lehrbuch der Soziologie. Edited by Gottfried Eisermann. Stuttgart, Germany: Ferdinand Enke Verlag, 1958, pp. xi+452.

The present volume was designed for teaching purposes and encompasses fields which the American sociologist rarely touches or does not consider as "sociology" proper. The book contains nine chapters, each being an entity in itself, which can be read separately as a monograph. The chapters (three of which are written by the editor) deal with the history of sociology, general or pure (*reine*) sociology, sociology of religion, sociology of law, sociology of economics, sociology of political science, sociology of the arts, music, and literature, urban and nonurban sociology, and the sociology of science. As is often the case in anthologies, the contributions are uneven in content, length, and scholarship. Although there are copious footnotes, there is no bibliography or index. But the *Universalitaet* (the approach of the wholeness) is present everywhere. In the chapter on the "History of Sociology," a special section is devoted to the United States. Sumner, Bernard, Ward, Ellwood, Hayes, Giddings, Cooley, MacIver, Thomas, and Znaniecki are heavily relied on. Terms such as "applied anthropology" and "social psychology" are discussed, and foreign influences, such as the *Einbruch* (invasion) of Simmel, Troeltsch, and Max Weber through the repeated translations of their works into English, are "explained." On the whole, the volume makes a substantial contribution to the reasons for sociology's permeating all fields of life and both hemispheres.

HANS A. ILLING

FIRO: A THREE-DIMENSIONAL THEORY OF INTERPERSONAL BEHAVIOR. By William C. Schutz. New York: Rinehart & Company, Inc., 1958, pp. 276.

This book records an attempt to develop and substantiate a formal theory of interpersonal relations. The theory is presented in the language advocated by contemporary philosophers of scientific method and is substantiated principally by the administration of a battery of specially devised Guttman scales to college students. The unifying idea in the book is the postulate that every individual has three kinds of interpersonal needs, namely, for inclusion, control, and affection. The remaining three postulates may be briefly paraphrased as follows: adult interpersonal behavior recapitulates either childhood behavior toward parents or parents' behavior toward self, according to the situation (postulate of relational continuity); compatibility of group members in the three need areas facilitates group goal achievement (postulate of compatibility); a newly forming group follows a sequence of interpersonal preoccupation from inclusion to control to affection, and a terminating group follows the reverse sequence (postulate of group development).

The key concepts of inclusion, control, and affection, though mistakenly regarded as needs resident in the individual, merit attention as a logical and parsimonious statement of the axes of individual-group interaction. The group development postulate is a novel, provocative, and easily testable hypothesis, though it is unfortunately the only postulate for which systematic evidence is not adduced in the book. But the reader will find no theory of interpersonal behavior in the book. He will find merely three illustrative applications of the author's classification of needs in well-known hypotheses, which have been restated in oversimplified form. He will find neither argument nor evidence to show that the author's statement of needs is better than any of the many earlier lists. And he will find that underneath the precise language of postulates and theorems, of primitive and defined terms, and of hypotheses translated into mathematical formulae, there is no greater rigor in method or in thought than is customary in less pretentious works.

RALPH H. TURNER
University of California at Los Angeles

PIONEERING IN INDUSTRIAL RESEARCH. The Story of the General Electric Laboratory. By Kendall Birr. Washington, D.C.: Public Affairs Press, 1958, pp. vii+204.

For those who enjoy the adventures of science in the technological laboratory, this book may serve as a kind of research feast. Professor Birr brings to it something of the artistry of the enthusiastic historian while telling of the inception and major purposes of the General Electric Laboratory, both as an institution and as an organization. There are about 4,834 industrial research laboratories in the United States performing "every imaginable scientific and technological operation" and playing an "important role in the economic life" of the nation. The author gives a fine historical account of the roots of industrial research and the pioneers related to it in various countries. Phenomena connected with light, vacuum tubes and radio, X rays, metallurgy and magnetism, and electronics are discussed along with the men responsible for the early and later development of these. An evaluation of the General Electric Laboratory successes and accomplishments concludes the survey.

M.J.V.

INQUIRY. An Interdisciplinary Journal of Philosophy and the Social Sciences. Oslo, Sweden: Oslo University Press, Vol. 1, No. 1, Spring, 1958, pp. 84.

This new Journal is a welcome addition to the social science publications of the world. It represents one more important step in the development of social science as a unitary, united, and international science.

The Journal aims "to stimulate research on problems common to philosophy and the various disciplines in the behavioral and social sciences." It is "intended for all those who are trying to cut across the boundaries of the various disciplines and to tackle analytically and empirically problems which cannot be solved within any single tradition of scholarship or research."

One of the major articles in the initial issue of this Journal discusses the differences between the physical and social sciences. A list of ten of these differences is presented and analyzed. It is concluded that "it seems that the social sciences must go on finding their own methods and frames of reference, and that the unified science movement must try to find or define a common minimum for a procedure to be called scientific rather than a common maximum which may be a barrier to progress in the various fields." In another article, Professor Ofstad of the University of Stockholm makes a strong plea for "an integration of philosophical analysis and empirical research." E.S.B.

THE AMERICAN LABOR FORCE. Its Growth and Changing Composition. By Gertrude Bancroft. New York: John Wiley & Sons, Inc., 1958, pp. xiv+256.

This is a skilled full-dress rehearsal of the census details about the American labor force with competent interpretations by one of the members of the Bureau of the Census. In the Preface she declares that the "work done by John D. Durand in his 1948 study, 'The Labor Force in the United States, 1890-1960,' " has laid the foundation for all who do research in this field. What she does here she notes as an extension "of his analysis on the basis of later data," with an added determination to show how "the unprecedented economic and demographic events that have occurred since 1940 have changed the patterns of labor force behavior of the American people." Discussed are the economic activities of the population, the trends in the labor force, changing patterns of labor force participation, and family employment patterns. Numerous interesting demographic facts are pointed out: (1) other motives aside from wages have assumed importance in recent years, (2) the number of women in the labor force who are wives of household or family heads increased substantially between 1940 and 1950, (3) the patterns of labor force activity changes are dominated by the increase in employment of women outside the home. Significant here is the method for handling and interpreting the facts that have been accumulated. M.J.V.

THE FERTILITY OF AMERICAN WOMEN. By Wilson H. Grahill, Clyde V. Kiser, and Pascal K. Whelpton. New York: John Wiley & Sons, 1958, pp. xvi+448.

This volume is one of the census monograph series for the Social Science Research Council, in cooperation with the U.S. Department of Commerce, Bureau of the Census. Its findings are based not only on census tabulations but also on use of specialized tables from the Scripps Foundation for Research in Population.

After two concise but illuminating introductory chapters which deal with historical demographic trends, the authors concentrate upon the significant gradients of population in the twentieth century. Following a period of high fertility from the 1600's to 1820, fertility gradually declined during the nineteenth century. It reached its lowest point in the 1930's, when for the first time in our history the balance sheet of birth and death rates was slightly below that essential to maintain a population. There was a sharp reversal of the last two decades when the birth rate shifted from 18 to 19 per 1,000 (as it was from 1933 to 1940) to about 25 per 1,000 (for 1946 to 1956). Due to increasing conscious control of reproduction, it is increasingly difficult to project trends, but it appears that there will be between 64 and 96 million births in the next twenty years or a population of from 244 to 266 million. This has profound meaning for our economic, political, and social institutions.

There is little doubt that many of the past generalizations which adequately described population composition will soon be out of date. The outlook is for a continued differential between rural and urban birth ratios, but the difference is diminishing. Further, there is now little difference by nativity in the urban white population. Equally remarkable is the convergence of fertility rates by color. There has been a "striking" decrease of differentials in fertility rates by education of the wife and by occupation of the husband, so that the trend is away from the inverse relation of socioeconomic status and fertility. A note referable to methodological problems has profound relevance when the authors suggest that "since increasing proportions of the families are exercising some degree of planning—there may be more and larger short-term fluctuations in the birth rate." This means that a whole new dimension has been introduced, by birth control, into the determination of population trends. With this factor in mind, it is not surprising to note an almost 300 per cent increase in childlessness, from 6 per cent in 1920 to 19 per cent in the present population of women in the age group 45 to 49, who have generally completed their families. This book is exceptional in its comprehensive treatment of both general and specific fertility trends. J.A.P.

THE WORLD OF WORK. **Industrial Society and Human Relations. By Robert Dubin. Edgewood Cliffs, New Jersey: Prentice-Hall, Inc., 1958, pp. xiii+448.**

Profusely illustrated and well documented, this text offers some significant insights into the workaday world and its human relations that are a resultant of personalities being caught in the meshes of an industrial society. Well-detailed analyses are distributed throughout; and, as a whole, they succeed in giving an excellent comprehension of the ways in which the structure of human relations is woven into the particular organizations under scrutiny. Dubin is generally meticulous in his care about definitions of terms, which is meritorious. However, there are a few definitions which suffer sometimes, such as the following: "By basic human relations we mean the established types of human interaction that are independent of the personalities of the people involved." Is this a scientifically proven social-psychological statement? Of course, he means the structure of basic human relations.

The structure of the text contains four principal divisions, these embracing organization of work, working population, getting work done, and management of work organizations. In the first of these, human relations, with emphasis upon power, authority, and status, are discussed along with such behavior systems as the formal, nonformal, informal, and technological. The second presents a graphic picture of the labor force and the backgrounds of the working population. In the third, automation, incentives, discontents, grievances, and communication find pivotal places, while the concluding part deals with work rules, management as bureaucracy and as leadership.

One of the best assets of the book is the excellent incorporation of the pertinent social-psychological materials, noted particularly in the chapters on status and authority and power relationships. The explanatory reference notes at the end of each chapter are worthy of attention. The text should captivate students, especially those oriented to visual education. Finally, Dubin insists that he is "not concerned with personality or its components" but wishes to discover "the processes of interaction and their structuring at work." Does it make any difference who are the persons interacting? Moreover, he follows Weber's definition of power as " 'the extent to which [the *power holder*] influences the behavior of others in accordance with his own intentions.' " Nonetheless, the text is most commendable. M.J.V.

ZECHE UND GEMEINDE. Untersuchungen ueber den Strukturwandel einer Zechengemeinde im noerdlichen Ruhrgebiet. By Helmuth Croon and Kurt Utermann. Tuebingen, Germany: J. C. B. Mohr (Paul Siebeck), 1958, pp. ix+305.

This book contains the results of a lengthy research devoted to a section of a coal-mine in the Northern Ruhr Territory in Western Germany. The aim and the scope of the research was to examine the interrelations during working hours in the mine with the life in the community. Very soon the examiners found themselves saddled with additional difficulties, mainly problems centering around the community and its peculiar structure. The town had developed from a village of 4,000 at the beginning of this century into a community of 25,000 at the time of the survey. The town went through difficult stages from an isolated town to and through a center of industrialization. However, the town retained its "own life," despite a growing system of rail and other communications. Since the change of the community had occurred during the last 40 to 50 years, the researchers were able to interview a great many "eye-witnesses," who had seen the town grow to its present size. Therefore, the major aim of the present research was focused on the *veraenderte Sozialstruktur* (changed social structure). Hence, according to the authors, the title, *Zeche und Gemeinde*, expresses a *polare Spannung* (extreme tension). HANS A. ILLING

SOCIAL WORK IN THE AMERICAN TRADITION. By Nathan E. Cohen. New York: The Dryden Press, 1958, pp. 404.

The author has accomplished at least two important aims: one, to write a history of the social work movement in the United States and, two, to discuss social work's changing philosophy.

The historical part covers eight of the eleven chapters and traverses the subject from the colonial period to the present. The concluding three chapters deal with the philosophy, professional aspects, and future of social work.

If the discussion of the philosophy of social work is piecemeal and lacking in organization, it is reflecting a past weakness and, to a considerable extent, a current deficiency in social work. Only since World War II ended have social work leaders, as a whole, been disturbed by the fact that their profession has had no adequate philosophy of what it is doing. It has had dominant themes, special methods, but no carefully thought-out philosophy. It is still in a dilemma, with "social reform as a mother and psychological individualization as a father." It has given attention to helping individuals to help themselves, but it has tended to forget the importance of the term "social" in "social work." It has lacked an interdisciplinary approach. It is only now beginning to develop a philosophy of responsibility for determining public social policies, of wholesale efforts to study the causes of social as well as individual maladjustment, and to assume responsibility for assisting in determining public policies. In dealing "with the consequences rather than the causes of social breakdown," it has neglected important aspects of its field. In short, social work training needs to be broadened and "to reflect the holistic approach of the social sciences." E.S.B.

BODY IMAGE AND PERSONALITY. By Seymour Fisher and Sidney E. Cleveland. Princeton, New Jersey: D. Van Nostrand Company, Inc., 1958, pp. xi+420.

A much neglected aspect of the study of personality and behavior is that which is related to those experiences which may be organized by an individual with reference to his body or the image he has of his body. The authors of this new book dealing with "body image" are psychologists associated with Baylor University's College of Medicine. They have developed a program involving a "series of research projects concerning the relationship of body image to such diverse variables as need for achievement, site of psychosomatic symptomatology, response to therapy, behavior in groups, culture patterns, and modes of physiological response." This should be significant for those interested in theories of personality, since few theorists have incorporated into their theories anything but "the simplest formulations regarding how the individual organizes his perceptions of his own body and how these perceptions affect his behavior."

In a brief introduction, a short review of the meanings which the term "body" has assumed in the literature on personality appears. These have been body type, physiological functions of body, handicap or deformity of body, and malfunctioning of body. Least explored has been that of body as psychological experience, that is, with focalization on the attitudes and feelings toward one's own body. Through their research projects, the authors have attempted to develop and test a theory relative to the influence of body image characteristics on the various adjustments made by a person. Their theoretical formulations have indicated that the "body image boundary dimension has shown itself to have a powerful potential for predicting a wide range of behaviors." The study is worth while for giving insight into certain fields of behavior. M.J.V.

THE CHANGING AMERICAN PARENT: A STUDY IN THE DETROIT AREA. By Daniel R. Miller and Guy E. Swanson. New York: John Wiley and Sons, Inc., 1958, pp. ix+302.

This carefully researched report by a sociologist and a psychologist of the University of Michigan, together with a group of research assistants, should be of special interest to all who want to know how a new generation is probably developing, and why families and family training of the young are so different from what they were in the past. The authors, using the tools of sociology and personality psychology, draw a picture of current trends in child rearing, based on a sample of almost 600 children. Apparently, a new style of child rearing and training is evolving in our cities, at least in one American city—Detroit.

The parents under study, chiefly the mothers, were chosen as a representative sample of the greater Detroit metropolitan area. After giving a historical sketch of the old and the newer methods of child training, from about 1800 to the present, the authors present the details of their own findings. Six hundred mothers were interviewed to obtain the concrete data.

One of the most important and interesting parts of the study is the contrast between the "older" and "newer" middle classes, and in their occupations and the opportunities and problems afforded by the occupations they hold. The two types of middle classes are characterized as "individuated-entrepreneurial" and "welfare-bureaucratic." The former are composed chiefly of individual entrepreneurs, in which class the people tend to stress self-control, independence, and looking out for themselves. The "welfare bureaucracy," which began to emerge toward the end of the nineteenth century and the beginning of the twentieth, is characterized by large organizations employing many kinds of specialists; there is a greater coordination of activities by supervisors who follow more codified rules of conduct. In such a society accommodation and security are important elements. The "bureaucratized parents" train their children for this new world and treat them in terms of its values, even though they may not be conscious of this fact. Children are taught to be more accommodative and to seek direction from the organizational programs in which they participate. The concrete data are analyzed to ascertain the extent to which the training of the children substantiates the theoretical postulates and to what extent they indicate variations from them. The major portion of the book is devoted to the analysis of the data obtained by means of the interviews.

The study has made available data on a wide range of child-training practices. Special effort was made to locate some of the sources of the newer ways of child training and to forecast possible consequences they may have for family life and for the personalities of children.

M.H.N.

GROUP DYNAMICS. PRINCIPLES AND APPLICATIONS. By Hubert Bonner. New York: The Ronald Press Company, 1959, pp. viii+531.

This book offers what appears to be the clearest and most comprehensive explanation of what is now implied by its subject, group dynamics. It is disciplinary, salutary, and challenging. Professor Bonner has taken the most significant theories, methodological studies, and experimental researches in the field and obtained the essence resident in these. He has expanded "the horizon of group dynamics to include educational, industrial, community, and political organizations." Always indulging in terms and phrases readily comprehended, the book should prove to be a boon and a kind of catechism for students in the field. In a sense, group dynamics as a subject is not new, but the attempts to enlarge its scope and significance are. Outlined here are those aspects of group dynamics which are being furthered by study, namely, "group structure, group cohesiveness, intergroup tensions, group learning, group problem solving, and group leadership." Group dynamics has been defined by Bonner as "that division of social psychology which investigates the formation and change in the structure and functions of the psychological grouping of people into self-directing wholes." Some problems which face the investigator of group potentials may be found in the many variables which must be dealt with, such as the intelligence of the various members, their age and sex, their variety of temperament, their knowledge of the discussion subject, and the like.

The final chapter presents a critique in which Bonner summarizes the subject as developed thus far, pointing out some misconceptions of Lewin's inappropriate use of physical and mathematical constructs in his field theory, first suggested to Bonner by I. D. London. Some sharp criticisms of the extreme enthusiasts are forthcoming, i.e., "Group integration, which is a normal social process, has been inflated to the point where it has become an all-encompassing ethic." Group dynamics as plotted by many research agents has lost sight of the individual, and nowhere is this more evident than in those reseearches having to do with group discussions and leadership. This is somewhat reminiscent of the old struggle anent group mind. This last chapter, which stresses the limitations and weaknesses of the subject and what it promises, is well worth the price of the book. The whole book is a fine appraisal of the field. M.J.V.

THE AMERICAN FAMILY SYSTEM. By Sister Frances Jerome Woods. New York: Harper and Brothers, 1959, pp. xv+585.

Using the social system as a frame of reference, this study relates the American family at each stage of its life cycle to other social systems—church, state, economy, and school. *Social system* is defined as "an orderly arrangement of parts having certain boundaries, unity, and endurance through time, within which meaningful interaction takes place whereby one part tangibly influences another." The first part of the book deals with the family as a social system, including an analysis of family variations and the historical development of the family. This is followed by an analysis of social configurations, notably value orientations and family norms, demographic trends, types of American families, and variations in family life in accordance with the social class structure. In describing the family life cycle, the stages of development are traced from the "beginning family" to the expanding and contracting families, and a chapter is devoted to the disintegrating factors in family life. One of the unique features of the book is the description of the family in relation to other social systems. The respective roles and influences of religion, government and law, the economic order, education, and social welfare are described to indicate their relation to family life and the interrelatedness of the constituent parts of the total social system.

Material is drawn from various disciplines—sociology, anthropology, history, economics, political science, and social psychology. The data used are well integrated, concisely presented, and extensively documented. The chapter summaries, discussion topics, and annotated bibliographies are especially helpful for teaching purposes. A selected bibliography of standard textbooks on the family is given at the beginning of the book, together with a table of cross references to these sources for the various chapters. M.H.N.

DEFINITIONS OF SOCIOMETRY. By Ake Bjerstedt. New York: Beacon House, Sociometry Monographs, 1958, pp. 20.

The author compares definitions of the term *sociometry* found in texts and scientific works with an "expert" vote on these definitions by leading sociologists. The term *sociometry* is recommended for use in a broad meaning to refer to measurement of every kind of interhuman and interanimal relation, whereas the term *preferential sociometry* is recommended for use when we want to refer specifically to measurement of those interhuman and interanimal relations which can be described in terms of preferences (attraction-neutrality-rejection in a choice situation). E.C.M.

THE IDEA OF A SOCIAL SCIENCE AND ITS RELATION TO PHILOSOPHY. By Peter Winch. New York: The Humanities Press, Inc., 1958, pp. 143.

Five unique and distinctively challenging chapters comprise this discourse on the relationship between the social studies and philosophy as the author conceives it. Winch, a lecturer in philosophy at the University College of Swansea, holds that misconceptions about the nature of philosophy, because of an incorrect assessment of the significance of some of Wittgenstein's contributions, has resulted in misunderstandings about the true relationships between philosophy and the social sciences. The scientist "investigates the nature, causes, and effects of particular real things and processes; the philosopher is concerned with the nature of reality as such. . ." Further, "social relations are expressions of ideas about reality." Therefore, "the central problem of sociology, that of giving an account of the nature of social phenomena in general is really misbegotten epistemology." With this point of view, some of the difficulties arising from basing understanding of societies on the methods of natural science are pointed out, especially those methods dealing with motives, causes, social institutions, and prediction. Of the latter, Winch avers "that the central concepts which belong to our understanding of social life are incompatible with concepts central to the activity of scientific prediction."

Chapter Four is devoted to a critique of Pareto and his attempt to show empirically "that the ideas which people have, in behaving as they do, influence the nature and outcome of their behavior far less fundamentally than is usually thought; and that, therefore, the sociologist must develop his own concepts *de novo* and pay as little attention as possible to the ideas of participants." Here is shown that "first, Pareto mistakes what is essentially a philosophical issue for an empirical scientific one; second, that the conclusion of his argument is in fact, false." In a sense, the discussions should have a kind of salutary effect upon those who misuse or overemphasize abstract mathematics in the formulation of social findings from inadequate data. M.J.V.

PSYCHOLOGY OF THE CHILD: PERSONAL, SOCIAL, AND DISTURBED CHILD DEVELOPMENT. By Robert I. Watson. New York: John Wiley & Sons, Inc., 1959, pp. xiii+662.

As a textbook in child psychology, this book has considerable merit. The author approaches child psychology, not as a separate or isolated subdivision, but as an integral part of the subject matter of general psychology. The discussions of socialization, personality, psychosocial developments of the child, and behavior disorders are of interest to the social scientist. In fact, the author draws material from a wide range of sources, especially educational, clinical, social, and general psychology. He attempts to integrate learning theory with psychoanalysis and discusses aspects of personality in relation to every phase of child development.

After a description of historic developments of the study of the child, and the various principles and methods of child psychology, including a chapter on the psychoanalytic theory of the early and later developments of personality, the major portion of the book is devoted to a more detailed analysis of infancy, early childhood, later childhood, and the psychological disturbances that may occur during childhood. Normal developments of a child are related to disturbed aspects. On the whole, the book is a well-integrated treatise on child development.

M.H.N.

OTHER PUBLICATIONS RECEIVED

COMMUNITY ORGANIZATION FOR CITIZEN PARTICIPATION IN URBAN RENEWAL. By William C. Loring, Jr., Frank L. Sweetser, and Charles F. Ernst. Prepared by Housing Association of Metropolitan Boston, Inc., for the Massachusetts Department of Commerce, Boston, Massachusetts, 1957, pp. viii+246.

The report describes how administrators and volunteer leaders may participate effectively in urban renewal at city-wide and neighborhood levels. Comparisons are made of a variety of reactions to renewal programs, ranging all the way from no citizen participation to extensive participation through city-wide district and community councils or committees. The cases cited demonstrate that more effective planning and organization are possible if the citizens of the area have a part in urban renewal.

WHAT'S HAPPENED TO OUR HIGH SCHOOLS? By John F. Latimer. Washington, D.C.: Public Affairs Press, 1958, pp. 196.

This book is a kind of historical review of the development and programs of the high school in the United States, with attention being given to important questions, such as: Should we stress mathematics and science and languages as much as the USSR does? Among the conclusions is this: The need for specialists will increase and "the quality of the education they receive will depend in large measure on the fusion of liberal arts and sciences."

WHO RUNS OUR SCHOOLS? By Neal Gross. New York: John Wiley & Sons, 1958, pp. xvi+195.

Chapters 5 and 6 fall within the field of social control and yield concrete data of importance on the subjects of who applies what kind of pressures and who is subjected to pressures.

THE ART OF PERSUASION. By Wayne C. Minnick. Boston: Houghton Mifflin Company, 1957, pp. 295.

This book deals with such subjects as how behavior is determined, getting and holding attention, ensuring accurate perception, the roles of wants and values and emotion, audience analysis, the ethics of persuasion.

THE CHANGING OF ORGANIZATIONAL BEHAVIOR PATTERNS. A Case Study of Decentralization. By Paul R. Lawrence. Cambridge: Harvard University, 1958, pp. 237.

Deals "with organizational change affecting personnel at management levels" in connection with "a medium-sized supermarket chain in which staff members were shifted from the home office to newly created store managers."

PROBLEM SOLVING IN DALTON. By Olive M. Stone. New York: Council on Social Work Education, 1958, pp. 86.

This monograph aims to provide "a generic approach to social work theory and practice" in the five methods of social work. Dalton is "a small conservative city of approximately 80,000 on the outskirts of a rapidly expanding and changing metropolitan area."

DICTIONARY OF PERSONNEL AND INDUSTRIAL RELATIONS. By Esther R. Becker. New York: Philosophical Library, 1958, pp. 366.

In this reference work and handbook as well as dictionary appear over 2,400 entries, with numerous cross references, covering many subjects and management techniques and listings of personnel and industrial relations associations, publications dealing with industrial relations, and colleges and universities offering courses and doing research in industrial relations.

CASE STUDY OF A FLOOD-STRICKEN CITY. By Seymour S. Weisman. New York: Graduate School of Public Administration and Social Service, New York University, 1958, pp. 149.

This is an excellent study of the results of the flood that struck Norwalk, Connecticut, in October 1955. It describes the city when the flood hit it, the clean-up after the flood, the losses, the redevelopment of the city, an evaluation of the total experience; and gives recommendations.

THE EDUCATION OF THE INDIVIDUAL. By Alfred Adler. New York: Philosophical Library, 1958, pp. 143.

In words quoted by Carleton Washburne in the Foreword, this book deals with "four problems an individual has to face: his relationship with others, his sense of equality, the possibility of an escape from the ephemeral, and the meaning of his actions."

THE FEMALE OFFENDER. By Caesar Lombroso and William Ferrero. New York: Philosophical Library, 1958, pp. 313.

This work, reprinted now nearly a hundred years after it was written, distinguishes between "the casual offender and the habitual as well as hereditary, pathological offender." It is viewed as counterbalancing "the mainly analytical and psychologically dynamic hypotheses of today."

THE WORLD CRISIS AND AMERICAN RESPONSIBILITY. Selected and Edited by Ernest W. Lefever. Analysis by Reinhold Niebuhr. New York: Association Press, 1958, pp. xix+128.

SELECTED BIBLIOGRAPHY OF NORTH AMERICAN SOCIAL WELFARE LITERATURE. New York: Council on Social Work Education, 1958, pp. 66.

Contains brief annotations of about 300 carefully selected references.

INTERVIEWING PROCEDURES. A Manual for Survey Interviewers. By J. Stacy Adams. Chapel Hill: The University of North Carolina Press, 1958, pp. 56.

The major topics include phases of an interview survey, the interviewing procedure, sampling, and common sources of interviewer bias.

CORRECTION

In the article by Robert J. Dwyer on "The Administrative Role in Desegregation" in the January-February issue of this Journal the word "no" was inadvertently omitted on page 186, seventh line from the bottom of the page. The sentence should have read. "There were *no* restrictive policies with reference to lunchrooms, toilets, drinking fountains, gymnasium or shower facilities."

Sociology and Social . . . Research . . .

AN INTERNATIONAL JOURNAL

Sociology of John L. Gillin 327
STUART A. QUEEN

Theory of Culture Change 333
OTAKAR MACHOTKA

Self-Tattooing Among Delinquents . . . 341
JOHN H. BURMA

Division of Labor of Communal Groups . . 346
HENRY ZENTNER

Student Attitudes Toward the Family . . 352
PANOS D. BARDIS

Politics of Orientals in Hawaii 359
GEORGE K. YAMAMOTO

W. I. Thomas and Social Origins 365
EMORY S. BOGARDUS

Peoples and Culture . . . 370
Social Problems and Welfare 378
Social Theory and Research 386
Other Publications Received 398

VOL. 43 MAY-JUNE 1959 No. 5

YEARLY SUBSCRIPTION, $3.50 SINGLE COPIES, 70 CENTS

Sociology and Social Research

AN INTERNATIONAL JOURNAL

PUBLISHED BIMONTHLY AT THE UNIVERSITY OF SOUTHERN CALIFORNIA
UNIVERSITY PARK, LOS ANGELES 7, CALIFORNIA

YEARLY SUBSCRIPTION, $3.50 SINGLE COPIES, 70¢

Entered as second-class matter March 31, 1936, at the post office at Los Angeles, California, under the act of March 3, 1879.

PUBLISHED BY

UNIVERSITY OF SOUTHERN CALIFORNIA PRESS

UNIVERSITY PARK LOS ANGELES 7, CALIFORNIA

SOCIOLOGY AND SOCIAL RESEARCH
May-June 1959

THE SOCIOLOGY OF JOHN L. GILLIN (1871-1958)

STUART A. QUEEN
Washington University

John L. Gillin, sixteenth president of the American Sociological Society, was one of a group of vigorous young men trained by Giddings at Columbia in the early years of this century. Gillin, like some others of his day, had come from a small college in the Midwest and had spent several years as a Protestant clergyman. After receiving his Ph.D. in 1906 he was on the faculties of Ashland College, Iowa State College, and, from 1912, the University of Wisconsin. He was the author of nine books and some forty articles. In 1921 Gillin, as Director of Educational Service for the American Red Cross—on leave from the University of Wisconsin—visited me at the Simmons College School of Social Work. From that time on I was proud to count him among my friends.

The thesis of this article, if it needs one, is that John L. Gillin served well through nearly two generations of American sociology. He was a prodigious worker, gathering enormous bodies of concrete data to support, challenge, or revise the similarly large bodies of social theory extant in the early twentieth century but not yet well founded on solid facts and clear analysis. During the most active forty years of Gillin's professional career, he grew in the quality of his work and in the range of his influence. Of course, he could hardly be expected to leap from Giddings' consciousness of kind, Ward's synergy, Small's six interests, and Sumner's mores to mid-century group dynamics, role-playing, structural-functional analysis, and sociometry. But he did grow and develop in substantial ways, as I shall demonstrate in the three sections which follow.

From *Poverty and Dependency* to *Social Pathology.* These two titles symbolize some of the changes in Gillin's frame of reference for dealing with human experiences variously labeled today "deviant behavior," "social disorganization," "conflict of values," and the like. When Gillin's professional work began, masses of Americans were struggling to keep the wolf from the door, while middle- and upper-class city dwellers were organizing charities to help the poor out of their misery. Since this was a major issue in American life, it was quite natural for a young Ph.D. in sociology to focus his attention on poverty and philanthropy.

With the trained scholar's predilection for definition and classification, Gillin identified several types of dependency: "natural," as of a child unready to care for himself, or an elderly person no longer able to endure the heat of the day; "customary," as involving the mutual aid of guilds, lodges, and unions; and "legal," as when law reinforces the traditional obligations of family or other group, or when detached persons are aided by the state "in the interest of the general welfare." Gillin also sought to distinguish "normal" and "abnormal" dependency, the former being that which is expected and dealt with according to the folkways and mores, the latter being unexpected and hence requiring some new kind of action. That poverty is a relative thing is clear in his statement about "a person who . . . does not maintain a standard of living high enough . . . to function usefully according to the standards of the society of which he is a member."

In the opening sentence of Chapter I, Gillin offered a clue which might well have been the basis of a very profitable inquiry: "Poverty and dependency did not appear as social problems until tribal society began to give place to civil society." As a Monday morning quarterback, I wish that my friend had followed this lead and searched through available historical and anthropological materials for the factors related to organized public concern about individuals in distress. Certainly nonliterate peoples have endured hunger, disease, and varied disasters, but it appears that they had no charitable societies or public assistance programs.

In the book *Poverty and Dependency* (1921) Gillin assembled a large body of important material which was used by many persons in their effort to understand and deal with human beings in distress. But, like other books of the period—my own included—this one contains something of a hodgepodge: the aged, the insane, mothers' pensions, unemployment, state supervision and administration. Let us see how different was *Social Pathology* (second edition, 1939).

Social pathology, said Gillin, "arises out of the maladjustment between the individual and the social structure." The influence may come from either side. Social change may take the form of invention, new natural resources, "new techniques in political, economic, and social life." Such changes may be disturbing, make people uncomfortable or fearful, or even incite them to riot. But sometimes it is the individual who changes or fails to meet the expectations of his society. This may worry him or other people or both. The "pathology of the individual" may involve physical illness or handicap, mental deficiency or disorder, or violation of the mores, as in alcoholism or prostitution.

Younger sociologists may note with interest the titles to Parts III, IV, and V: "Pathology of Social Organization," "Breakdown of Economic Relationships," and "Pathology of Cultural Relationships." Clearly Gillin was striving to achieve a new frame of reference, one more definitely sociological. But while I think that he made real headway, some of my young friends will be disappointed in his implicit value orientation—pathology implies a norm, nowhere clearly defined by Gillin—his focus on individuals rather than on groups, his concern about social services rather than sociological processes, and his impressionistic interpretation of causation. I fear they will judge him academicocentrically from the standpoint of their 1959 sophistication, rather than in terms of *his* starting point and *his* achievement.

From *Taming the Criminal* to *The Wisconsin Prisoner.* In the Introduction to *The Wisconsin Prisoner* Gillin wrote, "Ever since my graduate school days I have been interested in the criminal." In fact, the time he devoted to study of delinquency and its treatment, and the three books he published in this field, are evidence of his major concern with criminology.

Actually, his first book in this area was the general textbook *Criminology and Penology* (1926), but "logically" *Taming the Criminal* (1931) should precede, since it is a descriptive account of his visits to prisons in several countries of Europe and Asia, plus some states of our own country.

In *Criminology and Penology* Gillin offered the usual legal definition of crime as "any action by an individual in contravention of law." But he added a sociological definition which, for 1926, was quite significant: "Crime is an act which is *believed* to be socially harmful by a group of people which has the power to enforce its beliefs, and which places such act under the ban of positive penalties." However, he did not discuss the possible applicability of this definition to churches, trade unions, and other groups not organized as states.

About a fourth of this book was devoted to "the making of the criminal," and three fourths to "history of punishment," "penal institutions," and "the machinery of justice." In the treatment of causation Gillin discussed categories of supposed factors, after the fashion of that day, rather impressionistically. Thus he wrote of the "indirect influence of the physical environment," the high proportion of feeble-minded, epileptic, and constitutional inferiors, and physical abnormalities. Under economic factors he laid special stress on unemployment and occupations which provide "opportunities for committing different kinds of crimes." But he missed Sutherland's "white collar crime." However, he did make a real start toward describing the "mechanisms by which economic conditions influence criminality." (See pages 142-43 of the 1935 edition.) Also he gave a rather good account of the relation of culture conflict to emotional conflict, and of both to delinquency. On the other hand, his discussion of broken homes, "lack of wholesome recreation," "lack of proper direction," use of alcohol and narcotics did not go much beyond popular impressions of the 1920's.

In 1946 Gillin published *The Wisconsin Prisoner*, a research monograph that represented a marked advance over the two earlier books. His principal hypothesis was "that the early experiences of prisoners have a bearing on their later involvement with the law." He gathered his data by examining prison records, by interviewing prisoners and other persons who could provide information, and by inducing some of the men to write autobiographies in accordance with a mimeographed outline which he provided. His sample included practically all "lifers" at the Wisconsin State Penitentiary, all sentenced for rape or sodomy, and every third prisoner sentenced for a crime against property. Then he gathered corresponding data about brothers of 172 convicts, so that he might discover differences between criminal and noncriminal siblings. He also showed some differences between prisoners and the total male population of Wisconsin.

Space forbids a detailed review of the differences which were found to be statistically significant. We can only report that these include such factors as attachment to mother, job stability, marital status, and marital conflict. In his concluding chapter Gillin listed "conditions that seem to create a hazard" and "circumstances that appear to have a steadying effect"—both more modest and more useful than the impressionistic statements of his earlier books.

From *Outlines of Sociology* to *Cultural Sociology*. The friends of John L. Gillin—and he had many—have probably wished that his professional growth and contributions had been as great in general sociology as in the field of social problems, and especially in criminology. But even here there was development.

Outlines of Sociology (1915), written with Frank W. Blackmar, was not very different from the texts of Hayes, Ellwood, and others of the period. It set forth as a goal "to describe society as we find it, ascertain how it developed," not guessing but gathering live facts, not restricting ourselves to the United States but studying "the world around," "ascertaining how men actually live in groups," and "noticing the processes by which relationships are established." Despite this brave declaration, the *Outlines* turned out to be pretty much a collection of generalizations, some rather hazy, illustrated rather than established by varied sorts of data.

In the chapter on "Social Origins and Evolution" there is easily seen the influence of evolutionism, against which anthropologists were already rebelling. In discussing "the Aims of Society" the authors displayed their subjective value orientation. "Sociology," they said, "attempts to ascertain not only the ends which serve social welfare, but to understand by scientific methods the ways in which these aims may be realized. By means of these ideals progress is possible."

In *Cultural Sociology* (1948), written with his anthropologist son, John P. Gillin, our discipline is defined as "the study of interaction arising from the association of living beings." Its basic assumptions are "the essential orderliness of the universe," and the possibility of studying social relationships as "natural phenomena." Such study, the Gillins told us, calls for objectivity, patience, hard work, skepticism concerning popular beliefs, and creative imagination. Fallacies to be avoided include the ideas (1) that we know social reality because we live in it, (2) that all knowledge must have an immediate practical application, (3) that repeated concomitance or sequence establishes a causal relationship, (4) that science is impossible without laboratory or experimentation. Surely these ideas represent a long day's journey beyond anything in the *Outlines*.

But when we come to specific discussion of social institutions and processes, our enthusiasm is a bit dampened. Let me illustrate this from Chapter 28 on "Social Control." This is defined as "that system of measures . . . by which a society brings into conformity to the approved pattern of behavior a subgroup, or by which a group molds into conformity its members." The need for social control arises out of variations among individuals and among groups, maladjustments (related to circumstances as diverse as insanity and immigration), conflicts of values, and cultural change. The agencies of social control include beliefs, suggestion through example and propaganda, religion, social ideals, ceremony, art, leadership, intellectual factors, education, law, administration, and force. To me this is a crude list of overlapping and poorly identified items which may appear in the operation of social control. And discussion of "results of social control on values and institutions" is even more disappointing. Instead of important generalizations based on empirical data, we are offered a warning that through "certain violent methods of social control . . . our fundamental institutions are threatened," and "too much control may result in loss of values."

Thus *Cultural Sociology* employed some new words and some new data, but not very different ways of handling them. Like the *Outlines of Sociology*, it was a sort of social philosophy, eclectic in the use of concepts and concrete illustrations, with a North American, middle-class value orientation. However, it would be unfair to expect Gillin to have made himself over into a Kingsley Davis, Ronald Freedman, or Leonard Broom. Who of us can really renew his intellectual life with two separate generations?

In conclusion, John L. Gillin made a real contribution to the development of our growing discipline through research, writing, and teaching. In addition, he was a friendly person, genuinely interested in other people, ready to listen to their views and eager to be helpful. By those who had the privilege of personal contact, he will be missed. Those who have come lately to the field will do well to learn how Gillin and others of his generation helped to build American sociology.

A CONTRIBUTION TO THE THEORY OF CULTURE CHANGE

OTAKAR MACHOTKA
Harpur College

In everyday experience culture changes are evident which occur without the awareness of the people involved (who, for instance, pick up a local mannerism or develop new fashionable interests). They receive little attention because they seem too unimportant or too familiar to us. My attention was drawn to such changes, rather incidentally, during World War II. At that time the Germans attempted to impose their culture on the occupied nations. At the beginning only a very small number of opportunists accepted some traits of the Nazi culture. But, to my surprise, later on even some honest individuals accepted bona fide some of its traits. They did it often unconsciously, unwittingly, and without thinking about it. The changes in their convictions occurred unconsciously and to a certain extent remained unconscious.

Since that time I have given attention to the unconscious acceptance of new cultural traits and to unconscious culture changes in general. I felt that the explanations of concrete culture changes as well as the general theories of culture changes were not rigorous enough. Each of the theories made one omission: they did not give enough or any attention to the unconscious processes of the human mind, which, in my opinion, may explain a substantial portion of the unknown causes of culture process.

Let us discuss briefly the most important unconscious processes of the human mind which are relevant to culture change.

BASIC PSYCHOLOGICAL PROCESSES

1. *Perceiving*. From a number of experiments,[1] it may be seen that subliminal sensations may influence our behavior, particularly if there are many sensations of the same kind. The subliminal experiences may summate; a good example of such summation is the general impression the speaker forms of the audience; small changes in the facial and eye expressions of a mass of relatively distant individuals may produce the impression of interest, indifference, surprise, or resentment. The speaker may not know how to substantiate such an impression.

---

[1] See J. G. Miller, *Unconsciousness* (New York: John Wiley & Sons, Inc., 1942), pp. 149, 151, 152.

More important are marginal perceptions which are strong enough to reach the realm of consciousness but do not do so because of lack of attention. These furnish rich information about people around us. Due to them we feel, after coming to our office, that everything is as usual or that a new acquaintance is not a really dependable person or that our boss was pleased by our work, though in none of these cases was there a conscious reason for such a feeling.

Both subliminal and marginal perceptions yield a continuous flow of information about the social life around us, and we draw conclusions from them which may unconsciously change our personal values and behavior patterns. If similar small-scale changes are produced by similar external causes in a number of people and these changes become objects of social interaction, they may result in permanent culture change.

2. *Use of Forgotten and Unrecollected Experiences.* Even forgotten experiences leave traces which may influence our behavior. Many of our seemingly irrational attitudes are based on experiences we have forgotten. Likewise, we often use as our own a number of ideas, arguments, or reasons we have heard or read previously but have forgotten. Sometimes we imitate social models we have watched years ago, without being able to recall them. We make correct estimates of the size or weight of objects, though we have completely forgotten our previous experience with objects of similar size or weight upon which we base our estimate.

We do not recall hundreds of well-known facts in our physical and social environment, though we act as if we thought of them. We act as fathers, teachers, or citizens with certain rights without often recalling that we are these. Likewise, we unconsciously act according to certain stable or new conditions such as the assumption that we live in the twentieth century, that we are married, that we were promoted, etc.

Forgotten experiences, then, may lead to new behavior patterns of a large number of people, and unrecollected changes in the social life may change social values or other culture patterns.

3. *Learning.* Unconscious, unwitting learning from watching people or by handling objects may lead to culture changes. Lower-class people may unconsciously learn certain upper-class subcultural patterns (besides learning other upper-class patterns consciously). We become skillful photographers by taking a large number of pictures, without knowing how we developed certain parts of our skill. We also learn, often unconsciously, how to adjust to new physical or social conditions. If many people learn the same skills a new cultural pattern may arise.

4. *Habit, Routine, Automatic Behavior.* Habit, routine, and automatic behavior are also often established unconsciously. If changed or newly developed in a number of people, they may produce culture change.

5. *Imitation.* We unconsciously imitate a number of behavior patterns such as simple gestures, phrases, uses of certain implements, and many other patterns, which may be performed without learning. The imitated behavior patterns of a leading individual or a group may be accepted as new cultural patterns.

Likewise, unconscious imitation may produce acceptance of a new invention or of a foreign cultural pattern (diffusion) and thus bring cultural change.

6. *Thinking.* We have mentioned already one of the unconscious thinking processes, unconscious assumptions. But there are a number of others. Every day we make, for instance, hundreds of comparisons without consciously comparing. We know that our boss is in a better mood today than yesterday, that one person is more capable than another, or that one performance is more strenuous than another.

Likewise, people make unconscious judgments. For instance, they feel directly and without gathering the necessary facts and judging them that the rewarded student well deserves the reward. In other instances they may know all the relevant facts but produce the judgment without any conscious thinking. Either of the judgments appears in the form of a convincing "feeling." "Feelings" of this kind may produce culture changes: it may be generally felt that it is no longer necessary to be as formal as previously, or that the previously usual behavior pattern in general no longer seems adequate.

Generalization, transfer, and the drawing of conclusions are also largely unconscious. If permanently shared by a number of people, all three may lead to culture changes which may be either gradual and inconspicuous or fast and easily noticeable.

The unconscious establishment of a frame of reference from the behavior of the members of the group has been well demonstrated by M. Sherif. Human personality produces an enormous number of them from all kinds of behavior of other people. Through reaction or assimilation to the frame of reference, new subcultural or cultural traits may be established or the old ones modified.

Another kind of relevant unconscious thinking process is what we call the computing service. The human mind establishes automatically a more or less correct figure about how many times a certain event occurred. This happens even if we are not especially interested in the event. Thus we know that in the last month we went to movies about three times, that in the last year we got about ten letters from our friend, or that during our vacation we went swimming about a dozen times. The computing service, which is generally completely unconscious, helps change many social norms, values (especially fads), attitudes, and other cultural patterns. The mere unconscious cognizance of a less frequent occurrence of a culture pattern weakens it and a more frequent occurrence strengthens it. A more or less frequent occurrence of an event also changes the social attitudes toward it, its social value, and the norms of behavior toward it.

7. *Establishment of Sentiments and Social Ties.* It is well known that group life produces certain emotional experiences. These may eventually change the appropriate part of the culture such as patterns of acceptable emotions or emotional expressions. Football fans have developed new emotional patterns which had not been in existence in Western culture previously. They have been unconsciously produced by common excitement of the masses of onlookers.

Repeated emotional experiences of a certain kind may also unconsciously produce a new sentiment, which may become an enduring part of culture. The repeated strong frustrations of the local population by the German occupants in World War II produced an enduring hatred of Germans.

All of these processes are largely unconscious. We are either wholly or only partially unaware of them, but sooner or later their product—the new sentiment—may come into awareness.

As a rule, all the above-discussed processes are supported by other concurrent psychic processes or social-psychological factors. Social learning, for instance, is supported by thinking processes, norms, levels of aspiration, group belongingness, and by certain social values and depends on certain social concepts, expectations, pressures, and so on. Its product, then, is rather a complex social-psychological configuration.

Configuration to the writer is any psychological structure organized permanently or temporarily from a number of psychic or social-psychological components. The Gestalts of the Gestaltist school are only one kind of these, as we shall see later.

In the previously discussed configurations, generally one basic factor is the leading component. In a sentiment, for instance, it is its emotional content, while the appropriate norms, concepts, etc., are secondary components. Nevertheless, there are other configurations in which two or more components are leading, while other components have only a secondary role.

CONFIGURATIONS WITH SEVERAL LEADING COMPONENTS

1. *Attitudes.* Besides a strong emotional content (which makes them similar to emotions), attitudes generally have a strong conative component aiming at a certain reaction to the appropriate object, person, group, or situation and include a rather clear conception of the object. Many attitudes also include appropriate psychological sets. Besides these leading components, some other, secondary ones may be included in their structure as, for instance, habits, unrecollected, forgotten, and subliminal experiences, learned behavior, and the like.

Social attitudes may develop from similar personal attitudes of a number of persons through reshaping, through group stimulation, interaction, and assimilation. Other social attitudes develop through imitation, social pressure, and learning as well as through the creative power of common group activities. All of these processes may be unconscious.

Changes in attitudes may result in culture changes that are noticed only after they have occurred.

2. *Values.* The leading components of a value may be, for instance, the prestige of an object (old china or an old violin), the need for it (for display at home or for playing), and the emotional attachment to it (it has been in the family for generations). Generally, values have another main component: preference of higher valued to lower valued objects. Frequently they include also moral and aesthetic judgments, legal concepts, attitudes (or some of their above-mentioned components), assumptions, and expectations (for instance, that we may use the object for years, that it will be useful to our family, etc.) as main or as secondary components.

The organization of the components into a value configuration is often unconscious. So may be the product of the organizing process—the value itself. We simply deal with the valued object according to the valuation which occurred without our awareness. Changes in social values, of course, mean changes in culture.

3. *Norms and Obligations.* Though similar to each other, obligations are not formulated as such, whereas norms are. Obligations may be unconscious derivatives of certain social ties or attitudes, or they may be (often unconsciously) established through generalization, transfer, reasoning, or other processes. We may not know that we have certain specific obligations toward a friend of ours. But when he gets into trouble, we feel we have to help him. Likewise, our "feelings" tell us that our help has to go to a certain limit but not farther. The basic framework of such an obligation has evidently been established previously

to our helping the person. His friendly behavior toward us, his prestige, his personal qualities, his attractive personality, and our social or business relations toward him may be the leading parts of this framework, complemented by the state of our finances, by the attitude of our wife toward him, etc., as secondary components.

Not being clearly formulated, the obligations change easily. They are very sensitive to all the changes in our physical and social environment, as well as to the changes in our own situation. They are in a state of continuous reshaping. Whenever this occurs in a number of individuals, certain modifications in culture content are induced.

Though formulated and generally conscious, norms may be based on unconsciously developed obligations. Likewise, certain components of norms and their interpretation may be unconscious.

ORGANIZATION AND MAINTENANCE OF CONFIGURATIONS

Knowledge of the personality's ability to organize configurations is rather limited. The Gestaltists have not gone much farther than analyzing perceptions and insight and giving a very limited treatment to learning and emotions.

It seems that, tentatively, configurations may be classified into four groups. Into the first category may be put those produced by psychological laws. The second category includes configurations produced by culture. The personality may develop specific configurations of its own; this will be the third category. Finally, there are other specific configurations based on the unique conditions of the group.

The perception of an interrupted circular line as a circle is an example of the first category. Linguistic patterns are examples of the second type. An example of a personal configuration is the high valuation of a novelist who is not valued by other people. A group in a minority condition which develops special configurations of its own is an instance of the fourth category.

The most important configurations for the life of culture are those of the second, third, and fourth types. The second type is basic for the existence and maintenance of culture. Cultural traits consist chiefly of configurations of this kind. The third type is basic to changes of culture. Also the special group configurations may influence culture changes.

As a rule, the components of a configuration are held together by the continuing existence of the condition (or conditions) which initiated the process of organization and the meaning that the configuration has for the individual and the group. But some of the components of the configuration may develop their own reasons for existence, and by this they may considerably support the whole structure. Such are, for instance, habits, learned behavior, concepts, and possibly other components. They may maintain the configuration even when it does not suit the changing conditions. Cultural lags and survivals are due partly to these factors.

The continuous, generally unconscious, knowing of the existence of the conditions which stimulated the establishment of the configuration generally maintains it in full strength. A frequent and repeated checking on them, generally automatic and unconscious, is one of the important characteristics of the personality. Any possible change in any relevant condition may induce the appropriate (though often unconscious) restructuring or abandonment of the configuration.

The most important property of configurations is that each of them operates as a whole when conditions suitable for their operation arise. Nevertheless, even this property is flexible. For the sake of better functioning, some of the components of the configuration may momentarily occupy a more important place than others in accordance with the requirements of the situation. Thus, religiousness may display more of its emotional components or more of its refined conceptual aspects according to the situation and to the nature of the group in which we currently participate. Likewise, patriotism may be more sentimental than rationalistic or vice versa, according to the situation.

BEHAVIOR OF THE PERSONALITY AS A WHOLE

All the unconscious processes discussed above help to regulate the relation of the personality toward its environment. The human personality is an uninterrupted stream of a large number of such processes,[2] some of which cooperate and produce new configurations, readjust the old ones, and appropriately use the existing ones.

This continuous and rich stream enables the personality to meet the physical, social, and cultural necessities and harmonize them with the satisfaction of its own needs and wishes. It enables the individual to be a full member of his group, his society, and his culture by participating in and shaping the life of all of these.

The stream of spontaneous automatic processes operates as long as the person is alive. It may perhaps be compared to an imaginary factory incessantly producing the goods required by the market. The (per-

[2] G. A. Kelly says: ". . . . the person is not an object which is temporarily in a moving state but is himself a form of motion" (New York: W. W. Norton and Co., *The Psychology of Personal Constructs*, 1955), p. 48.

sonality) factory spontaneously adapts to the changing requirements of the market, for the most part without any supervision by conscious mental processes, and creates new products. The variety of products is incomparably larger than in any existing factory, and the social situations to which these are to be adapted are generally much more complex than any market situation. The adaptations and new creations do not cover only one (economic) field but a number of very different fields. They are not guided by only one motive (profit) but by a large number of motives, needs, pressures, and cultural requirements, and by many of these often simultaneously. Likewise, the appropriate distribution of products (use of configurations) is generally unconscious.

The picture of the total personality acting and reacting (to a large extent unconsciously) amidst the totality of the physical, social, and cultural conditions is what neither sociology nor anthropology, social psychology, personology, or psychology has given to us yet. Doubtless such a picture is long overdue, and it may be that the future development of these sciences will produce it gradually. It is of utmost importance for the understanding of the life of society and culture. Only such a picture of personality can explain the creation and maintenance of culture, the personality's enjoyment of it, its living in it and for it.

The unconscious structuring ability of the human mind using unconscious factors and processes to produce configurations is the fantastic workshop where so many cultural changes are produced. Here, with the help of group interactions, and other social processes, the new cultural patterns are formed and kept alive. Here also they may be reshaped or discarded if necessary. This unconscious personality workshop constitutes the long-sought-after link between personality and culture.

Unfortunately, it is not yet possible to indicate the laws of the operation of this workshop. These are to be discovered by empirical research. The major aim in this paper has been to point out the need for research in this unexplored area as well as to denote its direction.

SELF-TATTOOING AMONG DELINQUENTS
A Research Note

JOHN H. BURMA
Grinnell College

The culture trait of tattooing has a long history and is widespread throughout the world. The only scientific studies which have been reported are by anthropologists, who have concerned themselves with primitive societies. At least one generalization seems clear: generally tattooing appears to be a subcultural practice found in particular population categories (class, occupation, age, sex, etc.) rather than an established trait uniformly characteristic of a whole society. Little except of a popular nature has been written about tattooing among people of Western European extraction.

Nonstatistical, lay reports of the situation in America, commonly based on interviews with professional tattooers, suggest the following: (1) possibly one person in ten has a tattoo; (2) three to five times as many men are tattooed as women; (3) the basic motive is exhibitionistic; (4) the frequency rises in periods of crises, large-scale movements, the "holiday spirit"; (5) tattooing occurs most often when the client has been drinking; and (6) about one third of the tattooer's work involves requests to erase, cover, or "clean up" existing tattoos.[1]

On a preliminary basis it seems reasonable to hypothesize that in our culture persons who have certain types of self-concepts will be more likely to tattoo themselves than persons with other self-concepts. Because of the increasing significance of self-concepts in the study of delinquency,[2] it becomes a matter of interest whether or not there may be a relationship between the self-concepts related to delinquency and those related to self-tattooing. Although no analysis of this possible relationship has been made, Marshall Clinard and others have commented on it.

Before a major study of the possible relationship of various self-concepts to delinquency and to self-tattooing can be undertaken, it is first necessary to prove that a significant amount of tattooing does, in fact, occur among delinquents. The pilot study reported here attempts

---

[1] H. Ebersten, *Pierced Hearts and True Love* (London: Verscholye, 1953); *Literary Digest*, March 27, 1937, pp. 22 ff; "Skins and Needles," *Time*, 41:65, March 1, 1943; "War Booms the Tattooing Art," *New York Times*, Section M, p. 38, September 19, 1943; "Old Tattooer Talks Shop," *Science Digest*, 17: 21-23, March 1945; "Jap Gamblers Tattoo Selves," *Life*, 20: 12-14, March 11, 1946.

[2] For example, W. C. Reckless, S. Dinitz, B. Kay, "The Self Component in Potential Delinquency and Potential Non-Delinquency," *American Sociological Review*, 22:566-60, October 1957.

to do this, and in addition to learn something of the kinds of tattoos which exist; how, why, and under what circumstances the tattooing occurred; and something of the delinquent's attitude toward his tattoos. This study is neither definitive nor complete, yet it does present considerable data on the basis of which the hypotheses for a more conclusive study might be constructed.

Subjects for this report were inmates of the New Mexico Boys Training School, the Iowa Training School for Boys, and the Harwood School for delinquent girls at Albuquerque, New Mexico. In none of these institutions were all inmates or even all tattooed inmates interviewed. This might cast doubt upon the validity of some of the findings were it not that most of the data related not to persons, but to individual tattoos, of which well over 900 were observed and on 883 of which data were secured.[3]

The most overwhelming of the findings was that these were amateur "self-tattoos"; less than one half of 1 per cent were applied by professionals. Over two thirds were applied by the person himself, and the others by a boy or girl friend, sometimes on a "swapping" basis. Over 90 per cent were made by the use of ordinary sewing needle and India ink. Occasionally a razor blade or knife and fountain pen ink or graphite were used, usually because needle and India ink were temporarily unavailable.

Because not all inmates could be examined, no true statistical proportions of tattooed and nontattooed could be determined. The most accurate estimate the author can make is that at the New Mexico boys' school about 2 in 3 boys were tattooed, at the Iowa boys' school about 1 in 6 was tattooed, at the New Mexico girls' school possibly 1 in 3 was tattooed, and at the Iowa girls' training school, where only a cursory investigation was conducted, only about 1 in 25 was tattooed.

The data on number of tattoos per person were only exploratory, owing to less than 100 per cent coverage and the fact that a person with only 1 tattoo was more likely to be overlooked than a person with 10. However, the data are as follows: for the New Mexico boys (over 90 per cent coverage), the number of tattoos ranged from 1 to 25, and the median number was 5; for the Iowa boys (80 per cent coverage), the range was 1 to 14, and the median was 3; for the New Mexico girls (probably 60 per cent coverage), the range was 2 to 25, and the median was 10. These data show incontrovertibly that a large number of delinquents did have a significantly large number of tattoos.

[3] Special thanks for their assistance is due Rupert Trujillo, Ted Fiebiger, Marie Aiken, Jean Fowler, Arthur Tenorio, Jack DeRyke, and Elvira Pacheco.

The location of the 883 tattoos was determined with accuracy: about 32 per cent were between the wrist and the elbow, 23 per cent on the hands, about 17 per cent between elbow and shoulder, and the remainder on the fingers, face, and other parts of the body. The boys were considerably less likely to have tattoos where shirt sleeves could not cover their arms. The girls' samples showed them to have a higher proportion than the boys in visible spots like hands, fingers, and face, and also on their legs and thighs. Two thirds of all tattoos were on the left side and 80 per cent on the outer parts of arms. The single most common spot was between the thumb and forefinger on the left hand. None of the Iowa boys interviewed had face tattoos; 15 per cent of the New Mexico girls interviewed had 1 or more, and a full count of the New Mexico boys showed 12 per cent to have 1 or more such tattoos. Those who had only 1 or 2 tattoos usually had them where they could be covered up by shirt sleeves. Those with face tattoos usually had a considerable number of other tattoos, also.

By far the most common marks consisted of letters, most often the subject's own initials, but frequently the initials of a girl or boy, "Mom," or other words. Symbols were also frequent, with the most common being some variation of the "pachuco cross." Eight per cent of the tattoos studied had been left incomplete. Less than 1 per cent of the tattoos could be considered lewd in character. A number of tattoos had been marked out by new tattooing or by scars.

The interviewers attempted to learn the meaning of each tattoo, but with less than complete success. Frequently the answers were clear: "my initials," "my girl's initials," "all our gang had this," "pachuco cross." Often, however, the answers were vague, and, even discounting for evasiveness, it seems clear that many of the marks have little if any real significance and are in fact "just marks," much as ordinary 10- or 12-year-olds draw on their arms in schoolrooms throughout the nation—that is, except for the boys' initials on girls' arms, and vice versa, and for true gang symbols (which probably fail to exceed 10 per cent), the actual "content" of the tattoo seems of little use in analyzing self-concepts; certainly it seems less important than the fact of the tattooing itself. The chief exception seems to be the "pachuco cross" which, at least throughout the Southwest, has wide currency and is widely recognized by adults and by nondelinquents as well as by delinquents. It does serve as a gang sign for a few scattered groups, but it certainly does not indicate any nation-wide gang. That it does serve as a recognition sign for reference groups seems widely true. That is to say, a youngster in Albuquerque with a "pachuco cross" on his left hand may not belong to any gang at all, but if he moves to Los Angeles, or even Chicago, this symbol will serve to make it easier for him to set up relationships with some peer groups and more difficult with others. As a generalization it may be said that the subjects usually were far more concerned with the neatness or artistry of their tattoos than with their symbolism.

For all three groups the age at first tattooing was early. The age range for the New Mexico boys and girls was from six to eighteen years, and for the Iowa boys eleven to seventeen. For each of the three groups the median age was fourteen and the modal age was fifteen. Exactly 100 of the 883 tattoos were acquired before their owners were in their teens.

As to the circumstances under which the tattoo was made, no information is available for the Iowa boys, but for the New Mexico boys and girls, over 40 per cent were applied in their own homes or the homes of friends, with about an equal number being acquired while in a training school or jail (despite rigid training school rules). None resulted from formal gang initiation.

The majority of tattoos, at least according to the informants, were applied "for fun," because of "wanting something to do," "just fooling around," "no particular reason." For those tattoos for which a clear reason could be elicited, the chief reason given by girls was because of a boy friend, with copying someone they saw, as the second reason. For boys, gang reasons and girl friends were the two chief motivations. Some informants indicated that when a boy or girl in tattooing used someone's initials, usually either sexual intimacy had occurred or "they want you to think it had."

About half of each group indicated all or most of their friends had tattoos, and about half had brothers who were tattooed. Nearly half of the girls and nearly one fourth of the New Mexico boys said they had sisters who were tattooed, but only 4 per cent of the Iowa boys had tattooed sisters. About one half of each group stated as their immediate reaction to their tattooing that they "felt good," were proud, or felt "tough." About one fourth of the individuals of each group suffered remorse shortly after the tattooing. Questions were asked concerning the reaction of the subject's family to his tattooing, but the results could not be handled statistically because in a large number of cases the subject's parents still did not know, or the subject had no parents. In less than 5 per cent of the cases was the parent's reaction strongly unfavorable. In most cases where the subject's family knew about it, he was "fussed at" but not punished.

The subjects were also asked which tattoo they liked best, which least, whether they would like to have any tattoos removed and whether they expected to put on other tattoos later. The replies to these queries overlapped considerably, were conflicting in some cases, and frequently were hedged by "if." In each group the great majority judged the quality of tattooing and what the tattoo stands for as being paramount. Tattoos that were neat or artistic were liked; those that were of poor quality or incomplete were disliked. A considerable group of tattoos were disliked because they did not apply now—have a new girl or boy friend, moved from town, gang broke up.

Removal of all tattoos was desired by 75 per cent of the boys and 60 per cent of the girls. About 1 in 10 boys and 1 in 6 girls did not want any tattoos removed, and the remainder wanted some removed and some to remain. One in 3 girls said she "probably might" have more tattoos put on later, as compared to about 1 in 5 boys. The reasons given for wishing the removal of some or all tattoos were many, varied, and often vague. The two clearest and most common reasons were that they interfered with job possibilities, and that the particular tattoos were themselves unsightly and/or of poor quality. When asked why *other* boys had tattoos, the three most commonly given answers were: first, gang affiliation (although this varied from 45 per cent of the New Mexico boys to 5 per cent of the Iowa boys); second, that it made them feel "big" and "tough"; and third, copying others. In general, the boys seemed to show little insight into why girls were tattooed, but when urged to guess, their guesses matched the reasons actually given by the girls, namely, gang affiliation and boy friends.

Although this study is obviously an exploratory one, the author would like to conclude with the following general hypotheses: (1) Significantly more delinquents than nondelinquents tattoo themselves. (2) Significantly more boys than girls tattoo themselves, but when girls tattoo themselves they use at least as many tattoos as do boys. (3) The idea of tattooing oneself occurs to some people early, and is carried out at an early age, probably without much thought for the future. (4) Tattooing frequently, but not always, serves as a status symbol in certain peer groups, and it is only later that the subject realizes it is a negative status symbol in other groups. (5) Once tattooed, subsequent tattoos are put on with less compunction. (6) There is a close relationship between the kind of symbols most boys and girls *draw* on their arms and the symbols *tattooed* on by delinquents. (7) Self-tattooing is partial, but not certain, evidence of gang membership. (8) For some delinquents, tattooing is the result of certain self-concepts, and hence is a partial index of such concepts.

THE DIVISION OF LABOR AMONG COMMUNAL GROUPS: A FUNCTIONAL CLASSIFICATION

HENRY ZENTNER
Long Beach State College

This paper assays a classification of the functions performed by communal groups. As herein employed, the term *communal group* refers to that conceptually discrete organizational system, constructed by the inhabitants of a socially defined area or locality, which becomes functionally integrated around the problems and issues arising in the collective occupation and exploitation of the physical space comprising the defined area.[1] This definition, it may be noted, rests upon a classification of organizational systems based on considerations of the functions performed by the unit in question, i.e., the contribution it makes to the larger social system in which it is implicated, rather than upon considerations of its structural properties as is the case in the *gemeinschaft-gesellschaft*, primary-secondary, and other traditional classificatory schemes.

Accordingly, inasmuch as such organizational structures as the neighborhood, the district, the city, the county may be regarded as being integrated around the goals, objectives, and values arising in the collective occupation and exploitation of an area of given size and given symbolic identity, they may be conceived as falling into a single, more general type of organizational structure called *communal*—a type which can be further distinguished from other general types such as the recreational and commercial. Within the limits of this general type, however, there is evident a cultural ordering of socially defined areas involving greater and lesser degrees of spatial inclusiveness as well as a logical and symbolic ordering of the organizational units corresponding to each such culturally recognized spatial level.[2] For clarity of exposition, there-

---

[1] The notion of community as a functional type of social group or social system derives from Hiller's system of postulates relating to community. See E. T. Hiller, "The Community as a Social Group," *American Sociological Review*, 6: 189-202.

[2] The notion of multiple levels of communal organization, ranging from the household, seen as the smallest communal unit in an expanding hierarchy, to the nation as a whole, at the apex of the hierarchy, appears as a logical projection both from Hiller's definition of community and from the theoretical principles and typologies employed by R. M. MacIver and Charles H. Page, *Society: An*

fore, the nominally discrete organizational unit corresponding to each level of spatial inclusiveness will be termed the *communal group*; variations in the type of communal group corresponding to socially defined areas of varying degree of spatial inclusiveness will be articulated by reference to the notion of *levels of communal organization.*

The classification of communal group functions here suggested developed out of a research in progress concerning the use of time and space at various levels of communal organization and the problems of coordinating their activities in time and in space which confront the membership of communal groups. These activities may be regarded as problematic on both the intragroup and intergroup levels of communal organization comprising what the writer has elsewhere termed a system of habitational institutions.[3] In other words, the pursuit of the above-mentioned research objective, predicated as it is upon an organizational or sociocultural frame of reference, unavoidably necessitated a prior resolution of the problem concerning the particular functions culturally assigned to each of the several levels of communal organization as well as an understanding of the mechanisms which govern this division of labor between diverse levels or types of communal groups.

A search of the sociological literature relating to community disclosed that few attempts at systematic classification of these phenomena had as yet been reported. Moreover, such classificatory schemes of communal functions as were found proved of little operational utility for the problem in hand. Their utility proved limited for the reason that these schemes were derived from other definitions of community or other frames of reference than the one employed in the current research project. As it turned out, they either were entirely confined to the city or metropolitan community levels or were inclusive of all functions performed in the local society corresponding to these levels.[4]

---

[3] Henry Zentner, "Logical Difficulties in Relating the Concepts of Community, Society, and Institutions," *Alpha Kappa Deltan*, 28: 35-36.

[4] Such a classification appears in Wilbur C. Hallenbeck, *American Urban Communities* (New York: Harper and Brothers, 1951), pp. 261 ff. A conceptual distinction between community, as a limited and specific group which is integrated around the problems of occupying the locality, and the local society, which refers to all other systems of social relationships constructed by the inhabitants of the socially defined area, appears in Hiller, *op. cit.*

Introductory Analysis (New York: Rinehart, 1949); David Snedden, "Communities, Associate and Federate," *American Journal of Sociology*, 28: 681-93; and Betty W. Starr, "Levels of Communal Relations," *American Journal of Sociology*, 60: 125-36. These several propositions are analyzed and more fully developed by the writer elsewhere. See Henry Zentner, "Toward a Reconstruction of Community Theory," *Alpha Kappa Deltan*, 27: 28-32, and "Logical Difficulties in Relating the Concepts of Community, Society, and Institutions," *Alpha Kappa Deltan*, 28: 28-37.

Approached from the standpoint of the premises and postulates constituting the frame of reference cited above, however, it appeared that what was required for the purpose in hand was a classificatory scheme which would serve to articulate those culturally assigned functions which are *unavoidably* associated with inhabitation of given types of socially defined spatial or habitational units. That is to say, what was needed was a classification of the spatially endemic functions performed by given types of communal groups, seen in abstraction from control, coordination, communication, education, and other group functions which are necessarily, though variably, performed by the group qua communal group as a consequence of occupying and exploiting a given habitational space. In the absence of any existing classification of such a stamp, the construction of a tentative classification of the major space-related functions culturally assigned to each specific communal group in the series comprising the habitational system as a whole had of necessity to be undertaken before a precise specification of data requisite to the research could be undertaken.

Preliminary analysis and general observation suggested that each of the several levels of communal organization in the series evidenced a somewhat unique cluster of space-related functions. Nevertheless, a number of general classes of functions appeared to be common to all levels of communal organization. Included were (1) protection of persons and property, (2) the production and consumption of *certain* limited categories of economic goods and services, (3) provisions for the maintenance of sanitary standards, (4) provisions for the maintenance of health, (5) the provision of transit avenues and/or facilities, (6) the provision of recreational facilities, (7) the provision of certain welfare services, (8) the provision of communication facilities, and (9) provisions for the administration of justice (in the generic sense and including informal procedures).

Despite the possibility of certain unique functions on some or all levels of communal organization, it would appear that the nine general classes enumerated have the property not only of abstract logical independence but also of empirically observable behavioral manifestations. Nevertheless, having selected the present level of abstraction for the purpose of constructing a general classificatory scheme, it was immediately apparent that each of the nine general categories comprising the system would necessarily subsume a large number of diverse subclasses.

The general class relating to the maintenance of health, for example, would be divisible immediately into physical and mental subclasses.

Each of these, in turn, would entail further subclasses, and so on. The physical subclass, for example, would include behavior patterns relating to medication, exercise, dieting, ventilation, and numerous others. The mental subclass would correspondingly include such behavior patterns as the maintenance of privacy, balanced sociability, the creation of opportunities for self-expression, culturally sanctioned channels of tension and aggression release, and many others. Again, the general category relating to the provision of recreational facilities would entail subdivision into physically active and physically passive subclasses. The active subclass would involve further subdivision into lesser categories including games, sports, hobbies, etc., while the passive subclass in the case of modern cultures would involve such activities as radio and Hi-Fi listening, TV viewing, and spectator sports. Space limitations preclude a full and detailed exploration of the inventory of subclasses which would logically appear under each of the nine general categories cited above. Indeed, it can be safely asserted that only further detailed research can presume to determine the total range of phenomena subsumable under these nine general categories. The present classification, therefore, may be regarded as nothing more than a logical starting point for further research.

Of greater immediate relevance here, however, is the fact that even in the case of those general classes of function which appear to be common to all levels of communal organization, the specific behavior patterns implied or manifest at differing levels of organization (and from which the general classes of function enumerated have been abstracted) appear to be quite varied. Taking, for example, the sanitary function, it is evident that while all households are culturally expected to maintain certain minimum standards of cleanliness, to make reasonable disposal of garbage and refuse, etc., no household group is culturally expected to sweep the street in front of its holding. This function, as well as the taking away of garbage and refuse, is customarily performed by the city level of communal organization. Alternately, no neighborhood group is expected to clean up the local park site or playground; yet all neighbors, by virtue of *informal* group standards and pressures, are expected to maintain collectively agreed upon sanitary standards and practices relating to the control of children, pets, pests, vermin, rodents, weeds. Finally, all city levels of communal organization are expected to provide certain sanitary standards as well as sanitary services, such as water, sewage disposal, garbage collection; yet no city is expected to resolve, with its own limited jurisdiction and resources, the problem of smog which envelops an entire metropolitan area. This function, by virtue of cultural definition, would appear to have been relegated in part to the county, in part to the state, and in part to the federal level of organization. Correspondingly, similar arrangements may be cited with reference to each of the nine general classes of function cited above.

Adopting this premise, it appears, in brief, that cultural definitions and sanctioned expectations operate to reduce the logically abstract general classes of space-related functions common to all levels of communal organization into more or less specific tasks. These tasks are diversely, though in a functionally complementary manner, assigned to given levels of organization in the habitational system in accordance with the controlling mechanisms inherent in established cultural norms pertaining to the ascription of an appropriate degree or measure of local autonomy and local control vis-a-vis a corresponding degree of local responsibility ascribed to each level or type of communal group.[5] Within this broadly encompassing framework of culturally established norms, however, further variability is manifest. Each type of communal group, within the confines of its own organizational structure, appears to perform its culturally assigned space-related functions in a manner which is in keeping with the membership's value concepts relating to time, space, social status, peace, freedom, privacy, equity, cleanliness, legality, morality, safety, order, stability, convenience, economy, etc., seen in a state of dynamic interdependence and as conditioned by the unique and peculiar history of the local group in question.

Undoubtedly, it is the presence and interdependence between such group values as these which, operating within the limitations enjoined by the mechanisms of local autonomy, control, responsibility, and history, explains the fact that at all higher, i.e., spatially and numerically more inclusive, levels of organization many of the space-related functions nominally assigned to the communal group as such are not directly performed by the bulk of its membership. They are performed, rather, by specialized functionaries whose efficiency is greater and who act under the aegis and direction of properly constituted communal authority vested in spatially corresponding and formally constituted political or governmental group structures.

---

[5] These concepts are of course familiar to the political scientist and other students of government. It requires only a recognition of the fact that they may be structured both formally and informally to accept their assimilation to community theory. Indeed, in his early work on the community concept, MacIver made extensive use of these notions. Their subsequent disappearance from the sphere of community theory would appear to be in part explained by the persistent tendency in many quarters to confuse government with community. Analysis of this further problem, however, is beyond the scope of this paper.

The delegation by communal groups of certain space-related functions to other group structures, such as government, must be regarded, however, not as an abdication of responsibility, but rather as a culturally sanctioned and organizationally convenient division of labor. That is to say, the resident member of the communal group in question is not thereby entirely absolved from further duties and obligations relating to the discharge of the delegated functions. On the contrary, by virtue of related cultural sanctions there devolves upon him the duty of participating in the formulation of rules and regulations which govern the delegation of powers and functions to other specialized groups and/or functionaries. There devolves upon him as well the duty of complying with the collectively established rules relating to the facilitation of such functionaries in the discharge of their delegated functions. That many are lax in their sense of obligation in this respect and renege or in other respects are found remiss in the discharge of their culturally sanctioned roles is a consideration notwithstanding.

A final observation may be made in relation to the matter of the stability of the habitational system as a whole. Presumably, as was noted above, the division of functions, on both the intragroup and intergroup levels of communal organization, achieves an order and a stability as a consequence of the mechanisms of autonomy, control, responsibility, and history which were seen to be operative throughout the entire system of communal groups. These mechanisms, in turn, serve to carry out their functions as a consequence of the fact that membership in each level or type of communal organization is held *simultaneously* by each and every member of society. The norms of each type of group, therefore, as well as the institutional norms governing the entire system of communal organization, thereby achieve a measure of unity and integration, since it is one and the same social actor who acts in reference to his concept of the structure of each group in the series comprising the system as a whole.

ATTITUDES TOWARD THE FAMILY AMONG COLLEGE STUDENTS AND THEIR PARENTS*

PANOS D. BARDIS
Albion College

According to Ernest W. Burgess and Harvey J. Locke, familism refers to strong in-group feelings, emphasis on family goals, common property, mutual support, and the desire to pursue the perpetuation of the family.[1] As several recent developments indicate, this type of organization is no longer so dominant among typical American families as it was a few decades ago.[2] Furthermore, it seems that the influence of modern means of transportation and communication, as well as of recent socioeconomic changes, is so extensive and pervasive that the attitudes of various groupings—parents and children, college graduates and noncollege graduates, upper and lower occupational classes, and the like—are about equally nonfamilistic.

The Problem. The purpose of the present study, which deals primarily with attitudes toward familism among college students and their parents, was to examine this theory by testing the following hypotheses: (1) College students and their parents do not differ significantly in their attitudes toward familism. (2) There is no significant relationship between familism and such variables as education, age, size of home town, occupation, and number of siblings.

Methodology. To measure attitudes toward familism, a scale[3] was constructed by means of the Likert scaling technique.[4] The validity and reliability of this device were tested repeatedly and proved satisfactory. A split-half test, for instance, applied to the responses of 30 males and females selected at random from the sample of the present study, gave a

---

*This project was financed by a grant from the Faculty Fellowship Fund of Albion College.

[1] *The Family*, second ed. (New York: American Book Company, 1953), p. 60.

[2] *Ibid.*, pp. 53-95.

[3] For a detailed description of this scale, see Panos D. Bardis, "A Familism Scale," *Marriage and Social Living*, in press. Valuable suggestions concerning the scale items were given by Drs. R. Blood, E. Burgess, R. Cavan, H. Christensen, E. and S. Duvall, R. Hill, J. and P. Landis, and M. Nimkoff. Copies are available upon request from the author.

[4] Rensis Likert, *A Technique for the Measurement of Attitudes* (New York: *Archives of Psychology*, 1932), No. 140, especially pp. 11-33 and 44-53.

raw reliability coefficient of .79, which, after it was corrected by means of the Spearman-Brown formula,[5] resulted in a value of .88. The 16 items[6] of this scale were preceded by a statement specifying that the subjects were not expected to describe their own families but to indicate the extent to which they approved of the practices expressed by these items with reference to the family institution in general. The theoretical range of a person's reaction to each item was 0.4, while that of his familism score resulting from all 16 items was 0-64—a high score always indicated a familistically minded individual.

Part of the group studied by means of this familism scale consisted of students enrolled in the writer's Introductory Sociology course in 1958. Only white native Americans whose parents were also white native Americans, living, and still married were included. In this way, the entire group studied consisted of 68 students and their 136 parents. Of the former, 18 were males and 50 females, their ages ranging between 18 and 24 years—the mean was 19.37. Moreover, 1 was Catholic, 66 were Protestants—of these, 31 were Methodist—and 1 was nonaffiliated. One was married, 2 engaged, and 65 single. Forty-two were sophomores, 23 juniors, and 3 seniors. Eight had spent most of their first 18 years in communities of less than 5,000 population, and 59 in cities of at least 5,000—1 failed to supply information concerning this matter. Eight were only children, 34 had one sibling each, 14 had two, 11 had three, and 1 had six. The ages of the fathers ranged between 41 and 69 years, the mean being 51.26. Four of them were Catholic, 61 were Protestant—of these 27 were Methodist—and 3 were nonaffiliated. Five had only a grade school education, 22 were high school graduates, 26 had some college training, and 15 had done graduate work. Twenty-eight had spent most of their first 18 years in communities of less than 5,000 population, and 40 in cities of at least 5,000. Twelve were skilled workers or foremen, 15 were clerks or kindred workers, 24 were proprietors, managers, or officials, and 17 were professional persons. The ages of the mothers ranged between 38 and 59 years, the mean being 48.99. Two of them were Catholic and 66 were Protestant—of these, 29 were Methodist. Six had only a grade school education, 23 were high school graduates, 34 had some college training, and 5 had done graduate work. Twenty-five had spent most of their first 18 years in communities of less than 5,000 population, and 43 in cities of at least 5,000. Finally, only 9 were gainfully employed—4 were clerks or kindred workers and

---

[5] Henry E. Garrett, *Statistics in Psychology and Education*, fourth ed. (New York: Longmans, Green and Company, 1953), p. 341.

[6] See Findings and Interpretation, *infra.*

5 were professional persons—while the remaining 59 were housewives.

All of the data secured from these three groups were collected through personal interviews and analyzed by means of several statistical tests.

Findings and Interpretation. The means of the subjects' responses to each of the 16 scale items were as follows—the first value always represents the fathers, the second the mothers, and the third the students: a person should always support his uncles or aunts if they are in need, 1.66, 1.50, 1.91; children below 18 should give almost all their earnings to their parents, .94, .91, .59; the family should consult close relatives (uncles, aunts, first cousins) concerning its important decisions, 1.51, 1.13, 1.13; children below 18 should almost always obey their older brothers and sisters, 1.75, 1.38, 1.57; a person should always consider the needs of his family as a whole more important than his own, 3.01, 2.79, 2.76; at least one married child should be expected to live in the parental home, .41, .47, .40; a person should always be expected to defend his family against outsiders even at the expense of his own personal safety, 3.01, 2.44, 2.85; the family should have the right to control the behavior of each of its members completely, 1.00, 1.28, .96; a person should always support his parents-in-law if they are in need, 2.32, 2.59, 2.38; a person should always avoid every action of which his family disapproves, 1.50, 1.50, 1.46; a person should always share his home with his uncles, aunts, or first cousins if they are in need, 1.22, 1.28, 1.44; a person should always be completely loyal to his family, 2.90, 2.68, 2.71; the members of a family should be expected to hold the same political, ethical, and religious beliefs, 1.18, 1.00, .90; children below 18 should always obey their parents, 2.81, 2.68, 2.50; a person should always help his parents with the support of his younger brothers and sisters if necessary, 2.93, 2.66, 3.00; a person should always share his home with his parents-in-law if they are in need, 2.01, 1.93, 1.94.

The above values lead to the following conclusions: (1) The relative uniformity of the means representing each item indicates some proximity between the students' attitudes toward familism and those of their parents. (2) The item represented by the highest means referred to helping one's parents with the support of one's younger siblings, while that with the lowest means pertained to the married child's living in the parental home. (3) In general, if we divide the items into three categories represented by means found primarily between 0 and 1, 1 and 2, and 2 and 3, we observe that (a) the subjects disapproved most of policies depriving the individual of his independence with reference to finances, residence, conduct, and ideologies; (b) they approved most of practices conducive to the general security of the immediate family as a whole; and (c) the intermediate responses referred primarily to helping close relatives other than parents and siblings.

The means of the subjects' familism scores were 30.16 for the fathers, 28.22 for the mothers, and 28.50 for the students. (A similar study involving young people residing in a rural community in southern Greece gave a mean of 46.95.) The difference between fathers and mothers was insignificant above the .05 level (t 1.81, df 134), that between fathers and students above the .10 level (t 1.63, df 134), and that between mothers and students above the .70 level (t .27, df 134), thus tending to confirm the hypothesis that "college students and their parents do not differ significantly in their attitudes toward familism." An additional test of the difference between the mean of the male students (29.89) and that of the female students (28.00) revealed that this difference was also insignificant above the .20 level (F 1.03, df 49 and 17, insignificant much above .10;[7] t 1.21, df 66). In other words, as far as familism is concerned, the female students were about as liberal as the males, although certain studies dealing with dating have revealed a significantly lower degree of liberalism among females.[8] It is interesting to note, however, that among both parents and students the males made consistently higher familism means, the order from the highest to the lowest being: fathers, sons, mothers, daughters.

A different pattern of attitudes was revealed when the responses to the question, "At what age do you think boys should start dating individually, that is, not in groups?———, Girls?———," were analyzed. Indeed, the fathers' means for boys and girls were 16.40 and 15.85 years, respectively, the difference between them being significant slightly above the .05 level (t 1.90, df 134), while the mothers' corresponding values were 16.22 and 15.56, the difference being significant much below the .001 level (t 3.65, df 134), and those of the students 15.29 and 14.82, the difference being also significant much below the .001 level (t 4.27, df 134). In other words, as various similar studies[9] have also shown, the tendency of females to mature and marry earlier than males as well as to be younger than their husbands seems to lead to the belief that girls should start dating earlier than boys. In addition, the fathers once again proved to be the most conservative group and the

---

[7] See Allen L. Edwards, *Experimental Design in Psychological Research* (New York: Rinehart and Company, Inc., 1950), pp. 162-70.

[8] See, for instance, Panos D. Bardis, "Attitudes Toward Dating Among the Students of a Michigan High School," *Sociology and Social Research*, 42: 276.

[9] *Ibid.*, p. 277.

students the least conservative, while the mothers were found between the two extremes, perhaps indicating that parents still tend to consider certain modern dating practices too liberal. Indeed, when the mean ages referring to boys were compared, the difference between fathers and mothers was insignificant almost at the .50 level (t .69, df 134), that between fathers and students significant much below the .001 level (t 4.83, df 134), and that between mothers and students also significant much below the .001 level (t 7.15, df 134). Again, the corresponding differences pertaining to girls were all significant much below the .001 level (t 5.37, 4.70, 4.48; df 134). In brief, although the hypothesis concerning familism was confirmed, the two generations differed significantly with reference to attitudes toward dating.

The second hypothesis, dealing with the relationship between familism and certain variables, was also confirmed. The familism-age correlation coefficients for fathers, mothers, and students, for instance, were .20, .19, and -.04, respectively, while the corresponding figures for familism and years of education were .13, -.06, and .05. Moreover, after assigning a value of 5 to professional persons, 4 to proprietors, managers, and officials, 3 to clerks and kindred workers, 2 to skilled workers and foremen, 1 to semiskilled workers, and 0 to unskilled workers,[10] the fathers' coefficient of correlation for familism and occupation proved to be as low as -.06, while that of the students—for paternal occupations—was .15. On the other hand, of the mothers, the housewives made a mean familism score of 28.46 and the nonhousewives 26.67, the difference between these means being insignificant above the .40 level (F 1.27, df 58 and 8, insignificant much above .10; t .80, df 66). Insignificant differences were also obtained when those coming from small communities (see methodology) were compared with those coming from large cities.[11] For the fathers, for example, the mean familism score of the former was 29.96 and of the latter, 30.28, the difference being insignificant above the .80 level (F 1.23, df 39 and 27, insignificant much above .10; t .21, df 66). The corresponding means for the mothers were 28.00 and 28.35, their difference being insignificant above the .80 level (F 1.20, df 42 and 24, insignificant much above .10; t .22, df 66), while those representing the students were 26.62 and 28.78, their difference being also insignificant above the .30 level (F 1.42, df 7 and 58, insignificant much above .10; t 1.00, df 65). Finally, the students' coefficient of

[10] For this classification of occupations, see Alba M. Edwards, *Comparative Occupational Statistics for the United States, 1870-1940* (Washington, D.C.: United States Government Printing Office, 1943), pp. 181-86.

[11] Cf. Burgess and Locke, *loc. cit.*

correlation for familism and number of siblings was only -.04. It seems then that, perhaps for the reasons mentioned previously, as far as the subjects of the present study are concerned, there is no significant relationship between familism and such variables as age, education, occupation, size of home town, and number of siblings.

When, however, familism scores and the ages considered desirable for the beginning of dating were correlated, the coefficients were as follows: for boys, the fathers' coefficient was .27 (significant between .01 and .05, df 66), the mothers' .07, and the students' .47 (significant much below .01, df 66), while the corresponding values for girls were .27 (significant as above), .18, and .12. In other words, there seems to be a slight positive correlation between liberalism concerning familism and liberalism concerning dating.

Finally, an effort to determine the extent of the parents' influence on their children led to what appears to be the most interesting finding of the present study.[12] Indeed, the father-son coefficients of correlation for familism, age at which boys should begin dating, and age at which girls should begin dating were .16, .08, and .01, respectively, while the corresponding father-daughter figures were .41, .47 (both significant below .01, df 48), and .04. On the other hand, the corresponding mother-son coefficients were .16, .29, and .24 (last two, insignificant much above .05, df 16), while those representing the mother-daughter data were .37, .66 (both significant below .01, df 48), and .05. In other words, because the family is ordinarily the first institution to receive the child, because the latter interacts with this group when he or she is most impressionable, because family contacts are intimate, emotional, and continual, and because parents usually satisfy many of their children's physical, psychological, and social needs, thus encouraging identification with, and imitation of, the sources of such satisfaction, it seems that, despite the atomism which is dominant in our society, this institution is still influential. As the above data indicate, however, such influence appears to be more extensive among daughters, since, although all twelve coefficients were positive, the average of those representing the female students was .33, whereas that of the male students was only .16. Furthermore, mothers seem more influential than fathers, since their average was .30, that of the fathers being .20. Finally, the averages representing the four parent-child relationships were as follows: mother-daughter .36, father-daughter .31, mother-son .23, and father-son .08.

[12] Cf. Hugh Hartshorne *et al.*, "Testing the Knowledge of Right and Wrong," *Religious Education*, 21: 539-54, especially p. 545.

Summary and Conclusion. In brief, a study of attitudes toward the family among 68 Michigan college students and their 136 parents has revealed that (1) the two generations do not differ significantly with reference to attitudes toward familism; (2) males tend to be more familistic than females; (3) both males and females believe that girls should begin to date earlier than boys; (4) fathers tend to be more conservative than their wives and children concerning familism and dating; (5) parents believe that dating should begin much later than the average age given by their children; (6) familism does not seem to be affected significantly and consistently by age, education, occupation, size of home town, and number of siblings; and (7) children's attitudes toward the family are definitely influenced by their parents, the order from the strongest relationship to the weakest being mother-daughter, father-daughter, mother-son, father-son.

Further research by means of the familism scale employed in the present study may be conducted in various ways. Rural samples, for instance, may be compared with others obtained from cities. Moreover, it is possible for additional projects to include three generations as well as various racial, ethnic, or religious groups. Again, the scale may be administered before and after the completion of courses in Family Life Education to measure the influence of such work on familism. Finally, some of the effects of changing social conditions on the family could be ascertained by administering the scale in one and the same school or other institution every five or ten years.

POLITICAL PARTICIPATION AMONG ORIENTALS IN HAWAII

GEORGE K. YAMAMOTO
University of Hawaii

The assimilation of immigrant groups in America is frequently described with the use of certain kinds of population data that extend over a period of time, are relatively easy to obtain, and are reasonably accurate. As a facet of assimilation, the extent of political participation on the part of persons of Oriental ancestry in Hawaii may be made by utilizing United States Census and other more or less officially collected information.

Two limited types of political participation among Orientals[1] in Hawaii were selected for study: (1) that of serving as elected officials of the Territorial and County governments of Hawaii and (2) that of serving as appointed officials of the Territorial government, whose functions are "supervisory" or "administrative."[2]

Elected Officials. As indicated in Table 1, the percentage that all Orientals and also Japanese alone comprised in both categories of political participation was calculated for decade points from 1910 to 1950 and for the year 1955.[3] Among elected officials, the changes in percentage of participation by Orientals over the decades show no participation at all in 1910, then a minimal but rising amount of participation up to 1940, and then a rather sharp rise.

In order to give a sense of continuity and development for the whole period under discussion, including the years between decade points, pertinent information was obtained from *Thrum's Hawaiian Annual*,

---

[1] The term "Orientals," for the purpose of this paper, refers to persons of Japanese, Chinese, Korean, and Filipino ancestry. The Japanese have been singled out in the table because they constitute the largest ethnic group not only among Orientals but in Hawaii as a whole. The rest of Hawaii's population —non-Orientals—consists mainly of Caucasians and Hawaiians, including part Hawaiians, but also includes the numerically minor ethnic groups like the Puerto Ricans, Samoans, and American Negroes.

[2] The sources of information regarding both types of officials were (1) *Thrum's Hawaiian Annual* series and (2) *Directory of Agencies and Officers of the Territory of Hawaii*, a biennial Territorial government publication.

[3] The total number of elected officials varied little over the decades; it was 91 in 1910 and 93 in 1955. In the latter year Orientals, of whom there were 47, comprised 50.5 per cent of the total.

1900 to 1955.[4] It was not until 1920 that the first person of Oriental ancestry, a Chinese, was elected to any government office in Hawaii. In the decade following, a few other persons of Chinese ancestry were elected to both County and Territorial government offices, although as late as the year 1928 only four of the approximately ninety positions were held by Chinese. Japanese names among elected officials appeared for the first time in 1930, when two such persons were elected to the Territorial House of Representatives. In that year five persons of Japanese and Chinese ancestry made up, as the table indicates, about 6 per cent of the total number of elected officials. In 1932 eleven Orientals were elected to public office. This number remained unchanged during the middle 1930's, but in 1938 sixteen Orientals were elected, and in 1940 twenty-two, or about 24 per cent of the total, were Orientals. Thirteen of the twenty-two were of Japanese ancestry, and nine were of Chinese ancestry. One of the thirteen Japanese was the first Oriental to serve in the Senate of the Territorial Legislature. During the years of World War II, except for the holdover senator (1940 to 1944) and one other person who was elected to a County office in 1942 and 1944, no Japa-

TABLE 1

ORIENTALS IN HAWAII IN GOVERNMENT POSITIONS IN RELATION TO ADULT CITIZENSHIP, 1910-1955

	Elected Officials		Appointed Officials		Adult Citizens	
	Per Cent Orientals	Per Cent Japanese	Per Cent Orientals	Per Cent Japanese	Per Cent Orientals	Per Cent Japanese
1910	0	0	0	0	3.1	0.3
1920	1.1	0	0.8	0	12.7	5.5
1930	5.5	2.2	4.1	1.6	23.9	15.3
1940	24.2	14.3	6.3	2.9	35.9	26.6
1950	37.4	25.3	17.5	10.0	48.2	34.7
1955	50.5	43.0	29.7	19.1	54.0*	41.0*

*Estimated

[4] Hawaii's first election as an American Territory took place in 1900. Japanese and Chinese together made up well over half of the total population in 1900, but the overwhelming majority of these two groups consisted of immigrant aliens or their young citizen children who were not yet eligible to vote or to hold public office. Immigrants from Korea began to arrive in Hawaii from 1900 and from the Philippines from 1909.

nese ran for or held any elected office. Persons of Chinese ancestry made up about 10 per cent of the total of elected officials in 1942 and 1944. In 1946, the first election year after the close of the war, an equal number of Japanese and Chinese made up about 29 per cent of the total of 91 elected officials.

The increase in the Oriental percentage of elected officials that was observed before World War II continued in the postwar period, so that by 1955 slightly more than half of the elected officials were of Oriental ancestry. The increase, however, has been due almost entirely to an increase in the number of officials of Japanese ancestry, although in 1954 a candidate of Filipino ancestry and one of Korean ancestry were elected, each the first representative of his ethnic group to hold elective office in Hawaii.

Appointed Officials. The changes in the percentage of Orientals among appointed officials of the Territorial government take a form similar to that of the elected officials, from no Orientals in 1910 to about 30 per cent in 1955.[5] The first substantial increase, however, took place in 1940, a decade after Oriental participation in elective offices had first risen sharply. Throughout the period, participation as appointed officials lagged behind participation as elected officials; in 1955, while about half of the elected officials were Orientals, a little less than a third of the appointed officials were Orientals. Also, within the Oriental category, the proportion of Japanese appointees since the war is smaller than the proportion of Japanese elected officials.

Inspection of *Thrum's Annual* reveals that in the years before 1920 a few persons of Chinese and Japanese ancestry were employed in the lower white-collar ranks in the Territorial government but none in the ranks regarded in this paper as "officials." In 1920 there were two persons of Chinese ancestry listed as "chief clerk" and as "member of Board of Examiners of Optometry." In the late 1920's a few Oriental names began to appear in positions such as "field auditor," "assistant engineer," "chief termite inspector," "member of the Advisory Tax Appraisal Board," and the like. By 1940 Orientals were serving as officials in a number of departments and boards, including several in the Territorial courts, but Orientals as heads of departments or as chairmen of boards appear to be a post-World War II phenomenon.

Adult Citizens. The evaluation, or assessment, of the extent of participation on the part of Orientals in these types of government

[5] The total number of appointed officials of the Territorial government was 211 in 1910 and 931 in 1955.

offices calls for the use of some criterion with which the percentage of participation can be compared at each point during the period under consideration. From the information available in the United States Census reports for Hawaii, the percentage that Orientals comprised in the category "U.S. citizens 21 years of age and over" was selected as the most useful standard by which to gauge the extent of participation.[6] This "adult citizens" category in the table shows that Orientals made up 3 per cent of all such persons in 1910 and an estimated 54 per cent in 1955, with the Japanese comprising more than half of the Oriental adult citizen total from 1930 up to the present.

A comparison of the participation columns with the adult citizens column indicates that Orientals were "underrepresented"[7] in both types of government positions throughout the period; that is, Orientals were not up to their "expected" proportion and hence were not like the non-Orientals grouped together as a category (i.e., not assimilated). As a corollary, non-Orientals were "overrepresented." By 1950, however, the gap between the expected and observed percentages had become narrower, especially in the case of elected officials. Projected to 1955, it appears that Orientals had just about "caught up" in elective offices but still experienced a considerable lag in appointive offices. Considering the Japanese alone, this group's participation in elective offices in 1955 went slightly over the benchmark of an estimated 41 per cent with a 43 per cent representation; in the appointed officials category, this group's representation of 19 per cent of the total is less than half the "expected" of 41 per cent.

Summary. In an attempt to describe participation in government as a facet of assimilation among Orientals in Hawaii, the percentages that Orientals comprised in the total number of elective offices and of appointive offices were calculated for the period 1910 to 1955. These per-

[6] The percentage of the *total* population of Hawaii who are Orientals may be used to assess their proportion of government participation, but this practice tends to give rise to unrealistic interpretations, since noneligibles formed a much greater proportion among Orientals than among Caucasians and Hawaiians, especially in the early decades of this century. The discrepancy between proportion of adult citizens and proportion of total population among Orientals, however, decreased with each succeeding decade; in 1950 Orientals formed 57 per cent of the total and 48 per cent of the adult citizen population. In another decade there will probably be no statistically significant difference between the two percentages.

[7] Taking 1940 as an example, if we divide 24.2 (per cent Orientals, elected officials) by 35.9 (per cent Orientals, adult citizens), we obtain .67, which may be read as an underrepresentation by approximately a third. The expected index number would be 1.0, a coinciding of the two percentages. The .67 may also be read as an overrepresentation by about a third on the part of non-Orientals.

centages were compared with the percentages for comparable years that Orientals comprised in the total adult citizen population. It was found that:

1. Orientals lagged behind their expected proportion of filling roles as elected government officials, although the lag decreased with each succeeding decade. As of 1955, Orientals had become almost indistinguishable from non-Orientals in this facet of participation in government. The Japanese, among the Orientals, contributed most to closing the gap after World War II, seemingly largely as a result of this large group "coming of age" with respect to adult citizenship.

2. Orientals lagged behind their expected proportion of participants among appointed officials to a greater extent than in the case of participation in elective offices. Here again, however, the lag or gap narrowed with each succeeding decade. As of 1955, Oriental participation had risen to almost three fifths of their expected extent of serving as appointed officials. Japanese participation had risen to about half of their "quota." A hypothesis that suggests itself is that in American local politics, new ethnic groups experience an increase in their percentage of *elected* officials before they experience an increase in their percentage of *appointed* officials.

3. For the Hawaiian situation, the percentage of Orientals in the "U.S. citizens 21 years of age and over" measure is useful both as a standard to gauge the extent of political participation and also as a crude predictor of the ethnic distribution of political participants. As the percentage of Orientals among adult citizens increased, the percentage of Orientals in the two types of government positions increased. How to account for the fact that the percentage of Oriental participants did not quite coincide throughout the period with the percentage of Oriental adult citizens and the fact that Oriental participation increased at a rising rate in the latter part of the period involves such unexamined factors as differences and changes in the age structure of adult citizens in the Oriental category as compared with that of non-Orientals, the degree to which ethnic discrimination has been a policy in making appointments, the extent of ethnic bloc voting in the election of officials, and the possible differences and shifts in status, values, and skills as between Orientals and non-Orientals.

The description of limited types of political participation as a facet of assimilation among Orientals in Hawaii is generally in line with the findings of other aspects of assimilation made by utilizing Census and other government information. Orientals have tended over time to approximate the standards of non-Orientals in characteristics such as birth rate, fertility ratio, infant mortality rate, median income, amount of education, and occupational distribution,[8] as well as in extent of participation in the more important local government positions.

---

[8] A. W. Lind, *Hawaii's People* (Honolulu: University of Hawaii Press, 1955), Chap. 4, "How Do They Live?" and Chap. 5, "What Are They Becoming?"

W. I. THOMAS AND SOCIAL ORIGINS

EMORY S. BOGARDUS
University of Southern California

From the standpoint of the history of sociological thought in the United States, I have made a sampling of my notes taken in the class in Social Origins given by William I. Thomas at the University of Chicago during the academic year of 1909-10. This paper is no attempt to repeat those notes either in whole or in part except to illustrate the general trend of the lecturer's thinking regarding social origins.

Thomas' former students know that he rarely indulged in statistics, but sought to present the inner meanings of events from the standpoint of the participants in these events as disclosed by the participants' behavior. He perceived evolutionary trends in the development of culture and in the ability of primitive people to develop step by step, building new behavior patterns on the basis of antecedent patterns and insights. The method could be called sociopsychological. There was some organization around specific subtopics of "social origins," but no general system of thought was attempted.

There was, however, a definite point of view or approach, which might be labeled socioevolutionary. There was a comparative method, comparing what was with what later developed. There was a type of case analysis of one social situation after another, drawn from a large amount of data which Thomas was in a continual process of accumulating and having typed on slips of paper of different colors about four by six inches in size (these slips of paper were cut in terms of centimeters and were carried in a wallet of appropriate size). He continually referred to this storehouse of materials which he could easily organize and reorganize, for he recorded only one item on each slip of paper.

The notes on which this article is based were taken in long hand and hence are not always complete, even though the lecturer spoke slowly (in contrast with the rapid-fire method of George E. Vincent, who was also a member at that time of the sociology staff of the University of Chicago). Some of the ideas which are quoted here are extracted from what is at times an extended context, but the writer has been careful to quote only those ideas which can stand by themselves without being misunderstood by thoughtful readers.

An appropriate and available context for the ideas quoted in this paper is Thomas' *Source Book for Social Origins*,[1] published in the fall of

[1] Chicago: The University of Chicago Press.

1909 when the course was being given. During this time the writer's notes were taken. On the title page of this 932-page book on social origins appears a significant quotation: "In good faith my masters, this is no door. Yet it is a little window that looketh upon a great world" (quoted in Risley, *The People of India*, title page). Through little windows that Thomas opened four days a week, his students, who in the particular course given in 1909-10 included, besides the writer, Ernest W. Burgess, Luther L. Bernard, and others, obtained meaningful glimpses of the world of primitive men and women.

The socioevolutionary view was presented at the very beginning of the course of study. It was explained that there are three stages involved in this view, namely, the prehuman, the postanimal and prewhite civilization, and the civilization stages. Although the discussion of social origins centered in the prewhite civilization stage, references were made from time to time related to prehuman origins and also to current expressions of the prewhite civilization culture patterns.

It was noted, for example, that animals post sentinels and have leaders, usually the best and strongest fighters. They drive the ill-dispositioned members out of the group and maintain a kind of "group morality." Warm-blooded animals with lungs develop squeak-squeak sounds, the predecessors of vocal language. Chicks learn to run from shadows, and thus the survival of the fittest runners begins. Animals have no conception of danger but are "built up to avoid it."

The subject of social origins was related chiefly to living and extinct primitive peoples. The former were described as a kind of "delayed ancestors," or people who have not had the same opportunities as other people to develop. The chief difference between primitives and civilized peoples is "cultural, not biological." However, Thomas pointed out that social origins are not confined to the lives of primitive people. They occur at every stage of social life and they are occurring today.

Social change is and has been going on continually since the advent of man on earth. To primitive people change seemed to be beyond their control. It was inevitable. It was very real and the problem was how to meet it. Wherever it ran counter to established habits of the individuals, "change was met by a maximum of resistance." When times were bad, change was welcome. Hence primitive people on the one hand "were afraid of change" (because of its defiance of habit), and on the other hand they "prized it highly" (when it might bring better times). Even today great change takes place from generation to generation, for "the books of your father you keep for affection."

A few glimpses will now be given of Thomas' approach to such topics as origins of intelligence, of invention, of language, of emotions, of personal control, and of social control.

Origins of Intelligence. A few examples of Thomas' interpretation of how intelligence began and developed as a result of various kinds of stimuli will indicate his unique way of interpreting social origins. Since these statements are largely self-explanatory, they will not be prefaced or followed by comments:

The head of an animal goes first, not because it is the head, but because that which started first became the head. It got a head start.

The head got heavy and so man stood up; this rising to stand was man's grandest stand in life. It released his fore feet for all kinds of useful activities.

The erect posture came rather late, for nature didn't think of it at first.

The revolution of the seasons develops a series of pushes to get things done.

Mind is made up of pursuing and escaping.

You can't have a high state of mind in a low state of society.

Occupations represent the modes in which mind expresses itself. Specialization of occupation is an important mode of developing mind.

Primitive religion illustrates the logical process of mind working illogically.

Of Invention. The origins of invention are aspects of intelligence. Thomas had a great deal to suggest on this theme, and his incisive observations had a far-reaching significance for social evolution. He often left his students to furnish connecting links in their thinking about evolutionary processes.

Invention starts from an accidental discovery and involves abstraction.

The sword is a long, piercing tooth.

The spear is a longer, piercing tooth.

The arrow (and bow) is a still longer, piercing tooth.

The rifle pierces much farther.

Explosives multiply the piercing process at multiplied distances.

Man has kept adding handles to the killing instruments. In that way he has secured greater force. At the same time he has been able to kill at greater and greater distances.

Specialization may stimulate invention or it may deaden invention, especially when it takes nine men to make a pin, for the making of one ninth of a pin is not very stimulating.

Invention is a pacemaker—everyone catches up after a time.

Of Language. Thomas recognized the role of language as an expression of intelligence, as consisting of inventions, and as a form of communication. He pointed out some of the origins of meaning that are found in behavior and in gestures which may be "truncated acts" (Mead).

Bowing the head is a diminished approach.

"Yes" involves shaking the head, and rigidity.

Tithes developed by counting on the hands.

Group life is regulated by signals.

In certain remote regions distance is signified by two "whoops" and a "holler" (half a "whoop").

Language is a social control instrument, for through it traditions, knowledge, standpoints are passed along and increased.

Of Emotions. The origins of emotions are deep-seated and difficult to locate. They are related to favorable and unfavorable environmental experiences. They are widespread uniformities in their origins relating to the individual's gains and losses or anticipated gains and losses or imagined gains and losses.

The yelp of a dog at not being allowed to join in a hunt indicates a breaking of the emotions.

Primitive man away from home may die of homesickness because of the disrupting of so many of his habits.

Romantic affection is based partly on newness.

Temperament varies more than mind; emotionally you are not separable from your surroundings.

Primitive man's literature emphasizes emotions, not intelligence.

Emotions are bases of religion and the arts.

Of Races. The inherited mind of the different races is about the same. Racial differences, according to Thomas, are largely related to culture differences. The differences between the members of a race may be greater than differences between races. Racial prejudices are acquired or learned by each individual in his lifetime.

Our ancestors were once "savages."

The African black thinks that the first white man that he sees is frightfully anemic and to be pitied.

The favored color by primitive colored people is a chocolate brown.

The native African prefers a snug well-fitting nose. He deplores a beaklike projecting nose.

No Negro has ever been raised from birth as a white child in a white family.

The Oriental is more filial than the Occidental.

The time may come when all the world may be of a chocolate color, but what difference will that make?

Of Personal Control. Personal control begins in the arousing of inner processes by stimuli from surroundings. It has emotional aspects and is represented in habits. It is motivated by attention. It is broken in crises and made over by crises.

The control of life is a matter of personal attention.

Attention is both inhibited and freed by habit.

Attention is aroused by crises.

Animals have no conception of danger except as they are built up by experience to avoid it.

A trained tiger has a terrible history, for he has been trained to inhibit by punishment.

Ornaments were worn first, then clothing, that is, you get something on that will attract attention to yourself.
It is dangerous suddenly to break habits without first having developed a technique of inner control.
The "gaming instinct" means that everything takes on a plan of personal pursuit.
Obtaining personal control is the object of actions that have a purpose.

Of Social Control. While social control and personal control are partially inseparable, the former reaches into the field of social justice, morality, and religion. It includes a responsibility for social well-being and it may reach beyond mundane forces. It has many practical facets; in fact, social control among primitives arose out of personal and group needs.

Among primitives one may not marry inside certain limits (the clan), and one must marry inside certain larger limits (the race).
In primitive times a man was forced to settle in his wife's home; a woman was not allowed to follow a man and settle in his home.
Mind is the only instrument necessary to control the world.
The problem of society is how to get the individual to assume responsibility for the welfare of others as well as for his own.
If all persons were Jane Addamses, then there would be no need for government's heavy hand in social control.
"Justice" is often a case of clever lawyers (you never can tell what will be sprung in a given legal case).
Nobody gets up a code of morals; codes grow out of the stresses of group life; morality is a growth; morality grows out of social activities.
Cannibalism was rooted out because groups could not afford to lose their members.
Religion among primitive people was an attempt at control by making alliances with superhuman spirits, who must exist because things happen which no man does; in seeking causes primitive man was forced to believe in other spirits.

In conclusion, a reference may be made to Thomas' subtle sense of humor which cropped out in class lectures most unexpectedly. It was friendly, never sarcastic. It was pointed, but never punishing. It was polite, but its meaning was clear, e.g., "I courteously assume that most of you know all about the theory of evolution, but I presume that most of you do not," or "I don't let anyone sleep in this class except visitors." He often put over his point by startling and sweeping contrasts in ideas: "I'll think of the answer to your question in a moment, but in the meanwhile I don't know anything either."

PEOPLES AND CULTURE

WHAT'S RIGHT WITH RACE RELATIONS. By Harriet Harmon Dexter. New York: Harper and Brothers, 1958, pp. 248.

This encouraging book reports on the progress that has been made in overcoming racial discrimination in the United States. The author, a free-lance writer and professor of English at Northland College in Wisconsin, has had many years of experience in intercultural, interracial, and community relations.

Professor Dexter bases her study on a firsthand study of present conditions in schools and colleges, labor, housing, churches, transportation, the courts, athletics and recreation, and the armed forces. Her book contains a wealth of information obtained from interviews, case studies, and historical sources. Many data are included on such ethnic groups as Negroes, American Indians, Jews, Japanese, Chinese, and Mexicans.

Mrs. Dexter makes the point that "things don't just happen." Whether dramatic or unobtrusive, each action indicates the willingness of some individual or group to take the leadership or initiative. At times the author tends to be carried away by her enthusiasm for ethical and moral considerations. However, this does not detract from the fact that this readable book, which is designed for the general public, is a valuable addition to the literature available on ethnic relations in the United States.

I. ROGER YOSHINO
University of Arizona

POWER AND PROPERTY IN INCA PERU. By Sally Falk Moore. New York: Columbia University Press, 1958, pp. xii+190.

This study of the political, social, and economic structure of the Inca state reviews and interprets anew the forms of tenure of land, the tax system, the nature of the substantive law, the political system and its judicial functions, and, finally, there is a brief appraisal of theory and practice in Inca law. Throughout the book there is an effort to avoid errors in generalization which have been made by some former writers about the Incas. As features in the Inca culture pattern, the decimal structure from the Inca downward, the hierarchical power system with its privileges and obligations at different levels, the taxing and judicial functions characteristic within the entire Inca empire—all seem to gain in objectivity and clarity as elements in Inca life. J.E.N.

WEST OF THE HINDUS. By William O. Douglas. New York: Doubleday & Company, 1958, pp. xiii+513.

From the facile pen of Associate Justice Douglas has come another travel book, full of detailed and close observation, chiefly of the common people of interesting Asian countries, namely, Pakistan, Afghanistan, Iraq, Iran, and Turkey. The journey that is described took place in the summer of 1957 and was made chiefly by station wagon. Although there were rough roads, broken springs, great clouds of dust, unbearable heat, difficulties with food and water, the author maintained a fine equipoise.

The author found that the common people in each country visited showed a warmth of feeling, a "longing for equality," and a "great pride in race and culture." He found them needing friends without condescension. The Asian likes foreigners "who will eat his bread and rice," who will "sleep on his rice mats," who will "drink his tea and share his worries," and who "will not lord it over him."

The Associate Justice ended his journey with the belief that Europe, Asia, and Africa are becoming one, and that a great gulf is isolating America. He found evidence "of the growing gulf between America and the East, the gulf that threatens to leave us in lonely isolation."

E.S.B.

DESEGREGATION AND THE SOUTHERN STATES 1957. Legal Action and Voluntary Group Action. By Jessie P. Guzman and Woodrow W. Hall. Tuskegee Institute, Alabama: The Department of Records and Research, 1958, pp. 59.

This important and timely document contains "representative items for persons interested in the main developments of Negro-white relations in the areas covered." The data relate chiefly to the year 1957 and indicate how the nonsegregation principle was furthered by the judicial, legislative, and executive branches of the Federal government. The citations give examples of both noncompliance and compliance by the three branches of state governments in the South.

These materials are accompanied by citations of voluntary group action of Southern groups favoring integration and also of Southern groups opposing integration. A few cases of mob action are cited. The ensemble seems to show considerable social movement toward nonsegregation in the areas covered, namely, of education, transportation, recreation, voting, and employment. A.R.R.

DURBAN, A STUDY IN RACIAL ECOLOGY. By Leo Kuper, H. Watts, and R. Davies. Introduction by Alan Paton. New York: Columbia University Press, 1958, pp. 254.

This is a unique study dealing with Durban, a city of half a million, the third largest city of South Africa, and composed about equally of "Europeans," "Indians," "Africans." The city is committed to a policy of racial segregation which calls for plans of racial zoning, with reference not only to residences but also to places of business and in a degree to places of work.

The survey reveals that "the distribution of income, religious, and language groups within each race shows a pattern related to the climate and topography of the city." Natural segregation which is voluntary is to be supplanted by planned and compulsory segregation. The natural type "is now to be replaced by a planned resegregation," which is to "secure maximum racial 'purity.' " It is pointed out that "in the proposed rewriting of the ecology of Durban" the Europeans will be affected least and the Indians most, and hence the latter are objecting strenuously. It is proposed to incorporate additional areas into the city and resettle the Indians and Africans there and to arrange the transportation system so that these groups will not travel through areas occupied by Europeans. It is assumed that absence of racial contact will make for peace. However, the authors hold to a view common in many parts of the world that racial contacts can create better human relations than compulsory segregation. E.S.B.

THE SOUTHERN HERITAGE. By James McBride Dabbs. New York: Alfred A. Knopf, Inc., 1958, pp. 270.

This remarkable book was written by a South Carolina businessman and writer. It is a classic statement of the enlightened Southern view of race relations in the long perspective of history. Mr. Dabbs is a Southerner to the core. He is indeed proud of the South's great heritage, yet he has searched his mind objectively in a realistic and honest attempt to find the truth regarding the crisis between the races. The volume presents an abundance of data based on history and the sociological contributions of Howard W. Odum and his colleagues at the University of North Carolina.

In an excellent analysis the author very skillfully brings the reader to the realization of the great burden of guilt which has fixed itself upon the South because of the years of injustice forced upon the Negro through the practice of exploitation and discrimination. He eloquently and successfully presents a well-rounded picture of the South, including the harmonious antebellum plantation life, the devastating Civil War, the heartbreaking days of recovery, the establishment of Jim Crowism, the South's determination to segregate and defranchise the Negro and put him back in his place as a worker, and the new problems growing out of recent development symbolized by the Negro entering industry and his militant demand for integration.

Mr. Dabbs reminds us that segregation is extremely expensive and a great handicap to Southern industrialization, consequently a retarding influence to the progress of the South. Although the South has a divided heart, there is a new day ahead, for behind the problems that face the South are unimaginable opportunities waiting to test our gallantry and courage. This is a challenge which the South will accept. Many old attitudes and long-cherished traditions are vanishing and are destined eventually to give way to the democratic and the Christian traditions which are gradually but surely working toward the elimination of racial discrimination and a new day for the South.

FLOYD A. POLLOCK
Stephen F. Austin State College

A BLACK CIVILIZATION. A Story of an Australian Tribe. Revised edition. By W. Lloyd Warner. New York: Harper and Brothers, 1958, pp. xx+618.

In this revision of a book first published in 1937 and based on three years research, 1926-29, among the Murngin people of North Australia, the author has made a number of revisions. These are based on the literature which appeared in the years that followed the publication of the first edition and that deal with more or less controversial issues. The points under fresh consideration involve such themes as asymmetrical marriage, methods of regulating marriage and descent, the relation of "the nuclear families of orientation and procreation to the kinship system," the unilateral local organization, and the relation of the clans to the kinship system.

The book gives much attention to the nature and roles of magic, the totemic system, and to the extent, uses, and meanings of symbols. It may be noted in this work of almost countless facts that the social institutions of the Murngin people have been little influenced by the neighboring Malay race and culture, although some changes in the Murngin's material culture were noted. A.R.R.

CULTURAL ANTHROPOLOGY. THE SCIENCE OF CUSTOM. By Felix M. Keesing. New York: Rinehart & Company, Inc., 1958, pp. xxvii+477.

A feature of this text is its unique manner of presenting in a developmental sequence eighty-four problem-questions, each of which is analyzed and discussed at length, in place of the usual chapter subheadings. The problems are grouped under a wide range of topics emphasizing the nature of cultural anthropology, basic concepts of culture and people, the growth of culture from its earliest phases to the present machine age, the geographic distribution of culture, the interrelations of culture, society and personality, and the universal patterning of culture. Material culture is surveyed in terms of food customs, clothing, housing, transportation, tools, weapons and machines, ceramics, textiles, and metallurgy. Institutional aspects of culture are considered as related to economic, social, political, and religious organization. Language is examined as a culture system. Several of the problems deal with social control and deviant behavior. Eight of the problems discuss cultural change.

Many of these problems are on the borderline between anthropology and sociology, and justly so, owing to their mutual concern with cultural processes. The work is more essentially anthropological in its comparative method, in its tracing of culture from its earliest known stages, and in the nature of its examples and illustrations of cultural forms. The glossary of terms and the bibliography should prove of value for students. J.E.N.

MOONLIGHT AT MIDDAY. By Sally Carrighar. New York: Alfred A. Knopf, 1958, pp. xix+392.

The author, a naturalist, went to Alaska to study wild life for a couple of years but remained over nine years, and in addition studied and wrote about the Eskimo. Nearly two thirds of the book describes and interprets the lives of these "fine, complete people," as well as an anthropologist or sociologist might do. A great deal of the material comes from the Eskimo village of Unalakleet, near Nome, although the data presented afford the reader a fair sampling of the 15,000 Eskimos of Arctic Alaska.

The Alaskan Eskimos are seen as essentially a race adrift between the traditional Eskimo culture and the invading "Western" culture. "They are adrift and, through no fault of their own, almost helpless."

In their culture "all relationships have been based on cooperation," but now "in place of trust, they must develop wariness." They find it difficult to acquire the ability that some white Americans have of feeling "good will towards others while attempting to get ahead of them."

Some missionaries with a grounding in sociology and psychology have been of great help to the Eskimos in making their difficult adjustments to the coming of white Americans and "to a world that is less pure, less responsible, than their own has been." Other missionaries have brought "threats of hell, demands for money, and scoldings for giving in to temptations the white men have brought."

Special attention is given to teachers and the educational problems; to the rigors of the climate in the northern half of Alaska; to the cities like Fairbanks, Anchorage, Nome; to agriculture, mining, fishing; to the mistakes of the Bureau of Indian Affairs in dealing with the Eskimos; to the "bush" fliers; to the idealism, the quiet mind, and the spirit of sharing of the Eskimos. The book gives a dramatic account of a people accustomed to hardship, trying to hold off "civilized pressures."

E.S.B.

WORLD POPULATION PRESSURES. By Harold L. Geissert. Washington, D.C.: The George Washington University, 1958, pp. 46.

POPULATION PRESSURES IN AFRICA SOUTH OF THE SAHARA. By Richard W. Stephens. Washington, D.C.: The George Washington University, 1958, pp. 48.

The document on *World Population Pressures* gives figures on the population growth of the world by countries and by regions, and the birth and death rates by underdeveloped and developed countries, likewise the age composition and the degree of urbanization, country by country. It is pointed out that the population of Latin America "is growing more rapidly than any other major region of the world." Another of the important observations made by Professor Geissert is that the effectiveness of the technical aid programs of the United States "is hampered by our official inability to help these countries limit their population," and that some of the underdeveloped countries are more advanced in the willingness of "the public to accept the idea of birth control" than are the Western nations.

The brochure by Professor Stephens, which centers attention on population problems in Africa south of the Sahara, notes that stable economic systems are hindered from developing because "Africans by the tens of thousands are leaving their native villages and families for months and sometimes years at a time to work in the mines or the plantations, or wherever the Europeans will hire them." The vast majority are living under primitive conditions, "and each year there are more people." An underlying question is this, How can a nation become great if it allows no stable labor force to develop and no "stable wage-earning middle class"? E.S.B.

YEAR BOOK AND GUIDE TO SOUTHERN AFRICA, 1959. Edited by A. Gordon-Brown. London: Robert Hale, Ltd., 1959, pp. xlix+712+154 (supplement), 24 double-page maps in color, 26 photographs, one folding road map.

YEAR BOOK AND GUIDE TO EAST AFRICA, 1959. Edited by A. Gordon-Brown. London: Robert Hale, Ltd., 1959, pp. xxxiv+341+112 (supplement), 8 maps, 12 photographs, 2 folding maps.

These yearbooks provide a wealth of facts relating to the customs, history, religion, education, populations, communications of the countries of southern and eastern Africa, such as the Union of South Africa, the Rhodesias, Nyasaland, Uganda, Tanganyika, Kenya.

INTRODUCTION TO CULTURAL ANTHROPOLOGY. By Mischa Titiev. New York: Henry Holt and Company, 1959, pp. xvi+464.

This text begins with the definition of man as an animal with culture, a consideration of man's forerunners, the emergence of Homo sapiens, and the biological foundations of culture. This orientation of culture in general is followed by a survey of cultural development from its earliest phases, through the Old Stone Age, New Stone Age, and the so-called metal phases. The author demonstrates well the value of knowledge concerning primitive societies and their cultures so that the social and cultural influences shaping our own culture may be understood functionally.

From the institutional standpoint, the author gives some attention to kinship and nonkinship aspects of social organization, marriage, religion and magic, language, and the verbal arts. Music, the dance, and the playing of games are considered as nonverbal cultural elements. Finally, three cultures are compared in certain particulars—those of Tikopia, the Hopi Indians, and the United States. Though not so comprehensive in range as several other textbooks now current in this field, the approach taken and the manner of discussion are of interest. J.E.N.

RICE ROOTS. An American in Asia. By Arthur Goodfriend. New York: Simon and Schuster, 1958, pp. 209.

The author, who with his wife and children lived for a time "as a plain American trying to understand people at the rice roots" in Indonesia, gives a vivid and enlightening interpretation of what the common people of that new republic are thinking about with reference to capitalism, imperialism, communism, Americanism. He went to live at the "rice roots" level because he had become convinced that American dollars "were not reaching the people" in Asia, and that trying to reshape Asia "in America's image" was wasted effort. To deal with "the big wheels and count on them to reach the masses" is a misconception.

Living at the "rice roots" in Indonesia, the author found that many of the peasants think of America in terms of machinery, guns, and Marilyn Monroe. Judging from certain movies, they think of Americans as having a "lust for kissing and killing." The United States is thought of in terms of "big business, money, capitalism," that "the inner philosophy of the United States is money," and that the government is "subservient to political bosses and big corporations." Some ask, "What is free enterprise but the right of one man to overpower another?" The free enterprise system is conceived of as "the greatest imperialist of all times." Moreover, these misconceptions of America are played up and magnified throughout Indonesia by Communist agitators.

Indonesia's cooperatives, which have "risen to over ten thousand," have stimulated the members to become self-reliant, as indicated by the following firsthand report. In a cooperative "each of us keeps what he has and manages his own land or shop. But each puts a little into a common fund. We use the fund to buy seed cheaply at harvest time. We store our rice, selling it at a higher price in planting time. We put the profits back into the fund. Little by little, through saving and wise investment, we raise our own capital. Then we make this capital work for us, like a buffalo or a mule."

The author found the impoverished Indonesians to be "just as proud; as self-respecting, as chary about charity" as the people, for example, of New Hampshire (the author's home state). It is pointed out that Asians want understanding and partnership "on a basis of utter equality." It is urged that no American be sent abroad in any capacity "without thorough instruction in Asian culture and character." It is even suggested that the American moving picture industry make one picture in ten that is "truly reflective of the real America." E.S.B.

SOCIAL PROBLEMS AND WELFARE

FAMILY ALLOWANCES. By James C. Vadakin. Miami, Florida: University of Miami Press, 1958, pp. xiii+185.

Although all the important industrialized nations of the world have adopted family allowances for children, the United States has not yet given full-scale consideration and study to such a measure. The present book, which is Number 3 in the University of Miami Publications in Economics, offers an analysis of family allowances which is one of the most recent significant developments in the field of social security and child welfare.

This book covers the historical development of family allowances; the administration of the Canadian program; the implications of these measures in the fields of child welfare, demography, and economics; and the significance of family allowances for the United States. Also of interest is the discussion of current legislation and the reproduction of the resolution introduced in the Senate by Senator Richard L. Neuberger.

Sociologists concerned with the impact of an industrialized society upon family life will find this a compact analysis of the subject. And although the author presents the favorable and unfavorable views of family allowances, his own attitude, which appears to be shaped by the meliorist tradition in American sociology, seems to be that subsidies for our children are at least as important as subsidies to farmers, industrialists, corporations—and baseball teams. NATHAN HURVITZ

TRAINING FOR SOCIAL WORK. Third International Survey. New York: Department of Economic and Social Affairs, United Nations, 1958, pp. viii+349.

This meaty document deals first with training for social work with individuals, with groups, and with communities, and then with content materials concerning man and society. The importance of field work is emphasized, and social work theory and practice are discussed. Curriculum planning and content of courses are given attention. Proposals are made for "progressively raising the level of training for social work" on both the national and the international levels. One of the interesting sources of data for this document was a series of seminars (held in Montevideo, Uruguay; Lahore, Pakistan; and Athens, Greece) as a means of obtaining a wide coverage of social work activities.

NEW HORIZONS IN CRIMINOLOGY. Third Edition. By Harry Elmer Barnes and Negley K. Teeters. Englewood Cliffs, New Jersey: Prentice-Hall, Inc., 1959, pp. xxxvii+654.

This edition of a popular textbook in criminology and penology is comprehensive in scope, the content has been brought up to date, and the material has been presented in a concise and interesting manner. It is an informative source book, with extensive summaries of both theories and research findings. It is really two books in one, dealing respectively with Crime and the Criminal and Penal and Correctional Procedures.

After a provocative discussion of the crime situation in America, the authors present an analysis of the main theories and factors in causation of criminal behavior, which is one of the most valuable sections of the book. The theories and factors are grouped under the constitutional school of theorists, the geographic and economic factors in crime causation, modern sociological theories, minority group tensions, home and community influences, and emotional disturbances. An attempt is made to synthesize the various theories and research findings, using the "multiple-causation" approach. However, no comprehensive theoretical frame of reference is presented.

Approximately two thirds of the book is devoted to correctional programs, including a survey of criminal justice by the police system and the courts, the penal and correctional procedures, particularly reforms in criminal law and in penal institutions, and the rehabilitative process within the framework of imprisonment and the resocialization of the offender in the community. Only one chapter is devoted to the prevention of crime, which would seem to be a topic of major importance. A greater emphasis is placed on the new developments in prison and correctional programs, also in probation and parole philosophy. M.H.N.

RECRUITMENT TO SKILLED TRADES. By Gertrude Williams. New York: The Humanities Press, Inc., 1957, pp. vii+216.

Written by an English woman, the book begins with the Statute of 1582, which established a national system of apprenticeship, reviews the activities of the Poor Law authorities in the early 1800's with reference to farmed-out children to cotton mills, and takes up the Employment and Training Act of 1948. The procedure of integrating work with the employers' "day release" created some dissatisfaction. As a result, the following industries were studied in order to obtain the needed information: printing, building, motor vehicle, iron and steel, iron foundries, mechanical and electrical engineering, and shipbuilding.

Although the apprenticeship system in these various industries has many common features, the author deemed it wise to discuss each industry separately because of technical and historical variations. As a result of the superiority in technical education shown by other countries at the national exhibitions in the nineteenth century, concern in England resulted in the establishment in 1944 of junior technical schools. So small a proportion of the boys, however, have had a previous grammar school education that the results have not proved satisfactory.

The present system of recruiting and training workers for skilled industries, says the author, is essentially the same as that existing 800 years ago. New methods must be learned, and several other countries—notably the United States, France, Germany, and Holland—have given illustrations. In America men can become apprentices up to the age of 35 instead of 16 as is usual in Great Britain. In France a 3-year craft training course is provided. Germany requires apprentices to serve from 3 to 3½ years. If found unsatisfactory, they are reduced to unskilled labor. In Holland, the boys spend the last 2 years of their compulsory 8-year school training at a junior technical school. Then they are apprenticed at full-time employment for 2 or 3 years.

Consideration of these various methods of education enables the British Government to select the methods most suitable for local use and to gradually perfect its system of recruitment to the skilled trades.

G.B.M.

THE GANG: A STUDY IN ADOLESCENT BEHAVIOR. By Herbert A. Bloch and Arthur Niederhoffer. New York: Philosophical Library, 1958, pp. xviii+231.

Owing to prevalent misconceptions of the gang and the adolescent group, some general considerations are presented first to define basic terms and social situations which are essential in this study. Insight concerning the practices of contemporary juvenile groups and gangs is provided through cross-cultural comparison with comparable behavior among primitive peoples. Thus puberty rites of primitives are compared with contemporary "rites" of adolescence. The ganging process becomes understandable as a symbol of the urge to manhood. The relation of this process to delinquency is explained in terms of its psychological aspects and its philosophy of rationalization. The influence of the automobile, the significance of leadership and power, and other common factors in gang behavior objectify the study. J.E.N.

PERMANENT PEACE. A Check and Balance Plan. By Tom Slick. New York: Prentice-Hall, Inc., 1958, pp. x+181.

The author, described as a Texas businessman with considerable civic, government, and research experience, has developed a plan for permanent peace that is based in part on the Clark and Sohn book on *World Peace Through World Law.* It is based on the principle of gradualism, on "strictly limiting that portion of national authority turned over to international control to the minimum necessary for an effective program to function," and on a system of checks and balances between the power of nations and international authority, involving the establishment of an international police force, an international reserve force, and having these balanced on a fifty-fifty basis by national forces. After setting up the machinery for gradual disarmament, the author would have people unite for its adoption and for procedures to remove the causes of war.

An extensive emphasis on social machinery for preventing war seems to be given precedence over educational procedures for getting people to communicate with one another, to understand one another, and to work together by the use of discussion methods. Hence, two questions may be raised: Should the educational methods precede the legal and military ones? Or should they be developed simultaneously with the legal and military proposals? E.S.B.

WORK IN THE LIVES OF MARRIED WOMEN. By National Manpower Council. New York: Columbia University Press, 1958, pp. ix+220.

This volume presents the proceedings of a conference on womanpower sponsored by the National Manpower Council, which has as its purposes to study significant manpower problems and to contribute to the more effective development and utilization of the nation's human resources. Since one third of all the women in the United States work outside the home, since half of the women who work are over 40 years of age, since 3 out of every 5 of the 22 million women in the labor force are married, and since about 2.5 million women whose children are under six are in the labor force—work plays a most significant role in the lives of married women in the United States.

Four major themes were considered by the participants in the conference: "Education, Training, and Guidance of Women for Re-entry into the Labor Force," "The Utilization of Womanpower," "Income Earned by Married Women," and "Working Mothers and the Development of

Children." The conference findings are presented by Dr. Henry David, Executive Director of the National Manpower Council, in the final chapter of this book. These are so general, diluted, and attuned to prevailing attitudes and philosophies that one wonders why a conference was needed to give them further authority.

Although this book has significance for sociologists concerned with working women as a social problem, it does not have a meaningful sociological orientation. Thus, there is no serious evaluation of the work of married women in relation to the family as a social institution, the material presented is not related to the growing body of theory and research regarding marital roles, and there is no analysis of the place of women's work in relation to social structure. NATHAN HURVITZ

HIGH SCHOOL SOCIOLOGY. **A Study in Social and Human Relations. By William E. Cole and Charles S. Montgomery. Boston: Allyn Bacon, 1959, pp. viii+406.**

Although this book is a successor to *School Sociology* (1936), it is new in materials, format, illustrations, and supplementary aids. One part deals with "historical, cultural, and biological backgrounds of society." A second part follows on "our social roles and our social worlds." The third part describes important "major social problems facing our society." Many teaching aids are given and a glossary of nearly a hundred terms is given. A general bibliography is added. This text merits widespread use in high schools throughout the United States.

DATING, MATING, AND MARRIAGE. **By Jessie Bernard, Helen E. Buckanan, and William M. Smith, Jr. Cleveland, Ohio: Howard Allen, Inc., 1958, pp. xi+410.**

A new approach to the study of dating, mating, and marriage is presented in that the authors make exclusive use of personal documents. Similar documents have been used by other writers in the field, but none have assembled such a wide variety of personal case data as is found in the present treatise. The personal documents that are used reveal the participant's experiences and views of the dating, courting, and marriage procedures.

After introductory chapters dealing with the present-day challenges that the family must meet, and the community background of dating, a series of narratives of dating experiences, including the dating by service men abroad, are presented. This is followed by an analysis, through case records and personal documents, of family relations at the launching stage, student marriages, the problems of money matters faced by newly married couples, how certain individuals and couples dealt with differences in backgrounds and personalities, the respective roles played by men and women in modern society, and how individuals and families have met crisis situations.

Personal documents are interesting to read, for they reveal the inner reactions of persons to various types of situations. The authors did a good job of selecting these personal documents. The book can be used as a basic text in courses dealing with marriage and the family, and it is an excellent supplementary source book. The bibliography contains selected sources, including chapter references to standard treatises. Also, the cases and personal documents given in the book are keyed to nineteen textbooks on courtship, marriage, and the family. M.H.N.

VOCATION DE LA SOCIOLOGIE RELIGIEUSE—SOCIOLOGIE DES VOCATIONS. Edited by E. Collard and Others. Tournai, Belgium: Establissements Casterman, 1958, pp. 241.

PAROISSES URBAINES, PAROISSES RURALES. Edited by F. Boulard and Others. Tournai, Belgium: Establissements Casterman, 1958, pp. 222.

These two volumes represent the Fifth International Conference for the Sociology of Religion, held in Belgium in 1956. Naturally, the volumes can hardly fail to arouse some interest, as they treat a relatively neglected area of sociology. However, their value is reduced somewhat by the scope of the conference, which was largely European, with particular stress on the Low Countries, and almost exclusively Roman Catholic. As with most works of multiple authors, the quality of the papers varies considerably.

The volume on vocations would appear to be the more general of the two, as there is an introduction to the sociology of religion with notes on a variety of theorists, ranging from Freud to Durkheim. Of the research studies reported, Pickering's investigation with an English sample appears to be the most significant. The second part of the volume treats the clergy as a profession, particularly the factors influencing vocational choice in this area. Probably most interesting to the American reader is the research of Harte on the priesthood of the United States.

The volume on parishes is divided into two parts: the urban and the rural. In the various papers there are significant vignettes of life from Brussels to Chicago, from Rome to Buenos Aires. There is some noteworthy material on parish planning, including its ecological aspects. Boulard's study of optimum population within the parish is outstanding as is Laloux's study of a Belgian rural parish. Excellent, too, is Fichter's paper on social groups.

In evaluating the two works, which represent some thirty contributors, it is hardly original to suggest that there might have been more attention to methodology and documentation, since this is the favorite criticism of the American as he reviews foreign sociology. Despite its empirical limitations, the present volume is welcome in the fairly infant sociology of religion. Certainly some of the papers with their maps, tables, and references will be most useful to researchers in this field.

ROBERT C. WILLIAMSON
Los Angeles City College

MARRIAGE AND FAMILY RELATIONS: AN INTERDISCIPLINARY APPROACH. By Lawrence S. Bee. New York: Harper and Brothers, 1959, pp. xviii+500.

The main parts of the book deal with what individuals bring to marriage, including both cross-sectional and developmental aspects of personality; dating, courting, and engagement as preparatory steps toward marriage; growing together in marriage, especially the problems of family interaction and adjustment; patterns of faulty and productive marriages, illustrated by the sociopsychological portraits of three contrasting families; and the disorganization and reconstruction of marriage. The impacts of social change on courtship, marriage, and family living in America are discussed by way of introduction. The distinctive feature of the study is the description of the personality patterns that different people bring to courtship and marriage, including basic personality traits, the psychosexual development of personality, sex problems, the degree of emotional maturity, and the element of love. The influence of personality traits on courtship and marriage is stressed through the book and is illustrated by case material, including several extended case studies.

Even though the material is drawn from such fields as sociology, psychology, psychiatry, anthropology, physiology, social work, home economics, education, and literature, it can hardly be regarded as an integrated interdisciplinary approach. However, the wide range of material that is included enriches the content. Considerable attention is given to the components of basic personality, the psychosexual development of personality and sex problems, also certain emotional factors, which are regarded as crucial to marriage. The discussion of the problem of divorce is limited to one short chapter, and only a few pages are devoted to the "real causes" of divorce.

That the American family is undergoing changes has long been recognized. The trend from "institutionalism" to "personalism" is evident. New problems of the family have arisen in the wake of these changes. However, certain movements designed to help the modern family have emerged. The author has described briefly the family life movement in the schools and in religious organizations, family-centered medical practice, the family court, marriage counseling, and family service agencies. M.H.N.

PRIMER OF FREE GOVERNMENT. By William B. Chalfant. New York: Philosophical Library, 1959, pp. 160.

The basic contention in this essay is that free government, or what Americans understand as democracy, has never yet been constituted and the present troubles of the free world are attributable to this fact. To launch his argument, the author defines liberty, freedom, and equalitarianism, and states his conception of the ethics of free government. It is held that free government requires three groups of doctrines which give meaning to justice, to organization, and to practice, but the woes of free government as now imperfectly constituted spring from the lack of appreciation of the principles of free social life.

The signs of social dissatisfaction with "free government," or democracy as Americans think of it, are socialism and communism, which pointedly attack capitalism, free enterprise, and public government. The author regards it as tragic that the American dynamic will to the good life is hopelessly fettered by the bondage of social incompetency. The need for the organization of fully qualified free government must be recognized if the social, economic, and political problems of democracy are to be solved. J.E.N.

SOCIAL THEORY AND RESEARCH

LABOR AND ECONOMIC DEVELOPMENT. Edited by Walter Galenson. New York: John Wiley & Sons, Inc., 1959, pp. xiii+304.

Beginning with an exploratory introduction by the editor, this book offers five essays dealing with the growth and development of labor movements in five countries—India, Japan, Egypt, French West Africa, and the British West Indies. The essays are mainly reports of research studies financed by the Inter-University Study of Labor Problems in Economic Development. They have been undertaken and written by experts in the field, namely, Charles A. Myers, Robert A. Scalapino, Frederick H. Harbison, Elliot Berg, and William H. Knowles.

Interestingly conceived, the essays, though centered about the several different countries, manage to maintain a kind of central unity in that they describe the effects of labor problems on economic patterns that differ markedly from the British and American systems. Each of the countries under discussion has been more or less confronted with lack of experience in collective action, with problems of unemployment, poverty, much illiteracy, superstitions, and racial differences, and with unique cultural folkways and mores.

Egypt, asserting its proprietorship and control over labor problems, "seems to be fairly well supplied with native entrepreneurs and with educational facilities of turning out qualified engineers." Both in India and in Egypt, "great pressure exists to get rid of foreign management personnel." In Japan, the industrial revolution is nearly a century old, but its evolution has been uneven due in part to a high selection of certain Western techniques and experience. The Japanese state with its great power "was able more successfully than in the past to borrow from and interrelate with the values of a familial system that placed its emphases upon loyalty, obedience, and status-derived obligations." French West Africa, marked by colonialism, slave trade, tribal wars, diseases, and a dominant village system, offers still another picture of labor economics.

The essays are enlightening on almost every phase of the entire scene of economic growth, and they explore the many factors that influence industrial relations in their mode of development in diverse cultural milieus with different political settings. M.J.V.

INDIVIDUAL BEHAVIOR AND GROUP ACHIEVEMENT. By Ralph M. Stogdill. New York: Oxford University Press, 1959, pp. vi+352.

The author attempts to combine theory with experimental evidence. The main objective is to develop a theory of social achievement. In doing so, a vast amount of theoretical literature and research reports was canvassed. A total of 794 references are cited. The underlying assumption is that "a social group can be described in terms of performances, interactions, and expectations of the members." In analyzing the structure of organizational achievement, the member "inputs" (behavioral performances, interactions, and expectations) are described, followed by an analysis of mediating variables, including both formal and role structures. The group outputs or achievements consist of productivity, morale, and integration. Even though performances, interactions, and expectations are exhibited by varying degrees of independence, there is a wholeness and continuity of behavior. The achievements of the group represent a totality of the outcomes it experiences as the result of the interrelationships of the types of outputs. Thus, a group is an input-output system. The input variables in combination account for the development of the structure of the group and for the initiation and maintenance of group operations.

This attempt to develop a theory based upon research findings is a large undertaking. The theoretical frame of reference is mainly social psychological. Sociological findings are used to explain how member roles emerge in social groups. The study is psychological in that it seeks to explain how the behavior of individuals exerts effects upon the group.

M.H.N.

PARENTAL AUTHORITY: THE COMMUNITY AND THE LAW. By Julius Cohen, Reginald A. H. Robson, and Alan Bates. New Brunswick, New Jersey: Rutgers University Press, 1958, pp. xii+301.

A joint team from the fields of law and sociology, using parental authority as a test area, have developed a unique and reliable instrument that can be used in future studies to measure the community's moral sense in relation to the law. Among the issues investigated are the parental authority to control the child's property or earnings, to determine whether or not the child may have a college education, to determine the child's religious affiliation, his career, to refuse consent to his marriage, etc. Some questions deal with the willingness to grant autonomy to the child, and others concern familial versus governmental financial support of family members.

In about two thirds of the issues investigated the community viewpoint disagrees with that of the law. The investigators were therefore led to consider other related questions—for example, whether the community would grant more freedom from parental control than the law now permits. It was also found essential to learn whether people differ in their views because of variations in social backgrounds, whether urban and rural views may differ, whether Protestant views differ from those of Catholics, and whether such factors as sex, age, schooling, income, and kind of job make for difference in people's views toward the law. The practical value of research of this kind becomes obvious at once, and the authors are to be commended for their insight and initiative.

J.E.N.

SOZIOLOGIE. Vol. II: Die Vollzahl der Zeiten. By Eugen-Rosenstock-Huessy. Stuttgart, Germany: W. Kohlhammer, 1958, pp. 774.

The author (whose first volume has already been reviewed in this Journal) aims to give answers, desired by the youth of Germany as well as elsewhere, with respect to the crises and armed conflicts which the world has undergone. The first part, entitled "Die Wiederkehr der Erlebnisse" (the return of the experiences and events from Augustinus to the present), traces our present-day mores—such as the calendar, structure and ethics of the family, architecture—back to the old days, and compares tensions of bygone days with present ones. The second part, entitled "Der Gang der Erlebnisse" (the course of events), deals with new events of mankind, the Uralphabet of political forms: tribe, nation, people, the public, and the genius.

The second volume has an encyclopedic nature and demonstrates the author's universal thinking, knowledge, and feeling. If one accepts a limited definition of "sociology," the title is correct. Actually, however, the book's thinking goes far beyond sociology and presents a statement embracing thoughts of ancient and modern times, incorporating the knowledge, which in Germany was taught in *humanistiechen Schulen* (high schools with the majors in Latin and Greek) and which gave Germany the name of Das Land der Dichter und Denker (the country of the poets and philosophers). The absence of a bibliography and occasional footnotes may be noted.

HANS A. ILLING

SOCIOLOGY, A SYNOPSIS OF PRINCIPLES. Fourth Edition. By John F. Cuber. New York: Appleton-Century-Crofts, Inc., 1959, pp. xv+663.

The following changes in this new edition of Cuber's *Sociology* may be noted. New data and new treatment of data appear. The annotated bibliographies have been somewhat enlarged. A discussion of sociology as a profession has been added to the first chapter. The treatment of social stratification has been doubled. Deletions have been made in order to accommodate the new materials without unduly enlarging the size of the book. Although the term *principles* is an important part of the title of the book, it does not appear in the index. Sociology is defined as "a body of scientific knowledge about human relationships," but "principles of sociology" are not discussed, as such, and no classifications of them are given. A.R.R.

THE FAMILY AND POPULATION CONTROL. A Puerto Rican Experiment in Social Change. By Reuben Hill, J. Mayone Stycos, and Kurt W. Black. Chapel Hill, North Carolina: The University of North Carolina Press, 1959, pp. xiii+481.

Puerto Rico is one of the world's most densely populated areas and the population is still increasing. The declining death rate without comparable changes in the birth rate accounts for the steadily increasing population. The possibilities of fertility control have been the concern of government planners, population scientists, and civic-minded citizens. The study of family life and population control was designed to ascertain the prevailing conditions and to develop an integrated research program for understanding and controlling the fertility aspects of population growth. Practical research and population theory were combined to spell out the details for a public policy in fertility control. The basic data were obtained by a variety of research methods. The survey of the prevailing conditions included field experiments based on sampling methods.

After an introductory section in which the demographic setting, the development of the research project, and previous studies are described, the authors present detail data regarding family size preferences, fertility planning, and the incidence of birth control. This is followed by a description of the steps toward a model of family dynamics, experimental validations in field studies, and the implications of the findings for future programs in fertility control.

Explanations for the country's high birth rate, such as the desire for large families, religion, ignorance of contraceptive methods, or unavailability of materials, are shown to be inapplicable; yet the birth rate is declining very slowly and remains higher than in most countries. The focus of the study was the treatment of population control as a phenomenon of family planning and action. The key to the understanding and control of the fertility rate seems to lie in the decisions of husbands and wives and in the methods by which they solve their problem.

M.H.N.

READINGS IN SOCIAL PSYCHOLOGY. Third Edition. By Eleanor E. Maccoby, Theodore M. Newcomb, and Eugene L. Hartley. New York: Henry Holt and Company, 1958, pp. xi+674.

This new and third edition of the well-established *Readings in Social Psychology* emphasizes a number of changes that have left their impressions recently upon the field herein covered. Most important, perhaps, is the attention bestowed upon the added inclusions of empirical research materials relevant to the theoretical expositions. The organization of the readings has not been altered from the previous editions so far as the major headings are concerned, but, say the editors, "the arrangement of articles" is more "eclectic; less systematic," for the reason that "there is no single organizing concept nor theoretical point of view that would be satisfactory to all." The selections have been chosen with an eye on what they purport to represent. One of the latest meritorious selections is an article by Edgar H. Schein entitled "The Chinese Indoctrination Program for Prisoners of War: A Study of Attempted Brainwashing." Another welcome article pertains to the epidemiology of a new drug rehearsed in "Social Relations and Innovation in the Medical Profession." Still another good piece of reporting may be found in Yarrow, Campbell and Yarrow's "Interpersonal Dynamics in Racial Integration." An excellent presentation in the area of the perception of persons may be found in "Changes in Social Perception as a Function of the Personal Relevance of Behavior," by Jones and de Charms. Kurt Lewin is represented by an article written shortly before his death. It has been labeled "Group Decision and Social Change," and reports upon experiments on group decisions, these being defined as representing a process "of social management or self-management by groups." The new edition is sure to find a useful place upon social-psychological shelves, pointing as it does to the evolutionary development and growth of social psychology.

M.J.V.

THE ATOM AND THE ENERGY REVOLUTION. By Norman Lansdell. New York: Philosophical Library, Inc., 1958, pp. 200.

The object of this study was to present in brief a broad, balanced appreciation of the role of atomic energy in the world of today and tomorrow. The author first considers the present world position of energy resources and demands, and new sources of energy being developed. The rest of the report deals with significant elements in what may be called the atomic culture complex—the methods of releasing atomic energy, the development of natural materials for atomic energy, the applications made of atomic energy, the present status of development of atomic power by specific countries, and both international and national organizations for atomic energy development. Radiation risks and insurance proposals also are considered. The book as a whole is a valuable contribution to the study of technological change. J.E.N.

SOCIOLOGY TODAY: PROBLEMS AND PROSPECTS. By Robert K. Merton, Leonard Broom, and Leonard Cottrell, Jr., Editors. New York: Basic Books, Inc., 1959, pp. xxv+623.

An attempt is made in this new work to point out the trends, unsolved problems, and future prospects of contemporary sociology. The volume of articles was prepared under the auspices of the American Sociological Society. The first section deals with the general theory of sociology and with methodological problems. This is followed by eight articles that emphasize the problems of the sociology of institutions, two that deal with the group and the person, seven which emphasize demographic behavior and aspects of social structure, and five devoted to selected applications of sociology. Altogether, twenty-seven contributors participated in the preparation of the volume, each of them recognized as an authority on certain phases of sociological theory, methodology, and application.

It is difficult to appraise fully a work of this type. Obviously, there are differences in the quality of the various chapters, and one may find objections to certain details or to the general thesis of a particular article. Even though an effort was made to select sociologists with widely different training and emphasis, it is obvious that certain "schools of thought" predominate. Some of the contributors are vigorous exponents of the theories presented.

The wide range of subjects covered indicates the growing specialization in the field of sociology. "The book treats most but not all of the more than thirty sociological specialties." With the increasing number of areas of research and theory, it is necessary to periodically integrate at least some of the major theoretical and methodological developments. The present volume serves a useful purpose in that the main phases of concern are described and analyzed briefly and attention is called to developments in the specialized fields. The book obviously was prepared for sociologists, but others who wish to keep abreast with new developments in sociology will find this book stimulating and enlightening.

M.H.N.

MENTAL SUBNORMALITY. Biological, Psychological, and Cultural Factors. By Richard L. Masland, Seymour B. Sarason, and Thomas Gladwin. New York: Basic Books, Inc., 1958, pp. 442.

Calling mental subnormality the most significant handicap that affects more than 142,000 of the children born annually in the United States, the authors of this book have dedicated themselves to the task of presenting some of the salient results of research into its causal factors. The research was sponsored by the National Association for Retarded Children and was undertaken jointly by three professional men representing medicine, psychology, and anthropology. The organization of the report includes an introduction and two parts entitled "The Prevention of Mental Subnormality" and "Psychological and Cultural Problems in Mental Subnormality." Part I, written by Dr. Masland, deals with those "factors which produce anatomical or chemical abnormalities of the nervous system." One of these factors is that which deals with the chemical changes forming the basis of genetically produced human variations and abnormalities occurring in association with genetically determined disorders of the nervous system. This excursion into the genetics involved in mental subnormality will be of profound interest to eugenists, educators, and marriage counselors as well as social psychologists.

Part II, by psychologist Sarason and anthropologist Goodwin, gives the results of research into the psychological and cultural problems affecting subnormality. Concerned primarily with the "sources of retardation rooted in the individual and his environment," the reports reveal the involvements of society and the ways in which mental retardation is defined, perceived, and reacted to by society. In what ways do cultural factors sometimes interfere with normal development? This phase of the problem has not been systematically studied, and the authors conclude with a plea for the "establishment of a fully staffed research unit to investigate the problems of mental subnormality through the full range of its medical, biochemical, psychological, social, and other aspects. These well-presented findings are significantly important guide-posts for future research projects dealing with this crucial problem.

M.J.V.

TELEVISION AND THE CHILD. An Empirical Study of the Effects of Television on the Young. By Hilde T. Himmelweit, A. N. Oppenheim, and Pamela Vince. London and New York: Oxford University Press, 1958, pp. xxxv+522.

This study, financed by and published for The Nuffield Foundation (a British Ford-like foundation), is the most comprehensive and thoroughgoing research undertaking that has thus far been made to ascertain the effects of television broadcasting on children and young people. The series of studies reported in this book were carefully planned and carried out by a staff of research experts and by many cooperating individuals and organizations. The basic material was derived from a detailed examination of the reactions of over 4,000 children to television programs. Five English cities cooperated in the project. The observations of teachers and parents were used to supplement the basic data gotten from the children by means of diaries, questionnaires, and interviews. The project was originally planned in 1954, but the main survey was conducted in 1955 and in subsequent years. In one of the cities it was possible to examine children before and after television had come to the area to any appreciable extent. This made it possible to compare an experimental (television-viewing) group with a control (nonviewing) group.

The design of the study was carefully planned after a review of previous studies of the impact of television and other mass media of communication and entertainment. It was found that the types or areas of effects are chiefly the displacement effects (activities dropped after television came) and the effects of program content, including the influence that television may exert on children's knowledge and school performance, and on their outlook and values. Other areas of effects included the family life of these children and the emotional reactions of the children themselves.

The "Child Audience" is described in detail, including the first viewers, the amount of viewing, favorite programs, actual choice of programs, patterns of taste, and the attractions of viewing. The major portion of the research report deals with the reactions of children to conflict, crime, and violence on television; effects on children's values and outlook; effects on knowledge and school performance, including general knowledge, recall of information, cultural interests, and school work; effects on leisure and interests, including patterns of leisure, reading, radio and cinema, and other leisure activities; and certain special effects.

It is impossible to give a résumé of the findings in this review, for the "Summary of Main Findings" covers twenty-four pages, and three additional chapters are devoted to implications and suggestions that grew out of the study. The first to buy television sets are those with the strongest need for ready-made entertainment. After a family has a television receiving set, the children spend from 11 to 13 hours a week viewing programs, which is more time than that devoted to any other single leisure activity. However, the popular image of children "glued to television sets" did not fit the facts. Most children viewed reasonably selectively. The higher the child's intelligence, the less his viewing. For many children, except the television fans, television is something to fall back on when nothing more interesting is available. The social level of the home proved of little importance, except that the younger children of the working class view more than those of the middle-class families. Viewing rapidly becomes a habit. About three quarters of the children studied favored adult rather than children's programs. Their taste in television reflects their taste in other mass media. Where two channels (BBC and ITV) are available, the children were found to be more selective. Television appeals in different ways to different children, but its chief appeal lies in its easy availability and its subsequent value as a time filler.

The staple fare of the evening television broadcasts consists chiefly of Westerns, crime, and adventure. Drama plays an important part in broadcasts. Westerns tend to frighten the very young and the insecure; but detective, murder, and crime thrillers often frighten the older as well as the younger children. Viewers of these types of programs are not necessarily more aggressive or maladjusted than the nonviewers. While *Fabian of the Scotland Yard* was the first favorite, as many as two thirds of the children mentioned a variety of other favorites. The study seems to indicate that gains in knowledge come mainly from noninformation programs. Most viewers held their own with classmates of similar age, sex, social class, and intelligence in their school work. The findings suggest that viewing does not lead to poor concentration at school or reduce interest in school. Children who have access to television listen less to radio. At first, there usually is less reading; but television, especially the dramatization of books, was found to stimulate reading. Television keeps members of the family at home more, but it is doubtful whether it actually binds the family together more closely, except physically. Sometimes it causes conflicts of choices of programs. Children do not "absorb television like a sponge," and it does not dull their imagination. Some programs were found to stimulate children's interests. A considerable proportion of the findings indicate that the way children react to television depends upon their intelligence, age, sex, and general personality make-up. M.H.N.

THE FOUNDATIONS OF CAPITALISM. By Oliver C. Cox. New York: Philosophical Library, 1959, pp. 500.

The author of this study is particularly concerned with the structural designs of capitalist societies, their integration in a world-wide system, and their cultural potentialities. Part I deals with the historical origins of capitalism. The city of Venice is dealt with at length as the progenitor of capitalism, with further development attributed to Florence, Genoa, the Hanseatic League, Amsterdam and other Dutch cities. Part II describes the process of expansion of capitalist society into the modern nation and the place of industrialization. The principal topics in this part are the theoretical and practical considerations of nationalist ideology, English commercial and industrial strategy, mercantilism, and the Industrial Revolution. The work is not a traditional economic history, but is a more broadly social history of the capitalist system and the factors which influenced its development. The author combines the methods of social psychology, sociology, and history. The result is a readable and refreshing survey of a concept that needs revitalization—capitalism. J.E.N.

MODERN SCIENCE AND THE HUMAN FERTILITY PROBLEM. By Richard L. Meier. New York: John Wiley & Sons, Inc., 1959, pp. xiii+263.

Accelerated population growth in the world today is looked upon, "barring war and revolution," as "the greatest single deterrent to economic development over the long run." Demographers and many social scientists concerned with human fertility have been duly alarmed by the so-called population bomb which has exploded upon the earth, giving rise to the estimate that the "overall growth rate has now reached one and one-fourth percent per year, and that, therefore, should the rate continue for a half-century, the world population would come close to six billion persons." What is needed for the world then is the hand of science extended in the direction of finding a contraceptive cheap enough to place in the hands of people, coupled with another hand, that of philosophy, possibly to point out the essential change in values that must accompany the introduction of such a device. The author has made thoroughgoing analyses of the various implications and ramifications attendant upon the problem of reducing birth rates among the populations of both great and small nations. This reduction will be dependent in part upon what "laboratory scientists, administrative scientists, demographers, family sociologists, planners, and policy makers still need to do if economic improvement is ever to become possible for the densely populated resource-shy societies." The author introduces the research studies now being made in the field of oral contraceptives which may possibly hold out the promise of effectiveness and cheapness. Although he does not state it, policy makers might through taxation make considerable changes in birth rates. M.J.V.

RURAL SOCIOLOGY. An Analysis of Contemporary Rural Life. By Alvin L. Bertrand, Editor, and Associates. New York: McGraw-Hill Book Company, Inc., 1958, pp. xxix+454.

The editor and sixteen associates endeavored to produce a textbook that embodies some of the main trends in rural sociology. Some of the unique features of the book are the emphases on a sound theoretical frame of reference, a great reliance on current research findings, and the changing character of rural society. The introductory section is devoted to general sociological theory, including a consideration of social organization, rural-urban differentials, and rural social values and norms. The major portion of the book is devoted to a study of the rural population factors and locality groups (neighborhoods, communities, and regional areas); social differentiation and participation in rural areas; major social institutions; social processes and special interest groups; and social movements, including mass communication, in rural society. One of the special features of the book is the emphasis on the effects of technological developments.

Rural life has undergone tremendous changes during the present century. At the beginning of the century the population was predominantly rural. By 1957, only about 12.0 per cent of the population was classified as rural-farm, and this percentage is steadily declining; but

20.7 per cent were classed as rural-nonfarm, which group is slowly increasing. A considerable proportion of the farm population is concentrated in the South and in the Corn Belt. Even though the rural reproduction rate is still higher than the urban reproduction rate, farm people have steadily migrated to cities. Besides, the tremendous growth of the metropolitan areas has resulted in a spilling over of the urban population into the fringe and suburban areas, including areas formerly classified as chiefly agricultural territories. The authors emphasize the importance of the regional approach to the study of rural society, including the studies of the rural-nonfarm population and the suburbanization movement. Running through the book is the repeated emphasis on social change which has affected every phase of rural life.

The closing chapter is devoted to a concise review of rural sociology during the first half of the present century, especially its status and role at mid-century. Rural sociology has made great advances. The number and comprehensiveness of studies of rural society are increasing, and the focus of rural sociological research has been broadened to include rural-nonfarm and suburban groups. Rural societies in other lands are also studied with increasing frequency. Rural sociologists recognize that a thorough grounding in general theory and the use of scientific methods of research are essential for progress in this field. The authors conclude that if the nearly 500 members of the Rural Sociological Society of America were asked to specify the order of importance of the sociological roles they prefer to play, the chances are that they would list them in the following order: research, teaching, policy, and action. On the whole, this is one of the most thorough analyses available of rural society from the point of view of sociological theory and methodology.

M.H.N.

OTHER PUBLICATIONS RECEIVED

TOWARDS A NEW WORLD. By Richard Lombardi, S.J. New York: Philosophical Library, 1958, pp. 276.

DIRECTORY OF FARMERS' COOPERATIVES IN WASHINGTON. By Laszlo Valko. Pullman: Washington Agricultural Experiment Stations, State College of Washington, 1958, pp. 69.

ESSAYS IN SOCIAL SCIENCE. In Memory of Jacob Saposnekow. Edited by Henry Miller and Philip Shorr. New York: Jacob Saposnekow Memorial Volume Committee, 1958, pp. 157.

STATISTICS OF ALCOHOL USE AND ALCOHOLISM IN CANADA, 1871-1956. Compiled by R. E. Popham and W. Schmidt. Toronto: University of Toronto Press, 1958, pp. xv+155.

STATISTICS OF FARMER COOPERATIVES, 1955-56. By Anne L. Gessner. Washington, D.C.: Farmer Cooperative Service, U.S. Department of Agriculture, General Report 48, July 1958, pp. 74.

MORAL PRINCIPLES IN EDUCATION. By John Dewey. New York: Philosophical Library, 1959, pp. 61.

THE GROWTH OF MODERN THOUGHT AND CULTURE. By Herbert Wender. New York: Philosophical Library, 1959, pp. 215.

THE D.A.R. AN INFORMAL HISTORY. By Martha Strayer. Washington, D.C.: Public Affairs Press, 1958, pp. 262.

Although evidently eligible, the author has never joined the D.A.R., partly because she has wished to remain objective, as a reporter, to an organization, such as the D.A.R., which she has "covered" for "a longer period than any other American journalist." Consequently, while expressing appreciation of their good works, she also makes references to what she calls the "silly things" she has seen them do.

THE VOCATIONAL REHABILITATION PROBLEMS OF DISABLED PUERTO RICANS IN NEW YORK CITY. By V. D. Sanua and Others. New York: New York University, 1957, pp. 69.

ANTON SEMYONOVITCH. An Analysis of His Educational Ideas in the Context of Soviet Society. By Frederic Lilge. Berkeley and Los Angeles: University of California Press, 1958, pp. 52.

Sociology and Social . . . Research . . .

AN INTERNATIONAL JOURNAL

Social Philosophy of "It Doesn't Matter" . 403
WILLIAM F. OGBURN

Bilingualism in Island Legislatures 408
NORMAN MELLER

Attitudes of Teen-Agers 415
T. B. JOHANNIS AND JAMES ROLLINS

Population Dynamics in El Salvador . . . 421
ROBERT C. WILLIAMSON

Groups Versus the Individual 427
FRANK T. CARLTON

Conformity and the Middle Class 432
MARVIN E. WOLFGANG

Race Reactions by Sexes 439
EMORY S. BOGARDUS

Pacific Sociological News Notes 442

Peoples and Culture . . . 443
Social Problems and Welfare 447
Social Theory and Research 453
Index 467

VOL. 43 JULY-AUGUST 1959 No. 6

YEARLY SUBSCRIPTION, $3.50 SINGLE COPIES, 70 CENTS

Sociology and Social Research

AN INTERNATIONAL JOURNAL

PUBLISHED BIMONTHLY AT THE UNIVERSITY OF SOUTHERN CALIFORNIA
UNIVERSITY PARK, LOS ANGELES 7, CALIFORNIA

YEARLY SUBSCRIPTION, $3.50 SINGLE COPIES, 70¢

Entered as second-class matter March 31, 1936, at the post office at Los Angeles, California, under the act of March 3, 1879.

Articles published in this journal are indexed in *The International Index to Periodicals*, and abstracted in *Sociological Abstracts* and *Psychological Abstracts*.

PUBLISHED BY

UNIVERSITY OF SOUTHERN CALIFORNIA PRESS

UNIVERSITY PARK LOS ANGELES 7, CALIFORNIA

SOCIOLOGY AND SOCIAL RESEARCH
July-August 1959

THE SOCIAL PHILOSOPHY OF "IT DOESN'T MATTER"

WILLIAM FIELDING OGBURN
The Florida State University

On my way to Papeete, city of joy, I read a book of short stories about the native island peoples of the South Pacific. One of these stories had the title "Aita Pea Pea" (ah-eé-ta pé-a pé-a), which is not the name of a Polynesian maiden, but is an expression meaning "never mind," or "it does not matter." The story dealt with several instances of hard luck suffered by the islanders in fishing, in storms, in sickness, and in marketing copra. After each misfortune they say "aita pea pea." What if a storm delays reaching the mussel beds and the haul by the divers for mother-of-pearl is light—aita pea pea.

The story was informative to me, who, like many Americans these days, was a traveler in a far country among people with a very different culture from our own. For such travelers it is not easy to learn the values and attitudes toward life of a people; not as easy as to learn from statistics about population and foreign trade.

Further observation elsewhere led me to think that in aita pea pea there is wrapped up quite a philosophy of life which sets off the (once) mysterious East from the West.

In Bangkok I visited an American colleague who had lived there a year. I asked him what he had observed to be the outstanding attitude toward life of the Thai people. He said they were an "easygoing," hedonistic people, who cherished above other values smooth personal relations, and that seldom was heard the word "no." If an awkward situation arose, you would likely hear the expression "mai pen rai," meaning "never mind," "it does not matter." This phrase, he said, was also heard on many other occasions when something went wrong.

In Djakarta I asked my American host and hostess what expression in the Javanese language they heard most often. Both replied without hesitation and in full agreement that it was "ora apa apa" and meant "never mind," "it doesn't matter."

I then recalled that several years earlier, when exploring the sal jungles of Orissa with an Indian geographer from the University of Calcutta, he said many times in English "it doesn't matter," when I thought it did matter very much. I then thought it was a personal peculiarity of that individual. It did not occur to me that it might be a cultural trait of Bengal, and that any other Bengalese would have often repeated the same expression. After visiting Papeete and Bangkok, I inquired of an Indian from Calcutta about the expression "it does not matter" in the Bengalese language and was told it was "tate ki hayeche" and was commonly used in conversation in Bengal.

In Luzon I was driven along the countryside by a Philippine judge and his daughter. I asked them if there was any phrase in a native Philippine language that was used a great deal, more so than in English. They did not know of any such expression. Then I asked if there was a saying for "it does not matter." It was "ba hala na," and they said, "It is heard all the time."

Back in the U.S.A. at a dinner party one evening a Fulbright scholar who had spent a year in Greece was telling us of his observations and experiences. He said he met a woman tourist in Athens who made her way around Greece knowing only one expression in the Greek language, which he said was "them bi ra zi" and meant "never mind, it doesn't matter." It served her well, except on one occasion, a glorious Easter morning, when a Greek said to her in Greek, thinking she understood the language, "Christ is risen," to which she replied in Greek in the one expression she knew, "them bi ra zi."

Probably all languages have an expression for "it doesn't matter." In Burma it is "cakesa me shibu"; in Syria, "ma' lish," etc. The significance lies in the frequency of its use. What is strange is that visitors to the Asian countries, not knowing the language but trying to learn a few phrases, would so often hear "it doesn't matter" that the term would stick in their memories. A visitor from Thailand to the United States, not knowing the English language, would not hear "never mind" enough to take note of it. The expression is heard some in Western Europe and in England, particularly in the lower income groups, but apparently not as much as in Asia. He would more likely note "okay."

One other observation is that the great frequency of the remark "it doesn't matter" applies largely to the lesser irritations such as a derogatory remark, the loss of a small piece of property, the failure of a trade to take place, a minor injury. We should hardly expect to hear the remark "it doesn't matter" when a loved one dies or when a dwelling is destroyed by a tornado. Whenever the expression is used a great deal, it must apply largely to minor events, for the major catastrophes are too infrequent.

But in the United States and in Western Europe minor disturbances often loom rather large. For in the Western culture, competition is vigorous and the rewards of success are great. When the race is close and the slightest detail goes wrong, it becomes of major importance; and it does matter. Then, too, there are available so many ways of measuring our progress, with time pieces, scales, record keeping, statistics, progress charts, and schedule making, which do not exist in peasant cultures. With these we measure our efficiency and can detect the details that do matter. Thus the sector of our life in which we in the West can say "it doesn't matter" is reduced.

But, whatever may be the reasons why in Southeast Asia "it doesn't matter" is said so much and why in the U.S.A. it is said so little, it is the effect of the practice that is important.

If the blow of adversity is serious, to say "aita pea pea" helps one to roll with the punch, as the boxer sometimes does. Instead of "feeling sorry for himself," it means "better luck next time." In mishaps that are less serious, aita pea pea tends to operate as an insurance against worry. If a depression cuts the market for copra, "don't cry over spilt milk." Aita pea pea. They can return to the native custom of living off of fish and postpone buying a bicycle.

Aita pea pea would seem to be especially useful in maintaining cordial social relations, in that it discounts sensitiveness to slights, gossip, and supposed insults. For people who live in little communities quarreling and feuding are grievously disruptive. In such communities if the hazards of life are great and the death rate high, a village cannot afford to have much disruption, and fighting is particularly bad. Especially is it discouraged in children. Opposite traits of kindliness, manners, and cooperation are highly praised and of great value to the community. Aita pea pea, by encouraging indifference or dulling sensitiveness to malicious remarks, discourages friction in personal relations.

Aita pea pea may appear to travelers as a quaint mannerism of a happy-go-lucky people, especially by ethnocentric visitors who see the customs of other peoples as inferior to their own. By doing so they miss much of the pleasure and profit of travel. Looking for the good in other cultures, we find it interesting to speculate about the values of this Eastern culture trait for the West.

As a summarization, aita pea pea appears to be a cushion for worry. If it lessens worry in the East, would it not lessen worry in the West? Worry is a curse of vast scope in our civilization, and any suggestion that gives even a slight hope of reducing worry should be considered. We do not have any statistics of the number of worriers we have. If the census taker or a pollster asked the question "Do you worry?" it is doubtful if anyone would answer "no." But such an answer would give no indication of how serious the worries were. We have statistics on the number of psychotics entering our hospitals for mental disorder. But, contrary to popular opinion, many psychotics probably do not worry, as is indicated by the following definition: A psychotic is one who believes that 2 plus 2 equals 5; a neurotic knows that 2 plus 2 equals 4 but worries about it. And the neurotics are probably more numerous than the psychotics. Of course, aita pea pea would not cure a neurosis, the causes of which lie deep. Perhaps, though, it would make the suffering of a neurotic less intolerable.

There are worries not so serious as those of a neurotic, and many of these could be avoided. If the airplane is late, if the picnic is rained out, if the guest for dinner does not arrive, if the letter gets lost in the mail, if one's pocket is picked, what is the use in worrying when nothing can be done about it? But much worrying is about imaginary happenings of the future. We certainly should look into the future, but the vague and the unknown have a way of eliciting excessive worry about possible future consequences, many of which never occur. Then, too, much worry is about self, when what we need is to get away from self, as all of the great religions advise us.

That there is a vast number of such worries less serious than those of neurotics is shown by the consumption of sedatives and stimulants. In the United States the people take every year 500 tons of tranquilizers and barbituric sleeping tablets and 7,000 tons of aspirin, though not all headaches are caused by worry. Nor do all whiskey drinkers drink to forget, though of 700,000,000 gallons of distilled liquors drunk annually a sizable portion is from the "cup that cheers." Perhaps the mental attitude back of aita pea pea would reduce our consumption of tranquilizers.

We may divide our worries into two kinds, those that are precipitated in our work and those that arise outside. For the worries about our work it is shocking to think what would happen if we adopted aita pea pea in our business, where efficiency is the watchword, scheduling the practice, and success the goal. Imagine a production manager in a munitions plant which makes electric fuses saying to a worker who has failed to produce his quota of parts, "aita pea pea." Aita pea pea would wreck our industrial system, whose achievements are the envy of the world. We would rather have our worries and take our tranquilizers than to lose any of our efficiency.

Can we not exclude aita pea pea from our business but adopt it elsewhere? Outside the workshop we spend our time at home (which is a part-time place of work for wives), in places of recreation, or at social gatherings. There the pursuit of efficiency and success, though not wholly undesirable, may not be worth the price we pay in increasing strains in the home, anxieties about our children to the detriment of their personalities, tenseness at mealtime that does not help the digestion, tensions that mar the golf stroke, in taking the fun out of play, in increasing our sensitiveness to critical insinuations by others, and in making us feel a lack of ease at social gatherings. Just how efficient should a social gathering be? The test in Thailand is not efficiency but "sanug," that is, fun.

We wear evening clothes at a dinner party and sports clothing on the athletic field. Our language at church is different from our language at the bar of a cocktail lounge. The manners of the drawing room are not those of the seminar. So why should not the behavior in the factory differ from that in the family? Can we not taboo aita pea pea in our business but use it extensively outside? Perhaps we can exchange with the underdeveloped countries some of our technological know-how for some of their ancient wisdom on how to live. One of the expected advantages of our increasing travel is that travelers learn from every culture.

BILINGUALISM IN ISLAND LEGISLATURES OF THE PACIFIC AS AN INDEX OF ACCULTURATION—A HYPOTHESIS*

NORMAN MELLER
University of Hawaii

Students of culture change recognize that language not alone serves as a medium for communicating cultural elements but itself furnishes an insight into the dynamics of culture transfer.[1] Language usage has been suggested as a possible index of acculturation.[2] It is here proposed that the bilingual abilities of persons staffing political institutions may be used as a measure of the direction and rate of assimilation and, possibly, of cultural fusion. More specifically, it is hypothesized that the quantified language skills of legislators may be employed as a rough index of the progressive cultural adjustment occurring in the conjunction of two autonomous cultural systems, when one exerts a dominant effect upon the direction of the adjustment.

The hypothesis rests upon two assumptions: (1) that bilingualism is of itself evidence of acculturation and (2) that as assimilation occurs, the ancestral language will be supplanted by that of the dominant culture. Moving toward bilingualism, as the population adopts the language of the dominant culture, the language abilities of the membership of a legislative body anticipate the culture change; once the citizenry has achieved bilingualism and command of the ancestral language begins disappearing, the legislature will retain a higher, although decreasing, proportion of dual-language-skilled persons than characterizes the adult population as a whole.

In the administration of a colonial people, the metropolitan government charged with the governance of the area must wrestle with the semantic and cultural difficulties of translating its concepts for understanding by the local population. Local residents possessed of bilingual

* The field research necessary for this paper was made possible by grants from the Tri-Institutional Pacific Program. It will be incorporated into an expanded work on the Legislative Process in the Pacific.

[1] The Social Science Research Council Summer Seminar on Acculturation, 1953, "Acculturation: An Explanatory Formulation," *American Anthropologist,* 56:973-1002, p. 995.

[2] See J. Samora and W. N. Deane, "Language Usage as a Possible Index of Acculturation," *Sociology and Social Research,* 40:307-11; George C. Barker, "Social Functions of Language in a Mexican-American Community," *Acta Americana,* 5:184-202.

skills gravitate to the fore in government service to fill this need. What tends to be lost sight of is that the native population faces the same problem, aiding bilingual persons to assume roles of political leadership. Should the setting be changed so that instead of a handful of administrators in a colonial area, the situation be posited as a minority enclave surrounded by a numerically dominant majority, the same forces work to encourage bilingualism of the minority members in governmental posts and leadership positions. Legislators, and legislative bodies, in particular, appear to be peculiarly sensitive to these pressures, and thus offer promise as an index of their constituents' acculturation.

During the period 1956-58, the language skills of legislators in four island areas of the Pacific—Guam, Hawaii, Marshalls, Samoa—were ascertained.[3] All four (as to the Samoas, this applies to American Samoa; Western Samoa is administered by New Zealand as a Trust Territory) enjoy central representative bodies functioning under American tutelage, although the legislatures in the Marshalls and American Samoa are as yet wholly advisory and Guam's is recently removed from that status. In contrast, Hawaii instituted legislative government over a century ago, during the period of the Hawaiian Monarchy. In none is English-speaking ability legally mandatory to hold legislative office;[4] legislative business in Hawaii and Guam is conducted wholly in English, almost completely in the ancestral language in the Marshalls, and predominantly in Samoan in American Samoa.

In terms of stage of acculturation, unquestionably the people of the Marshalls and the Samoas stand toward one extreme, Hawaii to the other, and Guam somewhere in between. The legislative bodies of the

---

[3] *Methodological footnotes*: Data on 1956 Guamanian and 1957 Hawaiian legislatures from personal interview with all legislators, supplemented by informants for the latter; 1956 Marshall Legislature from personal interview supplemented by questionnaire and informants; 1958 Samoan Fono (American Samoa) from personal interview supplemented by informants; and 1958 Legislative Assembly of Western Samoa through official records supplemented by informants. The language classifications are based upon observed performance during interview, legislators' self-rating when furnished, and informants' evaluation; the division between "fluent" and "limited" is wholly subjective and not based upon any objective technique. All legislatures but that of Western Samoa were observed in session.

Legislators in Hawaii and Guam are chosen in secret election by the adult citizenry. In American Samoa the lower house is similarly selected, but the Senate is chosen through *Fa'a Samoa* ways by the *matai.* Although Western Samoa restricts the suffrage to *matais* for the 41 "Samoan" members, only 31 were chosen *Fa'a Samoa* while 10 were secretly elected by *matais.* The Marshallese House of Assembly for the most part was chosen through indirect selection by the atoll council, some members through indigenous modification of secret ballot and adult suffrage.

[4] However, in Hawaii, only Hawaiian may be substituted.

four areas fall into a similar alignment when the bilingual skills of their members are tabulated. Of the 70 members of the Marshallese bicameral legislature, all conversed in Marshallese, while 37 could speak no English, 10 only limited English, and 23 fluent English. Similarly, all 32 members of American Samoa's bicameral body spoke Samoan, but their English skill could be classified into 12 no English, 10 limited, and 10 fluent. At the other extreme, in Hawaii, all 33 non-*haoles* (non-Caucasians, including Portuguese) of the Territory's 45-membered, bicameral legislature were fluent in English but evidenced restricted abilities in their "ancestral" languages: 11 fluent, 17 limited, and 5 no control of the "ancestral" tongue.[5] Befitting their Island's stage of acculturation, all 21 legislators in Guam's unicameral legislature were fluent in both Chamorro and English.

The spread of the language of the dominant group must normally be reckoned in generations. As a result, it is to be expected that the younger members of the legislative bodies surveyed would generally possess more developed bilingual skills. This was demonstrated by the legislative bodies surveyed in those areas closest to the "ancestral" way of life. American Samoan legislators with a median age of 49, divided into median ages of 43 for the fluent English group, 50 for limited, and 55 for no English skill. The same phenomena characterized the "Samoan" legislators of Western Samoa: median age of 55 for all, but when grouped by language-speaking ability, fluent English 48½, limited English 55½, and for the no English group a median age of 60.[6] The 42 members of the Marshallese House of Assembly evidenced the same general age distribution, but not so neatly: the median age of the whole House was 44 years, and the fluent English group's low age of 39 at one extreme contrasted with the median age of 48 for the Marshallese assemblymen with no command of English. Seemingly disconcertingly, the limited English group's median age did not fall between the other two Marshallese groups, but rather was higher—49; however, the median age of the combined fluent and limited English groups was but 41, emphasizing the fact that Marshallese assemblymen with English language ability of some sort, as a whole, were considerably younger than legislators unable to converse in English.

Correspondingly, in an area where assimilation is almost complete, it is only the elders who will be expected to possess bilingual ability, while the younger generations are limited to use of the dominant language.

---

[5] Part-Hawaiians classified as of Hawaiian ancestry.

[6] Only the 41 "Samoan" members are included; "European" members representing the "European" electorate are excluded.

In Hawaii, an area of "advanced" acculturation, language skill thus must be measured in movement away from the "ancestral" tongue. As anticipated, the younger legislators in Hawaii displayed less command of their "ancestral" language than their seniors in the legislative chambers. All non-*haole* legislators in the 1957 legislature had a median age of 44 years; those with fluent command of their "ancestral" tongue reported a significantly higher median age—50, while those who could speak only English or English and the second language with limited ability approximated the median (44 and 43 years, respectively). The only sizable subgroup in the Hawaiian legislature—legislators of Japanese ancestry, 22 in number—evidenced a comparable relationship: median age 40; fluent Japanese, 40; limited or no Japanese language skill, 37.

Inherent acceleration and lag factors need be taken into account for legislative language skills to be utilized as an index of acculturation. The 1956 Marshallese legislature serves as illustration of the former, and Hawaii of the latter; Guam probably represents an area just going over the "hump." Far more than half of the Marshallese adults cannot speak English in any form, so that the legislators' skill was anticipating that of their constituents; it is doubtful that 85 per cent of non-*haole,* adult citizens of Hawaii can still speak their "ancestral" tongues, so that here the Hawaiian legislature appears to evidence a lag. Every member of the 1956 Guamanian legislature when interviewed proved fluent in English; a visitor to Guam at that time easily could observe that no such language ability distinguished all adult Guamanians.

A legislator's selection tends to depend upon segmental support; dual language skill does not alienate that portion of the citizenry which identifies with him due to his speaking the ancestral tongue. For an area moving toward bilingualism, command of the dominant language, and all attributes associated with it, weigh heavily in a candidate's favor; once over the "bilingual hump," normally command of ancestral language would continue to be of political advantage, although of decreasing importance relative to the size of his constituency valuing its use. In short, the forces at work encourage bilingualism in legislatures and help to explain both initial acceleration and subsequent lag.

Re-election depends upon many factors, so that for any one legislature it is unwarranted to causally associate success of its re-elected members solely with dual language ability. Then, too, only a small number of legislators are encompassed within each language fluency group, so that the findings for any one of the legislatures surveyed may be attributed to coincidence. Notwithstanding, as turnover statistics for the legislatures of the Pacific studied all demonstrate the same tendency, they lend credence to the influence of bilingualism as well as the effects of acceleration and lag.[7] In areas of increasing bilingualism, re-elected members comprised larger shares of the total membership which spoke the dominant language; in Hawaii, as an area moving away from bilingualism in which the ancestral languages are disappearing, greater electoral success nevertheless seemed to be enjoyed by legislators commanding those languages.

Service in Previous Legislature. First, as to the language fluency of members with experience in the legislature next previous to that surveyed: In the 1956 Marshallese House of Assembly, 15 members (out of 42) had served in the 1954 session, the last previous sitting of that body; 14 members (out of 32) of the Fourth Legislature were re-elected to the Fifth Legislature of American Samoa. In the 1957 Hawaiian House of Representatives, 13 of the 21 non-*haole* members had served in the 1955 House. Classifying all legislators of the Marshallese and Samoan bodies into the three groups of fluent, limited, and no English, it was found that these re-elected members comprised greater percentages of the fluent (53 per cent, Marshallese; 54 per cent, American Samoa) than the limited English (33 per cent, Marshallese; 45 per cent, American Samoa), and proportionately double their share of the no English group (24 per cent, Marshallese; 25 per cent, American Samoa). In line with the lag hypothesis, in the Hawaiian House,[8] 87 per cent of the fluent "ancestral" language group and 62 per cent of the limited "ancestral" tongue group had served in the previous session. Only 40 per cent of the no "ancestral" language group in the 1957 Hawaiian House had been members of the 1955 House, a percentage not even half as great as that which characterized the fluent "ancestral" language group.

Any Legislative Experience. The same encouragement of bilingualism is evidenced when all members with any previous legislative experience in each language skill group are identified. Here, instead of centering attention solely upon service in the next previous legislature, all legislative experience was taken into account. Surprisingly, over-all turnover thus disclosed ran less than 40 per cent. In the Marshallese House, 26 out of 42 members had had some previous experience in earlier sessions of the House; in American Samoa this figure for previous legislative

---

[7] Guam is not here included, as all of its members are bilingual.

[8] Hawaiian Senate not included, to eliminate difficulty of allocating hold-over members, all members being elected for four-year terms.

experience in either house was 23 members out of 32. In both houses of the Hawaiian legislature, 26 of the 33 non-*haoles* were found to have had former legislative service. Breaking total membership down into fluency groups, in American Samoa 85 per cent of the fluent, 73 per cent of the limited, and 50 per cent of the no English groups had in the past enjoyed some legislative service. Much the same held true for the Marshallese House: former legislators comprised 87 per cent of the fluent English group and 52 per cent of the no English group. The 50 per cent figure for the limited English group appears to strike a discordant note; but here again, if all Marshallese assemblymen with English-speaking ability of some sort are counted as one group, that is, combining the fluent and limited English groups, 76 per cent were former legislators, markedly contrasting with the 52 per cent of the no English group. In Hawaii, all of the legislators in the fluent "ancestral" tongue group and three fourths of those in the limited group had previous legislative experience, in distinction to the three fifths of the no "ancestral" language group serving their first term. Unquestionably, legislative veterans comprised greater proportions of the groups with dual language skills.

Number of Terms Served. Among those legislators serving in the 1956 Marshallese House, the 1958 Legislature of American Samoa, and the Hawaiian Legislature in 1957, members with greater bilingual ability tended to have been sent back to the legislative halls more frequently than their colleagues with less language fluency. The mean number of times members in each fluency group had been elected in American Samoa was 2.6 terms for fluent English; limited English, 2.5, and no English, 2.1 terms. Approximately the same characterizes the difference between the mean terms of members of the Marshallese House in the fluent English group (2.5 terms) as compared with the no English group (2.1 terms). The limited English group for the Marshalls again does not neatly fit in between these two extremes (2.0 terms); but, similarly, if Marshallese legislators with any English language skills are collectively considered, they display a mean of 2.4 terms, markedly contrasting with the mean of the no English group.

The 1957 Hawaiian Legislature dramatically displayed the relation between language skill and length of legislative experience. Legislators in the fluent "ancestral" group had been elected on the average of 3.3 legislative terms apiece, while the mean number of times the limited "ancestral" group had been sent to the legislative halls was but 2.8, and the members of the no "ancestral" language group showed only a mean of 1.4 terms. Just as legislators skilled in the dominant language in an area moving toward bilingualism tend to remain legislators longer, so in areas moving away from bilingualism to the dominant language, do legislators speaking an ancestral tongue tend to remain longer in the legislative halls.

Quantifying legislative bilingualism as a device for measuring the direction and speed of acculturation being but a hypothesis, it needs testing elsewhere both to verify its conceptualization and to determine its utility. But first a word of warning. If legal fiat requires command of the dominant language as a condition for holding legislative office, the index may be employed only where the use of the ancestral language is decreasing in a bilingual situation. Representation appears to be a material element, and a degree of freedom of choice an essential part thereof. In the Marshallese House of Iroij, where heredity nominally determined membership, no significant difference distinguished the 12 members with English language skills (fluent, median age 51; limited, 51) from the 16 Iroij with none (median age 52). Nor may reliance be placed solely upon the technical method adopted for selection of legislators, as, for example, secret elections; of the 10 "Samoans" elected by secret ballot to the Western Samoan Legislative Assembly, more than a majority (6) spoke only Samoan, while this lack of English-speaking ability characterized less than a third (9 of 31) of the members chosen through *Fa'a Samoa* means.[9] In short, the index as hypothesized appears to possess utility in only those cross-cultural areas of mobile ingress and egress to legislative membership where representation has political import.

[9] However, the median age of the Western Samoa elected members with no ability to speak English was higher (60) than the elected bilingual members (limited, 58; fluent, 39).

ATTITUDES OF TEEN-AGERS TOWARD FAMILY RELATIONSHIPS AND HOMOGAMY OF SOCIAL CHARACTERISTICS OF THEIR PARENTS*

THEODORE B. JOHANNIS, JR.
AND
JAMES ROLLINS
University of Oregon

Many studies have shown a positive association between the child's rating of the happiness of his parents' marriage and his affection for them.[1] Studies of homogamy or assortive mating have indicated that couples with similar background characteristics tend to marry one another and that this similarity is associated with marital happiness or adjustment.[2] However, few studies dealing with the relationship between marital happiness and the affection of children for parents have included all three of these factors, i.e., marital happiness, affection of child for parents, and homogeneity in background characteristics of the married pair.

PROBLEM

In this paper the writers attempt to ascertain:

A. The extent to which male and female respondents report the background characteristics of their parents to be different and the extent to which they report the marital happiness of their parents, their attitudes toward home life, and their attitudes toward their fathers, mothers, and siblings to be different.

B. The association of the number of shared background characteristics of parents (1) with the teen-age child's rating of the marital happiness of his parents, (2) with the teen-age child's attitude toward home life, and (3) with how well the teen-age child gets along with his father, mother, and siblings.

---

*The authors wish to express their appreciation to the E. C. Brown Trust and the Graduate School of the University of Oregon for financial assistance in the data analysis phase of this study.

[1] For example, Ernest W. Burgess and Paul Wallin, *Engagement and Marriage* (New York: J. B. Lippincott Company, 1953), Chap. 2.

[2] For example, Munford H. Kuhn, "How Mates Are Sorted," in *Family, Marriage and Parenthood*, Howard Becker and Reuben Hill, eds. (Boston: D. C. Heath & Company, 1955), Chap. 8.

C. The difference in the degree of marital happiness of parents from the attitude of respondents toward home life, toward fathers, and toward mothers.

D. The difference in the attitude of the respondents toward home life from their attitude toward fathers and toward mothers.

E. The difference in the attitude of respondents toward siblings from the degree of marital happiness of parents, respondents' attitude toward home life, respondents' attitude toward fathers, and respondents' attitude toward mothers.

F. The difference in the attitude of respondents toward fathers from their attitude toward mothers.

PROCEDURE

The data were obtained in Tampa, Florida, as part of a broader study on the division of labor within the family.[3] The sample represents families with one or more children attending the eight high schools in Tampa during April 1953. The 1,584 respondents were enrolled in the tenth grade and represented 91 per cent of the community's enrolled tenth grade population. Only questionnaires answered by white respondents were utilized in the current analysis, thus reducing the total N to 1,400. The information used in this paper was taken from the 1,148 questionnaires containing complete answers to the questions on parental background characteristics.

The six background factors: i.e., age, region in which reared, rural-urban background, education, religious affiliation, and occupation were obtained from the questionnaires completed by our informants, tenth grade adolescents, as were the ratings of the happiness of thcir parents' marriage, the respondents' attitudes toward their home life, and their attitudes toward father, mother, and siblings.

RESULTS

The median age of the fathers was 44 years, of mothers 40 years, and of respondents 15 years. The fathers and mothers had been married a median of 19 years. The median education of the fathers and mothers was 9 years. More than two thirds of the fathers and mothers had been socialized in the southeastern section of the United States. These families

[3] See Theodore B. Johannis, Jr., "The Adolescent's View of Father Roles in Relation to Socio-economic Class" (unpublished Ph.D. dissertation, The Florida State University, 1955).

were found to be in the prelaunching and launching stages of the family life cycle.

It should be noted that the number of shared background characteristics was somewhat skewed in the direction of high similarity. In 28 per cent of the cases parents were found to be alike on four characteristics. Twenty-six per cent of the spouses fell in the three characteristics alike and 22 per cent in the five alike category. Six per cent of the couples were found to be alike on all six background items and 4 per cent had zero or one characteristic alike.

Like many other studies, the respondents tended to rate their parents' marriages as happy and to state that they got along well with their parents. Eighty per cent of the respondents rated the marriage of their parents as happy or very happy, and 82 per cent stated that they were either satisfied or very satisfied with their home life. The remainder of the responses fell in the less than happy or the less than satisfied category.

But 18 per cent of the respondents reported that they got along less than well with their fathers, and 11 per cent of the attitudes toward mothers fell in this same category. This compares with 39 per cent of those having brothers and sisters who stated that they got along less than well with their siblings.

Other findings are as follows:[4]

A. No significant differences were found between the responses of males and females to the questions on the background characteristics of their parents. About as many males as females reported that they were satisfied with their home life, that their parents were happily married, and that they got along well with their fathers, mothers, and siblings.

B. No significant differences were found between the number of shared background characteristics of parents and marital happiness, attitudes toward home life and toward fathers, mothers, and siblings.

C. No significant differences were found between the degree of marital happiness of parents and the attitude of respondents toward home life. A significant difference was found between the degree of marital happiness of parents and the attitude of respondents toward fathers and toward mothers. Respondents tended to rate the happiness of their parents' marriages lower than they did the level of getting along with their fathers and with their mothers.

D. A significant difference was found between the attitude of the

[4] Complete data tables may be obtained from the authors.

respondents toward home life and their attitude toward their fathers and toward their mothers. The respondents tended to have a less positive attitude toward home life than toward their fathers and toward their mothers.

E. A significant difference was found between the attitude of respondents toward siblings and the marital happiness of parents, attitudes toward home life, and attitudes toward fathers and toward mothers. From inspection of the tables in which these data were placed and of the corrected coefficients of contingencies ($\bar{C}$) derived from them, it would appear that an inverse association might be involved, but these data were not tabulated in such a way as to meet all the conditions for assigning a plus or a minus to this coefficient, which ordinarily has no sign.[5]

F. A significant difference was found between the attitude of the respondents toward their fathers and toward their mothers. The respondents' attitude toward mothers was more positive than toward fathers.

DISCUSSION

A. Like the current study, Burgess and Wallin[6] found no significant differences in the way that male and female respondents report the level of marital happiness of their parents. Vollmer[7] obtained a similar result for his Negro sample but did find a significant difference between the responses of his white males and females on this item. Lang[8] found that men rated marriage less happy than did women. Further research is needed in order to clarify these apparently contradictory findings.

B. The finding of no significant association between the number of shared background characteristics and the ratings of marital happiness of parents, ratings of satisfaction with home life, getting along with father, mother, and siblings brings into question those writers who stress "likeness" as the major criterion for mate selection and future marital bliss. This emphasis on homogamy is especially noticeable in high school

---

[5] See Thomas C. McCormick, *Elementary Social Statistics* (New York: McGraw-Hill Book Company, 1941), pp. 203-08.

[6] Paul Wallin and Howard M. Vollmer, "Marital Happiness of Parents and Their Children's Attitude to Them," *American Sociological Review*, 18: 427-29.

[7] Howard M. Vollmer, *Variations in Parental Preference of Negro and White College Students* (unpublished M.A. thesis, Stanford University, 1951), pp. 34-37.

[8] Richard O. Lang, *A Study of the Degree of Happiness or Unhappiness in Marriage* (unpublished M.A. thesis, University of Chicago, 1932), p. 75.

texts on marriage and family.[9] It is also found in some college texts.

C. The finding of no significant difference between the degree of marital happiness and the degree of the respondents' satisfaction with home life may indicate that the respondent perceives these as being synonymous. This would lend support to Slocum's finding that the Washington high school senior's perception of the degree of happiness of parents is highly correlated with his perception of the degree of happiness in the home as a generalized image.[10]

D. That a generalized attitude such as satisfaction of home life and attitude toward getting along with father and mother should differ significantly could have been expected more or less on the grounds that interpersonal relationships are of different order from satisfaction with home life. The latter is a generalized image, while getting along with father or mother may be more specific and concrete for the adolescent.

E. The finding of a significant difference between the attitude of the respondents toward siblings and the marital happiness of parents, satisfaction with home life, and getting along with father and mother is not too surprising in the light of evidence from studies of twins, delinquency, and sibling rivalry, which indicate that siblings experience different social environments and that family cliques may be furthered by sibling rivalry.[11] Thus, there is a possibility that sibling relationships are not too closely allied to father-mother relationships or generalized feelings of home satisfaction from the teen-age respondent's point of view.

F. The significant difference which was found between the attitudes of the respondents toward fathers and toward mothers agrees with the findings of a long list of studies which have analyzed the parental preferences of children. The studies of Simpson, Mott, and Gardiner found that children five to nine years of age preferred their mothers.[12] Duvall reported that in the twelve to seventeen age range, both males and females preferred their mothers.[13] College students also show the same

[9] For example, Paul H. Landis, *Your Marriage and Family Living*, rev. ed. (New York: McGraw-Hill Book Company, 1954), p. 181.

[10] Walter L. Slocum, "Some Factors Associated with Happiness in Unbroken Homes," *The Coordinator*, 6: 35-39.

[11] Clifford Kirkpatrick, *The Family* (New York: Ronald Press, 1955), pp. 230-32.

[12] Vollmer, *op. cit.*, p. 2.

[13] Evelyn M. Duvall, "Child-Parent Social Distance," *Sociology and Social Research*, 21: 458-63.

preference pattern according to Nimkoff,[14] Terman,[15] Winch,[16] and Vollmer.[17]

---

[14] Meyer F. Nimkoff, "Parent-Child Relationships," *University of Southern California Scholastic Research Studies*, 1935, No. 14.

[15] Lewis M. Terman *et al., Psychological Factors in Marital Happiness* (New York: McGraw-Hill Book Company, 1938), p. 223.

[16] Robert F. Winch, "The Relations Between Courtship Behavior and Attitudes Toward Parents Among College Men," *American Sociological Review*, 8: 164-74.

[17] Vollmer, *op. cit.*, p. 45.

POPULATION DYNAMICS IN EL SALVADOR

ROBERT C. WILLIAMSON
Los Angeles City College

No part of the world appears to grow at a faster rate than Latin America. In particular, El Salvador is approaching a crisis stage in contrast to the relatively unpopulated countries of Central America. In fact, only Puerto Rico and Haiti in the Western Hemisphere are more densely populated. This demographic revolution which is occurring in large parts of the underdeveloped areas of the world can be ascribed to lowering of the mortality rate without an appreciable change in birth rate. The ratio of a birth rate of more than forty per thousand and a death rate of lower than twenty per thousand means an annual increase of 2 per cent, and much of Latin America is well above that ratio. In reality, El Salvador has been experiencing an increase of approximately 4 per cent in the last ten years. With a population of 2,350,201 in 1957 and an area of 8,259 square miles, a demographic crisis is hardly escapable. Already the vitaminless diet of corn, beans, and rice for possibly 85 per cent of the population is reflected in health and other problems.

The tremendous growth of population in Latin America during the last two decades has resulted from slightly better standards of health, medicine, and sanitation than were present earlier in the century. However, a large part of this increment may be explained by more accurate census methods, at least in the more urbanized areas. It appears that both births and deaths are ignored in the remote departments of El Salvador. For example, it is hardly plausible that the highly urbanized department of San Salvador should have a birth rate of 54.7 and rural Cabañas only 43.2.[1]

Specifically, the purpose of this paper is to examine the demographic situation in El Salvador and to determine if any solution can be found to their problem of overpopulation. Our basic premise is that the demographic determinants of any society, and El Salvador is no exception, are the rates of natality, mortality, and migration. In this article these

[1] Individual communication from the Dirección General de Estadística y Censos (Ministerio de Economía). Generally speaking, unless otherwise noted, the figures cited in this paper are from the *Boletín Estadístico*, a quarterly of the above office.

factors will be examined along with the question of age structure and urban-rural distribution.

The Birth Rate. The birth rate for El Salvador was 48.9 per thousand in 1957 and has remained above 47 for all years since 1950. This rate is not markedly different from that of other countries: Mexico, 46.4; Venezuela, 46.7; Chile, 35.4, yet opposed to the United States, 24.9, and Argentina, 23.8.[2] Its fertility rate (children under five years per thousand women, aged 15 to 44) is high even for Latin America.

As in most of middle America, the majority of births are technically illegitimate. Less than half of the "marriages" are contracted legally, and of those which have been performed by civil authority a large number have not been accompanied by religious ceremony. The more familiar pattern is of a *union libre*, or common-law marriage. This arrangement may vary between comparatively tenuous relationships of a few months to the more frequent type of several years.

Urbanization has reduced the birth rate to some degree. Still more impressively, social class is correlated inversely with the birth rate. The emerging middle classes in towns and cities are generally restricting their families to five children or less, whereas the number is frequently twice as large in the lower classes, especially among the rural population.

Mortality. El Salvador, in line with most lesser developed areas of the world, exhibits a relatively high, although decreasing, death rate. Mortality statistics, it may be added, are particularly suspect as concerns validity, at least in the rural areas. In any case, the death rate for 1957 was 14 per thousand (male, 14.8; female, 13.2). It is well above the United States figure of 9.4 for the same year. Infant mortality rates have decreased from 129 per thousand in 1930 to 70.3 in 1956 (the United States rate for the same year being 26). For the other end of the life span, namely, those individuals above 65, death rates have risen from 9.7 to 16.6 per cent between 1930 and 1950. In the same period deaths for ages below 20 have decreased from 62.4 to 58.1 per cent.

The leading cause of death in El Salvador is gastroenteritis, in contrast to what it is in the more advanced areas of the world. Since 1950 there have been three to six thousand cases annually. A number of disorders vie for second place, for instance, malaria, measles, influenza, and infant infection. However, in 1956 homicide had the distinction of being the number two cause of death, with 954 cases listed. With the gradual rise of medical and sanitary standards, it is conceivable that

---

[2] *Statistical Abstract of the United States* (Washington, D.C.: Bureau of the Census, 1958), p. 927. The figures generally refer to 1956.

homicide will become relatively more important in mortality statistics unless there is a change in the mores or a more effective law enforcement than is observable at present.

Life expectancy as reported in 1950 was 49.9 for the male, 52.4 for the female as compared with 65.7 and 71.3, respectively, for the United States. Probably longevity will continue to improve; however, in El Salvador there are certain limits in that the food supply is restricted. Already the per capita consumption of a number of essential foodstuffs is less than half its desirable norm. For example, the monthly consumption of meat in a sample of workers' families is less than six pounds,[3] not to speak of deficiencies in eggs, dairy products, and the like. The present diet of corn, rice, and beans—procurable at $0.20 daily per person—for possibly 90 per cent of the population has little likelihood of alteration in view of population pressure on the land. Consequently, resistance to disease is distinctly limited.

Age Structure and Future Population Growth. It is hardly necessary to emphasize the youth of the population. A low average age assures the country of a high level of future growth and also means that the relatively few adults are responsible economically for the welfare of a large number of minors. The enormous burden placed on educational institutions in part explains why approximately half of the population (57.7 per cent in 1950) is illiterate. In the rural areas this educational crisis is particularly acute.

Predictions of future growth have been derived for the next few decades and are of three types: high, medium, and low assumptions.[4] The projection for 1960 is 2.7 million; for 1970, 3.1; and for 1980, 3.8. The high and low assumptions vary by approximately 12 per cent on either side of the figures cited. Already it appears that the figure for 1960 is a trifle high. In any case, the predictions presuppose that by 1980 there will be some aging of the population and a decelerated rate of growth. Moreover, for the nation to support a population of nearly four million by 1980 would mean either drastic socioeconomic change or extensive out-migration. Of course, any prediction of population is accompanied by the usual problems of projecting demographic trends, which has not been without its hazards.

Rural-urban Distribution. One aspect of Salvadorean demography is its low rate of urbanization, which is in keeping with much of Central

[3] Dirección General de Estadística y Censos, *Hechos y Cifras de El Salvador, 1956* (San Salvador: Ministerio de Economía, 1957), p. 4.

[4] *Population of Central America (Including Mexico), 1950-1980* (New York: United Nations Organization, 1954).

America and with underdeveloped areas in general. It also is in harmony with the Davis thesis of the negative association between urbanization and agricultural density.[5] The urban population of the country actually decreased from 38.3 to 36.5 per cent between 1930 and 1950 and remained at 36.7 in 1957. Although the census authorities in most of Latin America prefer centers of 2,000 or 2,500 as demarcating the urban, El Salvador prefers the figure 500; with this criterion the country can be considered as approximately one-third urban. If 5,000 is the designation, the country may be considered as 21.7 per cent urban, which is not far from the norm of most of Latin America. In any case, the persistence of a predominantly rural population, despite growing commercialization and incipient industrialization, is somewhat perplexing. Possibly this rural character can be explained by certain factors more or less unique to the Salvadorean scene: (1) The country is exclusively agricultural with individual households living in *champas*, or huts, distributed over the land. (2) The population enjoys quasi urbanization because of the relatively small size of the country. Specifically, more than 95 per cent of the population live within thirty miles of the three cities of thirty thousand or more inhabitants. (3) The fairly universal tendency of the urban population to restrict its birth rate may be significant; however, this interpretation must be observed with utmost caution in view of the inaccuracy of census data, i.e., the failure to report deaths accurately in the rural area, which again may tend to inflate the latter's proportion of the population.

The question remains as to why El Salvador and certain other Latin-American countries exhibit little growth of the urban population despite the development of commerce and some degree of industrialization. It is surprising that the heavy migration of young people to the urban centers has not raised the ratio of urbanites. San Salvador, the capital and major city, is obviously expanding at a faster rate than the other urban centers of the country. However, the exact pattern of rural-urban distribution will have to wait until more accurate census methods can be devised for the remote areas.

---

[5] Kingsley Davis and Hilda H. Golden, "Urbanization and the Development of Pre-industrial Areas," in Paul K. Hatt and Albert J. Reiss, Jr., *Cities and Society* (Glencoe: The Free Press, 1957), pp. 120-40. According to Jack P. Gibbs and Kingsley Davis, "Conventional Versus Metropolitan Data in the International Study of Urbanization," *American Sociological Review*, 23: 504-14, El Salvador is judged to be 36.5 per cent urban and 11.9 per cent living in metropolitan areas. In other words, it is urban to about the same extent as most of Latin America with the exception of Argentina, Cuba, and a few other countries.

Some Suggested Solutions. The social scientists can hardly view a demographic catastrophe as in the case of El Salvador and certain other of the overpopulated though underdeveloped areas of the world without suggesting some possible alternatives. One familiar solution for the impasse would be industrialization and modernization, as this process generally brings rapid change in the form of population increase in its early phases and decline in the later stages. However, there is hardly sufficient time for that solution in view of the urgency of the situation. Furthermore, the possibilities of industrialization are limited in Central America due to a lack of critical resources, skills, and readily available markets and purchasing power. Yet in the last decade there has been some medium industrialization, particularly in textiles, foodstuffs, and other consumer's items. The next decade will undoubtedly witness further development of light industries. This economic diversification is extremely necessary in view of the highly agricultural nature of the country, especially as it has been practically confined to one crop, namely, coffee.

Another solution is out-migration. Although figures are difficult to obtain, it appears that nearly one hundred thousand Salvadoreans are residing in underpopulated Honduras. Bureaucracy and various border restrictions along with certain economic barriers have restrained this migration to a fraction of what it should be ideally. If the long-awaited Central American federation or union can be initiated, this problem of emigration can be enormously facilitated. Also the union would make for a more effective economy throughout Central America. However, national pride and various rivalries will likely prevent the present Organization of Central America republics (ODECA) from becoming what it might be.

Certainly the most drastic attack on the problem of overpopulation would be a specific birth control program. Considering the mores and folkways of Latin America there appears to be little probability of success with a program of voluntary sterility. Nonetheless, the establishment of certain birth control clinics, as has occurred in Puerto Rico, may point the way of possible reform for other parts of Hispanic America. The teachings of the Catholic Church constitute only one obstacle to a birth control policy. More basic is the rural character of the country with its low standard of living. Consequently, a program of industrialization is desirable, as it probably means higher standards of education and health as well as the strengthening of the middle class. The Salvadorean government, along with the International Cooperation Administration (Point Four) of the United States government, and the United

Nations are at present attempting to improve the use of the land and to pave the way for industrialization to whatever its potential may be. As the most densely populated country on the American continent, there is little doubt as to the need of reform in El Salvador in a variety of directions.

GROUPS VERSUS THE INDIVIDUAL

FRANK T. CARLTON
Case Institute of Technology

Until recent generations a man belonged to few groups—the family, the tribe, a religious group—and these had only a small membership. Now, an individual usually belongs to many groups and some of these have many members—the nation, a labor union, a professional association, a political party, an insurance organization, an investment trust, a corporation, a business association, a cooperative establishment, a club, a fraternal body, or a gang. One rough-and-ready measure of civilization may be the number of groups to which the typical person belongs.

In the last three quarters of a century, certain groups, such as corporations, unions, and business associations, have become very influential in the political and economic fields. To get things done, the individual must tie in with certain organizations, old or new. When he becomes a member of a group, he is expected to be ready to discuss, to compromise, to do teamwork. In short, a good member must be a reasonable fellow. The extreme individualist is anathema.

The brainy boy and the man of unusual ability and initiative are likely to be outcasts from the groups to which they would normally belong. The nonconformist is distrusted. In other words, group ideals or "images" demand conformity rather than initiative from members, and "conformity breeds sterility." However, in too many instances, "success" appears to follow only if one becomes an "organization man." The emphasis often placed upon the good mixer may be a consequence of the rapid material development which quickly transformed pioneer and agricultural America into a complex industrial nation.

The captains of industry or the "robber barons" of the latter part of the nineteenth century and the first quarter of the twentieth were men of power interested primarily in making money. The broader view of community welfare taken by many corporation officials in recent years did not appeal to this earlier group of industrial and financial magnates. Money was power.

Today, the labor leader is in somewhat the same position as were the earlier captains of industry. Power comes through the ability to direct members of the union by means of strikes, picket lines, boycotts, political influence. When the leaders of one union can practically tie up transportation over a wide area—possibly nationwide—and when labor leaders control millions of dollars paid in by the members of unions, they approach or exceed the economic and political influence of financial giants of two generations ago. Corporations have been restricted in their business activities by law. Labor organizations are today favored by many special legal immunities.

Members of the management group in a big corporation are prone to become "organization men" who conform to the general pattern and who gradually lose the precious gifts of initiative and individuality. Teamwork rather than hard individual effort is demanded in many an organization. A major problem of today is that of maintaining a considerable modicum of independent individual effort while continuing as an active member of a group. Members of a labor organization are often forced to support the program of the officials.

Even in colleges and universities the exceptional thinker is too frequently pressured to conform to the orthodox mold. An observer, P. E. Jacobs, of recent college life holds that students emerge from four years of college more alike than when they entered. He asserts that the American college has become a "vehicle of conformity."

In the United States our public school system has failed to place sufficient stress upon the direction and education of the gifted student. This we must do in the immediate future or suffer in world competition. Many believe that American schools should stress "social conditioning." In other words, instead of emphasizing individual mental training and the ability to solve problems of sundry kinds, the school system should stress ability to conform to social standards and to get along with fellowmen. However, this point of view overemphasizes conformity and good fellowship. The age in which we are now living demands new skills and attitudes; it calls urgently for men and women who are able to initiate new programs and who act vigorously to overcome social inertia.

In 1959, a basic demand is for security. Young executives and staff members are in danger of becoming "comfortable, insignificant" cogs of an organization. Today, the corporation, the business, the plant, and the union are becoming centers of power to which the primary allegiance of all connected is demanded. Two common practices are also sapping freedom of action and of movement: installment buying, that is, mortgaging the future pay checks, and the swelling system of fringe benefits which tie an employee to one company. After he has worked for a firm for a few years, an employee hesitates to leave because he may forfeit certain pension and other rights.

Nevertheless, even in this era of automation, huge corporations, and powerful unions, progress appears to depend, in no small degree, upon individuals who have the courage to think new thoughts and to do things in a new and very different manner. This is true, not only in domestic affairs, such as politics, business, and educational institutions, but also in foreign affairs. In this dynamic epoch, a fresh outlook upon our relations with other nations is imperative. Men and women are needed with ideas geared to the new, strange, and rapidly changing world—individuals who are not afraid to challenge orthodox points of view.

Now is definitely a time for leadership which can draw Americans away from the worship of low, long, and high-powered automobiles, of comfort, and of a very short working week—from abject conformity to group patterns. Even though Americans are living in Patten's "pleasure economy" or in Galbraith's "affluent society," our leaders should demand efficient personal service from each and every person as well as devotion to the nation's and to humanity's welfare.

The growing size and the economic and political strength of large corporations and of big labor organizations necessitate a new survey of the role of government in order to preserve the essentials of a democratic form of government and of the "free enterprise" system. As the economy becomes more and more complex and interrelated and as the tempo of change becomes more rapid, the necessity for additional central direction becomes clear. One of the major difficulties in Communist Russia appears to be the increase in the hierarchy of officials, supervisors, accountants, bookkeepers, and secretaries. More effort is spent in "nonproductive labor" than in the countries of the "free world." Communism and other forms of highly centralized and autocratic control are extreme examples of compact centralized social organization in which the individual is reduced nearly to zero.

While the federal government of the United States is not as autocratic as that in a Communist or Fascist state, it has been growing in power over the local and state authorities and over the individual citizens. Since I was a boy, governmental interference with individuals and groups has multiplied; heavy taxation, central control over transportation, manufacture, and sale of products, and social security are examples.

In 1959, ownership of stock in a big corporation is far different from ownership of a farm or of a small business in 1890. My grandfather owned his large farm and made business decisions; no business executives or governmental officials told him what to do, such as how many acres he could plant. His direct taxes were local and state. He did not pay an income tax. His grandchildren and great grandchildren are employees.

Some of them own their homes and may own a few shares of stock in corporations, but their only functions in connection with their part ownership in corporate industry is to sign proxies and draw dividends, if declared.

Employees are obliged to conform to group requirements—corporate loyalty, union loyalty, and community customs and habits. It may also be pointed out that pension funds, insurance companies, investment trusts, and special trust funds own large blocks of corporate securities, still further modifying the control of corporations. Grandfather was an individualist. His grandchildren and great-grandchildren are almost inevitably conformists. If one of these deviates from the specific expectations of his corporate employer, his union, or his neighborhood, he will become a lonely individual.

When an instrumentality, whether a corporation or a labor organization, becomes powerful, very powerful—under the American Constitution, it should be subjected to governmental control and regulation, whether it be the Pennsylvania Railway or the Teamsters' Union, whether it be an insurance company or a huge pension fund.

For the welfare of the human race, it is far more important that humans learn how to live in peace without mass violence than it is to be able to land men on Mars or the Moon. Space ships may be very desirable, but the easing of world tensions between groups is today of major importance to mankind. As well as launching more and bigger satellites or exploring Mars, men and women of this sphere, called Earth, should be diligently and intelligently seeking the betterment of its inhabitants, individually and collectively. The old slogan of "make the world safe for democracy" should give place, in the words of General Omar Bradley, to that of "making the world safe for living." Devoted men and women are essential to transform such a slogan into a living reality.

Living in an era of rapid transportation and communication, men and women begin timidly to grasp the idea of a world group, including all peoples and all nations. When the welfare of this group becomes an important goal of mankind, we may hope for world peace and prosperity. If more of the world's brain power had been devoted in recent years to such programs, mankind might not be in grave danger of destruction. Basic research in human relations is now important. In the hysterical demand for scientists and engineers, the realms which alone may make for world peace may be overlooked.

In the near future, world peace may depend upon the establishment of a world group or a federation with the power to control recalcitrant nations and able to bring law and order into what is now called international relations. How sufficient strength may be given to a world federation without unduly dominating local and national groups, and also individuals, is a vital and urgent problem. As far as can now be seen, this world group or federation would be the ultimate in organized communities, unless there is finally needed a universe group or federation.

The organization of a world federation with a reasonable degree of stability will doubtless be delayed until the great differences in economic conditions and political outlooks are in some degree reduced. And such reduction will require earnest endeavors on the part of leading nations of the free world. Of course, no attempt should be made to mold all to the pattern of the present free world. Sincere endeavors should be the order of the day to bring about mutual understanding and to minimize extreme unlikeness and intolerance.

The radio and the airplane have made distant peoples neighbors in the physical sense, but little advance has been made in understanding and sympathy between these new neighbors. The times call for a universal language, a common monetary unit, and generally accepted units of measurement. The history and problems of different national, racial, and religious groups might well be studied in all colleges and universities. If men and women knew more about the new neighbors that technological advance has given them, mutual understanding and sympathy would normally follow. After looking at modern means of warfare, a world federation and an approach to the brotherhood of man appear to be essential for human survival on this shrinking globe.

CONFORMITY AND THE MIDDLE CLASS

MARVIN E. WOLFGANG
University of Pennsylvania

American writers of fiction, essay, and drama have long decried the middle class in our society, but especially since the last war has this numerically massive segment of our population been the subject of constant ridicule. The style of living, reading habits, consumption of household items, child-rearing practices, and the rituals of family living have been under unwarranted attack. The bourgeoisie, we are told, is a powerful force molding men to a similar pattern of conformity; yet few voices from this unfortunate group have risen above the increasing clamor of derision. It is time, therefore, to re-examine this middle class in order to see whether the prevailing sentiments of the intellectual literati are valid and to determine whether there are any middle-class virtues worth retaining.

It has become a standard cocktail joke to deride a particular form of behavior as "*so* bourgeois" or "decidedly middle class." So widespread is this type of phraseology that even the "decidedly middle class" has used it and has sought increasing but marginal differentiation in the consumption of goods (as David Riesman points out) in order to escape the heavy weight of conforming to patterned expectations of style, behavior, and furniture.

For decades literacy attacks have been made on what is referred to as the stolid, dull, conformistic mediocrity of the middle class. The justifiable concern of Sinclair Lewis with Babbitt only revived the general stream of essays deploring Philistinism and the inflexible reactionary. The *Death of A Salesman* by Miller and *The Organization Man* by Whyte point to the dangers of becoming a rutted, routinized conformist in industrial and other types of bureaucracies. But in the past few years there has been a *mentis gratissimus* error in the expansion and extension of these valid pronouncements of writers like Miller, Riesman, Whyte, *et al.*, for the entire middle class has become a label of conformity, a symbol of the Unimaginative Man. So far has this derision gone that recently Peter Viereck made a plea for the Unadjusted Man and invites us to escape from the mold of the masses.

How far we have come from the thirties and forties when the chief goal of psychological training was Adjustment—always with a capital A! Perhaps our adjustment to the collective group has indeed become extreme, but these are relative judgments and may be found among the luxuries permitted to a prosperous nation not at war. Fighting against the fears of mass unemployment and fear itself during the thirties, and then against totalitarian aggression during the forties required a degree of social consciousness, *esprit de corps*, and acceptance of prescribed institutionalized roles of thought and action such as our nation had never before witnessed. The present cold war does not present an immediate, direct threat. There have been suggestions that for the remainder of this century our tense international relations will be suspended between the idealized peace held in 1945 and the speculated total destruction of another war. Under these circumstances there is less pressure than during national emergencies to conform to a national pattern, and we can enjoy the democratic luxury of self-criticism which views conformity with alarm.

But blind conformity should not be confused with belonging to the middle class. Adherence to middle class values is not the same as "over-adjustment," Philistinism, or mediocrity. Yet it is this kind of association between the middle class and the common criticisms about the organization man and the lonely crowd that is unwarrantedly made by an increasingly abundant number of people who seek variegated ways to "express their individuality" and to "escape the middle-class mold." My chief contentions, therefore, are, first, that identifying unimaginative conformity with the middle class is an error of association of ideas, a lack of proper perception; and, second, that the middle class with its system of values constitutes the basic framework of our harmoniously functioning society.

Excessive conformity to cultural expectations has been a phenomenon common to almost every major historical period through which Western civilization has passed. Toynbee speaks of the development of the Universal State as a symptom of civilizational decay, and of the need for a new or revived challenge to stimulate appropriate response. In the past, whenever similar expectations of behavior became excessively universal and the institutional demands for conformity too oppressive for the creative, dynamic individual, some one or some group always appeared on the cultural scene and was able to break through, to produce a revolution of thought or action. Shakespeare revolutionized the form of drama and theater. Cimabue and Giotto broke through the formal stylization of medieval art. So deeply embedded in astronomic and religious thought was the Ptolemaic conception of the universe that Copernicus and Galileo were revolutionaries of their time. Guido d'Arezzo, like Plato's philosopher bringing us out of the cave into sunlight, led us beyond the monochromatic scale into a polyphony of unlimited variation. In religion, architecture, law, and many other similar fields where cultural change occurred, the geniuses of history have deviated from the demands to conform when an institutional trait reached classic perfection of form and style, or when the requirements to conform became unbearable to the renascent spirit of man. Nonconformity of this type has always been an active, positive force—a voice of dignity and reason. Not always among the instances in which a few men revolutionized a style can it be claimed that the old form was something necessarily to be discarded. There is much delight derived from the classic Greek drama, the Gregorian chant, Gothic architecture, and from forms of art, thought, and behavioral expectations of earlier periods in our history. The old is not always totally displaced by the new.

Deviation, then, almost by definition appears to arise out of excessive conformity in a culture. Deviation that endures and becomes a pattern has been productive and pragmatically successful. Quacks, quirks, and phrenetic fringes have always been with us, and the heroes of history may have been labeled horrible heretics at the time of their innovations, but each was promulgating a positive thought or action based upon the virtuous elements of the traditions from which they sprang. When a religious, political, or other social innovator stepped out of the bounds of rigid conformity, he was pushed by the tyranny of the institution whose demands were too oppressive and pulled by the dynamic quality of the human spirit.

Perhaps it is true that one of the major battles man faces today is that of increasing depersonalization and mechanization, of trends toward centralization and overadjustment. These may be valid assertions; but, when we are told that it is the "middle-class morality that places chains of restrictions on individuality," that it is the "stultifying middle class" that is responsible for these social ills, and that "the pressure to conform is a middle-class phenomenon," then an unjustifiable connection is made between some real dangers in contemporary society and a social class that happens to be numerically the largest. Although bureaucracy may sometimes be an efficient means of organizational functioning, the resulting personality-damaging aspects of it that have been under attack should not be associated with the meaning given to the middle class nor the prevailing middle-class system of values. The creative, autonomous individual who is universally admired appears on all levels of the social class structure, and neither intellectuality nor intelligence owes allegiance to any particular class.

There are certain forms of middle-class behavior and thought that are most often derided. The delusions of happiness that are used to cover deep-seated, seething discontent and frustrations *do* undoubtedly occur among many middle-class families. The poignancy and directness of *Death of A Salesman* make this play one of the most important in the modern theater. There is perhaps a certain amount of drudgery and dull routine in which a middle-class Sisyphus daily participates. C. Wright Mills has portrayed many white-collar workers in this way. But it is presumptuous speculation to contend that the majority of the middle class is unhappy, despairing, confused, and drab. There is just as much evidence to propose an opposite contention. Furthermore, it may be that some social analysts who emphasize the despairing nature of the middle class project their own psyche into the life situations of the group they analyze and that they imagine how they (the writers) would respond as a typical white-collar worker in an executive job in American business.

Because the average American middle-class male goes to work every morning on the 8:02, sits at the same desk every day, works and lunches with the same office corps, is met on the 5:45 by his middle-class wife and preschool child in middle-class suburbia, it does not follow that he is bulging with frustrations and is following a life that leads nowhere. The bare outline of a daily routine fails to indicate the many pleasures that may be had at work, with associates, and within the family circle. What if he is one of thousands of similar commuters living in a housing development and has a middle-class automobile and two or three typically middle-class kids? The fact that he is doing some productive work, that he supports a family, that he is capable of providing decent clothing, shelter, and affection for his children should be viewed as more than a patterned mold of conformity. Moreover, this pattern may be a pattern simply *because* it provides an ease of living, harmony, and comfort that previous generations of strivers sought and failed to attain.

This middle-class male, his wife, and children may in fact be quite happy and do not seek more than marginal differentiation because of their contentment. Perhaps it is a life of some mediocrity for many, but there is merit in an abundance of middle-class mediocrity. (Webster defines *mediocre* as moderate excellence.) We are not, nor can we all be, geniuses, leaders, or President. Our open-class society permits sufficient striving and leaves open the door to leadership and achievement without causing mass anxiety about the inability to rise among the leading few. Only under the totalitarian restraints of a tyrannical set of conduct norms is the individual forced to seek refuge entirely outside the group. Within a democratic framework and an open-class society, there is adequate opportunity for flexibility and variation as well as for social mobility. If some kind of generalized conformity exists within this framework, perhaps it is not so horrendous or oppressive as is often suggested. If it were, the underyling strength that historically gave rise to the middle class would rescue the group.

There are basic values in American culture that find roots in the Judeo-Christian tradition, that were incorporated into the spirit of the Italian Renaissance and the Protestant Ethic, nepotized in the French and American revolutions. English common law borne by the colonial forefathers was part of the American rising middle-class structure. Norms of conduct stemming from these sources have produced the predominant value system in our society—and this is a middle-class value system.

There are semantic and other problems involved in any attempt to identify empirically the middle class, but included among middle-class norms is the ethic of rationality, forethought, planning. Emphasis is placed on respect for property and for the dignity of the person, which implies self-control and control of physical violence and aggression. The qualities of industry and thrift, of economic and occupational skills, of individual responsibility, resourcefulness, and self-reliance are considered admirable in themselves. Ambition, or the desire to "get ahead," has grown side by side with the striving middle class. The students of social class have detailed these middle-class values and have analyzed their relationship to a variety of economic and political aspects of American society. These norms constitute a value system that may not be the best of all possible worlds; they may be ideals imperfectly performed in reality. Whether they are proper norms is a dilemma for the absolutist. That they have provided a workable and harmoniously functioning society capable of withstanding onslaughts from without and weaknesses from within, history can record.

Conformity to this value system may, in this light, be desirable. The middle class has an ontological stability sufficiently tested and secure, composed of lasting values shared by most creative individuals and groups. These are not ephemeral values of the moment crying for attention and making demands for conformity to a less flexible set of norms.

William Graham Sumner long ago pointed out that one can no more escape from the mores than he can from the laws of gravity. To divorce oneself from the prevailing mores simply means withdrawal into another set of mores. The middle-class mores have survived dynamic social change and have moved forward harmoniously with developments in the arts, science, and literature because one of the virtues of the middle-class value system is that it permits a wide range of behavior and attitude, including opportunities for innovation and change *within* the system.

What are the alternatives to this value system? The cult of the Beat and Angry men? As a way of life for a total society this kind of nihilism and vacuous negativism (which the middle class can tolerate quite easily) would result in mass nonproductive disorder. Some forms of Bohemian life are subcultural delights that provide refreshing vitality and constitute an expression of the alliance between the middle class and social and political freedom. It is interesting, however, how diffusive the prevailing middle-class value system is among many contemporary Bohemians and lesser sorts of deviants.

Another alternative, of course, is legal nonconformity—abrogation of middle-class norms that have been codified into law. Delinquency, crime, drug addiction, etc., certainly are deviations. The abiding interest the middle class has in literature, the cinema, and television that dwell on the themes of detective mysteries, crime and violence, indicates that the populace enjoys taking vicarious excursions into this type of nonconformity. We may smile at the vicariousness and economically profit from it; yet we are appalled at overt manifestations of this kind of nonconformity. When the delinquent or criminal is taken into custody, even the most ardent attackers of the "decidedly middle class" agree to the principle of reformation or rehabilitation. We seek to help the offender to adjust and to conform. And to what should he adjust? According to which set of values is he being reformed? We want him to conform to what kind of social expectations? Check the list of middle-class norms again and the answers are obvious. The reason society seeks to mold, to reform the delinquent and the criminal to this pattern is not only that it is the predominant pattern in American culture; it is also the pattern most likely to produce an integrated and socially useful human being.

The fight for individuality, personal differentiation, and the private life is a universal struggle. The genetic uniqueness of each individual and the wide range for personality development provided through middle-class values offer a continuity of optimism rather than despair. Conformity to this productive set of norms that results in social harmony and strength may be viewed as a virtue. Should the strictures toward conformity become too great or too rigid, the amorphous, unorganized, and flexible nature of the American middle class is such that it can permit changes to occur within the framework of the value system it supports.

RACE REACTIONS BY SEXES

EMORY S. BOGARDUS
University of Southern California

This paper deals with the question: Do men and women react in the same ways to given racial and cultural groups? The data which serve as a basis for discussing this question are found in the race relations study that was made by the writer in 1956 of a sample of 2,053 men and women from 33 different areas in the United States, ranging chiefly between the ages of 18 and 35 and divided about equally between college students and college graduates, most of whom were employed but taking one or more courses of advanced study.

The results of that study have been reported in part in a paper in which comparisons were made of the racial reactions of these persons with the reactions of similar persons in 1926 and in 1946 to a similar list of thirty selected racial groups, as that term is generally used by the public.[1]

In the 1956 study the racial reactions of 2,053 respondents have been broken down in a number of ways. One of these is described in these pages; namely, a division of the total number of participants was made in terms of the two sexes. Another reclassification was carried out in terms of the racial reactions of the subjects according to four main regions of the United States in which they lived. This report deals only with the findings when the breakdown by sexes is considered.

The 2,053 subjects in the 1956 study included 1,005 men and 1,048 women. The division is nearly equal in number, and the other factors are similar for both groups. That is to say, the men and women had similar amounts of education, they were nearly the same ages, and they came from the same localities in the United States. Their religious representation was similar, their economic status was similar, and their cultural backgrounds were similar. The main difference between the two classifications was sex, and hence the data have been tabulated so as to determine if any difference may be found between their racial reactions to the same list of thirty racial groupings.

When the racial distance reactions of the 1,005 men and the 1,048 women were compared, it was found that with one exception these re-

---

[1] "Racial Distance Changes in the United States During the Past Thirty Years," *Sociology and Social Research*, 43:127-35.

actions were higher for women than for men, signifying the expression of a greater distance toward 29 of the 30 races that were listed. The one exception was the reaction to the "Americans (U.S. white)," in which case the racial distance scores for the two sexes were the same, 1.08. In the reactions to the other 29 racial groups, the scores of the women ranged from 2 to 47 points higher. The arithmetic mean of the reactions of the 2,053 men and women considered as a unit was 2.07, of the 1,005 men considered by themselves was 1.97 and of the 1,048 women, 2.17. The reactions of the women represented about 20 points (19.8) more distance than did reactions of the men. However, the reactions of the women were not uniformly higher toward the different twenty-nine races. Toward 15 races the reactions of the women represented less than 20 points and toward 14 other races the reactions of the women represented more than 20 points of distance. With two exceptions the less-than-20 points difference in the scores were in the nearness half of the racial distance reactions. These exceptions were the Poles and Greeks. The greater-than-20 points difference in the racial reactions of the men and women was in the farness half of the racial distance scores, with three exceptions—the Jews, Armenians, and Negroes. The most significant exception is the low amount of difference in the scores of the men and the women toward Negroes.

The least difference between the reactions of the men and the women toward the 29 races was expressed toward the English and the Finns (2 points); French, 5 points; Irish, 7 points; Canadians and Swedish, 9 points; and Negroes, 10 points. The greatest difference in these reactions of the men and women was expressed toward the Koreans, 24 points; Japanese and Russians, 47 points each.

The question arises as to why the racial distance reactions of the women are greater than those of the men. This question cannot be answered finally here. Ordinary types of interviewing and data obtained from questionnaires will not suffice. Individuals cannot tell offhand in many instances why they react racially the way they do. Some do not know why. Some give a superficial answer, referring to the most recent striking racial experience that they have had. Few go back to conditioning experiences which throw light on why they have reacted in given ways to specific racial contacts. It is evident that in this field some form of depth interviewing is needed in order that the most important explanatory factors may be uncovered.

The interview data at hand, although inadequate, suggest four hypotheses that may be tested by further research. (1) The greater racial distance expressed by women than by men may be accounted for in part on the ground that men have more racial contacts than women have. (2) Men have more racial information, by virtue of these contacts, than do women. (3) Men meet members of other races more often in a business way than do women, while women meet other racial members in the more personal ways. (4) Custom and public opinion put more restraint on women than on men in meeting individuals of other races.

TABLE 1

RACIAL REACTIONS BY SEXES (Total N 2053)

Races	Of 2,053 Men and Women	Of 1,005 Men	Of 1,048 Women	Differences in Scores
Toward				
1. Americans (U.S.white)	1.08	1.08	1.08	.00
2. Canadians	1.16	1.12	1.21	.09
3. English	1.23	1.22	1.24	.02
4. French	1.47	1.44	1.49	.05
5. Irish	1.56	1.52	1.59	.07
6. Swedish	1.57	1.52	1.61	.09
7. Scots	1.60	1.52	1.68	.16
8. Germans	1.61	1.53	1.68	.15
9. Hollanders	1.63	1.54	1.71	.17
10. Norwegians	1.66	1.59	1.74	.15
11. Finns	1.80	1.79	1.81	.02
12. Italians	1.89	1.83	1.94	.11
13. Poles	2.07	1.92	2.20	.28
14. Spanish	2.08	2.01	2.14	.13
15. Greeks	2.09	1.98	2.19	.21
16. Jews	2.15	2.07	2.23	.16
17. Czechs	2.22	2.00	2.45	.45
18. Armenians	2.33	2.26	2.46	.14
19. Japanese Americans	2.34	2.21	2.47	.26
20. Indians, American	2.35	2.23	2.47	.24
21. Filipinos	2.46	2.34	2.58	.24
22. Mexican Americans	2.51	2.29	2.72	.43
23. Turks	2.56	2.37	2.75	.37
24. Russians	2.62	2.40	2.92	.52
25. Chinese	2.68	2.50	2.79	.29
26. Japanese	2.70	2.47	2.94	.47
27. Negroes	2.74	2.68	2.78	.10
28. Mexicans	2.79	2.65	2.91	.27
29. Indians from India	2.80	2.69	2.90	.21
30. Koreans	2.83	2.65	2.99	.34
Arithmetic means of 61,590 racial reactions	2.08	1.98	2.18	.20

PACIFIC SOCIOLOGICAL NEWS NOTES

Pacific Sociological Society. The 1960 annual meeting of the Pacific Sociological Society will be in Spokane under the joint sponsorship of Washington State University and the University of Idaho. President Donald Cressey has asked that a committee consisting of Leo Reeder of the UCLA Medical School and Edward McDonagh of SC assist him in screening the submitted papers for the Spokane meeting.

University of California, Berkeley. Professor Herbert Blumer returns to the Department from Brazil, where he has been serving as a research consultant to the center newly established there by UNESCO. Beginning July 1, 1959, he takes up his new part-time duties as director of the Institute of Social Science at Berkeley. Hanan Selvin will take part in an S.S.R.C. Summer Seminar on Peer Group Culture and Adolescence at Ann Arbor, Michigan. Seymour Lipset is teaching at the Salzburg Seminar in American Studies during June and July. William Petersen, associate professor of sociology at the University of Colorado, has been appointed associate professor in the department. Robert Alford and Inge Powell have been appointed lecturers for 1959-60. William O. Nicholls, now lecturer in sociology at Columbia University, has been appointed as an instructor. Philip Selznick has been appointed as vice-chairman of the department for 1959-60 succeeding Kingsley Davis.

University of Southern California. Dr. Thomas Ely Lasswell, professor of sociology, Grinnell College, has joined the department as an associate professor of sociology. Dr. Lasswell will continue to specialize in community stratification studies and assume some of the editorial responsibilities of *Sociology and Social Research.* Drs. Georges Sabagh and Maurice D. Van Arsdol, Jr., have received a substantial grant from the National Science Foundation to study the "Demographic Factors in the Growth of Urban Subareas." Dr. Harvey J. Locke returns to the department after a sabbatical leave. Dr. Bessie A. McClenahan, emeritus professor of sociology, received the Alumni Distinctive Service Award from Drake University on May 7. For a period of twenty-five years Dr. McClenahan served the Department of Sociology. The following graduate students passed their qualifying examinations for the Ph.D. degree: Harold Hubbard, Harold Nelson, Issis Istiphan, and Richard Udry. Three advanced graduate students received the doctorate in sociology: Abraham Rosenblum, Rabbi, Verdugo Hills Hebrew Temple; Alexander P. Runciman, Staff Director at KNXT, Columbia Broadcasting System; and Merle E. Fish, Jr., Director of Development, School of Religion, Columbia, Missouri.

Whittier College. Professor John Burma of Grinnell College is visiting summer professor of sociology. Professor Jerome Patton is in charge of the first group of Whittier College students living abroad with headquarters at the University of Copenhagen, Denmark. Robert O'Brien will spend the coming year in England as an exchange professor. Professor Lee M. Brooks of the University of North Carolina rejoins the Whittier College sociology staff.

PEOPLES AND CULTURE

THE WAIST-HIGH CULTURE. By Thomas Griffith. New York: Harper and Brothers, 1959, pp. vii+275.

The first third of the book is autobiographical; the remainder deals with a large variety of foreign and domestic issues including the American image at home and abroad.

Griffith describes his early life in a boardinghouse for children in Seattle, his paper-carrying days, and his adolescent experiences. As a youth he was a University of Washington student, New Dealer, idealist, and critic. He now wonders "whether some of that idealism with which I credited myself and fellow sword-bearers in that anonymous army got lost or was never really there." Much of his story is of course unique, but the broader setting is one common to a generation. The author's work as Foreign News Editor of *Time* has given him an unusual opportunity to analyze foreign affairs and American policy. This discussion makes up the second part of the book. A chapter title "Making Allies and Losing Friends" gives a cue to the critical tone of the analysis.

The third section, devoted to the American situation, is somewhat more sociological, if, some may think, less astute in analysis. Griffith is rightly concerned with the problems of mass culture. "Waist-high" refers to a culture that exalts the middle—the widest audience, the biggest market, the average man. The results are that "We are being done in by irrelevancies, levelled by palaver and coated with sham." He deplores ". . . the false leveling of equality in American life," and thinks that democracy is suspicious of high standards and may be inherently hostile to the "first rate." Griffith recognizes the existence of an economic elite that is "the most powerful element in the community." The elite, however, is not behaving as an elite should. Some may read into this discussion a secret desire for a "proper" elite; however, this would not be completely fair to Griffith. The elite are very likely to behave just as he describes them.

A remarkable aspect of the book is that the author identifies himself with the society and with many of the trends which disturb him. He is a part of it and makes no attempt to withdraw from American life and look in on it from the outside or down on it from above, as is usually the case when academicians attempt such an analysis.

JOEL B. MONTAGUE
Washington State University

ANCESTORS AND IMMIGRANTS. By Barbara M. Solomon. Cambridge: Harvard University Press, 1956, pp. 276.

This work attempts to examine the attitudes of Boston Brahmins toward themselves in their local society from 1850 to 1920. The proper Bostonians by 1850 had developed a distinctive code of values governing their relations with both man and God. This code came to a severe test when the Irish immigration rate reached a high tide in 1880. Lowell purported that the Irish could never become true patriots to their adopted land. In retrospect it is strange to learn that James Russell Lowell believed that "men of English blood" had a hereditary instinct for democracy. Solomon traces the development of the Immigration Restrictive League, which became responsible for the passage of the nationality quotas in the 1921 and 1924 immigration laws. One of the favorable aspects of the immigration process seems to have been the gradual acceptance of each ethnic group after an initial period of criticism.

E.C.M.

THE STUDY OF POPULATION. An Inventory and an Appraisal. Edited by Philip M. Hauser and Otis Dudley Duncan. Chicago: The University of Chicago Press, 1959, pp. xvi+864.

This is indeed a formidable volume on demography—its nature, its elements, scope, methods, and relationships to ecology, geography, anthropology, genetics, economics, and sociology. Thirty-three essays contributed by top-flight men in the field, including the editors, form the substance of the book. For a long time, it will probably be the chief aid and encyclopedia for those who wish to consult an authoritative demographical source.

Beginning with a chapter entitled "Overview and Conclusions" by the editors, the four major divisions of the book deal with demography as a science, the development and current status of demography, the elements of demography, population studies in various disciplines. Hauser and Duncan, in preparing the agenda and plan for the contributors, suggested the following definition for guidance: "Demography is the study of the size, territorial distribution, and composition of population changes therein, and the components of such changes, which may be identified as natality, mortality, territorial movement (migration), and social mobility (change of status)." The essays have generally followed this definition, observing its limitations as outlined by the editors, who have noted that "demographic research is conducted within an explicit and coherent frame of reference."

An interesting phase of demography as a science is that "it is dependent for its data on observation and recording of events occurring in the external world rather than on experiments under more or less controlled conditions in the laboratory." It is subjected to the weakness of gathering reliable and complete data, since, aver the editors, only 80 per cent of the world's population was enumerated in some kind of census during the decade between 1945 and 1954. For students interested in theory, there are some excellent notes on it under the caption of "Demographers' Conceptions of Theory" in the more general discussion of demography as a body of knowledge. Limitations of space ban an evaluation of the essays, but one may truly state that all are written expertly by experts.

M.J.V.

CITY LIFE IN JAPAN. A Study of a Tokyo Ward. By Donald P. Dore. University of California Press, 1958, pp. x+472.

This treatise is based on a social survey that was made in Japan in 1951. The author, an associate professor of Asian studies at the University of British Columbia, lived for several months in a Tokyo lower middle-class ward or precinct and collected his data primarily through the methods of participant observation and interviews.

In the early chapters of the study, Professor Dore describes the standards of living of the ward inhabitants. He includes a detailed description of their houses, family incomes, expenditures, and aspects of health and security. He depicts the means by which the people of this section of Tokyo accommodate their daily lives to different levels of income, what they look forward to, and what they fear.

Later chapters examine the family system, political attitudes, education, leisure, neighborhood groups, religion, and morality. The author shows that there have been changes in the modes of living and attitudes which have been brought about in part by the technological process and in part by the impact of Western influences. Throughout, Professor

Dore attempts to compare modern urban Japan both with the old culture of feudal Japan and with Western industrial societies, and to analyze the process of social change.

To the reviewer, the book seems to lack integration and it is somewhat lacking in structuralized research design, theoretical orientation, and conceptual scheme. On the other hand, the author does formulate hypotheses and test them, and he refrains from making unwarranted generalizations.

Despite the weaknesses mentioned above, this volume is an excellent and highly readable work. It contains a wealth of facts and information relating to the transition experienced in the life of the ordinary Japanese city-dweller. The book is a must for those who have a combined interest in the social sciences and the Far East.

I. ROGER YOSHINO
University of Arizona

ANALIS SOCIO-ECONOMICO DEL BARRIO "SAGRADA FAMILIA." By Sakari Sariola. San Jose, Costa Rica: Escuela Superior de Administracion Publica America Central, Universidad de Costa Rica, 1958, pp. 106.

The study represents a detailed analysis of a lower-class suburb of San Jose, the capital and largest city of Costa Rica. The work is a research project of an advanced university class. The graphs, statistical data, and some typical case material present an interesting picture of a rapidly changing Central American urbanized area. There are data and discussions on a variety of problems: rural-urban migration, unemployment, housing, inflation, alcoholism, and certain other tension areas. Social, political, and religious participation, as well as some of the details of family structure and behavior, receive attention.

In view of the nonempirical heritage of much of Latin-American sociology, it is refreshing to see the excellent statistical analyses (even though the chi-squares on class and rural-urban differences approached the obvious). As one who has been involved in a recent community study in Central America, the present previewer had some doubts about the validity of the interviewees' responses. Methodologically, however, the volume testifies to advanced knowledge on ecological and other techniques. On the whole, the author and his students should be congratulated for the fine organization and the inclusion of adequate tables, graphs, bibliography, and appendices. In addition, the findings are neatly summarized at the end of the book.

ROBERT C. WILLIAMSON
Los Angeles City College

VOTING-BEHAVIOR IN AN INDIAN VILLAGE. By A. H. Somjee. Baroda, India: M. S. University of Baroda, 1959, pp. 64.

In this interesting and important study special attention is given to interview methods in social situations where reliable and "objective" interviewing is very difficult. The theme is the significance of "vote-intention," or what in the United States would be called political polling. The author carefully examined the vote-intention of a voter in a given village (Gujarat) of 8,000 population near Bombay "against his social, economic, and religious background." His approach is that of both a political scientist and a social psychologist. His tool for gathering data is what may be called an interview-questionnaire. It was found, for instance, that "the economic factor considerably influenced the voting-behavior" in all occupations. A small minority were influenced chiefly by the urging of leaders. The influence of caste and religious sentiment "was considerable" but not "universally present." E.S.B.

SOCIAL PROBLEMS AND WELFARE

ESSAYS ON THE WELFARE STATE. By Richard M. Titmuss. New Haven: Yale University Press, 1959, pp. 282.

This book consists of ten lectures given at different times. Most of them dealt with conditions in Great Britain. The present distribution of social and economic rewards is out of balance with the pattern of needs. More of the national income goes to those without dependent children. Part of the confusion in Britain's social policy is due to the fact that some services are classed as social service while others of equal importance are not. Private old-age pensions are increasing and tend to divide the population into distinct groups based on contrasting social service programs.

The remarkable decrease in birth rates during the last fifty years has released women for other services than childbearing. The gradual emancipation of women has brought about intellectual and temperamental compatibilty between partners. It has also enabled women to achieve an independent life through the opening of work opportunities for all. One chapter deals with the anachronism found in the attitude of many doctors and nurses toward the hospital patients—a fact reminiscent of the conditions found in the hospitals by Florence Nightingale a century earlier. The National Health Service has been of social value in England to patients and doctors alike in spite of the propaganda launched against it by medical associations.

The author outlines the varieties of medical, hospital, and dental care provided. The principle of free access to medical care had to be somewhat limited. There is practical freedom to choose or change one's doctor. Specialization has widened the distance between the general practitioner and the specialist—a condition that has produced considerable anxiety. Scientific medicine has undermined personal and individual authoritarianism in medicine. Increasing intelligence among the people results in a greater recourse to preventive methods.

An appendix yields evidence on the quantity and quality of general practitioners' work. Another lists important references covering the years from 1904 to the present time. G.B.M.

FOUNDATIONS OF THE RESPONSIBLE SOCIETY. A Comprehensive Survey of Christian Social Ethics. By Walter G. Muelder. New York: Abingdon Press, 1959, pp. 304.

The materials for this book have come in the main from the pronouncements on social ethics by ecumenical and other church bodies, the teaching of Jesus, and the author's own analyses. Dean Muelder reports that he is writing "at the intersectional points of theological, philosophical and social science disciplines," and that his concern is for "emergent coherence."

The importance of mankind as constituting one world community is emphasized throughout the treatise. In the main chapters, certain basic "institutions of culture" are discussed, namely, the family and educational, political, economic, and religious institutions. The concluding chapters are entitled "Social Welfare and Church-State Relations" and "Responsible World Community."

The author effectively applies Christian ethics to important aspects of social life and institutions. Additional themes that might have received attention relate to the uses of leisure time and the extensive development of consumer, producer, credit union, housing, and health cooperatives in the United States today. The discussions throughout the book are fair minded, incisive, and thought arousing regarding the responsibilities of individuals for building a just social order and a world community.

E.S.B.

UNDERSTANDING AND PREVENTING JUVENILE DELINQUENCY. By Haskell M. Miller. New York and Nashville: Abingdon Press, 1958, pp. ix+190.

This book is intended as a practical resource book for individuals, church, family, and community. As such, it fulfills its function very well. The particular interest is what the churches can do to help prevent delinquency. To present the material objectively, the author discusses what delinquency is, how many delinquents there are, why be concerned about the problem, the available research data on the subject, and what can be done by parents, churches, and community agencies to prevent the spread of delinquency. A wide range of sources were consulted and the material is presented concisely and accurately, recognizing that the data on the subject are limited and that more research is needed to ascertain the full extent, causes, and difficulties of the problem. M.H.N.

TOWARD BETTER UNDERSTANDING OF THE AGING. New York: Council on Social Work Education, 1959, pp. 127.

This document gives a report on the "Seminar on the Aging," held in Aspen, Colorado, 1958. In addition to the Introduction by Katherine A. Kendall, associate director of the Council, a summary of discussion reports, and a bibliography, there are eight papers that treat of topics such as Aging in Modern Society, Emotional Functioning of Older People, Economic Functioning of Older People, and Some Sociological Research Findings About Older People (by Ethel Shanas and Ol A. Randall). Dr. Shanas, for instance, concludes her paper, perhaps the best of the group, with the assertion that the needs of older people are the needs of all people: economic security, something to do, a place to live, and a sense of physical and emotional well-being. The last term, emotional well-being, may be the most important of all. E.S.B.

RELATIONS HUMAINES ET RELATIONS INDUSTRIELLES. By Marcel Bolle De Bal. Brussels, Belgium: Institut de Sociologie Solvay, 1958, pp. vi+146.

The Belgian sociologist De Bal attempts in this volume to clarify two complex fields, namely, human relations and industrial relations. Apparently his work grew out of his dissatisfactions with the unclear thinking of certain publications in these areas. More specifically, the problem is one of introducing human relations to a society noted for industrial conflict.

The first section of the book treats some of the definitions basic to the field and reviews the history of industrial sociology from Taylorism to the Western Electric studies, along with the contributions of sociometry and group dynamics. Some recent European developments are also mentioned.

The second section turns to the problem of how various industrial relations programs can be accepted in a country like Belgium with its European tradition of class conflict. The basic question appears to be the inability to reconcile differences between the unions and the employers about the status and purposes of human relations. The problem of structuring goals and values in view of some of the limitations and barriers occupies the last section of the book. The author pays particular attention to the role of the sociologist in helping to solve some of the impasses.

Naturally, the brevity of the work can permit only a limited discussion of the literature of the field. However, it is surprising that certain authorities, like Caplow, Dubin, Moore, and Whyte, are given so little attention, while some relatively minor contributions are heavily stressed. Still, the book presents some significant perspectives and ends with an impressive bibliography of both European and American sources.

ROBERT C. WILLIAMSON
Los Angeles City College

STANDARDS AND GUIDES FOR THE DETENTION OF CHILDREN AND YOUTH. New York: National Probation and Parole Association, 1958, pp. 142.

This report, prepared by the Advisory Committee on Detention and Shelter Care of Children and Youth, sets forth standards and guides for the controlling of admissions, detention care, planning and building of detention homes and facilities, and plans for regional detention. The cardinal concepts of detention are defined. Even though this booklet is not intended as a blueprint to be followed rigidly, it is one of the most carefully planned guides of detention care for the children in physically restricted facilities pending court disposition or transfer to another jurisdiction or agency, especially for the 100,000 children from seven to seventeen years of age inclusive who are now held in jails and jaillike places of detention.

THE PROBLEM OF DELINQUENCY. By Sheldon Glueck, Editor. Boston: Houghton Mifflin Company, 1959, pp. xxx+1183.

This book of readings, together with the introductions to the various chapters by the editor, is one of the most extensive assemblies of materials of juvenile delinquency yet compiled in one volume. Altogether, 186 articles are included, and each of the chapters is prefaced by an introductory note in which the various articles are briefly summarized and evaluated. The book is divided into four parts: Part One, Incidence and Causation; Part Two, The Juvenile Court and the Law; Part Three, Treatment; and Part Four, Prevention of Delinquency.

The materials are admittedly eclectic in respect to the causes, treatment, and prevention of delinquency, with considerable emphasis being placed on the legal problems involved in society's effort to cope with the problem of maladjusted individuals. The editor is highly critical of writers who "stake out a claim" for a particular discipline. Even though he recognizes that psychiatrists have made exaggerated claims for the role of psychiatry in the understanding and treatment of delinquency, it is his opinion that dynamic psychiatry offers the best hope of ascertaining and understanding the complex motivations of delinquent behavior. The causes of delinquency are admittedly multifarious, yet it is believed that "certain areas, techniques, and tests give special promise of yielding causal involvements: namely, anthropologic measurements and classifications, psychiatric interviews, the Rorschach test, the Wechsler-Bellevue test, investigation of the parent-child relationships, examination of the boys' school history, study of the neighborhood influences." As in the previous Glueck studies, which are extensively quoted, the major emphasis is on individual rather than environmental factors. While a rigid theoretical frame of reference is deliberately avoided, the editor expresses a point of view which underlies both the emphasis and the selection of materials. The section on the causes of delinquency is concluded with a special chapter on Theories of Delinquency Causation, in which an attempt is made to synthesize the individual and group versions of delinquent behavior.

The last three parts, which make up the main portion of the book (pp. 269-1147), constitute the most important contribution of the book to the understanding of delinquency. In these sections are fairly detailed descriptions of the history, philosophy, and organization of the juvenile court; the basic legal issues, the problems of detention, investigation, and sentencing; the types of disposition and treatment of cases, including various techniques of treatment; and the methods of prevention. Extensive documentary and concrete judicial cases are included. The legal aspects of the problem are ably presented. The discussions of prevention are somewhat limited, with emphasis on the necessity of recognizing potential delinquents and special means of prevention. The book brings together a great variety of materials, including articles, legal documents, and excerpts from books. M.H.N.

THE LAWYER AND THE SOCIAL WORKER, GUIDES TO COOPERATION. New York: Family Service Association of America, 1959, pp. 36.

In this report of a committee on "lawyer-family agency cooperation," the situation is recognized that many lawyers as well as many social workers "deplore a considerable antipathy which has long existed between the members of these professions." The committee undertook "to explore ways and means of improving the relations of these two professions." A major obstacle to interprofessional cooperation is given as a "lack of knowledge of each other's aims and skills, misunderstanding, and even indifference." It is projected that the solution to the problem may be found if each profession will expand its horizon and look beyond its own members "for help in solving society's problems." E.S.B.

ALICE SALOMON. DIE BEGRUENDERIN DES SOZIALEN FRAUENBERUFS IN DEUTSCHLAND. Ihr Leben und Ihr Werk. Edited by Hans Muthesius for the Deutsche Verein fuer oeffentliche und private Fuersorge. Cologne, Germany: Carl Heymanns Verlag KG, 1959, pp. 348.

The monograph contains four parts. The first is written by Dora Peyser and contains a detailed biography, according to which Miss Salomon spent the last eleven years of her life in "exile" in America, refusing to return to her native country, even though new tasks awaited her there. The second, third, and fourth parts are written by Carl Ludwig Krug von Nidda and present excerpts from Miss Salomon's writings (about social legislation, social insurance, the ethical fundamentals and goals of social welfare, structure of the family, etc.). The book includes a bibliography of 247 titles and a biographical index of individuals to whom Miss Salomon has made reference in her writings, from Adolf Hitler to Goethe to Florence Nightingale and back to Pope Gregory the Great. A wealth of source material, data, and historical and sociological resources are all combined in one volume.

HANS A. ILLING

THE WOMAN EXECUTIVE. By Margaret Cussler. New York: Harcourt, Brace & Company, 1958, pp. xxi+165.

In this study based on a selected sample of fifty-five women executives living in the Boston and Washington areas, interesting descriptions are given of the activities and personalities of top women executives and junior executives. The married woman executive as a class is considered to be in a more advantageous position than the unmarried one. Sometimes the woman executive rises to the top by "finding a sponsor." She has to overcome the tradition that top executives must be men. She succeeds by working hard and "by taking what comes." She must contend with "differences in salary, in rank, in responsibility, in opportunity, in security—differences usually based not on merit but on sex."

SOCIAL THEORY AND RESEARCH

SOCIAL MOBILITY AND CLASS STRUCTURE. By Gösta Carlsson. Lund, Sweden: C. W. K. Gleerup, 1958, pp. 198.

Professor Gösta Carlsson of the University of Lund has written a most insightful document on the nature of social mobility and its relationship to social stratification theory. Social mobility is defined as the change of occupational status between two or more generations. The empirical data examined in this work were selected largely from the excellent material available in the Swedish Central Bureau of Statistics. An intensive analysis is presented of the changes in status of fathers and their sons for a number of selected years from 1899 to 1923. It is found that white-collar workers increased in a substantial manner during these years. Farmers and farm workers declined sharply in Sweden as they have declined in the American economy. Over the years, state employees remained about the same, which may seem a bit strange for a country that has increased its government-supported welfare practices. No doubt, some of the professional workers are employed by quasi-government services, and this fact may tend to reduce the actual number of civil servants listed as state employees. Carlsson has developed a number of mathematical models that will command respect and attention by students of social stratification. In general, Carlsson has done a superb job of presenting his own data and of weaving into his monograph materials from other sources. This is a mature and scholarly piece of sociological research and writing.

E.C.M.

THE MAKING OF AN AMERICAN COMMUNITY. A Case Study of Democracy in a Frontier County. By Merle Curti. Stanford, California: Stanford University Press, 1959, pp. xii+483.

In *The Making of an American Community,* historians join the growing variety of scholars engaged in "community studies." Curti and his assistants have chosen Trempealeau County, Wisconsin, during the mid-nineteenth century to test the hypothesis that the ready accessibility of free or almost free land promoted economic equality and thence political equality. He concludes that this hypothesis, with some qualifications, is supported by the case chosen.

The data to test Curti's hypothesis were gathered not only by the traditional techniques of history but also by techniques which are more often associated with sociology and social anthropology. While the study is ex post facto by a century more or less, its procedures are in many ways comparable to those used in studies of contemporary communities. While interdisciplinary studies sometimes have a tendency to become *a*disciplinary when a work is constructed by many and meaningful to few, Curti never leaves any doubt about the fact that he is a historian engaged in historical research. *The Making of an American Community* is strictly a history book. However, Curti's approach to the study of history tends to bridge some of the gap between history and the other social sciences and to add to the fund of general information accessible and useful to all of the social science disciplines.

THOMAS ELY LASSWELL
Grinnell College

SYMPOSIA ON CHILD AND JUVENILE DELINQUENCY. Chaired and edited by Benjamin Karpman. Washington, D. C.: Psychodynamics Monograph Series, 1959, pp. 364.

This volume is a compilation of papers presented at the American Orthopsychiatric Association by fifteen contributors, together with the discussions by sixteen others and the comments and summaries by the editor. Nearly all of the contributors and discussants have M.D. degrees, and many of them are psychiatrists with responsible positions in hospitals, clinics, institutes, and medical schools. The five round tables dealt with "The Psychopathic Delinquent Child," "Psychopathic Behavior," "A Differential Study of Psychopathic Behavior in Infants and Children," "Psychodynamics of Child Delinquency," and "Basic Emotional Factors in Delinquency." The chairman, in opening the series of symposia, states that "there is no nosological condition in the entire field of psychiatry on which there is so little agreement, and which is subject to so much misunderstanding and equivocation, as that of psychopathy and psychopathic personality." Through the discussions the contributors and discussion leaders struggled with the definitions of these concepts, as well as with the concept "delinquency," especially as conceived of from the standpoint of psychiatry. One wonders why such terms as "psychopathy" and "psychopathic personality" are used at all. The concept "psychopathic delinquent" is a misnomer, a vague generality that is better known by what it is not than by any specific positive factor. However, the discussions and the concrete cases used in analyzing the various phases of the subject, and the illustrations by Wesley R. Wilkins, are apparently designed to clarify not only the conceptional framework but to throw light on the varied behavior phenomena involved in this type of behavior.

Most of the material deals with items of special interest to psychiatrists and psychoanalysts, but pathology in relationships within the family is quite frequently referred to and some attention is given to "delinquency founded primarily on social dislocation," as illustrated by the case of the App family. In the final symposium the participants come to grips with the matters of definition, characteristics, and types of delinquents, possible antecedents of delinquency in infancy and childhood, the atypical children, psychodynamics as related to delinquency, and how to deal with delinquency. M.H.N.

SOCIOLOGY AND THE MILITARY ESTABLISHMENT. By Morris Janowitz. New York: Russell Sage Foundation, 1959, pp. 112.

"This bulletin is the fourth in a series of bulletins, each dealing with a single area in which the sociologist is a practitioner or his work relevant to practice. . . . The intention," we are told in the Foreword by Dr. Leonard S. Cottrell, Jr., "is to stimulate the development of more adequate conceptions of the basic sociological problems presented by the United States military institution, its internal functioning, and its relation to the total social system." He also indicates that despite sociological contributions in World War II, "there still seems to be no clear conception on the part of the Department of Defense, or for that matter, most sociologists, of the possibilities of military sociology as an important contribution to military effectiveness. . . . It is therefore the purpose of this volume to impress upon sociologists and professional military officials alike the need for more effective utilization of sociological theory and research capability in the analysis of problems of vital importance to our military forces."

The only response possible to this laudable goal is emphatic endorsement. It is important for the military services that they take the fullest possible advantage of the research and consultative resources available in the social sciences; but it is equally important that the military institution which is so demanding of our manpower and material resources and which so intimately affects the conditions of life and the value orientations of all, civilian and military alike, be subjected to scientific investigation. Scientific inquiry should make it possible to judge the impact of the military institution on national ideals and objectives, and determine the degree, if any, to which military programs are dysfunctional from the standpoint of national goals.

Janowitz has done an acceptable job in reviewing the state-of-the-art in regard to the application of sociological research to a broad array of military problems. Of necessity, he reviews the military institution of World War II and Korea, and not the space-age military institution equipped with minute-man missiles, reconnaisance satellites, and multi-megaton hydrogen warheads with which we all must learn to live. At some point the social scientist should be prepared to suggest new ideas and concepts for the resolution of conflict, and not serve merely as a facilitator of the ideas developed by physical scientists and engineers.

This report should serve well in courses on the sociology of the professions, and will be utilized in courses erroneously designated as military sociology.

Two problems exist, and they are serious and worthy of research attention. They are the ones clearly identified by Cottrell: How do you encourage the military to support and utilize social science research at an adequate level, and how do you stimulate research interest in problems relevant to the military institution? It is to be hoped that Janowitz' excellent review of the "internal social organization of the military establishment; hierarchy and authority, assimilation of military roles, primary groups, and techniques of organizational control" and his good, though too brief, consideration of military applications of political sociology and cold war and psychological operations will recruit new and resourceful research efforts by a growing group of sociologists, and in particular some who will relate the military institution to the "total social system."

CHARLES E. HUTCHINSON
Washington, D.C.

ORIGINS OF CRIME: A NEW EVALUATION OF THE CAMBRIDGE-SOMERVILLE YOUTH STUDY. By William McCord and Joan McCord. New York: Columbia University Press, 1959, pp. ix+219.

This is essentially a re-examination of the Cambridge-Somerville Youth Study, a project that was begun in the 1930's. In 1948 Edwin Powers and Helen Witmer began a careful analysis of the experiment. Their report of the outcome of the project was presented in *An Experiment in the Prevention of Delinquency, 1951.* In 1955, ten years after the termination of the project, the McCords began their follow-up study of the Cambridge-Somerville boys. It was not possible to make a study of all cases, but through the cooperation of the Massachusetts Board of Probation, lifetime court records of the boys who committed crimes were obtained. A few of the total number of boys studied probably committed offenses outside Massachussetts, but only a small proportion of them had no records in Massachusetts.

The Cambridge-Somerville project was one of the most extensive and costly experiments in the prevention of delinquency. A total of 650 boys were ultimately selected as subjects for the experiment; 325 received intensive counseling service and 325 (the control group) received no special treatment by the project personnel. The two groups were matched in terms of physical health, intelligence, emotional adjustment, home background, neighborhood, and delinquency prognosis. The McCords confirm the conclusion by Powers and Witmer that the project largely failed to accomplish its goals. "It failed primarily because it did not affect the basic psychological and familial causes of crime." However, the McCords point out some positive findings about the causes and the course of deviant behavior. The case records made it possible to study the developmental nature of criminal behavior. The causes of criminality were not reconstructed retrospectively, after the men had become criminals; but the availability of a vast fund of case records, gathered before the onset of criminality, gave the authors data for the re-examination of possible causal factors.

It is not possible in this review to indicate in detail the findings, which are concisely summarized in the book, including nearly one hundred tables. Among the findings reported, it is significant to note the fact that the roots of crime are implanted early in life. The authors weigh the influence of particular elements of family life and social conditions on later behavior. Parental discipline, family emotional relationships, home atmosphere, parents' character, and type of neighborhood in which the boys lived are carefully weighed. Intelligence was not strongly related to the causation of crime, except that those who committed crimes against property were, most often, of average intelligence, and it is likely that those with high intelligence may have escaped detection of some crimes. The physical condition of the boys did not affect crime, except in cases of those who suffered from a distinct neurological disorder. Social factors were variously related to crime. Even though a slum neighborhood can mold a child's personality, the influence is conditioned by other factors in his background that make him susceptible to the subculture that surrounds him. Those who lived in good neighborhoods, even though they came from neglected families, tended to channel their frustrations in noncriminal ways, and even those who did commit offenses were more likely to change their behavior after the age of eighteen than those who lived in the poorer areas. On the other hand, cohesiveness in the family, consistent discipline, and parental affection tended to insulate children from gang influences. Home atmosphere, the type of discipline, the father's personality and his role model, the mother's personality, and the son's position in the family were significantly related to the behavior of the youth studied. Gang membership increased the chances of criminality. Neighborhood conditions affected juveniles more than they did adults as a factor in criminality.

The study indicates clearly that one cannot understand the origins of crime by concentrating on one factor only. To understand crime it is necessary to study the "complex interactions of such determinants as the parents of the individual, the parents in relation to the child, and the family as it combines with neighborhood influences." If both parents reject a child, or if they are bad parental models, if the discipline is inconsistent, and slum conditions are added to rejection, boys are especially prone to become criminal. M.H.N.

HOW TO INTERVIEW. Fourth Revised Edition. By Walter Van Dyke Bingham and Bruce V. Moore. New York: Harper and Brothers.

In this revised edition of a widely used elementary book on interviewing, the subject is treated in terms of general principles of interviewing and of interviewing for selection, for placement, for facts, and for opinions. The counseling interview receives special attention. New emphasis in this edition is included on the self concept, the psychodynamic concepts, the psychoanalytic concepts, Carl Roger's techniques, market research interviewing, and public opinion polling. E.S.B.

SYMPOSIUM ON SOCIOLOGICAL THEORY. Edited by Llewellyn Gross. Evanston, Illinois: Row, Peterson and Company, 1959, pp. ix+642.

Nineteen essays comprise this ambitious effort to present what might be held to be nineteen points of view on the nature and design of sociological method and theory. Editor Gross states that he offers the volume as "a review and as a promise of the kinds of theoretical considerations that warrant examination in the immediate future." With this in mind, he hoped that the contributors would explore such central concepts as postulates, explanations, models, types, levels, dispositions, transactions, functional relations, processes, probability, causality, verification, confirmation, and normative processes. Most of the contributors use some of these concepts but not always with the same meaning. Certain convergences and divergences, some imposed by the editor, make their appearances, and for the convenience of the reader as well as for his grasp of the materials, his introductory essay outlines these, which is most fortunate. Some of the convergences read as follows: "values play a significant role in the process of creating a social science"; "theoretical and methodological analysis must be anchored to human problems"; "the basic character of a scientific theory is determined by the set of concepts or principles that are chosen as central to its formulation"; and "though social science seeks to use language that is clear and correct, the current goal of analytic or procedural purity is questioned." Bierstedt shows clearly that there are different kinds of definitions and that different definitions perform different functions. As a consequence, he avers that definitional terms can or cannot operate in specific ways.

The essays are arranged under nine different headings: orientation, social types, social order, social change, functional theory, models in social science, formalization of theory, values and theory construction, and sociology of knowledge. Some of them are more valuable than others for their insights into the problems confronting sociology. Mills' essay, "On Intellectual Craftsmanship," should have a salutary effect upon those who would burden sociological writings with such affectiveness that a disguised profundity of thought results. He writes: "To overcome the academic prose... you have to overcome the academic pose." And further, "writing not imaginable as human speech is bad writing." Some of the included essayists may be found guilty on this score. Other essays that are very valuable as to content are Hempel's "Logic of Functional Analysis," Hart's "Social Theory and Social Change," Timasheff's "Order, Causality, Conjuncture," and Wolff's "Sociology of Knowledge and Sociological Theory." A few of the essays will be limited in value for students without excellent mathematical backgrounds, and one or two might even have the effect of driving some students into other areas of endeavor. M.J.V.

THE STATUS SEEKERS. By Vance Packard. New York: David McKay Company, Inc., 1959, pp. 376.

In this book Vance Packard has gone primarily to the sociologist for the facts to describe the processes and problems experienced by persons attempting to achieve status in contemporary America. One of the chief virtues of this work is that it will serve to broadcast the major findings of stratification research to the general public. As a generalist the author blends many facets of the stratification process to highlight the key factors in changing status, marks of status, strains of status, and some of the more significant trends in the art of seeking status.

Packard sees America as a society stratified into two large segments: the diploma elite and the supporting classes. In actual description the diploma elite is divided into the "real upper class," which may be considered synonymous with Mills' "power elite," and the "semi-upper class," consisting mainly of professional men and decision makers in business at about the manager level. The supporting classes are described as the "limited-success class," the "working class," and the "real lower class."

Some of the statements that may provoke the reader's attention: as a badge of status a residential address is more significant than the home, in matters of clothing the upper classes may be characterized by an elaborate casualness and the lower classes by an almost animallike faith in formality, and, finally, in the real upper class there seems to be a monumental casualness about paying bills which has been epitomized in Gloria Vanderbilt's autobiography when she learned that the family butcher bill had reached $40,000.

For some readers Vance Packard's new book may become something of a manual on how to appear to be in a higher social class than is actually the case. Inasmuch as this work will probably be read by a great many Americans, the degree of status consciousness will become sharper concerning such items as a "good address," "the proper behavior associated with a particular class," "the right political party," and the "totem poles of job prestige." The author, though writing a popular book, has maintained a scholarly respect for the findings of research in the field of social stratification. E.C.M.

SOCIOMETRY IN THE CLASSROOM. By Norman E. Gronlund. New York: Harper and Brothers, 1959, pp. xviii+340.

The author writes not just from a knowledge of the literature of the "sociometric movement in education," but as one who has contributed by frequent and steady publication to the development of the "movement." Since his cognizance of the utility of the technique stems from his actual experience of its adaptability, it is, therefore, not secondhand. Scientists now acknowledge that an adequate epistemology of events requires their interpreter to be caught up in their evolution. Because Gronlund meets this requirement, he writes with verve, perspicuity, and discernment.

The book begins with a description of the method, suggests uses, defines terms, and establishes connections with educational objectives. A particularly important contribution concerns the limitations of sociometry.

Following this introduction several chapters are devoted to the construction and the administration of the test, the analysis and presentation of results, and typical patterns of response given by students from the third-grade level through college. Further chapters consider the reliability of findings, the validity of the instrument, and the application of results to the solution of educational problems.

Altogether the book is a rich store of information, written with such detail and lucidity that it can be understood and utilized by students of every area of human interaction. Since learning is, among other things, a function of sociometric status, the work is of paramount interest to the teacher.

HAROLD T. DIEHL
Los Angeles State College

THE OBJECTIVE SOCIETY. By Everett Knight. London: Routledge and Kegan Paul, 1959, pp. 136.

While specific definitions of terms are not given, it appears that the essence of an objective society may be found in its cultural heritage and in the creative activities of its ablest minds. A dilemma arises from the fact that the masses of people are not particularly interested in giving attention to these characteristics. Except for a few people, the world is entering a space age while "entertaining ideas which have come down to us from antiquity." Likewise, it might be said we are developing a nuclear-ruled world while holding to provincial ideas. Hence, the author asserts "that our culture is now bankrupt," and thus we are not equipped culturally or otherwise to live in a world community or a space age. Further, the author believes that "western society is adrift" and "its relative material prosperity causes us to overlook its ideological emptiness." The language of the book is forceful but phrased in a way at times that is not likely to appeal to those who most need to think through its philosophical analyses. E.S.B.

AN EXPERIMENT IN MENTAL PATIENT REHABILITATION. By Henry J. Meyer and Edgar F. Borgatta. New York: Russell Sage Foundation, 1959, pp. 114.

This book represents one of the few scientific researches undertaken in the social welfare setting. The "Altro project," so-called because the data are from the Altro Health & Rehabilitation Services, Inc., was initially intended to evaluate the agency's program for rehabilitating posthospitalized psychiatric patients. As a consequence of the project directors' awareness that little is known of the characteristics of mental patients eligible for rehabilitation, and that little knowledge of community and agency procedures for handling patients released from mental hospitals exists, the project is conceived in a broad framework which extends beyond the limited focus of evaluative research.

The first three chapters, which constitute the first half of the book, deal with the research design, implementation of the research project, and the type of data utilized. Chapter 4 describes the sample of patients selected for investigation and presents extensive background and classification data. The final three chapters focus upon 36 background variables subjected to factor analysis, an assessment of the effectiveness of rehabilitation, and final conclusions. A total of twenty-three tables are presented, and the appendix contains the intercorrelation matrix for variables used in the factor analysis.

The researchers interpret their findings cautiously: they state on page 99, "the data suggest that participation in Altro might reduce to a modest degree the likelihood of rehospitalization." They hold that participation may function as a palliative, and, consequently, the effectiveness of the program is not more convincingly demonstrated. In conclusion, the reader is reminded that there may be other patient benefits from Altro, such as the development of "normal" adult activities, if criteria other than rehospitalization were used.

HAROLD G. HUBBARD
Extended Day Division
Los Angeles State College

SOCIAL CONTROL AND THE FOUNDATIONS OF SOCIOLOGY. Pioneer Contributions of Edward Alsworth Ross to the Study of Society. Edited by Edgar F. Borgatta and Henry J. Meyer. Boston: Beacon Press, 1959, pp. xii+211.

The editors have done a meritorious piece of work in selecting the original and most significant sections in Ross' two important early books (published in 1901 and 1905) for republication. In editing the materials, illustrative materials have been omitted to a large extent, thus emphasizing Ross' contributions to sociological theory. The reproduced writings of Ross give his discussion of such themes as the social person, with the role of sympathy, of sociability, of the sense of justice, and of individual reaction receiving emphasis. The selections of Ross' treatment of social control deal with the need for social control, the direction of social control, the radiant points of social control, and with "society as a persistent system that molds and limits the forms that may arise within it."

Ross is viewed by the editors as being "a power among pioneers, sharing their zeal for applying scientific inquiry to social problems and surpassing them all, perhaps, in the energetic promotion of sociology as an instrument for doing so." He is described as "a tireless observer of social changes which he investigated directly in his worldwide travels" and wrote about extensively. His primary interest, in his words, was in the "influences that reach men and women from without, that is, social influences." He analyzed extensively what today are called "social norms, role expectancies, cultural patterns." By omitting most of the illustrative examples, an aspect of Ross' style is lost, but there is a gain in the impression of greater theoretical worth that is given. E.S.B.

BASIC SOCIOLOGY. By E. J. Ross. Milwaukee: The Bruce Publishing Company, 1958, pp. vii+488.

This book is a revised and enlarged edition of the author's earlier work with the same title. Offered as a text for introductory college courses in sociology, it presents an informative and highly readable treatment of the principal areas generally covered in such courses. Sociological terms are defined as they are introduced, and central concepts are described and identified with their originators. Provision of numerous cross references in the text should serve to aid the beginning student in tying together the ideas developed in the various chapters.

While this book is frankly directed toward use in Catholic colleges, its general scope and readability might well recommend it for use in many other small liberal arts colleges offering only a single course in sociology. Instructors in colleges with more comprehensive sociology programs, however, may not care for the unusual topical arrangement of the book, its inclusion of extraneous material, and its omission of some important concepts.

JOHN F. CROWTHER
Compton College

THE IDEA OF THE UNIVERSITY. By Karl Jaspers. Edited by Karl W. Deutsch. Translated by H. A. T. Reiche and H. F. Vanderschmidt. Boston: Beacon Press, 1959, pp. xxiv+135.

This short book gives both a pragmatic and an idealistic conception of the nature and proper functions of the university. The basic conception of the university is that it is dedicated to the pursuit of science and scholarship, and its three essential and inseparable functions are research, the transmission of learning, and education to culture. The university owes its existence to society and the body politic. Only to the degree that the state respects the university and protects it from interference can the university fulfill its purposes and function as the intellectual conscience of an era. When completely recognized by society and the state without reservations or restrictions, the university exists virtually as a state within the state. This university ideal would be incompatible within a state which is intolerant of any restriction on its power for fear of the consequences of a pure search for truth.

J.E.N.

SOCIOLOGY AND SOCIAL LIFE. By Kimball Young and Raymond W. Mack. New York: American Book Company, 1959, pp. 472.

In this work a major revision of the senior author's earlier work has been accomplished with success and advantage. The authors have attempted to organize the subject matter of sociology around such major factors as "social relations," "social organization," and "social institutions." A sociological frame of reference of a conceptual type emerges to guide the thinking of the student. Attractive features of the book may be appreciated in its literary style, selection of illustrations, and for the most part a good coverage of topics considered in introductory sociology. However, some critics may fail to see a coherent frame of reference throughout the work. This book merits careful consideration by instructors of introductory sociology.

E.C.M.

WOVON LEBT DIE MUSIK: DIE PRINCIPIEN DER MUSIKSOZIOLOGIE. By Alphons Silbermann. Regensburg: Gustav Bosse Verlag, 1957, pp. 235.

The author, sociologist and musician, manifests concern about the fate of music in a world which is ostensibly committed to Renaissance values and virtues but which, simultaneously, seems bent on destroying the conditions that made these values both possible and appealing. In the author's opinion, music and man's involvement with music are related to specific sociocultural circumstances and the press of history and not, as some insist on believing, to a mystique or to a way of life unique to the creation of "mature" music. Thus it is, for example, that Handel is the alleged representative of an age of tranquillity; Beethoven, of anxiety.

It is Silbermann's view that music develops out of and reflects the underlying social structure. Two major groups dominate the field of music—producer and consumer. But neither can function effectively except as their values flow from the existing social milieu. Insisting on the sociocultural interpretation of musical creation and its consumption causes the author to question, for example, the frequent contention that the French Revolution "liberated" the creative artist from court control and patronage, thus enabling him to pursue whatever artistic ends were sought. Liberated or not, the artist and his public did not escape the dictates of traditional social controls and in some instances the democratic ethos.

Examining the contemporary scene, Dr. Silbermann argues that music and its enjoyment must be freed from the controls exercised by the professional critics, publishers, and philosophers of art. He believes this freedom necessary for the establishment of a more meaningful and productive relationship between artist and listener.

In 1954 Dr. Silbermann organized the first international congress dealing with sociological aspects and problems of music and radio. The meeting was held in Paris and sponsored by the French government. His previous works include *Of Musical Things*, Sydney: The Grahame Book Company, 1949; *La Musique, la radio et l'auditeur*, Paris: Presses Universitaires de France, 1954; *Introduction a une sociologie de la musique*, Paris: Presses Universitaires de France, 1955.

RICHARD O. NAHRENDORF
Los Angeles State College

FAMILY WORLDS: A PSYCHOSOCIAL APPROACH TO FAMILY LIFE. By Robert D. Hess and Gerald Handel. Chicago: The University of Chicago Press, 1959, pp. vii+306.

This book differs from most books on family life. It is a book of five cases and these families are analyzed from the viewpoint of family interactions. The stress is on the personality aspects of members of the families, family functions, mutual interaction, congruences of images, family theme, the family world, and other psychosocial aspects. The book offers a theory of the nature of family life and presents five cases to give a more minute portrayal of the psychosocial portrait of family life. The Clarks (husband and wife) had insecure pasts, coming from broken homes and moving from one home to another. Their own marriage and family life provided security and a more protective world for their children. The Lansons definitely strive for harmony and equanimity but are sometimes perplexed by the consequences. The Littletons desperately strive to balance emotional tensions and division by allowing each member of the family to build a separate world for himself (or herself). The Newbolds are a very energetic and self-sufficient family. They are the leadership type with all members actively participating in numerous activities. The Steeles are constantly wrestling with the problem of blending companionship and assertion.

The central aim of the project was to study families as groups of interacting persons. The main data were obtained by means of interviews with members of the family, accompanied by various tests. By studying small groups, the authors were able to ascertain the interplay between personality and family as each group attempted to work out its special way of coping with the problems of everyday living.

M.H.N.

INDEX TO VOLUME 43

SOCIOLOGY AND SOCIAL RESEARCH

1958-1959

UNIVERSITY PARK
LOS ANGELES

INDEX TO VOLUME 43

SOCIOLOGY AND SOCIAL RESEARCH

Abu-Laban, Baha, and A. T. V. Matthews, Job Satisfaction and Leisure-Time Activity 189

Bardis, Panos D., Attitudes Toward the Family Among College Students and Their Parents 352

Bogardus, Emory S., The Direction of Sociological Research 38

————, Racial Distance Changes in the United States During the Past Thirty Years 127

————, Mannheim and Systematic Sociology 213

————, Racial Reactions by Regions 286

————, William I. Thomas and Social Origins 365

————, Race Reactions by Sexes 439

Borgatta, E. F., and J. Robbin, Some Implications of High Speed Computers for the Methodology of Social Research 259

Borgatta, Marie L., The Concept of the Group 83

Burma, John H., Self-Tattooing Among Delinquents 341

Carlton, Frank T., The Group Versus the Individual 427

Chen, Theodore, and Wen-hui Chen, Changing Attitudes Toward Parents in Communist China 175

Christopherson, Victor A., and J. Walters, Responses of Protestants, Catholics, and Jews Concerning Marriage and Family Life 16

Dwyer, Robert J., The Administrative Role in Desegregation 183

Eaton, Joseph W., The Relevancy of Social Work for Sociology 197

Etzioni, Amitai, Lower Levels of Leadership in Industry 209

Helbrich, Margaret L., Occupations of Sociology Majors 276

Hoult, Thomas F., Teaching Sociology by Radio and Television 97

Hunt, Raymond G., and V. Synnerdahl, Social Influence Among Kindergarten Children 171

Ireland, Ralph R., The Role of Economic Motivation in Ethnic Relations 119

Jackman, Norman, and M. Sherif, Group Processes and Communication on the Prohibition Issue 265

Johannis, T. B., and James Rollins, Attitudes of Teen-Agers 415

Keedy, T. C., Jr., Anomie and Religious Orthodoxy 34

Machotka, Otakar, A Contribution to the Theory of Social Change 333

Matthews, A. T. V., and B. Abu-Laban, Job Satisfaction and Leisure-Time Activity 189

Meadows, Paul, and W. Torrence, American Culture Themes 3
Meller, Norman, Bilingualism in Island Legislatures 408
Montague, Joel B., Jr., A Problem of Remuneration of the British National Health Service 205
Neumeyer, Martin H., Areas for Research in Leisure and Recreation 90
Northwood, L. K., Measuring Group Opinion by Expert Estimates 113
Ogburn, William F., The Social Philosophy of "It Doesn't Matter" 403
Queen, Stuart A., The Sociology of John L. Gillin 327
Robbin, J., and E. F. Borgatta, Some Implications of High Speed Computers for the Methodology of Social Research 259
Rollins, James, and T. B. Johannis, Attitudes of Teen-Agers 415
Rosenblum, Abraham, Ethnic Prejudice as Related to Social Class and Religiosity 272
Schermerhorn, R. A., Techniques and Instruction in Teaching Sociology on Television 108
Sherif, Muzafer, and N. Jackman, Group Processes and Communication on the Prohibition Issue 265
Shippey, Frederick A., Social Class in Philadelphia Methodism 23
Stewart, Robert L., and G. M. Vernon, Four Correlates of Empathy in the Dating Situation 279
Sussman, Marvin B., Teaching Sociology via Television 102
Synnerdahl, Vonda, and R. G. Hunt, Social Influence Among Kindergarten Children 171
Torrence, William, and P. Meadows, American Culture Themes 3
Vernon, Glenn M., and R. L. Stewart, Four Correlates of Empathy in the Dating Situation 279
Vincent, Melvin J., Labor Under Review: 1957 8
Walters, James, and V. A. Christopherson, Responses of Protestants, Catholics, and Jews Concerning Marriage and Family Life 16
Watson, Bruce A., Art and Communication 28
Westie, Frank R., Social Distance Scales 251
Williamson, Robert C., Population Dynamics in El Salvador 421
Wolfgang, Marvin E., Conformity and the Social Class 432
Yamamoto, George K., Political Participation Among Orientals in Hawaii 359
Zentner, Henry, The Division of Labor Among Communal Groups 346

Sociology and Social Research

AN INTERNATIONAL JOURNAL

Articles in Forthcoming Issues . . .

September-October and later

Pro-Natal Influences in American Culture .... J. W. DYKSTRA
A Study of Community Values .... S. JOHN DACKAWICH
Stereotype of the Negro and His High-priced Car .... I. ROGER YOSHINO
Reactions of Television Viewers .... ALEXANDER RUNCIMAN
Social Problems in Pakistan .... JOHN E. OWEN
Institutional Planning for Social Change .... MARY LYSTAD
Distance Mechanisms of Stratification .... P. L. VAN DEN BERGHE
Development of Group Health Practice .... DENNIS C. MCELRATH
Attitudes Toward Social Class in India .... MEYER F. NIMKOFF
Differentials in Ideal Family Life .... C. A. YERACARIS
Measuring Marriage Satisfaction .... NATHAN HURVITZ
Theory of Social Movements .... J. W. VANDER ZANDEN
Sociology of Alfred Weber .... RUDOLF HEBERLE
Labor in 1958 .... M. J. VINCENT
Reappraisal of Comte's Sociology .... RUSSELL MIDDLETON
Status and Social Tropism .... E. C. MCDONAGH
Sociology for High Schools .... ARTHUR REPKE
The Nigerian Elite .... M. H. AND M. M. SMYTHE
Sociological Contributions of Znaniecki .... THEODORE ABEL

Articles in Preceding Issue . . .

May-June 1959

Sociology of John L. Gillin .... STUART A. QUEEN
Theory of Culture Change .... OTAKAR MACHOTKA
Self-Tattooing Among Delinquents .... JOHN H. BURMA
Division of Labor of Communal Groups .... HENRY ZENTNER
Student Attitudes Toward the Family .... PANOS D. BARDIS
Politics of Orientals in Hawaii .... GEORGE K. YAMAMOTO
W. I. Thomas and Social Origins .... EMORY S. BOGARDUS